THE ETHICS OF ŚAṄKARA AND ŚĀNTIDEVA

DIALOGUES IN SOUTH ASIAN TRADITIONS:
RELIGION, PHILOSOPHY, LITERATURE AND HISTORY

Face-to-face conversation and dialogue are defining features of South Asian traditional texts, rituals and practices. Not only has the region of South Asia always consisted of a multiplicity of peoples and cultures in communication with each other, but also performed and written dialogues have been indelible features within the religions of South Asia; Hinduism, Buddhism, Jainism, Sikhism, and Islam are all multi-vocal religions. Their doctrines, practices, and institutions have never had only one voice of authority, and dialogue has been a shared tactic for negotiating contesting interpretations within each tradition.

This series examines the use of the dialogical genre in South Asian religious and cultural traditions. Historical inquiries into the plurality of religious identity in South Asia, particularly when constructed by the dialogical genre, are crucial in an age when, as Amartya Sen has recently observed, singular identities seem to hold more destructive sway than multiple ones. This series will approach dialogue in its widest sense, including discussion, debate, argument, conversation, communication, confrontation, and negotiation. It will aim to open up a dynamic historical and literary mode of analysis, which assumes the plural dimensions of religious identities and communities from the start. In this way the series aims to challenge many outdated assumptions and representations of South Asian religions.

The Ethics of Śaṅkara and Śāntideva

A Selfless Response to an Illusory World

WARREN LEE TODD
University of South Wales

ASHGATE

Published by
Ashgate Publishing Limited
Wey Court East
Union Road
Farnham
Surrey, GU9 7PT
England

Ashgate Publishing Company
110 Cherry Street
Suite 3-1
Burlington, VT 05401-3818
USA

www.ashgate.com

British Library Cataloguing in Publication Data
Todd, Warren Lee.
The ethics of Śaṅkara and Śāntideva : a selfless response to an illusory world. – (Dialogues in South Asian traditions)
1. Sankaracarya–Ethics. 2. Śāntideva, 7th cent.–Ethics.
3. Self (Philosophy) 4. Altruism. 5. Buddhist ethics.
6. Hindu ethics. 7. Philosophy, Indic.
I. Title II. Series
181.4-dc23

The Library of Congress has cataloged the printed edition as follows:
Todd, Warren Lee.
The ethics of Śaṅkara and Śāntideva : a selfless response to an illusory world / by Warren Lee Todd.
pages cm. – (Dialogues in South Asian traditions: religion, philosophy, literature and history)
Includes bibliographical references and index.
ISBN 978-1-4094-6681-9 – ISBN 978-1-4094-6682-6 (ebook) – ISBN 978-1-4094-6683-3 (epub) 1. Sankaracarya–Ethics. 2. Santideva, 7th cent–Ethics. 3. Religious ethics–India–History. I. Title.
B133.S5T63 2013
170.92'234–dc23

2012049673

ISBN 9781409466819 (hbk)
ISBN 9781409466826 (ebk – PDF)
ISBN 9781409466833 (ebk – ePUB)

MIX Paper from responsible sources FSC® C013056

Printed and bound in Great Britain by
TJ International Ltd, Padstow, Cornwall.

Contents

Foreword by H.H. the Dalai Lama *vii*
Abbreviations *ix*
Acknowledgements *xi*

1 The Self 1

2 A New Ethical Model 17

3 Situating Śaṅkara and Śāntideva 47

4 Their Common Approach to the World 81

5 Knowledge and Liberation 121

6 A Selfless Response to the World 139

7 Marginal Cases 177

Conclusion 199

Bibliography *203*
Index *215*

Foreword:
H.H. the Dalai Lama

THE DALAI LAMA

FOREWORD

India has been for thousands of years the cradle of a multitude of religions and other schools of thought. What sets India apart from many other parts of the world is that it has consistently displayed an extraordinary aptitude for pluralism and intellectual openness, as a result of which, seemingly contradictory ways of thinking have coexisted in relative harmony. This is why, whenever I have the opportunity, I express my admiration for the religious pluralism and non-violence that exemplify India's unique cultural heritage.

As a result of the atmosphere of tolerance that has prevailed since early times, India's various schools of thought have engaged in vibrant doctrinal debate on the basis of mutual respect. This trend has been stimulating for all concerned, leading to a steady refinement of each other's points of view. There is no doubt that Buddhism and other ancient Indian schools of thought were enriched as a consequence.

Shankara's famous polemical debates with his various contemporaries, as well his treatises on advaita philosophy, are a case in point. Similarly, Shantideva's masterpiece the *Guide to the Bodhisattva's Way of Life* (skt. Bodhisattvacharyavatara) propounds the Prasangika Madhyamaka standpoint and is critical of other's points of view; it reveals intellectual rigour at its very best. Both these masters left an indelible mark on thought.

Shankara's advaita philosophy regards Brahman as the primal basis of the entire universe - an inherently existent ultimate truth. Shantideva, on the other hand, being a Prasangika Madhyamika, holds that nothing can be inherently existent, on the grounds that all conditioned things arise in dependence on something else. Apart from that, Sankara's views share many similarities with those of the Yogacara school of Buddhist philosophy. I welcome this book *The Ethics of Shankara and Shantidev* by Warren Todd in which, following the pattern of critical examination in which both masters participated, he provides a comparative study of various aspects of Shankara's and Shantideva's ideas, particularly their mutual focus on ethics.

April 26, 2013

Abbreviations

Ait.U. (Bh.)	*Aitareya Upaniṣad (Bhāṣya)*
A.N.	*Aṅguttara Nikāya*
BCA	*Bodhicaryāvatāra*
B.S. (Bh.)	*Brahma Sūtra (Bhāṣya)*
Bṛ.U. (Bh.)	*Bṛhadāraṇyaka Upaniṣad (Bhāṣya)*
Bh.G. (Bh.)	*Bhagavad Gītā (Bhāṣya)*
Ch.U. (Bh.)	*Chāndogya Upaniṣad (Bhāṣya)*
D.N.	*Dīgha Nikāya*
Dhp.	*Dhammapada*
EHU	*Enquiry concerning Human Understanding*
EPM	*Enquiry concerning Principles of Morals*
G.K. (Bh.)	*Gauḍapāda's Kārikā (Bhāṣya)*
G.S.	*Gay Science*
Gau.D.S.	*Gautama Dharma Sūtra*
Īś.U. (Bh.)	*Īśā Upaniṣad (Bhāṣya)*
Jā.U.	*Jābāla Upaniṣad*
Ka.U. (Bh.)	*Kaṭha Upaniṣad (Bhāṣya)*
Ken.U. (Bh.)	*Kena Upaniṣad (Bhāṣya)*
Mā.U. (Bh.)	*Māṇḍūkya Upaniṣad (Bhāṣya)*
Miln.	*Milinda Pañha*
MMA (Bh.)	*Madhyamakāvatāra (Bhāṣya)*
MMK	*Mūla-madhyamaka kārikā*
M.N.	*Majjhima Nikāya*
Mu.U. (Bh.)	*Muṇḍaka Upaniṣad (Bhāṣya)*
P.U. (Bh.)	*Praśna Upaniṣad (Bhāṣya)*
Ś.S.	*Śikṣā Samuccaya*

S.N.	*Saṃyutta Nikāya*
T.U. (Bh.)	*Taittirīya Upaniṣad (Bhāṣya)*
U.S.	*Upadeśa Sāhasrī*
Util.	*Utilitarianism*
V.C.	*Viveka Cūḍāmani*
Vin.	*Vinaya*
Vm.	*Visuddhimagga*
Vv.	*Vigrahavyāvartanī*

Acknowledgements

I acknowledge my deepest debt to the AHRC for their doctorate scholarship. I thank Ashgate for providing such a wonderful series in which to publish. I especially thank Dr Brian Black for his generous guidance and encouragement at the start of the project, and Matt Irving for so patiently guiding me through the whole publishing process. Respect and gratitude to my tutors: Prof. Peter Harvey, Prof. Chakravarthi Ram-Prasad and Dr Irina Kuznetsova, without whom this book would not have been possible. Special mention to Linda Gyatso for 'making things happen' in India. I bow to H.H. the Dalai Lama and to the late Chogye Trichen Rinpoche for placing me on the path. Thanks are also due to my friends and family for their constant support and humour. Finally, 'thank you Joly' for your endless patience and limitless passion. Warren.

Dedicated to Paul

Chapter 1
The Self

It is more than a hundred years since Nietzsche's 'madman' ran through the streets of Europe. And while the flames of atheism and doubt may well have been fuelled by science and scepticism alike, the 'old deep trust' (G.S. 343) in a personal God and for a necessary Absolute being is still very much alive. My interest here does not concern the 'gruesome shadows' (108) *per se*, but will necessarily involve the re-evaluation of their role. 'How much must collapse' asked Nietzsche; what will happen to 'our entire European morality' (343)? Barring Communism, that monstrous failure, has the European really been capable of an answer? Meanwhile, the American still calls on the Good Lord to protect their 'crusades'. Perhaps then, we should leave the West and travel east. Could it be that there are moral lessons to be learnt from somewhere as distant as 8th-century India?

From an Indian perspective, we do not have to consider God 'dead'; an agnostic stance will suffice. God may sing and dance in the shadows if he likes. The universe is here about us as a brute fact, a place of suffering. That is why Buddhism in India has often been labelled 'agnosticism' rather than 'atheism'. But if the Buddhist understanding of the world has been essentially 'man-centred', then my argument here is that the same may be said of the Hindu, Śaṅkara. This is especially true when we consider his views on liberation. In other words, Śaṅkara's central concern was the 'current bondage of the human condition' (Suthren Hirst 2005: 94). Liberation from this world is a *human* task, a gnoseological project.[1] Even Otto (1957: 189), the great defender of a theistic Śaṅkara, felt compelled to admit that 'Śaṅkara is so deeply interested in the subjective pole of salvation, that the other is scarcely noticed by him'. Śaṅkara is hardly interested in looking good in God's eyes. That is, when it comes to the ultimate means of liberation, God (Īśvara) has but little importance. Śaṅkara's interest lies more in a cognitive shift. As he puts it, the 'non-dual realization is a mere mental modification' (*advaita jñānaṃ manovṛtti mātram*) (Ch.U.Bh., intro). This discovery that one is in fact *brahman*-consciousness is followed by immediate liberation from suffering (*jīvan-mukti*), and the salvation of others who continue to suffer within transmigratory existence.

Suffering is thus the consequence of a basic misunderstanding. Hence, no devil, but ignorance (*avidyā*) shows itself to be the great enemy, and even God is subject to it (B.S.Bh. II.i.14). This ignorance, or not-knowing (*a-jñāna*), according to Śaṅkara, is the 'root' (*mūla*) of transmigratory existence (*saṃsāra*) (U.S. Metric, 1.4–5) and stems from the clinging to the transitory world of name and form

[1] No parallel with Gnosticism is implied here. By 'gnoseology', I simply mean a system which posits a type of 'saving knowledge' as its goal.

(*nāma-rūpa*) (B.S.Bh. II.i.14). For both Śaṅkara and Śāntideva, this ignorance shows itself as egoism (*ahaṃkāra*) and culminates in the clinging to a self as body, or as individuated soul (*jīva*). According to Śāntideva, all misfortunes in the world are due to clinging to such a false self (BCA. 8.134). Similarly, Śaṅkara sees the cause of suffering as ignorance of the nature of self. If one could only see that there were no difference between your self and the Self of *brahman*, one would be released from suffering. Hence, 'That one is other [than *brahman*] is due only to the [error of] accepting the doctrine of difference' (U.S. Prose, 1.30).

The gnoseological response then becomes threefold:

1. create doubt in the deep-seated belief in our ultimate individuality;
2. question the origin and validity of our private cognitions; and
3. re-evaluate our embodied existence.

For Śāntideva, the Mādhyamika Buddhist, there is no all-powerful God with his hands upon the world, and the Buddha remains as example and guide, not as Lord Creator. And even the Buddha is ultimately to be viewed as 'illusion-like', for 'Merit comes from a Conqueror [Buddha], who is like an illusion, as if he was truly existent' (BCA. 9.9a). But far from being a nihilistic thesis, Śāntideva adds perfect wisdom and compassion to Nietzsche's infinite nothing. For Śaṅkara, the Advaitin, the personal God (Īśvara) is likewise to be seen as part of the illusion (*māyā*) from which we must awaken, a construct, which along with individuation, awaits dissolution into universal consciousness. A popular Advaita text states, when ignorance and illusion is overcome, 'there is neither God nor soul' (V.C. 244).[2] And as for the attributeless (*nirguṇa*) *brahman*, it is so bare a concept, it can 'hardly be the Creator God' (Matilal 2004: 40). Again, this is no nihilistic thesis, for ethics remains paramount. As Black (2008: 3) suggests, the 'Upanishadic notion of the self is not merely a philosophical insight, but a way of being in the world'. In place of an infinite nothing, Śaṅkara speaks of 'infinite' (*anantaṃ*) 'knowledge and truth' (*satyaṃ jñānam*) (T.U.Bh. II.i.1). More in line with Nietzsche, both Śāntideva and Śaṅkara seek liberation in terms of gnoseological illumination, and all three are intent on producing their 'free-spirits'.

So the Western reader will begin to see the virtue in this debate if and when they consider the problem that arises when the *certainty* of a personal I-Thou relationship with God is seriously doubted. More specifically, as we become agnostic about God, the notion of a personal, God-given, 'soul' becomes a redundant concept. And consequently, we lose the line of reference on which to pin our certainty about the locus of our individual 'self'. This lack of ground,

[2] The *Viveka Cūḍāmaṇi* (*V.C.*) is treated here as probably not written by Śaṅkara. However, it may be assumed to be a gloss on Śaṅkara's authentic works. It will be drawn on to show how its views compare with Śaṅkara's, due to its ease of reference and extreme popularity.

coupled with a lack of historical anchor, lends itself to a sceptical attitude towards the question of whether or not there is any foundation at all for morality.

The problem, as framed here, is not an emotional one, nor is it necessarily existential. It is not whether one may live a life with more or less fear of death, though fearlessness is indeed a spiritual achievement, prized by both Advaita and Buddhism. It is not about freedom to act beyond the institutional walls. Nor is the problem about whether or not a lack of 'self' would take away our claim to individual rights. The problem, as framed here, is more philosophical, more 'global'. It is whether or not ethics has any meaningful place in a world where the individuated self is not simply doubted, but ultimately denied. With one eye on the current trends in cognitive science, I believe this question will come to play a major part in future ethical discussion. And an ethical question of particular interest to me is whether or not 'altruism' remains possible within a metaphysics of non-individuation. When I speak of 'altruism' here, I mean more than just the occasional jump into a lake to save a drowning child. Rather, I am pointing at a total outlook on being and beings, an ethical worldview. A detailed analysis of how we may qualify our terms of reference to allow for other-regarding ethics within such revisionary metaphysics will thus be offered. More generally, we might ask, just how do metaphysical claims impact upon our ethics?

If we are to understand the question from Śāntideva's or Śaṅkara's perspective, we need to be familiar with the distinction between what they call the 'ultimate' (*paramārtha*) truth and 'conventional' (*saṃvṛti, vyāvahārika*) truth. For simplicity, we might say that ultimate truth is that seen by the wise, and is the final description of what this world is like in 'reality' (*tattva*), essentially in terms of metaphysics. The conventional is the world of 'common people' (*prakṛtā janāḥ*), the 'worldly' (*loka*), and, in Indian terms, is the place of work, ritual and ethical action (*Dharma*). This sense of worldly convention is explicit in Nāgārjuna's notion of 'worldly conventional truth' (*loka saṃvṛti-satyaṃ*) (MMK. 24.8), and both Śāntideva and Śaṅkara will show their debt to Nāgārjuna, the founder of Madhyamaka.

Nevertheless, the wise look upon the conventional world as a dream-like world, a place where the seeming permanency of objects is likened to a magical display, a mirage. In this 'illusory' world, the majority of men and women go about their business, praying to their Gods, stoking their sacrificial fires, selling their wares. It is a world in need of a moral structure, and both the Mādhyamikas and the Advaitins will give provisional value to it. The question of just how much of this conventional world the wise really 'share' with us is a matter to be addressed throughout this book. For now, it is enough to say that conventional truth is not necessarily the same as consensus. It is the external world of 'things', where 'beings' are taken seriously. When we get to the ultimate level of discourse, the validity of 'beings-as-independent-subjects' will be put into question. At this level of understanding, to use the language of modern philosophers of the self, there is 'no underlying person' (Parfit 1971: 25), there is literally 'no one *in* the cave' (Metzinger 2004: 549).

But this does not mean that there is no person at all. For the Advaitin, it means that the person does not possess an individuated self (*jīvātman*) which would separate him from *brahman*. As for the Buddhist, it means that there is no need to posit any substratum that supposedly maintains one's individuality, one's identity over time. Of course, Śaṅkara thus supposes that the Mādhyamika Buddhist does indeed deny the person (Ch.U.Bh. II.xxiii.1), because a non-agency thesis combined with (what he took as) their non-existence (*asat*) thesis would amount to either nihilism or incoherence. But Śaṅkara consistently fails to take account of the Madhyamaka's acceptance of dependent origination. Emptiness, for the Mādhyamika Buddhist, is emptiness *of* something, just as consciousness is consciousness *of* something. Emptiness and phenomena are not two distinct things, but two characterizations of the same thing. Things are empty because they are dependently originated. If phenomena were not empty of inherent existence, it would be impossible for phenomena to be transformed in dependence on causes. So a constructed person is empty *because* he is a constructed person.

So Derek Parfit, who we may thank for reviving the analytical interest in the Buddhist non-self thesis, is wrong if he sees the Buddhists as totally denying the person (see Ganeri 2007: 162–6). The Buddha never denied the person that stands before you. Hayes states that the topic of one of the first of the Buddha's discourses was about 'why none of the constituents of a person qualifies as a self' (in Keown and Prebish 2007: 28). But how could one make any sense of this if the Buddha was also denying the 'person'? It is evident, even under Madhyamaka's revisions, that the mere imputed person is not to be refuted. Only by distinguishing between the notions of 'self' and 'person' can one make sense of the Buddhist concept of the selflessness of the person. Indologist Ram-Prasad (2012: 132) claims that Parfit has changed his mind about Buddhism and has come to see them as 'reductionists', and Ram-Prasad himself is generally correct when he states here that 'Buddhists are reductionists about persons' (p133). In fact, Buddhologists, like Mark Siderits (2007: 69), continue to liken Parfit's reductionism to Buddhism, which is why Parfit is of such interest to our debate.

However, while Siderits (2000: 417) has admitted that Śāntideva sometimes adopts 'Reductionist assumptions', he more generally argues that the 'Madhyamaka rejects Reductionism' (2003: 111, note c). This is so if we take 'reductionism' to be the view that things, like persons, can be reduced to other kinds of things, such as what Siderits has called 'psychophysical elements' (p24). So while the Mādhyamikas *do* deconstruct the body into its component parts, the deconstruction, unlike that of Abhidharma, does not end in a final list of true existents. King (1995: 112) has made the same point with regard to the *Prajñāpāramitā* texts, for which 'there is no level at which the reductionist process can conceivably end'. Such a deconstruction, then, for the Mādhyamika at least, is a sceptical one, leaving nothing in the place of the 'body' or 'being' it started out with; that is, nothing except dependent origination. Śāntideva, then, unlike Śaṅkara, would agree with modern philosophers of the mind, like Metzinger (2004: 563), who claim that there is no 'unchangeable essence' behind the notion of 'self'.

Even so, we should note, along with Perrett (2002: 377), that Indian Buddhist Reductionists 'were not *Eliminativists* about persons'. And while a distinction can be drawn between the general Buddhist view and the Prāsaṅgika (more minimalist) view, the Prāsaṅgikas (with whom Śāntideva has been historically lumped)[3] remained on a 'middle path with respect to the issue of personal identity' (p382). Now, Siderits (2003: 116) has argued that the 'distinction between Reductionism and Eliminativism cannot be drawn without using the distinction between conventional and ultimate truth'; but my argument is that Śāntideva can be read as *flickering* between the two. The distinction is thus non-graspable. For Śāntideva, then, the unenlightened person does indeed have enough ground to take care of their own livelihood, and so prudential concern is far from being 'irrational' (see Siderits 2003: 13). Prudence is only irrational if seen from an ultimate perspective, but when one shifts perspective, when one *flickers* between the Two Truths, prudence is rational indeed. In fact, prudence may go on to form the basis of a compassionate outlook (BCA. 8.92ff). Thus, Śāntideva writes:

> Even though my pain does not torment the body of others, that pain on the other hand is unbearable for me based on the love for myself. Although the suffering of another cannot be experienced by me personally, nevertheless, for him that pain is unbearable because of self-love. I should dispel the pain of others, just as I do my own, based on the fact that it is pain. And I should help others for they are beings like me (BCA. 8.92–4).[4]

Furthermore, in his call for a selfless response to the world of suffering beings, Śāntideva reconstructs his own deconstruction of the person, so the person is definitively reinstated. That is, the *bodhisattva* returns to the 'cave', as it were, and projects a fixed self onto other beings for their own sake.[5] This I label 'constructive altruism'. If his predecessor Nāgārjuna 'neither denies the world nor affirms it' (Bhattacharya 1998: 91), then Śāntideva, I argue, both denies it *and* confirms it.

Initially, Śāntideva establishes a rather negative view of people and society in order to persuade men to renounce the world of politics and desire. He then deconstructs the world of objects in order to bring on a glimpse of emptiness. Finally, he reconstructs the world of beings in order to convince monks into a compassionate response to others. We ought never to lose sight of these strategic means, for such manipulation requires that we contextualize each and every manoeuvre. Śāntideva thus begins with a provisional sense of the 'person', which includes their status and their gender. He later works from a self-imposed

---

3 The concept of sub-schools within the Mādhyamikas of India was likely a Tibetan invention (Williams 2009: 65), the terms 'Prāsaṅgika' and 'Svātantrika' never being employed by the Indian Mādhyamikas (Ruegg 2010: 160).

4 All translations from the Sanskrit are my own (unless otherwise stated).

5 The 'cave' metaphor is borrowed from Plato's *Republic*. For its modern application in the debate about self, see Kapstein (2001: 216) and Metzinger (2004: 547ff).

'delusional sense' of the person. So while the phenomenologist, James Giles (1993: 175) claims that the 'no-self theory lets the self lie where it has fallen', we will see that Śāntideva verily picks it up again! Ultimate truth (*paramārtha-satya*), then, does not, *pace* Sprung (1973: 44), bring the relative truth (*saṃvṛti-satya*) of persons to an end; it merely restructures the way in which one constructs the other (for we all construct others in one way or another).

Now, for Parfit, psychological continuity is more central to ethics than personal identity, and this continuity is a 'matter of degree' (1971: 25). This resonates with Buddhist thought, and equates with what Goodman (2009: 13) calls the 'loose unity' of our causal continuity. Peter Harvey thus identifies the false notion of a 'unitary' person, suggesting the Buddha accepted more a 'person as a cluster of changing physical and mental processes' (in Keown and Prebish 2007: 569). Of course, we should never presume that modern Western philosophers of the self (like Giles, Metzinger and Parfit) are speaking the same language as Buddhologists. For example, we should be careful not to misread Parfit to be saying that his 'matter of degree' also applies to rebirth, even when he says that psychological continuity can be regarded as 'more important than sameness of body' (Parfit 1971: 13); for Parfit clearly places the person within the brain (or parts of it) and seems to take 'body' as being everything bar the brain. For the pre-scientific, Indian tradition, the brain (if acknowledged) would be considered just another part of the body, along with the sense organs, of which the mind (*manas*) is but one. That is, according to Indian religions, mind is made of 'matter' (*bhautika*) (see Ch.U.Bh. VI.v.1),[6] and, though consciousness (*cit, vijñāna*) is said to interact with the body in this life, it would primarily be mental imprints/tendencies (*saṃskāras*) which gave rise to psychological continuity across lives (see B.S.Bh. III.i.1 and Ch.U.Bh. VI.ix.3).

Limiting our study to this life then, psychological continuity is not so much a question of whether me at t_1 is the same me at t_2. The question is flawed from the start by the assumption that 'me' picks out the individual. We would have already assumed too much. Nor is the Reductionist analysis a complete denial of the relationship between me (t_1) and me (t_2). Rather, what Parfit (along with the Indian tradition) is saying, is that both me (t_1) and me (t_2) are *constructed* by past states of affairs and by present conditions. If your name remains Derek through t_1 and t_2, then we have a legitimate right to pick you out with the name 'Derek' on both occasions. But we do not have the right to assume that you are unchanged. Nor should we fall prey to what Siderits (1997: 463) calls 'naïve semantic realism', believing Derek to be anything beyond that of a convenient designation. In arguing that the Buddhist allows for the convenient designation of the person on 'pragmatic grounds', Giles (1993: 176) thus inadvertently removes the Buddhist as a 'candidate for utter elimination' (Siderits 1997: 460): this manoeuvre is one of both Reduction and Construction. Through similar manoeuvres, Parfit (1984: 281–2) was able to

[6] Notably, the Upaniṣads say that the mind (*manas*) is made of 'food' (*annamaya*) (Ch.U. VI.v.4), a verse cited by Śaṅkara (U.S. Prose, 1.22) to prove to the pupil that the mind is part of the world of name and form (*nāma-rūpa*), and thus not an ultimate existent.

drop the concept of a permanent self, later making the emotional claim that he consequently had less fear of death. But more importantly, for my ethical thesis, he also claimed that he was 'more concerned about others' (p281). He therefore appears to agree with the Buddhists, who claim that letting go of the concept of 'self' leads to a greater degree of compassion for others, making one more prone to selfless action, or 'altruism'.

But what, you may ask, of Śaṅkara? While Western scholars are currently ready to admit that 'Buddhism has some valuable contributions to make' with regard to the question of personal identity (Giles 1993: 185), how is Śaṅkara to fit into this company of what we might assume to be self-denying atheists? For one, you might point out that Śaṅkara firmly believed in *ātman*. And two, you might think he believed this *ātman* to be God. These may seem like valid objections, but they are confused. For one thing, God as Lord (Īśvara) plays very little role in either Śaṅkara's soteriological or ethical project. To be liberated is simply to understand that one's consciousness is no other than *the one* consciousness (*brahman*). For the sharp-witted seeker of Self, it need have no further theological grounding. For such a seeker, it is not about sitting alongside God (Bṛ.U.Bh. III.v.1); it is not even about 'union' (*saṃyoga*) with *brahman* (U.S. Metric, 16.39–40). It is about knowing that one's 'apparent' (*ābhāsa*) individuality is not one's ultimate status. Indeed Metzinger (2004: 550) correctly noticed that Śaṅkara's intent was to avoid confusing ourselves with 'the shadow' self. But we should also realize that 'the shadow' (*chāyā*) for Advaita is more than just the body. It is also the apparent individuated self (*jīva*), which is taken to be true Self, like the 'reflection' (*chāyā*) of one's face in a mirror (U.S. Metric, 12.6). The task, for the Advaitin, is thus to 'de-individuate the *jīva*' (Ram-Prasad 2002: 7), that illusory subject which sets up a locus for relationships (*saṃbandha*) with God and the world (Ch.U.Bh. III. xiv.4). Only then does the seeker attain the 'shadowless' (*acchāyam*) *brahman* (P.U. 4.10).

As for ethics, Śaṅkara's main concern is with the freedom from socially imposed obligation that comes with a certain form of knowledge. This knowledge is then to be passed on. But this is not so much about doing God's work as about the continuation of lineage. In fact, he is explicitly rejecting the ritual that ties the *Brahmin* priest to the Gods. As for *brahman*, it plays no major part in Śaṅkara's ethical project other than the fact that when one sees *brahman* and *ātman* as non-dual, then one is beyond ethical obligations. Śaṅkara's soteriology, which is in fact a gnoseology, is less one of grace, faith and works, but more one of realization. One only need wake up and then wake up others. And here lies his principal ethic. Placed in these austere terms, the Buddhist would have no objections to such a life. I therefore believe that we could justifiably work with Śaṅkara's gnoseological and ethical project without reference to 'God' with all its Western connotations.

However, we may need to be more cautious when it comes to the case of Kṛṣṇa as Lord (*Bhagavan*). For there is no getting away from the fact that Śaṅkara looks up to Kṛṣṇa of the *Gītā*. He certainly never denies Kṛṣṇa his role of exemplary teacher of mankind, or as pure consciousness manifest. Nevertheless, while Kṛṣṇa is seen as the spokesman of social (egoless) ethics; the *brahman*-knower, as conceived by Śaṅkara, stands firmly outside this dutiful bond to Kṛṣṇa. Furthermore, the list of qualities that Śaṅkara applies to Kṛṣṇa (Bh.G.Bh., intro) are elsewhere, in his major works, denied applicability (B.S.Bh. II.ii.44–5). So once again, I feel we are justified in bracketing God (be it Īśvara, qualified (*saguṇa*) *brahman* or Kṛṣṇa) from Śaṅkara's main gnoseological concerns. We will, however, draw on the *Bhagavad-Gītā Bhāṣya* for his views on provisional ethics.[7]

Unlike other Brahmanical schools, Śaṅkara's Advaita does not hold to the theory of multiple 'selves', either standing in direct relation to a personal God (re: Dvaita Vedānta), or ritually working towards their own private salvation (re: Mīmāṃsa). In fact, even these non-Advaitic schools claim *ātman* in a 'purely formal' manner (Ram-Prasad, in Siderits et al. 2011: 220), where *ātman* pertains to essence rather than personhood. By personhood, I mean an individual with a unique psychological make-up, which emerges through social interactions. So Doniger (2010: 168) only confuses the issue by claiming that the 'person is the individual soul, the atman, or self, which is identical with the *brahman*'. While the average Hindu may well believe himself to have an ever-lasting individual 'soul' (*jīvātman*); this, according to Brahmanical tradition, is a mistaken view.

The mistake, as interpreted by the non-Advaitin, is to assume that one's actions relate to the *ātman* within, the mere witness (*sākṣin*) of actions (cf. *Bhagavad Gītā*).[8] The mistake, as interpreted by the Advaitin, is that the (socially and psychologically constructed) person takes consciousness as being their own, as 'mine', thus failing to recognize the singular nature of *brahman* (Ch.U.Bh. III.xiv.4): this mistake is what allows for the existence of *jīvas* (in the plural) and their transmigration. Here *jīva* is used in a manner similar to the Jains, and is comparable with the *ātman* of other Brahmanical schools. It is no more the pure witness, but is subject to phenomena through association with the individual person's mental apparatus. The best that such a person could hope for, that is, prior to *brahman*-knowledge, is a symbolic meditational and/or devotional relationship with God (Ch.U.Bh., intro).

On the other hand, to see *brahman* is to see the falsity of the *jīva* 'trope' of consciousness, putting an end to rebirth. For Śaṅkara, then, we are not given a 'soul' by God. Nor is it the 'soul' that sees and knows itself to be Self, as claimed in the *Bhagavad Gītā* (6.20) and echoed by Otto (1957: 4). To the *Gītā*'s (6.20) 'seeing the Self by the self' (*ātmanaṃ paśyann ātmanī*), Śaṅkara adds the words 'received through one's own mental apparatus' (*upalabha mānaḥ sve*) (Bh.G.Bh. 6.20), which is Śaṅkara's way of stressing that there is only one self which reveals itself locally. In the final analysis, there is only the attributeless (*nirguṇa*) all-oneness (*sarvathā-aikyam*). The liberated person, the *jīvan-mukta*, lives out his

---

7 Śaṅkara's commentary on the *Gītā* is the earliest extant version.

8 The *Gītā* accepts 'self-body dualism' and multiple 'indestructible selves' (Perrett 1998: 7, 18). Śaṅkara does not accept this view of multiple selves (Bh.G.Bh. 2.12; B.S.Bh. II.iii.50). For the extent to which this divides the various Schools of Vedānta, see Chari (2005).

days in this ultimate consciousness, not as an all-knowing soul, but as *brahman* embodied, until the *karma* which maintains his body runs out (B.S.Bh. III.iii.32; Ch.U.Bh. VI.xiv.2). For such a gnoseology, culminating in an ideal cognitive state, it is sufficient to reduce *ātman*-talk to consciousness-talk.

The consciousness in this consciousness-talk, according to Śaṅkara, is also your consciousness and mine. Derek's consciousness at t_1 and t_2 are nothing other than *brahman*. Consciousness, as true reality, has remained unchanged; only the (adventitious) mental imprints in Derek's mind have changed. That is, the 'consciousness of individuals is ontologically identical (though phenomenologically different) from that universal consciousness' (Ram-Prasad 2001a: 178). And so, at the conventional level of discourse, Śaṅkara admits psychological continuity in basically the same manner as the Buddhists do. Mental imprints (*saṃskāras*), deriving from action (*karma*), which itself derives from the mistaken belief in individual agency (*kṛtvā*), produces the clinging to individual goals. That is, all imprints are due to ignorance (*avidyā*). Thus, while accepting rebirth as a phenomenon, his assessment of it is essentially negative. This assessment is in accord with early Buddhism. However, we shall see how later Buddhists, like Śāntideva, gave a re-evaluation of rebirth in light of the compassionate wish to be reborn for the benefit of others.

It would seem then that any division of Indian philosophical schools into *ātmavādins* (Self-doctrine followers) and *anātmavādins* (Not-self-doctrine followers) (for example Perrett 2002: 377) is insufficient to bring out the import of Śaṅkara's non-dual move. For example, both Śāntideva and Śaṅkara must answer the (Nyāya) objection that 'connection between action and fruit is impossible without an [individuated] self' (BCA. 9.70). The Dalai Lama, perhaps before he became fully acquainted with Vedānta, also seems to overlook Śaṅkara when he writes:

> The non-Buddhists could not even assert the mere selflessness of persons, and from that, therefore, they derive the necessity of asserting a permanent, partless, independent person (Gyatso 1975: 73).

Buddhologist, Peter Harvey (1987), on the other hand, does draw the distinction between those that believe in an 'individual, inner self' (that is, non Advaita) and those that believe this self to be 'universal' (that is, Advaita).[9] He claims that, from a Buddhist point of view, the former 'encourages selfishness', while the latter 'can encourage impartiality to all' (p32). This seems to be based on the principle that, 'As we think the ultimate reality to be, so we behave' (Radhakrishnan 1989: 80). Yet, believing in an individual *ātman* would only encourage selfishness if one wrongly assumed it to be about a private self, somehow linked with one's own

---

9 Siderits et al. (2011: 4) have recently tried to overcome this category problem by dividing self-views into three types: substantialist (non-Advaitin), non-substantialist (Advaitin) and non-self (Buddhist).

history; that is, by confusing selfhood with personhood (see *Gītā*). In the words of Śāntideva: 'egoism [*ahaṃkāra*], which is the cause of suffering, increases from the delusion that there is a self [*ātma*]' (BCA. 9.77a). Here, he takes self to be the embodied person, 'this dream-like form' (9.87a), which consciousness grasps as being real.

In his *Brahma-Sūtra Bhāṣya* (I.i.1), Śaṅkara usefully lists all the different ways in which Indians have understood the meaning of 'self': as body-only (*deha-mātraṃ*) [Common people and the Lokāyata School], as mind (*cetana*), as momentary consciousness-only (*vijñāna-mātraṃ kṣaṇika*) [that is, Yogācāra], as empty (*śūnya*) [that is, Madhyamaka], as soul separate from the body and/or from God (Īśvara) [that is, other Vedāntins], and as *brahman* [Advaita]. Halbfass (1983: 91–2) interprets Śaṅkara here to be claiming that even the Madhyamaka are referring to an 'absolute *ātman*' when they speak of *śūnya*; however, he should not be taken this way. If we examine the *Upadeśa Sāhasrī*, we see that Śaṅkara's (mistaken) view is that the Madhyamaka are total nihilists (*vaināśika pakṣatvāt*), who believe the body *and* the self to be non-existent (U.S. Prose, 2.55).

But whilst accepting that everyone (barring the Mādhyamika) believes that, in one form or other, they have a self, and that no one believes, 'I do not exist' (B.S.Bh. I.i.1), Śaṅkara also denounces egoism (U.S. Prose, 1.6) and attachment to personhood. When claiming that, 'The existence of the self cannot be denied' (B.S.Bh. I.i.4), he need only be read as implying the mere 'inability to deny the particularity of consciousness' (Ram-Prasad 2001a: 165). This is so if the 'non-substantialist', by definition, 'sees the self as just consciousness itself' (Siderits et al. 2011: 4). And there is surely no controversy with the Buddhists here, for who could deny one's own consciousness?

For Advaita, then, the 'gnoseological project is the cultivation and disciplining of *jīva*-consciousness through analyzing away the inauthentic features of self found in egoity [*ahaṃkāra*]' (Ram-Prasad, in Siderits et al. 2011: 221). And it should also be pointed out that, just as knowledge of virtue may co-exist with non-virtuous action, so believing in non-self may co-exist with egoism. Thus, while extreme 'egoism' may well be the opposite of extreme 'altruism', it does not follow that a belief in non-self is necessarily altruistic.[10] The removal of egoity is a gradual affair, and so Buddhists are as prone to it as Hindus. Indeed, Śāntideva himself cries out, 'Oh, why do you not get rid of this "I" notion?' (BCA. 8.179b). Thus, a view acknowledged by both the Buddhist and the Advaitin is that negative emotions emerge from a wrong conception of self, and that one must therefore start by inhibiting one's identification with this false ego-sense.

Śaṅkara's philosophy would therefore, along with Śāntideva's, sit outside Parfit's (1971: 26) 'principle of self-interest' and, theoretically at least, should pass his 'principle of impartiality' (ibid.). In fact, we might note here how Śaṅkara, in his commentary to the *Īśā Upaniṣad* (5–6), links two Vedic verses to explicitly claim a potential view of impartiality and universalism. First he highlights the

---

[10] See Harris (2011).

verse 'The Self that is within all' (Bṛ.U. III.iv.1), and then links it with the verse 'When a man sees all beings in this Self, and the Self in all beings, he feels no hatred' (Īś.U. 6). It is also worth comparing this to the *Bhagavad Gītā*'s: 'One who has his mind self-absorbed through yoga, and who has the vision of universal sameness, sees his self existing in all things, and all things in his self' (6.29).

In his commentary (Bh.G.Bh. 6.29), Śaṅkara claims that such a sense of universal belonging even extends to 'inanimate' (*sthāvara*) objects. Besides presenting us with the potential for an Advaitin environmental ethics, two important teachings follow from this: 1) Just as one who is fully satisfied can have no desire (G.K. 1.9), so he who is one with the Self can feel no hatred; and 2) from the ultimate perspective of Self-knowledge, the other is non-different from oneself. This gives an interesting twist to the notion that a motivational model of altruism, which focuses on the person's intentions, must allow for 'combinations of self-in-others and others-in-self' (Krebs and van Hesteren 1994: 105).[11]

Śaṅkara's call for non-hatred can also be gleaned from the *Upadeśa Sāhasrī* (Prose, 1.4), where he illuminates us about the signs of true knowledge:

> When [the teacher] sees by signs that knowledge has not been grasped by the pupil, he should remove the causes of non-comprehension, which are: [past] sins, worldly heedlessness, lack of firm preliminary learning concerning the discrimination between what is eternal and non-eternal, listening to worldly opinion, pride of caste, etc – by means contrary to those causes, and enjoined by the scriptures, that is non-anger, etc., non-violence, etc., and those observances which are not contrary to knowledge.

Now Harvey (1987: 32) has claimed that the [Advaitin] universal view 'does not encourage respect for the individuality of different persons', by which he means 'different mind-and-body combinations' (ibid.). Here Harvey is defining an individual in the early Buddhist manner as a combination of mind and form (*nāma-rūpa*). When Perrett (2002) argues that 'Indian Buddhist Reductionists … were not *Eliminativists* about persons' (see above), he has in mind this definition of a person, with an implicit link to the concept of the five aggregates (the *skandhas*). I shall not take up this discussion of respect for individuality here, other than to note two things, one regarding Hinduism and the other Buddhism.

First of all, in revealing the concept of a singular *brahman*, the Advaitin indeed aims at the undermining of the conception of the individual, and this ought to be seen as a soteriological device. This need not affect their ethics. In fact, the *Bhagavad Gītā* specifically addresses its entire discourse to an individual, Arjuna, and Śaṅkara's commentary makes this even more explicit by arguing that certain individuals should be exempt from *Dharma* (as social ethics), whereas Arjuna, in his current state of gnosis, or lack of, should not. As we shall see, social ethics, for Śaṅkara, take place within a more preliminary conception of personhood,

---

11 Cf. Malinar (2007: 111ff) on the *Gītā*'s 'Self of the selves of all beings' (Bh.G. 5.7).

one which adopts a more 'extended sense of self' (Ram-Prasad, in Siderits et al. 2011: 222) which assumes social responsibilities. It is therefore not true that there is 'no "other" in Advaita Vedānta', as Krishna (in Bilimoria et al. 2007: 110) claims. Secondly, I will simply note that when the Madhyamaka School denies the five aggregates ultimate status (see MMK. 4.1–7), we may have to ask if this also jeopardizes their respect for the individuality of different persons. Given that Śāntideva did not *openly* endorse the *varṇa* (class) system, we will need to develop a more analytical method of investigation. However, his obvious gender bias and his even more obvious division of people into *bodhisattva* and *non-bodhisattva* categories does hint at the fact that distinctions still apply.

Now we are in a position to understand how both a Mādhyamika Buddhist, like Śāntideva, and an Advaitin, like Śaṅkara, are both going to deny individual personhood at the ultimate level, but are both willing to admit the person at the conventional level. They would both be content with Harvey's (1987: 45) description of a man as 'not just the sum of heredity and social, psychological … conditions', but as having a 'long past in a line of rebirths'. That is, the man is not only *socially constructed*, but is an *accumulation* of his own karmic history, and is therefore to be taken as a conventional person-as-continuity. While the name 'Derek' may pick out a specific embodied person in this life, it may not be used to pick that 'person' out in a future life. However, at the conventional level, the future being (human or otherwise), whose past *karma* is connected to Derek, will indeed be part of Derek's continuum (*saṃtāna*). Derek dies, but the continuum lives on. Just as it is for an understanding of modern thinkers like Parfit, so this model of continuity is central to understanding Advaita and Madhyamaka ethics.

To re-iterate, at the conventional level, man does enjoy the fruits of his actions and, according to the laws of *karma*, will benefit or suffer on the basis of past actions of body, speech and mind. Hence, both Śaṅkara and Śāntideva would accept the classical pan-Indian truth that a man 'becomes something good through good action and something bad through bad action' (Bṛ.U. III.ii.13). And while the Buddha may have shifted the nature of *karma* back to 'intention' (*cetanā*), the notion that 'people make their own "destiny" by their actions' (Harvey 1990: 40) remained a central tenet of Buddhism. For example, Śāntideva writes that, 'Suffering and happiness are the result of action' (*karmaṇaḥ sukha duḥkhe*) (BCA. 9.122a). However, at the ultimate level of analysis, there is no underlying entity to which all this happens. The belief that there is a single, unique, entity throughout life to which all these events happen is a mistaken one. Śāntideva *and* Śaṅkara, if they were alive today, would agree with Metzinger's (2004: 563) conclusion that,'No such thing as selves exist in the world'. These are all but shadows.

As we have already noted, Parfit suggests that through his insight into the lack of personhood, he was liberated from the fear of death and from a selfish attitude towards his own needs. This is understandable, for 'fear and attachment are closely interdependent and the absence of one inevitably leads to the nonoccurrence of the other' (Brassard 2000: 48). So we will find both Śaṅkara and Śāntideva stressing both the state of non-fear (*nirbhaya*) and non-attachment (*anāsakti*). To let go of the self is possibly the most fearful thing for man. But as we now know, Śāntideva and Śaṅkara are not denying our personhood, only the notion of a permanent individuated essence behind the person. It is this denial of the ultimacy of the individuated self by both traditions that gave rise to the 'Selfless Response' found in the title of this book. But a man free of attachment and fear is surely free to be 'selfless' in a more altruistic sense, for fear and attachment 'can stand in the way of acting on one's obligation to help others overcome suffering' (Siderits 2003: 201).

So, we can see how the term 'Selfless' may come to have three meanings:

1. I will use 'selfless' to indicate an ethical approach to the world, a form of conduct which aims to eradicate egoism, first by eliminating hatred and desire, and then by removing ignorance, especially the ignorance that leads to the assumption that one is an individuated self. For Śaṅkara, this ignorance, or nescience, takes the form of non-knowledge (*a-vidyā, a-jñāna*) of the true 'Self', which is *brahman*. Śaṅkara thus holds that our consciousness, our sense of presence, is but an aspect of *brahman*'s consciousness, which is all-pervading. For Śāntideva, ignorance may be taken as either a false belief in an individuated self (*ātman*), or again as *avidyā*, in the sense of non-realization of the inter-dependence of all phenomena, spoken of as emptiness (*śūnyatā*).
2. This leads to the second meaning of 'selfless' (better 'self-less'), the metaphysical view held by both Śaṅkara and Śāntideva that the individual has no permanent individuated 'self'. For Śaṅkara, this amounts to saying that when the true Self (*brahman*) is known, the 'imagined' individuated self (*jīva*) is no longer given any credence. However, this imagined self is given provisional status by Śaṅkara, who takes it to be that which transmigrates as a 'subtle self' (*liṅgātman*) for those who fail to know *brahman* (Bṛ.U.Bh. IV.iv.2). Here, the self is individuated in the sense that it the same 'self' that leaves one body and takes up another body, which accounts for karmic continuity. But such transmigration ends with knowledge of *brahman*, and with this knowledge the (illusory) *jīva* also ends. As such, this provisional self is impermanent. Even so, being provisional, it is not non-existent, and as such Śaṅkara may lean on the *jīva* (as well as the authority of the Vedas) as a focus of moral agency. The *jīva*, for Śaṅkara, was therefore a 'point of contact between metaphysics and ethics' (Isayeva 1993: 218). Of course, this 'agent' will be shrouded in nescience, and thus all action prior to the dawning knowledge of *brahman* is, to varying degrees, deluded action.

   For Śāntideva, there is no such provisional self, self-talk almost being a 'taboo' in Buddhism (Collins 1982: 12, 71–7), just as the doctrine of difference (*bheda*) is formally 'forbidden' (*pratiṣiddha*) in Advaita (U.S. Prose, 1.26–30). Nevertheless, Śāntideva will also make use of the fact that people *believe* themselves to be individuated in his call for a regime of daily meditation leading to a personal commitment to selfless conduct. Even here though, under ultimate meditational analysis, impermanence applies to every moment of consciousness. Hence, even though the 'person' who meditates and takes on the Bodhisattva Vow may be accepted as real, there is no permanent underlying self as *ātman* or as *jīva*. So, although consciousness is in some sense individual and eternal (in the sense of being both beginning-less and end-less), it is nevertheless to be seen as impermanent (*anitya*) due its momentariness (*kṣaṇikatva*). Transmigrations still take place, yet this is due to a consciousness-as-continuum rather than any permanent underlying individuated entity. In fact, due to the Vow demanded by Śāntideva's ethics, transmigrations ought never to come to an end, as the 'karmic potency of the vow falls upon successive' rebirths (Matics 1971: 18). This is true selflessness.

3. Finally, the third use of 'selfless' (or 'Self-less') applies only to Śāntideva, for his theory that all is inter-dependent also acts as a denial of any substratum. There is therefore no *brahman*, no universal ground of all consciousness, the only 'Self' that Śaṅkara acknowledges in the ultimate sense.

Due to the delusions of mankind, people are bound to this world, and so both Śaṅkara and Śāntideva are forced into accepting a conventional cultural reality. Both will argue that the way these average worldly beings see the world is fundamentally flawed. For Śaṅkara, this world is not made up of independent objects and beings, but is in fact all but a transformation of the one *brahman*. For Śāntideva, neither objects nor beings exist *from their own side*. Nothing has the independent existence assumed by the worldly; everything is inter-dependent, existing due to causes and conditions.

Both Śaṅkara and Śāntideva will argue that the worldly grasp at this world, imagining that by owning (impermanent) objects they will somehow find permanent happiness. Even the religious, who seek an (impermanent) divine realm for an (illusory) self, are surely deluded. However, it is here in this world of nescience that religion finds its true meaning. Therefore, both will equally denounce any attempt to deny this world of beings and physical objects. Hence, both will make strong appeals against any call for an idealism which might deny the role of ethical action and intention.

Both will go on to make use of a language of Two Truths (*satya-dvaya*), the conventional and the ultimate. Convention may be adopted in order to benefit those caught up in the 'false' or 'mistaken' (*mithyā*) image of the world, but these conventions are not to be taken as ultimately valid. The common aim of Śaṅkara and Śāntideva will be the liberation (*mokṣa, mukti*) of beings from nescience (*avidyā*). Liberation for Śaṅkara is a state of freedom which comes when one has dropped the mistaken belief in an individuated self and thus become one with the all-knowing universal consciousness. Liberation for Śāntideva is the state of freedom which comes when one has dropped the false notion of self and gained a realization of emptiness, the fact of dependent origination. Both will posit a living example, an embodied human being who is at once complete with the wisdom of the tradition, yet somehow *beyond* that tradition, an ideal of moral conduct, yet somehow *beyond* traditional moral law.

For Śaṅkara, the liberation which comes about when one sees that all is *brahman* is more than gnoseological, it is also the more final liberation from the cycle of rebirth. This is therefore the *brahman*-knower's last incarnation. Even so, whilst still embodied, the liberated Advaitin (*jīvan-mukta*) will act selflessly and without fear of death. For Śāntideva, liberation is purely in gnoseological terms. He will demand that the *bodhisattva* use this insight to liberate other beings, not just in this life, but in future lives. His insight into self-lessness is thus, paradoxically, a call to the 'self' to use that (ontological) self-lessness to be more actively selfless. The 'self' is maintained to a certain degree through what we might call a 'voluntary delusion'. Śāntideva then plays on the fact that we have now had an insight into non-self, but that we also remember what it was like to believe in a self. The *bodhisattva* thus has, what Metzinger (2004: 566) calls, the 'availability of earlier processing stages'. By fully adopting the ultimate view of emptiness (*śūnyatā*) towards one's own 'self', one is free to be (emotionally) selfless. By maintaining and accepting a deliberately delusional attitude towards the 'selves' of others, one is motivated into (ethically) selfless action. Such moments of volition, brought about by the general willingness to help others, generate the mental formations which guarantee rebirth.

In his response to Parfit and Buddhism, Jim Stone (1988: 532) has claimed that 'if we exist at all we come and go in a moment'. Whilst accepting Siderits' (1997: 461) critique that Stone mistakenly identifies the Buddha with Eliminativism, this statement of momentariness would have some appeal to a Mādhyamika like Śāntideva. Nevertheless, Śāntideva would want to add that the label 'person' has its value at the level of moral decision-making, thus reclaiming the Reductionist ground. Whilst developing my theory of 'flickering' in both Śāntideva and Śaṅkara, I will also be arguing that their basic acceptance of provisional reality allows for a much more permanent sense of the other, one which assumes fellow interlocutors.

Perhaps we can imagine Śaṅkara's non-dualistic response as being: 'We "exist" up until the moment that we realize that all is *brahman*, from whence "we" no longer exist'. But even here, the enlightened are entitled to turn back towards the world with sufficient compassion to see the 'we' in us. In either case, Madhyamaka and Advaita demonstrate a thesis which assumes an ultimate lack of individual agency combined with an acceptance of that agency on both conventional and ethical grounds. This being the case, we may feel uneasy with Siderits' (1997: 464) description of persons as 'conceptual fictions'. Even if Giles (1993: 176) turns out to be right in assigning such a view to Hume (on the basis of his 'bundle' theory) – a debate I will not pursue here – the ethical commitments of the Buddhist and Advaita traditions in India (as well as Tibet) should warn us against any such claim with regard to our Eastern counterparts. In fact, both Śāntideva and Śaṅkara wish to take these persons (as 'Derek' and 'Mark' and 'James' and 'you') as very much part of their reality. It would therefore seem that both Śāntideva and Śaṅkara are in an ideal position to answer those who know not how one could possibly live with such a counter-intuitive truth of non-individuation.

Let us see then how these two apparently opposing versions of revisionary metaphysics, espoused by Śaṅkara and Śāntideva, impact on the ethics of their traditions. How do these traditional ethical stances hold up to the theories of radical non-duality and emptiness, respectively? How indeed is one to live with the truth of non-individuation? What are the cognitive and emotive states of living liberation? Further, let us perhaps learn from their endeavours, and judge for ourselves whether their selfless models: 1) make sound sense, and 2) are of ethical value.

Chapter 2
A New Ethical Model

There is no doubt that a comparative ethical study of Indian Mahāyāna Buddhism and early Vedānta is long overdue. And it is quite evident that this particular metaphysical/ethical analysis of Śāntideva's Madhyamaka and Śaṅkara's Advaita Vedānta is just the beginning of what will hopefully be a sustained and probing recovery and rediscovery of the Sanskritic source material. Moreover, one anticipates that it will be a *practical* rediscovery; one which involves ethical questions as well as metaphysical ones, one which will hopefully lead on to novel approaches which aim at accessing the workings of consciousness and thus to the potential training of the human mind. With the advent of the cognitive sciences, it may well be that Indian philosophy has come of age and is finally being taken seriously in the Western academy. As well as the cognitive discoveries to be made from an analysis of Eastern systems and practitioners, one also hopes for an objective discussion of the ethical implications of such work.

Flickering Consciousness

The contribution made here continues a modern trend in Indian philosophy, the treatment of Buddhist and Brahmanical thinkers side by side, being subjected to analytic scrutiny. It is not my intention to show one system of thought to be superior to the other, nor to use one to show up the faults of the other. Rather I wish to present both on equal terms, as two answers to what they perceived as one fundamental question: how should one respond meaningfully to a world that is *like an illusion*, a world that is not quite what we perceive it to be? How ought we to react to this conscious, embodied existence that is fundamentally flawed, filled with suffering?

Yet this is no comparison for its own sake, simply placing two independent treatises side by side, showing up their similarities and differences. Rather, what I wish to demonstrate here is that two thinkers, from apparently conflicting religions, with radically opposite metaphysical starting points, may even so adopt a methodology that is remarkably similar, not only in structure, but in content and purpose. To reiterate, that a confirmed *ātmavādin* (self-doctrine follower) may so closely parallel an equally confirmed *anātmavādin* (not-self-doctrine follower) in the denial of individual agency and may so similarly argue for the ethical and soteriological consequences that follow from this intuition is nothing less than remarkable. Such a coincidence of philosophical analysis by two authoritative voices surely demands that we take a fresh look at how we distinguish Buddhists from their Brahmanical compatriots.

Furthermore, while this work is set up as a comparison of Śaṅkara and Śāntideva, it is also, by default, a comparison of the Hindu Advaita Vedānta School and the Indian-Buddhist Madhyamaka School. That I chose Śaṅkara to represent the views of Advaita Vedānta surely needs no explanation, his *Brahma-Sūtra Bhāṣya* generally being considered the School's foundational text. However, my choice of Śāntideva to represent the Indian Madhyamaka School may well come as a surprise to some. True, like Śaṅkara, Śāntideva is viewed as an 'authentic' voice within the tradition, a voice that continues to be quoted to this day. But unlike Śaṅkara, Śāntideva's pronouncements do not constitute the 'seeds' of his tradition's rhetoric, which (most scholars agree) are to be found in the writings of Nāgārjuna. Thus, most discussions of the Two Truths would take Śaṅkara and Nāgārjuna as their two major protagonists (for example Sprung 1973: 2–3). My choice then of Śāntideva (as opposed to Nāgārjuna) needs further explanation, and can thus be reduced to three broad reasons:

1. It is believed (by most modern historians) that Śāntideva was contemporary with Śaṅkara, which means that they were debating within the same Indian philosophical milieu. Nāgārjuna is presumed to have lived several centuries earlier.
2. I wish to demonstrate how both Advaita and Madhyamaka opposed and refuted the views of the Yogācāra. Nāgārjuna predates the rise of the Yogācāra School.[1]
3. I wish to highlight the value that both traditions put on embodied conduct, and Śāntideva is indeed the most dominant Mādhyamika voice on this issue.[2]

There are those who would like to obliterate the difference between Madhyamaka and Advaita Vedānta by collapsing one into the other. This is done by either making the emptiness (*śūnyatā*) of Madhyamaka into an Absolute (for example Murti, Conze and Ninian Smart), or else by taking the quality-less (*nirguṇa*) *brahman* of Advaita Vedānta to be a form of emptiness (for example Dasgupta) or by simply claiming that Buddhism is a *form* of Hinduism (for example Radhakrishnan and Vivekananda). But what I say here is, no, let emptiness be *empty* (even of itself) (BCA 9.32), and let the quality-less *brahman* be *full* of its being (*sat*) and its consciousness (*cit*) (U.S. Metric, 17.13). In other words, let these schools be the opponents, or even 'arch-antagonists' (Klostermaier 2007: 357), they themselves assumed they were. But having allowed them this much, let us then demonstrate just how close they were, not in doctrine or tradition, but in objectives and methodology.

---

[1] For an alternative view, which has Nāgārjuna living for 600 years (!) and thus witnessing the rise of the Yogācāra School, see Hopkins (1996: 356–64).

[2] The Wallaces state that Śāntideva's *Bodhicaryāvatāra* is the 'primary source of most of Tibetan Buddhist literature on the cultivation of altruism' (Wallace and Wallace 1997: 7). In contrast, Westerhoff (2009: 215) notes that, in Nāgārjuna, the 'specific ethical consequences of Madhyamaka thought are virtually absent'.

Hence, we will follow Śaṅkara and Śāntideva as they both struggle to construct a philosophy which will attempt to leave their respective conduct-oriented traditions intact, whilst at the same time putting forward a radical view of the absence of an ultimate moral agent. We will come to understand that both wish to:

1. deny the ultimacy of the individual agent;
2. deny the (Yogācāra) denial of the world;
3. leave intact a form of conduct consistent with moral agency.

In the broadest sense I see this comparison as having the following logic: having highlighted how radically opposite the metaphysics of Śāntideva and Śaṅkara are, I will go on to show how this, quite surprisingly, leads the two models to agree on their denial of the ultimacy of the individuated self, the philosophical core of the comparison. I will then propose that they both continue to subscribe to the ethics of their respective traditions. They will both insist that the ideal person, who truly knows reality (*tattva*), will *naturally* act according to the Law of moral correctness (*Dharma*), albeit in an unconventional manner. A liberated being approaches the world according to a Two-Truths (*satya-dvaya*) model, by which I mean a system whereby it is assumed that there are certain people who can see reality as-it-is (*yathā-bhūmata*) and who stand out against the vast majority who cannot. These people are aware of the ultimate truth (*paramārtha-satya*), of how things truly are. At the other end of the spectrum, there are the common folk, who are only privy to the relative world of objects and means. In taking this epistemological approach, I will be speaking of 'Truths' more often than 'Realities', though the notion of 'Two-Realities' will also feature in my analysis of Śaṅkara's view of the world. The relative truth is referred to under various Sanskrit terms, '*vyāvahārika*', '*prātibhāsika*', or '*saṃvṛtti*'. Often, however, the term adopted by both Śāntideva and Śaṅkara is '*loka*', the 'worldly'. Here they are either bowing to consensus or contrasting it with the views of the wise. Though never claiming to be liberated or enlightened, both Śāntideva and Śaṅkara will adopt this mode of epistemological and/or ontological analysis. Our first and primary hermeneutical tool then is this Two-Truths stance, and an awareness of the shifts in truth levels.

It is noteworthy that Śāntideva begins his chapter on wisdom (*prajñā*) in the *Bodhicaryāvatāra* (from here on, *BCA*) with these verses:

> It is declared that there are two truths, the conventional and the ultimate. Reality is not within the scope of the intellect. The intellect is said to be [grounded in the] conventional. Thus people are seen to be of two types, the ordinary and the *yogis*. The views of the ordinary are superseded by those of the *yogi* (BCA. 9.2–3).

The *yogi* then is not simply an intelligent person; he is one with a superior insight into nature. Likewise, Śaṅkara will state that only the *brahman*-knower (*brahma-jñānin, brahma-vid*) is privy to the ultimate view of things, not the ritualist, believing as he does in a separate God:

> Self-knowledge is to be attained, and the self – being devoid of the attributes of hunger, etc. – is to be distinguished from the means and fruits of ritual action. To understand the self as being identified with these is ignorance. As it says in [this] Upaniṣad [I.iv.9]: 'He [who worships another God thinking] "He is one, and I am another" does not know' (Bṛ.U.Bh. III.v.1).

Nor is the one who insists on relying on the intellect, privy to the ultimate:

> Moreover, this connection of the self with the adjunct of intellect has forever been associated with misunderstanding and misunderstanding cannot come to an end except through right knowledge. Hence, so long as there is no realization of the Self as *brahman*, so long does the connection with the intellect persist (B.S.Bh. II.iii.30).

There is a problem with this model however. It leads one to believe that something is either ultimate or relative. That is, it leads to an either/or methodology. But to jump to this conclusion would be to completely misinterpret both traditions. What we need to realize is that knowledge or wisdom is not an all or nothing situation. Both Śāntideva and Śaṅkara will offer a gradual approach to complete knowledge. Taber (1983: 5) has argued that Śaṅkara's philosophy is 'transformative', by which he means that he accepts certain virtues and practices as 'necessary means' to liberation. Śāntideva is working within the classic six-*pāramitā* (perfections) schema of means (that is, generosity, morality, patience, effort, meditation) and wisdom. Reaching a new stage of perfection implies a new level (*bhūmi*) of understanding, so there are clearly those that must partially know the whole truth.

It is interesting that Kohlberg's much discussed work on moral development (see Scott and Seglow 2007: 69–70) also describes six 'hard' stages (see Krebs and van Hesteren 1994: 106) of moral development which successively transform and displace each other. I do not intend to make too much of this here for two reasons: 1) Śāntideva's stages do seem to be 'softer' than those found in, say, the *Daśabhūmika Sūtra*, and 2) Kohlberg-like 'hard-stages' models seem to be going out of vogue (Krebs and van Hesteren 1994: 108). In fact, they were already coming under attack in the late 1970s for being too rigid and for ignoring social factors (Rosenthal and Zimmerman 1978: 22). Krebs and van Hesteren (1994: 107) prefer a model based on what they call a 'soft conception of stages' which implies 'quantitative increases in cognitive capacity or competence'. It is particularly interesting that they suggest that people 'may well behave at a high level in one domain and at a low level in another' (ibid.). This would presumably allow a *yogi*, who had reached a certain level of 'seeing', to remain prone to seeing the world in a manner more in line with the conventional norms of perception. It would also allow for someone to cognize the world in terms of 'old stage-structures' (p110). Also, given that people are able to 'flexibly shift' between stages (Rosenthal and Zimmerman 1978: 150–51), there seems no reason why we should not allow for involuntary and/or voluntary 'flickering' between levels.

In the Buddhist tradition, those that partially know the truth are sometimes referred to as '*bodhisattvas*', and at other times as '*yogis*'. It is therefore of paramount importance that Śāntideva follows the above introductory verses with the following line: 'Moreover, the views of some yogis are superseded by the views of others of even higher wisdom' (BCA. 9.4a).[3] Commentaries indicate that a *yogi* is anyone who has attained the path of seeing (*darśana mārga*)[4] (see Sweet 1977: 56–7). The Dalai Lama states that, 'when one cognises emptiness directly for the first time, the path of seeing is attained' (Gyatso 1975: 45), and one enters the first stage (*bhūmi*). In the *Śikṣā Samuccaya* (from here on, *Compendium*), Śāntideva distinguishes between those who have entered the stages (*bhūmi-praviṣṭa*) and 'ordinary' men (*pṛthag-jana*) (Ś.S. 140). Of these ordinary men, Śāntideva says that their minds waver (*cala cittatāyā*). But once we understand that 'even an ordinary man' (*pṛthag-jano 'pi*) can be a *bodhisattva* (Ś.S. 6), we see that they are only 'ordinary' when compared with those *bhūmi-praviṣṭa*, and are thus an intermediate category, the so-called 'commencing' *bodhisattva* (*ādikarmika-bodhisattva*).[5] But there is also an indication that one may fall back from a higher level of realization. In the *BCA*, Śāntideva says that a male *bodhisattva* may still fall under the spell of a beautiful woman because 'at the time of seeing her, the influence of emptiness [in him] is weak' (BCA. 9.31b). Thus, we see that meditation on emptiness can lead to different degrees of wisdom (*prajñā*) as it proceeds through a number of stages. It is due to such experience and development that one *yogi*'s wisdom may be said to be higher than another's.

With a similar stress on gradualism and levels of wisdom, Śaṅkara states that the scriptures, 'gradually remove [the pupil's] ignorance about [the Self]' (U.S. Prose, 1.42). And again:

> One hears about the Self – unchanging and eternally uniform though it is – that there remains a difference in the degree of manifestation of glory and power, caused by the gradation of the minds through which it is conditioned (B.S.Bh. I.i.11).

Moreover, 'It is known that the gradation of authorization is determined by people's abilities, predilections, etc' (B.S.Bh. I.4). Furthermore, Śaṅkara talks of those aspirants of slow (*manda*) or middling (*madhya*) understanding, who must rely on meditation and symbolic devices (Ka.U.Bh. I.ii.17). Again, Śaṅkara says of meditation on the letter 'OM', that: 'These recitations are supplementary aids

---

[3] The *Śikṣā Samuccaya* (*Compendium*) even divides the ignorant into categories (Ś.S. 180–81), speaking of the 'more deluded' types.

[4] This is the third path (*mārga*) of five, as described by the Yogācāra School. These are the paths of preparation, application, seeing, cultivation and completion.

[5] I take this to mean either a person who came to Buddhism through the Mahāyāna, or one who has converted from the Śrāvaka (individual liberation) path. The *Compendium* was intended for such people (Ś.S. 356).

towards a non-dual realization by way of presenting a flash of true reality through the purification of the mind' (Ch.U.Bh., intro).

Moreover, Śaṅkara even admits that a *brahman*-knower may remain with his wife and desire worldly objects due to deep-seated tendencies which 'cannot suddenly be dropped' (Ch.U.Bh. VIII, intro). But if the 'empirical world of multiplicity' truly disappeared from the consciousness of a *brahman*-knower (see Deutsch 1973: 84), how would this knower even recognize his wife or any other thing as being an object of particular value? Gandhi (2009: 150) once said:

> The idea that the Brahman is real and that the visible universe is illusory is simply beyond the capacity of our reason to comprehend. How difficult it must be, then, to live according to it, to live forever absorbed in the *Atman*.

Gandhi adopts this move to demonstrate the advantages of the path of *karma-yoga* in tandem with devotion to a personal God; but I adopt it to show that the majority of seers are simply *not* 'forever absorbed', be they Hindu or Buddhist. In fact, Gandhi later adopts such a view when he states that the free ethical reign given by Kṛṣṇa to one without a sense of 'I' (Bh.G. 18.17) is in fact written about an 'imaginary, ideal' figure (Gandhi 2009: 191). In other words, no such person exists. And we should note that Śaṅkara speaks of 'teachers who are almost omniscient' (*sarva-jña kalpair ācāryaiḥ*) being capable of imparting *brahman* knowledge (P.U.Bh., intro). So when comparing the Advaitin teacher with their students and others, we are talking about relative wisdom rather than omniscience versus ignorance.

This calls for a second hermeneutical tool, for we now have those that *fully* know reality, those that *partially* know reality (through glimpses of its nature) and those that simply *know not*. While the first tool was ontological in nature, this will need to be more epistemological. It is of paramount importance to realize that both Śāntideva and Śaṅkara assume the average person to be epistemically deluded. As Śāntideva puts it:

> Ordinary people see existent things and imagine them to be real. They do not see them as illusion-like. This is where there is dispute between the worldly and the *yogis* (BCA. 9.5).

And even the *Brahmins* come under attack from Śaṅkara:

> Rites are enjoined for a person who naturally has the notion of being an agent and an enjoyer, and who is possessed of the defects of attraction for and aversion against the results of such rites … Therefore rites are enjoined only for those who have such defects as ignorance, etc., but not for one who is possessed of non-dual knowledge (Ch.U.Bh., intro).

But the *yogis* themselves are prone to certain errors until they are fully enlightened. And though not as explicit as Śāntideva about levels of knowledge, Śaṅkara will also note this tendency to err by those who have yet to be fully established (*sthita*) in *brahman* (Bṛ.U. Bh. I.iv.10). And as we have just seen, these errors can compromise the ascetic ideals of Śaṅkara. Flaws aside, they are still to be known as men of realization.

I will refer to these people in the middle category as having a 'flickering' consciousness, that is, one which flickers between common delusions and knowing the ultimate truth. In the case of Śāntideva, we see that flickering is apparently imposed on the *bodhisattva* in order to maintain a focus for a compassionate response to those who suffer:

> [If you argue] 'For whom is compassion if no beings exist?' [We respond] For anyone who [our voluntary] delusion projects for the sake of what must be done. [Objection] Whose is the task to be done if there are no beings? [Response] True, the work is indeed delusional, but in order to bring about the end of suffering, the delusion which conceives the task is not restrained (BCA. 9.75–6).

In the case of Śaṅkara, flickering is my way of saving him from contradiction when he claims that one needs to have given up the world of form in order to be enlightened, but then speaks of those enlightened ones who still fall under the illusion of form. Śaṅkara's ingenious solution is to speak of the strength of past tendencies (*saṃskāras*) which, once in a while, may create obstacles to clear seeing:

> However, mistaken cognition, even when annulled, continues for a while owing to the influence of past tendencies, like the cognition of two moons [due to an eye condition][6] (B.S.Bh. IV.i.15).

Again, in the *Bṛ.U.Bh*, Śaṅkara says that there are those who hold that *brahman*-knowers maintain desire for sexual union (*saṃbandha*) and accuses them of not having listened to the Upaniṣad (Bṛ.U.Bh. II.iv., intro). And yet, in the *Ch.U.Bh*, Śaṅkara makes what appear to be two contradictory statements about the relationship between men of knowledge and women. First he tells us that a man of knowledge (*viduṣa*), unlike the worldly, does not amuse (*krīḍati*) himself with women (VII.xxv.2), and then he tells us that, due to past habits dying hard, the spontaneous detachment brought about by realization may not be sufficient to hold back the force of lustful tendencies, and so injunctions of celibacy and so on become necessary (VIII, intro). But if one who desires after women cannot possibly know the Self, then how does this situation arise? The answer lies in the above notion of latent tendencies.

6 The two-moon (*dvi-candra*) analogy is repeated at B.S.Bh. III.ii.21 and C.U.Bh. II.xxiii.1, where the eye condition is given as '*timira*' and '*taimirika*' respectively. The same condition is mentioned in Candrakīrti's *Prasannapadā* (58.7–9). It is also found in the *Diamond-Sūtra* (32) as one of the nine analogies of illusion.

Here I wish to note that my concept of 'flickering' is more useful than Marcaurelle's either/or interpretation of Śaṅkara's position. Marcaurelle (2000: 132) states that, for Śaṅkara, 'one can either identify with the desireless and actionless Self or with the personality of a householder nourished by desire, but not with both at the same time'. But where there are latent tendencies, there is also flickering, and as such one can indeed live as a householder with desire for one's wife whilst at the same time having periods of *brahman*-consciousness.

As well as these temporary losses of *brahman*-consciousness, there are also temporary breakthroughs. Thus, Śaṅkara speaks of those who chant certain *mantras* having a 'flash' (*avabhāsaka*) of true reality (Ch.U.Bh., intro). Śaṅkara's view is that *brahman*-consciousness can be both gained and lost. The monastic life (without wife, sons or duties) is the best way of ensuring that most of one's time is spent in *brahman*-consciousness, guaranteeing final liberation. He writes:

> And a man who wishes to attain this view of the ultimate truth should abandon the … desire for sons, wealth and worlds, which result from misconceptions about caste and life order, etc. (U.S. Prose, 1.44).

Flickering consciousness, or temporary lapses, is therefore a most useful means of interpreting Śaṅkara's way of allowing for the behaviour of the enlightened householders. In fact, as I will argue throughout this book, Śaṅkara's moves with regard to the actions of knowers will not do *unless* one accepts the notion of flickering. In other words, the issue is not whether the person is fully enlightened or not, the point is that the person can be enlightened at $time_x$ and slightly deluded at $time_y$, and that he may flicker between these states.

In the case of Śāntideva, this flickering is admitted, and is said to go 'unrestrained'. In other words, it is voluntary. In the case of Śaṅkara, it seems less than voluntary. The *brahman*-knower, who Śaṅkara feels should be celibate, lapses into lustful thoughts due to past habits. However, when we consider the case of teaching, we will come to understand that Śaṅkara's ideal teacher must be capable of distinguishing a *Brahmin* male from a non-*Brahmin* female *even though* the *brahman*-knower is said to be beyond seeing the world in such dualistic terms. My theory of flickering would allow for this level of conventional seeing by claiming that the knower switches to a more provisional view of reality. In a sense, this is more a case of *oscillating* between two realities, but because Śaṅkara has already admitted the negative effect of past tendencies, I prefer to stay with the notion of flickering, which is perhaps a more dynamic form of switching. Whether this mode of switching is also to be seen as *erratic* is another question and is beyond our knowledge. Whatever the speed or frequency of switching, my argument is that it must take place.

Now Śaṅkara may be comforted by recent research that seems to show that the 'higher a person's level of development, the lower the probability that he or she will invoke low stage forms of thought and behaviour' (Krebs and van Hesteren 1994: 110). Nevertheless, the point has been made that enlightenment is not an all or nothing situation and this is another essential point which will help us understand the question of self. To repeat, I am claiming that both Śāntideva and Śaṅkara can be saved from contradiction if we assume that their knowers of reality flicker between seeing the world in ultimate terms and in seeing it provisionally. By seeing the world in ultimate terms, they are capable of its transcendence. And by seeing the world provisionally, they allow themselves the ability to act compassionately for others. Flickering also allows them to see themselves as having no individuated self whilst maintaining the notion of an individuated self in the other. Also, through the notion of flickering, we can gather that those of less than perfect understanding may still have moments or flashes of absolute truth which provide them with religious authority.

When we come to the ethical implications of such epistemological assumptions, it may also be worth bearing in mind that Monroe (1998: 7, 16–18) has come to similar conclusions with regard to altruism, which she describes as 'running along a continuum'. Behaviour is never purely altruistic or purely self-interested, but always lies somewhere between. Both our models refuse *either/or* categorizations. Krebs and van Hesteren (1994: 104) also see this as a key feature of their model, claiming that it 'supplies a basis for surmounting problems with either-or, egoism-altruism dichotomies, implying that most helping behaviours are guided by both egoistic and altruistic goals'.

De Silva (in Ames 1994: 312) brings the gnoseological and the ethical fields together, when he says that 'the more penetrating our insight into the no-self doctrine is, the more vibrant becomes the self-transcending emotions of compassion and kindness'. As the self here is the ego-centred (illusory) individuated self, this is equally capable of incorporating the Advaitin realization of the 'nothing' that one is (Deutsch 1973: 48). Both the affective and the cognitive faculties, including the ability to see reality as-it-is, are thus meaningfully tied to the denial of the individuated self. It is only compassion for others that prevents the Mādhyamika and the Advaitin from seeing them as, what Krishna (in Bilimoria et al. 2007: 110) has called, 'absolute ontological nullities'.

Krebs and van Hesteren's (1994: 114–15) 'Stage Alignments' are of much interest here, for it shows theorists positing completion stages with regard to self and to morality. According to Krebs and van Hesteren (1994: 134), the first social scientist to study altruism was Harvard Sociologist, Sorokin, who argued for a 'supraconscious' level of development, which, he claimed, leads to cases of 'supreme altruists'. Now, two of the examples he gave were, interestingly enough, Gandhi and the Buddha. So it would seem that Hinduism and Buddhism do indeed have much to offer in the field of ethics, especially in the domain of altruism.

Unlike our Western theorists, with regard to ethics, both Śaṅkara and Śāntideva will both face the same paradox of why selfless persons should be concerned with following the ethical prescriptions at the conventional level. Both will need to answer why a liberated being should even bother to help those who are seen as being without individuated selfhood. They will both mix ultimate and conventional truth in their responses in what may *seem* like a paradoxical manner, both relying on the analogy of dream and illusion. However, they will both strongly deny idealistic theories of reality, which, I will argue, are potentially dangerous to their ethical systems, for such theories might be seen as questioning the reality of persons even at the conventional level. By comparing Śāntideva's worldview with Śaṅkara's, it will be shown that a selfless response to an illusion-like world is a common factor in both models. A critical reflection on these models will assess whether the lack of moral agency is a meaningful notion and whether it is a positive factor in the pursuit of ethics.

It will therefore be shown that both Śāntideva and Śaṅkara prescribe forms of ethical conduct which seem to assume an agent whilst also insisting on the lack of ultimacy of this agent. They will both open themselves to similar criticisms, namely 'Who is the actor?' and 'Who are they acting for?'. If these criticisms can be overcome, both models might suggest that a denial of an ultimate individual-as-moral agent is a notion worthy of consideration. I will argue that the way to overcome them is through the notion of Two Truths and the implied flickering between them.

Comparison and Tension

In a recently published book on Śāntideva, Clayton (2006) felt the need to give a lengthy explanation of the validity of comparison as a human act. She concluded that it is through comparison that 'we come to know, integrate, and articulate knowledge of anything' (p12). To a certain extent, as an academic seeking my own comparative methodology, I am happy to accept her conclusion. However, I would like to add some 'tension' to this conclusion, for it all seems a little too neat, too *positivist*, and there remains in me a certain degree of disquiet.

Three questions keep arising: 1) Can these philosophies actually be understood by the 'uncommitted' mind?; 2) Can we actually compare systems which deal in non-dualistic frameworks and Two-Truth hierarchies and come away with anything like certain knowledge?; and 3) Should we, as academics, even be aiming so high?

It is beyond question that we must aim for clarity of articulation, but we ought never to assume that what we articulate is *fact*. After all, metaphysics and ethics are not mathematics. Our interpretation can only ever be tentative. The interpretive (mystical) question – 'Do relative matters filter back into the ultimate?' may have to be restated academically as – 'Do those truths accepted within provisional reality have an effect on the ultimate truths being posited?' The thesis here is that they do, but only partially. In order to remain coherent to the world, the relative discourse must put pressure on the ultimate view, but the ultimate view can only be allowed to *bend*, never to break. The resulting 'tension', generated by the awareness of these two views, shall always be there, not only in all truth claims, but in all prescriptions to act. Both Śāntideva and Śaṅkara are equally subject to this model, for they equally flicker between the Two Truths in their description of the world. All we can do then is try to give each philosopher the best reading we can, and to articulate our findings in the clearest manner possible, being as sympathetic to their project as possible, whilst remaining objectively critical. Comparison, at its best, helps to tease out features of one model which are more evident in the other model.

It would be wonderful if we could overcome the temptation to use such labels as 'contradictory' or 'ambiguous' or 'paradoxical' for the philosophy of Advaita and Madhyamaka. Although the temptation is indeed great, we need to resist it for two important reasons: 1) it offers an essentially negative account of the overall system, and 2) it actually says nothing. And so Taber (1983: 52) wrote of Śaṅkara, 'His statements only appear as contradictions when one interprets them rigidly in terms of the ordinary human conceptual system'. Śaṅkara was trying to express the concept of *brahman*, while believing that '*brahman* is inexpressible' (Bh.G.Bh. 13.12). On Madhyamaka, Inada (1993: 13) wrote: 'It is trite to say that language can never reach reality per se, and yet we must remind ourselves of this to restitute the Śūnyavāda from the charge of nihilism'. Of course, Śaṅkara was one of those who made the charge, and so we need to offer a sympathetic reading of the thesis that 'all is empty'. Likewise, we must try to explain what Śaṅkara meant by 'all is Self'. Further, we must attempt to articulate the differences in these competing Two-Truth hierarchies. The problem that both reader and writer face is how to understand something that is 'presented in a way that deviates from the only mode of understanding we know' (Taber 1983: 52); hence, the disquiet.

And so, I wish to hereby introduce the notion of 'tension'. I will often return to this 'tension' as my third hermeneutical tool (the others being the 'Two Truths' and 'flickering'). It will act dynamically throughout, often hidden from view, primarily as a *warning* that the Two Truths are *not* totally distinct fields of analysis, but cross over into each other's domains. We can therefore see how this discursive notion of 'tension' is closely related to the psychological notion of 'flickering', a phenomenological feature of those who are on the path.

In working out this model, I am of course indebted to others who have puzzled over similar problems. With regard to the ultimate mode of being, and my notion of 'flickering', I am indebted to Peter Harvey's work on the final state of a Buddhist practitioner (the *arhat*) according to the Pāli Suttas. I wish to quote Harvey (1995: 222) at length here:

> [W]hereas the 'early Suttas' see the full realization of *nibbāna* as an 'unsupported', objectless state of discernment, where other mental factors are absent and activity in the world does not seem possible, the Mahāyāna sees 'non-abiding' *nirvāṇa* as compatible with action in the world. Only if the Arahat rapidly alternated between objectless, nibbānic discernment and object-directed states of discernment could these two perspectives be brought together … The 'early Suttas', though, contain no hint of an enlightened person choosing to remain in *saṃsāra* after death. From the perspective of the 'early Suttas', the unsupported nibbānic state would be either dwelt in for specific, limited periods, or perhaps a state which rapidly alternated with normal consciousness.

Now I am aware that this interpretation of *nibbāna* as a beyond death continuation of 'unsupported discernment' is highly contested (see Gethin 1997, and Bodhi 2000: 421, n314), but we need not enter into this debate. All we need for our purposes is the concept of 'flickering' between a relative state and an absolute state of seeing. Now Harvey does not actually use the term 'flickering' here, though 'rapidly alternated with normal consciousness' may surely be taken as synonymous. Harvey does, however, use the term 'flickering' in his translation of the canonical *Dhammapada* verse '*Phandanaṃ capalaṃ cittaṃ durakkhaṃ dunnivārayaṃ*' (33a), which Harvey (1995: 114) translates as 'The flickering fickle *citta*, difficult to guard, difficult to control'. The context of the verse shows that 'flickering' (*capalaṃ*) here is to be seen as negative, and might well be translated as 'wavering'. In other words, it matches Śāntideva's use of the term '*cala*' to describe ordinary men who waver in thought (Ś.S. 140). In a similar vein, Harvey (1995: 114) speaks of 'competing mind-sets' and 'empirical, functioning *selves*', which need to be controlled. Perrett (1998: 30) usefully talks of a 'scrutinizing subset' of beliefs which, changing over time, leads to 'self-revision'. Śāntideva sees the task of the will in similar terms: 'Freed from all other concerns, with one-pointed mind, I shall exert myself in taming this mind and towards meditative concentration' (BCA. 8.39).

Eventually, according to certain Mahāyāna texts, such as the *Daśabhūmika Sūtra*, when one has reached the eighth *bhūmi*, one is '*acala*', unwavering, firm and immovable; one's knowledge is non-regressive (see Cleary 1993: 764–76). So we might reasonably talk of two types of 'flickering': the first being the minds of common folk which flicker between one thought and another, which I will refer to as 'wavering', and the second being the mind of a partially enlightened being which flickers or oscillates between objectless consciousness and relative existence. For both Śaṅkara and Śāntideva, the former is to be overcome via a single-minded approach to liberation from nescience. As for the latter, I argue that both Śaṅkara and Śāntideva will rely on it for the sake of compassionate activity.

My second debt, though more indirect, goes to the Scottish philosopher, David Hume (1711–76). In one place, Hume tells us that 'existence and non-existence destroy each other, and are perfectly incompatible and contrary' (Treatise, I.iii.1). This seems a reasonable enough argument and one that Paul Williams (1998a: 107–12) draws on in his critique of Śāntideva. However, Hume later goes on to state that it is 'easy for us to conceive any object to be non-existent this moment, and existent the next' (Treatise, I.iii.3). Elsewhere, Hume also states that, 'whatever is intelligible, and can be distinctly conceived, implies no contradiction' (EHU, IV.ii.18).

So, for example, we might imagine a virtual car race. When a child is about to enter into the game, they do not actually believe they are entering a truly existent race. However, midway through, they might find themselves believing the race to be real. At other moments, they see that it is *only* a game. They thus flicker between existence and non-existence. Hume wishes to use this capacity of our imagination to question the necessity of a causal account of phenomena, whereas I wish the reader to note that a flickering consciousness may well see 'objects' and 'social games' as alternatively existent and non-existent, and may thus learn to see things as empty of inherent existence or as illusion-like. In other words, to stretch the analogy, noticing that the game is a virtual one does not deny the car's conventional existence. Unlike Hume then, I adopt his statement about conception as a *response* to his statement about existence and non-existence, and thus deny his either/or interpretation. Again, this demonstrates how the 'tension' between the ultimate and the relative view might be approached through the notion of 'flickering'.

My third debt goes to the British moral philosopher, Bernard Williams (1929–2003) and his inspirational collection of essays, *Problems of the Self* (1976), and particularly his famous hypothetical experiment, whereby two people agree to undertake an exchange of 'selves' (1976: 46–63). This may be taken to imply either an exchange of bodies, or an exchange of brains, or an exchange of memories. One body is to be given a prize; the other is to be tortured. These people, A and B, are to decide which body should get which treatment (assuming the choice is made on 'selfish grounds'). The problem, of course, is whether we see our 'self' to be the body or whether we see it to be mental data. Williams' treatment of this experiment is fascinating, and I will return to it later. But here I simply wish to highlight three points: 1) Williams refuses to merely acknowledge these as 'borderline cases' and leave it at that; 2) He refuses to sit comfortably with the notion of 'ambivalent concern' for the self; and 3) He acknowledges the 'artificial' neatness of the experiment. Where Williams (1976: 63) talks of the 'risk' in making such a choice about a future self, I would like to talk of the 'tension' in this choice.

In terms of ethics, one might feel a little uneasy about the language of 'tension' and 'flickering' and the lack of fixity that these terms conjure. It could be argued that ethics demands a firmer, more objective base. One may even feel that 'flickering' conjures up an erratic state of mind. But like Bernard Williams, I feel we must accept that the ground on which we state these problems of the self is indeed 'shaky' by nature. Not only is the ground generally 'shaky', but, more specifically, it is the concern for the 'ambivalent' self that provides the starting point for the ground of Śāntideva's case for selfless conduct; and of course the question 'What is the nature of this "ambivalent" self?' is the catalyst of Śaṅkara's gnoseology. Indeed, it is the fact that they both so ardently deny our reality and yet so fervently reaffirm it that makes their work so relevant. For Śaṅkara and Śāntideva, these were no 'effete intellectual puzzles' (see Solomon, in Ames 1994: 9). In fact, I believe that we modern philosophers of self can learn much from these medieval thinkers, who positively grasped both horns of the bull of Two-Truths, who overcame the ambivalence of either A or B by affirming the 'tension' of both A *and* B.

I therefore urge the reader to keep the above-mentioned hermeneutical devices in mind as they reflect on the teachings of these two fascinating, and at times, puzzling systems of thought and practice. To repeat, these are:

1. The ontological Two-Truth models
2. The epistemological notion of:
   - those who know reality as-it-is,
   - those who are deluded, and

   – those whose cognitions flicker between these two
3. The discursive notion of 'tension' between the Two Truths

The Virtue Model of Comparison

One model of comparison, which was made particularly dominant in Buddhist ethics by Damien Keown, is that of Virtue Ethics. Now, a virtue ethics, in simple terms, may be taken as an approach to ethics which focuses on the moral subject and the kind of life they ought to lead. As the name suggests, the subject's attention should be on the cultivation of a particular set of 'virtues' which aim at the development of *character* rather than at the development of discrete behaviour. The set of virtues one ought to cultivate is often thought to be a matter of culture and tradition. It may also be taken to be a question of refining one's human nature or of grooming our God-given qualities. Nevertheless, one would expect that a virtuous person is one who we (or those with the authority to judge) would conclude was of 'good' character. Such a person would also be expected to reach some stage of completeness, whereby they lived a flourishing human existence, ending perhaps in the fulfilment of certain capacities, both moral and cognitive. Thus, Keown (2001: 193) defines it as 'man fulfilling his function through the development of his potentiality in accordance with a specific conception of a goal or end'.

In such a scheme, however, the focus remains not so much on what the person does for others, but on what kind of person they are, or are seen to be. In this way, it differs from a Consequentialist Ethics, which, in theory, judges actions by the effect that they have on the world rather than on the agent. The classic example of a virtue ethics is that expounded by Aristotle (384–322 BC) in Ancient Greece. It is often contrasted with the Utilitarian Ethics of Britain's John Stuart Mill (1806–1873) and other Consequentialists.

Having seen Keown parallel Buddhist Ethics with those of Aristotle, might we not be tempted here to use the same virtue ethics model to compare Śāntideva and Śaṅkara? Might we not start by collecting a list of virtues in each of their writings, and from there make our conclusions as to their shared ethics? Might we not claim that both saw knowledge as their ultimate goal? My answer is a resounding 'no', and I would like to take some time to explain why.

First of all, most scholars would agree that Keown allocates a disproportionate amount of space to the thesis that Buddhist ethics is analogous to an Aristotelian virtue ethics. To some extent, this is Keown's own affair; but due to the prominent (and no doubt deserved) position he now holds within the field of Buddhist ethics, all are now forced into answering his claim. For example, Clayton (2006: 100) feels the need to label Śāntideva's moral theory as 'a type of virtue ethics', going on to call it a 'supererogatory virtue ethic' (p101) despite the fact that she later claims that the 'concept of virtue ethics … is not adequate' (p109). The confusion in her thesis clearly comes from her explicit attempt to answer Keown (p90). The fact is that Śāntideva's ethics, when taken as a whole, are simply *not* a type of virtue ethics. Śāntideva asks us to focus on others, not on ourselves. Our own happiness is secondary to the happiness of others. He writes: 'May there be in me no root of good or knowledge of *Dharma* or skilfulness which is not of benefit to all beings' (Ś.S. 33).

Rather than call this a 'supererogatory virtue ethic', Clayton would have done better to have stayed with 'extreme altruism' (2006: 100). In fact, Keown (2001: 138) himself equates 'supererogation' with 'altruism'. But, as I will argue throughout this book, active altruism *does not* represent a virtue ethics. Virtue ethics stops with the subject and hardly considers the object, the other. Śāntideva's ethics, on the other hand, are consistently directed towards benefitting the other. And so, contra Clayton (2006: 100), I would argue that Śāntideva *is* ultimately asking us, 'What is the right thing to do?', rather than 'What kind of person should I be?'. In fact, Clayton seems to do a U-turn, and later claims that the main question the *bodhisattva* asks is: 'What will be the best thing for other beings?' (p113). Here she is quite correct. But this question does not arise from a virtue ethics.

This is not to say that Śāntideva ignores the virtues. In fact, Clayton (2006: 100) rightly suggests that the virtues are emphasized at the 'commencement of the spiritual path'. However, as Clayton further points out, at a certain point along the *bodhisattva*-path, Śāntideva's ethics begin to 'resemble utilitarianism' (p117). And so it is clearly this model that we should pay more attention to. Clayton also notes how, for Śāntideva, anger is seen as wrong because of its 'overall loss of benefit to beings' and that this is the 'deciding factor' (p108). In summary, Clayton states that, 'There is a definite sense that the bodhisattva should try to maximize the benefits to sentient beings' (ibid.). And so, along with Osto (2008), who reviewed Clayton's book, I was a little confused by Clayton's allegiance to virtue ethics as a means of explaining Śāntideva. Thankfully, a more recent article (in Powers and Prebish 2009: 15–29) shows Clayton moving much closer to the consequentialist side of her "hybrid" thesis.

More problematically, from a comparative point of view, Keown (in Schweiker 2005: 286) claims that Buddhist ethics shares 'many features with Aristotle's notion of the good life being one devoted to the cultivation of virtue and culminating in a condition of happiness'. But surely, this pays too little respect to the two cultures involved in the comparison. As Ram-Prasad (2007: 102) notes, 'there is no comparison between what Aristotle would define as a good and what our Indian philosophers would'. In fact, even those scholars who accept Buddhism as a virtue ethics play down the parallel with Aristotle (Cooper and James 2005: 83). But more importantly, happiness is simply *not* the culmination of Śāntideva's ethics or of Mahāyāna Buddhism in general. The *bodhisattva* would willingly give up his own happiness for the good of others. Śāntideva writes:

> If the suffering of many disappears through the suffering of one, then that suffering must definitely be made to arise by one with compassion for oneself and for others (BCA. 8.105).

If happiness were the *telos* of Mahāyāna Buddhism in general, then why is Śāntideva trying to, if you will forgive the phrase, get idle monks off their behinds? I will return to this below. For now, it needs emphasizing that Śāntideva goes much further than a virtue ethics model would allow. That is, he asks us to put these virtues to good use. It is the 'other' that is primary in Śāntideva's ethics. The *Compendium* thus prays that the virtues be kept hidden (Ś.S. 33). For Śāntideva, virtues are not for display or self-fulfilment, but must be put at the service of others.

One scholar who has recently spoken out against Keown's model is Charles Goodman, stating that 'no form of Buddhist ethics is as similar to Aristotelianism as Keown claims' (Goodman 2008: 17). He rightly concludes that the 'analogy with virtue ethics … does not represent a very valuable interpretive strategy when it comes to Mahāyāna ethical thought' (p31). We seem to have come to this conclusion independently, yet we differ in what we want to put in its place. Goodman (2008 and 2009) wishes to make his own case that Mahāyāna ethics is in fact a form of consequentialist ethics. Now, while it may be agreed that Mahāyāna ethics, when it comes to activism, sit closer to consequentialism than virtue ethics, I fail to see why we have to pigeon-hole them at all. It is not an either/or proposition. Mahāyāna ethics requires the virtues as a base, but asks us to put those virtues to good use. That is all we need grasp. For me, that is a call to altruism.

Mark Siderits has also spoken out against Keown's virtue ethics model, and, like Goodman, calls for a consequentialist interpretation. However, his call for an 'Aretaic Conseqentialism' (2003: 110, note b) appears to allow the virtues more of a role than Goodman does. It also allows for the 'cognitive limitations' (Siderits, in Bilimoria et al. 2007: 292) of our commencing-*bodhisattvas*, who may not have the foresight to see all the consequences of their actions. For it should be noted that consequentialism asks far too much of us if we are expected to foresee all the effects of our actions. In the altruistic model I argue for, the virtues combine with consequentialist thinking, and a *bodhisattva* is meant to know at what level of knowledge and power he stands at.

I will join Siderits in his praise of Keown, not so much for reclaiming *nirvāṇa* as a 'positive state of human fulfillment' (Siderits 2003: 110, note b), but for playing down the 'transcendency thesis' of Buddhist ethics (see Keown 2001: 83ff). This is essentially the thesis that Buddhist moral precepts have only instrumental value in achieving *nirvāṇa*, a thesis which Śāntideva's ethics of compassion and altruism prove wrong. Keown is also to be praised for almost single-handedly opening the 'western gate' for Buddhist ethics, allowing it to enter into the *maṇḍala* of modern academia. However, it is time for a paradigm shift, one which focuses more on an altruistic interpretation of Mahāyāna Buddhism.

One scholar who has provided Buddhist ethics with a modern paradigm shift is Christopher Queen in his work on 'Engaged Buddhism'. Queen (2000: 11–17) offers a four-fold categorization of Buddhist ethics, leading through 'discipline', 'virtue', 'altruism' and 'engagement'. These (largely) chronological categories are most useful. Queen takes 'Engaged Buddhism' to be a modern (essentially post-1960s) phenomenon, going one step beyond altruism in that it takes account of the 'social and institutional dimensions of suffering' (Queen and King 1996: 10). Queen sees early Buddhism as focusing its attention on discipline and virtue. The rise of Mahāyāna Buddhism brought altruism into the foreground. However, this altruism does not 'ignore self-cultivation' (Queen 2000: 14). I thus agree with Queen that pre-modern Mahāyāna ethics, and especially the ethics of Śāntideva, are best represented by the term 'altruism', but an altruism that depends upon the ripening of certain virtues.

I will also show that Śaṅkara's ethics should also be seen as altruistic. But we should not forget that most of the followers that Śāntideva and Śaṅkara address are monks. Thus, Śāntideva's ethics, especially those aimed at the commencing-*bodhisattva*, and Śaṅkara's ethics, aimed at the Advaitin teacher, are a type of altruism largely bridled by the need for discipline. Their ethics are best defined then as a monastically-informed altruism. Needless to say, Śāntideva, like Śaṅkara, was essentially non-political, and his writings should not be used to justify arguments for 'Engaged Buddhism', a mistake that Goodman (2009) sometimes commits.

In trying to collapse all Buddhist ethics into the category of consequentialism, Goodman also falls into a similar trap as Keown, skipping over and re-interpreting those examples that are clearly virtue- or duty-orientated, or else adding a qualifier such as 'character' to the term consequentialism (Goodman 2009: 41), thus claiming the entire moral field. As Meyers (2010: 2), in her review of Goodman's book, notes, Goodman's work 'tends to efface elements of Buddhist ethics that do not fit neatly into the consequentialist model'. Marcia Baron, in the *Three Methods of Ethics*, wrote:

> It is a little silly to ask whether a theory is more concerned with action or with character, as if theorists have to favour one over the other. One would expect any reasonably rich ethical theory to be concerned with both (Baron et al. 1997: 36).

We need to heed Harvey's (2000: 51) warning that, 'Overall, the rich field of Buddhist ethics would be narrowed by wholly collapsing it into any single one of the Kantian, Aristotelian or Utilitarian models'.

Naturally, this is not to deny the fact that we cannot always avoid making reference to these three dominant paradigms. In fact, we may need to make reference to all three, along with appropriate qualifications. For this reason, I will not get involved in the Hallisey methodological debate on 'ethical particularism' (see Clayton 2006: 5ff). Rather, let me simply note, with Harvey (2000: 51), how Buddhism makes equal demands on: 1) a good motivating will; 2) cultivation of character; and 3) the reduction of suffering in others and oneself. It will later be shown that Śāntideva's, and indeed Śaṅkara's, ethics include all three.

We should also bear in mind that monasteries in India are very much a communal culture, and the sight of an undisciplined monastic may well have a detrimental effect on other monks. Thus, it is rather inappropriate to suggest the title of 'act-consequentialist' for a monk like Śāntideva, as Goodman (2009: 90) does. It becomes especially irresponsible when one ponders on the possibility of 'humanitarian military intervention' by an army of *bodhisattvas* (p81). The ethical conduct of ascetic monks, of which Śāntideva (and Śaṅkara) are extreme cases, will be heavily influenced by their social context. While the rules are frequently disregarded, in line with act-utilitarianism, the moral of non-harming (*ahiṃsā*) is never disregarded. The actual life of the monk is likely to be far more cautious than certain rhetoric would have us believe. According to Prajñākaramati (the 10–11th-century Indian commentator on the *BCA*), the *bodhisattva* ought not to be too heroic (*vīrya*) (BCA. Pañjikā, 143). In such a communal culture, an act of misconduct by a single monk could cast a shadow over the whole community. Thus, Mrozik (2007: 54) speaks of 'communal ripening' and the pressure on the monks to be inspirational (p76). Hence, the *bodhisattva* reflects, 'I must please my fellow-students' (Ś.S. 150). The *Compendium* adds that the *bodhisattva* should be 'modest' (*salajja*), 'cautious' (*sabhaya*) and 'peaceful' (*śānta*). Through possessing a collection of virtues (*śīla-skandha*), the *bodhisattva* becomes a great being (*mahā-sattva*) (Ś.S. 147). His karmic merit (*puṇya*) is said to be pure when his morality (*śīla*) is pure. Hence, we can detect an equal stress on traditional 'monkish virtues' as well as on certain rule-breaking scenarios. One may think of a *monastically-informed altruistic ethics* which constantly seeks to benefit, first oneself, and then others. If Buddhism was indeed 'decadent' at this time (Klostermaier 2007: 302), it does not show itself in Śāntideva's ethics.

The temptation here, of course, is to follow up this discussion of Śāntideva's list of virtues with a whole list of similar virtues in the writing of Śaṅkara, and indeed it would not be difficult to do so (see Cenkner 1983: 50–54). But my whole point here is that it would be futile. For example, the way one 'pleases' one's fellow students may vary in the two camps, as might their definitions of what it means to be 'peaceful' or 'modest'. Even Śāntideva himself has two types of 'modesty' in mind in his writing, one for monks and another for lay women. More generally, Chappell (1996: 57) notes that the 'same value … can function in different soteriological contexts that result in different expressions'. And we might also note here how the Buddha often implied that the *Brahmins* even failed to understand the meaning of *their own* language of virtue ethics and he thus reinterpreted them for their own sake (see Gombrich 2009: 183). Similarly, within Vedānta, Lipner (2010: 213) has pointed out how the charge of lacking 'moral integrity' was made against Śaṅkara by Rāmānuja, who felt that the Advaitin was incapable of grasping the proper meaning of ethics from scripture.

What we can offer then, as a compromise, is that, in Advaita, 'Moral virtues, such as compassion, charity, self-control, and non-injury, may be supports for the attainment of the spiritual end, although they are not the end themselves' (Deutsch 1973: 102). These 'spiritual' qualities are not the cause of liberation, but act as associate causes to knowledge. Śaṅkara says that the student 'should also be guided in humility, etc., the virtues which are means to knowledge' (U.S. Prose, 1.5). These virtues, then, are merely a 'means to knowledge'. In other words, this is not a virtue ethics, but a particular form of soteriological consequentialism. However, like Śāntideva's consequentialist thought, it certainly requires the virtues as a basis, virtues which have their basis in tradition. Hence, *pace* Rāmānuja, Potter (1981: 36) feels that Śaṅkara's ideal renouncer 'must be imbued with strong positive moral inclinations'. One look at Śaṅkara's description of the ideal teacher proves Potter right:

> Now the teacher is one who is able to grasp the pros and cons of an argument, who understands and remembers them, who has tranquillity, self-control, compassion, kindness, etc., versed in the scriptures, unattached to enjoyments (visible or invisible), having abandoned all ritual actions, he is a knower of *brahman*, he is established in *brahman*, breaking not the rules of conduct, free from faults such as: deceit, pride, trickery, wickedness, deception, envy, falsehood, egoism and selfishness. With the sole aim of helping others, he wishes to make use of knowledge (U.S. Prose, 1.6).

And again, as with Śāntideva, it is when one begins to pass on this highest good that the true 'ethical' work begins, and this I take to be a form of duty (*Dharma*). Once again, we see a complete mix of ethical systems.

As we can gather, the issue with Keown's virtue ethics model goes much further than whether we can rightly translate from the Greek or the Pāli. While we may accept MacIntyre's (1966: 59) point, that a 'change in language is also a change in concepts', my position is more akin to another of his arguments, that 'different forms of social life will provide different roles for concepts to play' (p2). Keown (2001: 193), well aware of this problem, merely insists on a 'formal' parallel with Aristotle. But such a formal parallel tells us next to nothing.

It might of course be tempting to imagine that because Śāntideva and Śaṅkara share a common language and a common culture that we could go beyond this formal parallel; but so-called virtuous traits and their allocated words are forever open to various interpretations. After all, what do we mean by calling somebody 'nice'? This problem becomes particularly acute when we try to make sense of one of the so-called 'cardinal virtues' of Buddhism, which Keown (2005: 13) translates as 'understanding'. What exactly does it mean to be or to have understanding? Indeed, when we look at the Sanskrit, we see that 'understanding' is in fact a negative noun '*a-moha*', which more literally means 'non-delusion'. But what am I to be non-deluded about? Surely this is tradition-specific. A non-deluded Buddhist understands there to be no abiding self. A non-deluded Advaitin understands the self to be non-dual with *brahman*. A non-deluded Cartesian understands that the self is a thinking thing which is distinguishable from the material body.

In fact, Śāntideva provides us with a perfect example of this in his attack on the Sāṃkhya's so-called 'knowers' of reality. And as those that supposedly know (*jñā*) are being compared with those that are deluded (*moha*), we can take 'knowing' here to be synonymous with 'non-delusion':

> If you argue that the worldly do not see [the true state of things] due to delusion, [we say that] those that [you claim] 'know' reality are in the same position (BCA. 9.136b).

For the Buddhists, the Buddha is the only perfect teacher and his teaching is unique to him. Similarly, the *Gauḍapāda Kārikā* (4.99) drives a wedge between the Buddha's knowledge and the knowledge of Vedānta. Even the Buddha (lit. the awakened one) remains deluded:

> Even though the view [of the Buddha], which rejects the existence of external objects and asserts the doctrine of consciousness-only, is said to be similar to the notion of non-duality; the ultimate non-dual reality is, however, only known through the Upaniṣads. This is the meaning (G.K.Bh. 4.99).

This demonstrates that it is not simply *that* we understand that is of relevance, but *what* we understand and *how* we came to understand it. As Steven Collins once reportedly said, the Buddha is not saying 'Make your own truth', but 'Make *the* Truth your own' (in Gombrich 1988: 72). It is for such reasons that we cannot simply compare, say, the Buddha's categories of 'the immature' and 'the wise' (Dhp. Chapters 5 and 6) with Hume's categories of 'the vulgar' and 'the wise' (Treatise).

Now we may be tempted to think that the situation is different for Śaṅkara and Śāntideva, for they both posit a Two-Truths model, and so, 'the wise', for them, are those that know the ultimate as well as the relative. But even here we should tread very carefully. Both Śaṅkara and Śāntideva will indeed proclaim their traditions' understanding of reality in these epistemological terms, but as far as Śaṅkara is concerned, Śāntideva falls far short of the knowledge or understanding he has in mind, and *vice versa*. Neither of them understands the other's form of 'ultimate'. Their knowledge may well place them within the 'wise' category of their own tradition, but they still fall within the 'immature' category of their opponent's tradition. To make the basic claim then that Śaṅkara and Śāntideva both see 'non-delusion' (*amoha*) or 'knowledge' (*jñāna*) or 'wisdom' (*prajñā*) as a virtue would be quite meaningless, even from within the common parameters of a Two-Truths model. Here we see just how powerful metaphysics is in dividing traditions and just how weak the comparison of virtue models is.

Likewise, when it comes to the ethical life, Aristotle may tell us that *eudaimonia* (happiness?) is the final goal (Nicomachean Ethics, 1095a), and that this, in its highest form, lies in a certain kind of contemplation (*theoria*), of which, incidentally, he says so little that it would be impossible to compare his notion with the vast literature that the Buddhists have produced on this matter. Certainly, if Flew (2005: 126) is correct in thinking that, for Aristotle, 'goods exist by choice rather than by nature'; then we would find ourselves embroiled in a most complex parallel with *nirvāṇa*. But assuming that Aristotle is indeed advocating a life of contemplation over action, and Stalley, for example, thinks he is (in Aristotle 2009: xiii); would Śāntideva be happy with this mode of life? Would Śāntideva praise the 'wise', detached monk who sat there all day enjoying his own blissful contemplation? There is textual proof that he would not: 'Having cultivated the virtue of solitude in this way, discursive thought being calmed; one should now cultivate *bodhicitta*' (BCA. 8.89). Furthermore:

> Being able to remain in cyclic existence, free from attachment and fear, for the benefit of those suffering through their delusion – such is the fruit of emptiness (BCA. 9.52).

By cultivating *bodhicitta* (thought of enlightenment), Śāntideva has in mind the need to generate compassion for all sentient beings and to act on this compassion. It is this capacity to act for others that justifies the view of emptiness. *Bodhicitta* thus stresses the altruistic motive of the *bodhisattva*. But it is only with the view of emptiness that selflessness is truly self-less. In the final analysis, it is the *bodhisattva*'s ability to remain in the relative world (without defilements) that justifies the search for ultimate knowledge. Śāntideva never takes epistemic certainty as an end in itself, but sees its value in terms of its power to overcome suffering, especially the suffering of others. No doubt, if he knew of it, Śāntideva would strive to turn Aristotle's hierarchy of contemplative and practical wisdom (Nicomachean Ethics, 1177a) on its head and demand an altruistic response to the suffering of beings: 'If all sentient beings were to have their wish fulfilled, no one would suffer. No one wishes for [their own] suffering' (BCA. 6.34). And again:

> If the suffering of many disappears through the suffering of one, then that suffering must definitely be made to arise by one with compassion for oneself and for others (BCA. 8.105).

That is, if one has pity (*daya*) for one's own suffering, including the slight suffering that is brought on by having compassion (*daya*) for others, then that suffering must be taken on as a duty to others. This shows the need for a more positive, altruistic approach to Buddhist ethics, one which goes beyond seeing *nirvāṇa* as the goal of Buddhism. And needless to say, the *nirvāṇa* of which Buddhism speaks is not the *brahma-nirvāṇa* the Hindu seeks (cf. Bh.G. 2.72).

Altruism as an Alternative Model of Comparison

Returning then to the question of comparative ethics; one occasion where I feel Western ethical categories may come to our aid is when we consider more deeply the meaning of 'altruism', and especially the act of self-sacrifice for the good of others. Borrowing from Oliner's (2003: 15) recent interpretation of Auguste Comte (1798–1857), we might take altruism to have two main phases: 1) the eradication of self-centred desire, and 2) a life devoted to the good of others. It is my contention that both these phases can be found in the ethics of Śaṅkara and Śāntideva. Indeed, I believe that most Advaitins and Mahāyāna Buddhists would agree with John Stuart Mill's statement that the readiness to self-sacrifice was 'the highest virtue which can be found in man' (Util. II.16).

Nevertheless, having been so demanding on virtue ethics, perhaps we need to be just as critical of 'altruism'. For while it may be true that, 'All world religions concur that altruism … is virtuous' (Neusner and Chilton 2005: vii); would all religions condone the 'self-sacrifice' of a suicide bomber? I think not. Similarly, when we are told that the regard for others is 'almost universally hailed as a virtue' (Rushton 1980: 2), we need to ask whether that regard is limited to certain others, or whether it is universal in scope. For example, would all religions condone the donation of one's wealth to the rich at the exclusion of the poor? I think not. And so we will need to ask whether the altruism of Śaṅkara and Śāntideva may rightly be called 'moral', and we will also need to ask how universal their ethics are. Hence, it is not so much the *fact* of altruism which must drive our comparison, but the *structure* of that altruism.

Going back to the problem of comparing Buddhism with Aristotle's virtue ethics, it is very interesting that Ryan claims that Mill's sentiments about self-sacrifice and a 'life of goodness' were 'entirely foreign' to Aristotle (in Mill and Bentham 2004: 21). Goodman, who incidentally refers to Śāntideva's ethics as 'radical altruism' (Goodman 2008: 12 and 2009: 90), states that, 'for Aristotle, the foundational justification for virtuous acts is their contribution to the flourishing of the agent' (Goodman 2008: 19). Goodman (2009: 42) also states that the welfare of all beings, which is so central to the ethics of Śāntideva, is 'not found in Aristotle'. In fact, Berchman (in Neusner and Chilton 2005: 10) has suggested that Aristotle's ethics may be seen as 'decidedly self-centred'. Should we really be comparing Buddhist ethics with a self-centred ethics? Surely altruism is a better contender.

That a utilitarian, like Mill, should give us an apparent parallel to Śāntideva is perhaps not so surprising when we note that Krebs and van Hesteren (1994: 136) have defined 'high-quality altruism' as that which maximizes the 'greatest good for the greatest number'. But even here, we need to be careful, for we should not confuse Mill's *Greatest Happiness Principle* with the Mahāyāna call to benefit all beings. Firstly, a multiplicity of socially active lives, full of temporary moments of contentment, is not what Śāntideva is asking his fellow monks to sacrifice their own happiness for. This is so, for, like Śaṅkara, he has denounced such a social life as one of suffering, and feels that he (along with all others) must be led to a more ultimate form of bliss, even if that 'bliss' is but a negation of worldly suffering. While Śāntideva's rhetoric on aiding the poor and the weak often has the feel of 'social service' (Clayton 2006: 59) about it (for example Ś.S. 274), transcendence of society is his ultimate aim, and such a view demands a negative evaluation of existence.

More important, however, is the question of the term 'self' in 'self-sacrifice'. If we are to talk meaningfully about the place of altruism in Śāntideva and Śaṅkara, then this is the key problem to address. Śāntideva, for his part, will play on the notion that there is no *self* from the side of the *bodhisattva* involved in the sacrifice of time and effort. Śaṅkara will also claim that there is no (individuated) self coming from the side of the *brahman*-knower who has 'no need of living' (C.U.Bh. VI.xiv.2) and who lives on with 'the sole aim of helping others' (U.S. Prose, 1.6). So the very meaning of 'self-sacrifice' is brought into doubt. Hence, we need to be aware of the fact that altruism, in its original Western context, referred to the conscious attempt to override one's selfish inclinations in order to act selflessly. In other words, one puts one's own self aside. This self was never in doubt; it was merely downplayed. The self of others, or the desires of those selves, were thereby put first.

But Śāntideva and Śaṅkara are making a much stronger (metaphysical) claim. They are saying that there *simply is no self* which needs putting to one side. The bare recognition of non-self (*anātman*) or non-duality (*advaita*) leads to selflessness. Thus metaphysical assumptions along with their differing concepts of 'common good' make comparison with Mill problematic to say the least. Nevertheless, a further look into utilitarian-defined altruism shows that what matters is not simply that one is other-centred, but also that one helps others in 'less superficial and less transient ways' (Krebs and van Hesteren 1994: 136). That is, higher stages of altruism are 1) purer, and 2) deeper. That Śaṅkara and Śāntideva wish to remove *all* of one's suffering *forevermore* is surely testimony to their depth.

There is still a major problem with comparing their models with those of Mill. It is indeed their condemnation of the superficial and transient nature of worldly life that gives them their depth, but it is this very same feature that commits them to a transcendence of that very world. Even though the end justifies the means in Advaita, this is only so if the end in question is self-realization. Hence, the Upaniṣads distinguish the 'good' (*śreyas*) from the merely 'pleasant' (*preyas*) (Ka.U. I.ii.1). Liberation (*mokṣa*) is hereby considered the highest good, a 'good outside this miserable world' (Otto 1957: 191). It might therefore be argued that the ultimate goals of Buddhism and Advaita are, to borrow Mill's words, 'pernicious to society' (Util. II.19). Both find themselves centre stage in the conflict between societal and renunciatory values. Despite implicitly sharing with Śāntideva and Śaṅkara the belief that certain voices are 'more authoritative than others' (Skorupski 1998: 23), and despite therefore being an 'elitist' (p29), we still might reasonably cast Mill as a 'social egalitarian' (p2). On the other hand, neither Śāntideva nor Śaṅkara were 'egalitarian', nor were they ever politically minded. And they clearly go against the current (politically correct) notion that 'Religious individuals are committed to the preservation of the family unit' (Barnes 2008: 205).

To bring this conflict to life, let us imagine that a certain *bodhisattva* or *jīvan-mukta* was so successful in his call for renunciation that a substantial sector of society left their families and jobs in the search of liberation. What would be the outcome on society? Disastrous, one would assume.[7] Not that this is anti-social behaviour. One might still coherently claim that Buddhism and Advaita would, along with Hume's average citizen, prefer what is 'useful and serviceable to mankind, above what is pernicious' (EPM, IX.1). And like J.J.C. Smart's (in Smart and Williams 1973: 31) sympathetic and benevolent men, both might maintain an 'ultimate pro-attitude to human happiness in general'. Thus, unlike Olson (1997: xiv), I do not see how the renouncer, be he Buddhist or Hindu, could be taken as 'anti-social', though perhaps he is 'unsocial' (p2) or, more accurately, 'asocial' (Bilimoria 2007: 45). Certainly,

[7] Brodbeck assumes that the writers of the *Gītā* took this threat very seriously and that the *Gītā* was an explicit reaction to the pursuit of ultimate liberation (*mokṣa*), which 'threatened social, cultural and economic continuity' (in Mascaró 2003: xvi).

if altruism is necessarily 'prosocial' (Rushton 1980), then the ideal of inactivity (*nivṛtti*) of the renouncer appears to stand outside this domain.

Yet, as we will see in both Śaṅkara's and Śāntideva's selfless ethics, despite their aloofness from society, there is adequate room for wilful engagement and other-regarding responses. But while it might be true that 'complex societies cannot exist without a large degree of concern for others' (Rushton 1980: 10), could it not also be true that these societies would stop existing if this 'concern' were taken to Buddhist and Advaitic extremes? Thus, Radhakrishnan (1989: 381) prefers the term 'super-social man' to describe the Indian renouncer, who has seen reality as-it-is. The Advaitin and the Buddhist would argue against Rushton (1980: 197) that it is more than the 'flexibility of our intelligence' which distinguishes us from 'social insects'. We are also capable of the transcendence of that intelligence and thus the transcendence of the technological society which modern sociologists, like Rushton, envisage. And it may even be argued that the monk who goes about teaching these truths to others performs the most important 'social service' of all.

Such inner complexities confirm the above statement that we cannot entirely rely on ethical categories, be they 'virtue ethics', or 'consequentialist ethics', or even Western-derived 'altruistic ethics' in our comparative frameworks. Instead, we must forever keep an eye on the *structure* of those ethics: the metaphysics, the soteriology, the gradualism and the social traditions which underpin the author's values, qualifying their ethics accordingly. Thus, the altruism I want to link with Śaṅkara and Śāntideva is very much a 'qualified' altruism.

To be other-regarding, according to Śaṅkara and Śāntideva, one has to *delude* oneself that the 'other' is in fact there as a separate independent entity. One needs to *reconstruct* their fixed personhood, as it were. To regard the other at all is to agree to play by the rules of conventionality. That is, to be selfless on their account is a metaphysical game. Thus, the altruistic model presented here will not be a Western one, but a *radically qualified* one, requiring much attention to detail. So whilst drawing upon Western models of altruism, I cannot over-emphasize the *structural* differences; namely the metaphysical underpinnings and the epistemological manipulations. I call this ethical model 'constructive altruism'.

I therefore agree with Dharmasiri (1989: xii) that Buddhist ethics 'cannot be satisfactorily analyzed through Western categories', and I believe the same goes for Advaitin ethics. Dharmasiri talks of Western categories as being too 'narrow' (ibid.) to account for Buddhist metaphysics, and so I believe my model of constructive altruism may well help to widen these categories. Dharmasiri is indeed correct to say that the distinction between [Western] 'altruism and egoism breaks down' (p15), but not for the reasons he offers. The real issue is not that, in Buddhism, 'helping others is a way of helping oneself' (p16), but that, in Madhyamaka (and Advaita), helping others is about *constructing* others. This is the key difference between Western models and my Indian-derived model. Constructive altruism, then, is a model that allows for notions of moral action within a framework of ultimate non-individuation.

Inter-religious Comparison

The modern moral theorist is (and should be) less concerned with the actual norms of a system and more concerned with the Nietzschean question of *why we ought to be moral at all*. Hindery (1996), in his *Comparative Ethics in Hindu and Buddhist Traditions*, sees it as the first question that must be asked of any moral tradition. And given the metaphysical revisions which underlie the model of constructive altruism proposed here, the *why* question would seem especially urgent.

The question as to why we ought to be moral might arise from a multitude of subjective or objective starting points. For example, it could be taken as a sceptical one, essentially challenging ethical discourse *en masse* (à la Nietzsche). For Hindery (1996), it is an epistemological question. Alternatively, it might be asked existentially. Here, the departure will be taken from the grounds of Śāntideva's and Śaṅkara's competing metaphysics. The question then is, if I were one or other of these two thinkers, if I held either of their metaphysical views, why would I wish others to follow a particular ethical code? How could I justify such prescriptions? This metaphysical approach will be taken for two reasons.

In the first place, ethics seems to me to be inseparable from metaphysics. If we are going to compare how two religious thinkers ask their disciples and peers to live within the world, then it would seem unquestionably necessary to first define just what those worlds are like. That is, authors and believers do not simply live within the world as we currently define it, but exist within a *worldview*. That worldview will of course depend on time and place, and so we can note from the start that Śaṅkara and Śāntideva both inhabited an 8th-century India.

Also, as the concern here has little to do with how morality functioned on the ground, it is even more justifiable to give primary value to worldview. This is especially justified in the case of Śaṅkara and Śāntideva, for they both offered a radical metaphysical revision. Thus, Deutsch (1973: 99) went so far as to claim that ethical questions for Advaita are present in 'every metaphysical or epistemological question' they ask. With regard to Śaṅkara's broader epistemological concerns, this is no doubt an exaggeration. However, we can interpret Deutsch to mean that Śaṅkara was more interested in searching for the 'right' knowledge (*saṃyag-jñāna*) than in verifying that his knowledge was 'right' (that is, justified). In other words, right knowledge, being *brahman*-knowledge, is its own justification. Śaṅkara writes:

> For when somebody feels in his heart that he has realized *brahman*, and yet bears a body, how can this be contested by anyone else? (B.S.Bh. IV.i.15).

Thus Taber (1983: 13) translates *saṃyag-jñāna* as 'self-verifying knowledge'. In fact, Śaṅkara borrows this notion of 'self-validating' (*sva-pramāṇaka*) knowing from the Pūrva-Mīmāṃsā School, but adds the further *pramāṇa* of 'experience' (*anubhava*) to the list of validating means of knowledge (Suthren Hirst 2005: 66–7), a move that Ram-Prasad (2001a: 170–71) describes as 'unfortunate', given that an experience needs an experiencer, which, in Advaitic terms, implies *jīva*-consciousness. Be that as it may, Śaṅkara states that: 'The knowledge of *brahman* culminates in experience which relates to an actual entity' (B.S.Bh. I.1.2).

As for the metaphysics of self, we have already noted how the concept of self was so pivotal to Śaṅkara's ethics, the rejection of egoism being directly linked with his metaphysics of *ātman*. One reaches *brahman* through a complete destruction of egocentricity. Thus, Hopkins (1996: 187) points out the apparent contradiction in the Prāsaṅgika's suggestion that labelling the highest reality 'Self' would increase egocentricity. In fact, Śaṅkara clears the way for a life of selfless service through an insight into Self:

> It must be accepted that [the self] is 'self-evident', which is synonymous with 'self-knowable'. And the experience of one's [true] Self is established along with the cessation of the [false] notion of 'I' (U.S. Metric, 18.200/203).[8]

And as we have already noted, Śaṅkara's metaphysics and ethics meet through the following verse from the Upaniṣads: 'When a man sees all beings in this Self, and the Self in all beings, he feels no hatred' (Īś.U. 6).

If we fail to understand Śaṅkara's views on self, it is simply impossible to understand his ethics. Likewise, as Goodman (contra Keown) has pointed out, 'The doctrine of no self is at the heart of Mahāyāna ethics' (Goodman 2009: 96). Finnigan and Tanaka (in Cowherds 2011: 231) have also concluded that both Candrakīrti and Śāntideva 'explicitly connect Madhyamaka metaphysics with Mahāyāna ethics'. Śāntideva writes that, 'the *bodhisattva* who thus sees reality as-it-is feels a profound compassion for all beings' (Ś.S. 119). In Śāntideva's hands, metaphysical self-lessness becomes 'the tool of altruistic service' (Matics 1971: 89), that is, ethical selflessness:

> If one does not let go of self, one cannot free oneself from suffering, as one who does not remove themselves from fire cannot avoid being burnt. Thus, in order to alleviate my own suffering and put an end to the suffering of others, I devote myself to others and accept them as 'myself' (BCA. 8.135–6).

The doctrine of selflessness is thus a 'philosophical concept, an ethical principle, and a soteriological device' (Huntington 1989: 70). Only when we understand Śāntideva's manipulations of the concept of self can we ever come to understand his ethics. If I am confusing ethics with metaphysics, then so did Śaṅkara and Śāntideva.

And not only did they link ethics with a radical metaphysics, but they both offered an ideal type, a liberated being, who is said to act correctly because of an insight into the true nature of reality. This ideal type is also based on a common ascetic/monastic stance functioning within a network of norms. We may call this network '*Dharma*', though Śaṅkara and Śāntideva will have different definitions of what this means to their traditions. We can therefore respond to MacIntyre's (1996: 1) warning that 'Moral concepts are embodied in and are partially

[8] In Mayeda's edition it is verse 18.200; in Jagadānanda's edition it is verse 18.203.

constitutive of forms of social life', by pointing out that the two traditions under analysis share a huge amount of social ground, yet differ in religious lineage. It could be claimed of both systems that their ethics were metaphysically grounded in a realist sense, that is, both confirm a common moral realism, the law of *karma*, which is highly deterministic.[9] Furthermore, there are truths out there to be known, and there are humans who have exemplified such a realization.

The critical question for both systems is this: do the descriptions of their modes of conduct make sense within their respective metaphysical descriptions? That is, we will need to ask whether an altruistic ethical stance is at all compatible with the respective metaphysical revisions offered. This will include both the apparent discontinuity of a confirmation of worldly tradition with the goal of liberation from that very world, along with the more subtle problem of whether persons (as individuated agents) are accepted as truly existent or not, and indeed what 'truly existent' means. Readers of Little and Twiss' *Comparative Religious Ethics* might recognize the former feature as parallel to the problem of transcendent morality, and the second feature as parallel to the so-called 'paradoxical element' (1978: 231) in the teachings of Theravāda Buddhism. An attempt will be made here to show how the transcendent morality thesis fails to apply to the ethics of Śāntideva or, for different reasons, to those of Śaṅkara. It is also hoped that the 'paradox' might be solved by introducing the concept of a 'voluntary' delusion on the part of Śāntideva and by examining the complex question of residual (*prārabdha*) *karma* in Śaṅkara.

Stating the case briefly here, comparing the two systems, we might note that at the universal level, their metaphysics are radically opposed, whilst at the level of agency, their metaphysics quite unexpectedly converge. Neither level is compatible with the realist's view of the world. And it should be noted that the ultimate denial of individual agency was as equally counter-intuitive in 8th-century India as it is now in the 21st-century west. Nevertheless, for Śaṅkara, all is *brahman*, and as such, anything other than *brahman* fails to have independent existence, including the so-called individuated self (*jīva*), whose personal agency is the result of a mistaken cognition. For Śāntideva, all is empty (*śūnya*), that is, empty of inherent or independent existence; hence an agreement with Śaṅkara that there is no individuated self. The shocking conclusion is that the foundational ethics of these two systems turn out to be remarkably similar despite the radically opposed metaphysics which ground them. They both respond with a call for ethical, even compassionate, action, yet they are both open to the 'why' question.

Summary of Aims

The reader may take my aims as threefold: one *philosophical*, one *historiographical* and one *disciplinary*.

---

[9] By this I mean 'doing x typically leads to y', rather than, 'one had no choice but to do x'.

The first aim is to show how two very different – even radically opposite – views on the cosmology of self can generate strikingly similar accounts of the relationship between human conduct and the world within a 'selfless framework'. The philosophical point to be captured is that neither Śāntideva nor Śaṅkara will require a view of the person as a stable individuated agent in order to posit a system of moral values that ought to be followed. In fact, they will both conclude that the very belief in oneself as a unified moral agent is counter-productive to other-regarding moral thought. The outline of their models presented here should therefore impact on the way philosophers of the self approach the question of ethics.

The second aim, which I regard as *historiographical*, is to show how committed these two thinkers were to the continuity of their lineages, both in terms of doctrinal commitments and normative conduct. It will demonstrate how the language of ultimate truth sets the limits on these commitments, but also how the seemingly opposing language of conventional truth tends to balance the weight of any ultimate assertions. We may see this as a partial resolution of the 'tension' introduced earlier. For example, Śāntideva will use ultimate-style logic to put the very idea of selfhood under question, but will then adopt conventional-style rhetoric to reinstate the 'other' as the *raison d'être* of the ethical life. In like manner, Śaṅkara will use ultimate-style rhetoric to shift the focus of the seeker's awareness from the relative world to the absolute realization of *brahman*-consciousness, whilst later reinstating those very cultural categories he criticizes in order to maintain traditional social class norms, and thus the 'purity' of his lineage, both in terms of social background and education.

The third aim, which is *disciplinary*, has two parts. The first *disciplinary* objective is basically to warn those who would over-stress the *ātman/anātman* distinction as a way of categorizing Hinduism versus Buddhism. It will be highlighted how their ultimate views lead both thinkers into a denial of *jīvātman* as individuated self, and also how their call for a 'selfless' response to others demands that they pay lip service to a provisional level of individuated self. That they both shift between these two levels, and for the same reasons, is demonstration enough that we need to reconsider the commonly voiced view that *ātman/anātman* is the major distinguishing feature of these two religions (for example Hayes, in Keown and Prebish 2007: 28). To do justice to the Sanskrit material, we need a more nuanced approach to the question of self, which has to consider not just the Two-Truths mode of discourse, but also the persuasive, even voluntary self-deluding, form of emotive ethical rhetoric taken up by both Buddhist and Hindu traditions.

The second *disciplinary* objective overlaps the others. Here I wish to point out how Śāntideva and Śaṅkara, as representatives of two often competing religions, actually share far more ground than their ultimate stances would first indicate. It will be shown how their methodologies and aims, and even their inter-sectarian differences, are in fact *cross-cutting*. This will show itself in the way that both ultimately deny the individuated self, both adopt the concept of Two-Truths or Two-Realities, and both then posit a teacher who can distinguish between these realities and who can equally lead others to an understanding of the Two Truths. It will also show itself in their mutual attack on the Yogācāra School of Buddhism. Furthermore, it will be demonstrated how the conventional, and thus moral-making ground of each tradition consistently manages to survive the ultimate level of discourse.

Chapter 3
Situating Śaṅkara and Śāntideva

There are essentially two major doctrinal differences between Brahmanism and Buddhism which have forever held them apart as separate, even opposing religions. The first is the Buddhist denial of the validity of the Vedic view of the cosmos and its sacrificial rites, and thus the authoritative testimony (*śabda*) of the Vedic literature. The second is the Buddhist denial of a permanent, essential self, be it *brahman*, *ātman* or *jīva*. Both of these Buddhist positions, in one form or other, go right back to the Buddha himself, and thus precede the Mahāyāna.

The contrast between Śaṅkara and Śāntideva is thus, in the main, one inherited from their traditions. However, it is further sharpened by the radical (re)formulations which later take place; on one side, the Advaita doctrine which states that 'all is *brahman*', and on the other, the Madhyamaka doctrine which states that 'all is empty'. These radical metaphysical positions do two things: first, they place Śaṅkara and Śāntideva at opposite ends of the 'Self-spectrum'; second, they threaten to undermine their own traditions. Before we can judge how much they each threaten their own traditions, we first need to lay out the doctrines and modes of conduct that Śaṅkara and Śāntideva inherited from their respective traditions.

3.1 Approaching Śaṅkara

In India, it is not so much originality, but fidelity to tradition that is prized most. While Śaṅkara may well be called an innovative philosopher, he did not claim to be the inventor or expounder of an original system. The tradition that Śaṅkara wishes to defend has its origins in the Vedas. Śaṅkara wishes to *provisionally* defend the early (*pūrva*) Vedic scriptures, with their sacrificial rites and associated social systems, whilst wishing to *ultimately* defend the later (*uttara*) Vedic scriptures, otherwise known as the Upaniṣads. Śaṅkara asks us to accept the prescriptions with regard to actions as found in the early Vedas, whilst also understanding that the non-dual (*advaita*) description of *brahman* given in the Upaniṣads (in his interpretation) is the ultimate truth (*paramārtha-satya*), and that the attainment of this knowledge leads to liberation from the conventional (*vyāvahārika*), and is verily the final goal. And so: 'Absolute liberation cannot be achieved without the realization of the non-dual self' (Ch.U.Bh., intro).

At the conventional level, Śaṅkara essentially follows the Pūrva-Mīmāṃsa. For this school, the Vedic revelation must be interpreted solely as injunction (*vidhi*) to action. That is, Vedic sentences are an incitement (*codana*) to ritual action (*karma*). Thus, Jaimini's *Mīmāṃsā Sūtra* (I.i.2) defines '*Dharma*' as *incitements to action*. Furthermore, the Vedas are said to be the only source which can teach us about *Dharma* (see Mohanty, in Bilimoria et al. 2007: 57–78). Yet, for Śaṅkara, the Vedic sayings are most potent when they speak of knowledge (*jñāna*) rather than ritual action.

Śaṅkara has been called the greatest representative and interpreter of Eastern mysticism (Otto 1957: xvi). Others have suggested that his exegesis was 'too rational' to be classed as mystical (Cenkner 1983: 82). Some have stressed that Śaṅkara was, first and foremost, a teacher (Suthren Hirst 2005: 1). He will be treated here primarily as an exegete. As for the teaching aspect, the focus will be on his insistence that one needs a qualified teacher, and on the notion that the teacher himself, having realized *brahman*, is in need of nothing. The *brahman-knower-cum-teacher*, the living-liberated being (*jīvan-mukta*),[1] being a voluntary actor, solely responding to the needs of others, will be described as 'altruistic'. The basis of this altruism, I will argue, is a sense of compassion.

The exegetical focus will be on his commentaries to the so-called Triple Canon of the Vedānta tradition: the major *Upaniṣads*, the *Bhagavad Gītā* and the *Brahma Sūtra*. Attention will also be paid to his principal (authentic)[2] non-commentarial work, the *Upadeśa Sāhasrī*, where Śaṅkara pays most attention to the role of the teacher. This text is divided into two parts, the Prose-section, which is a 'handy guide for teachers', and the Metrical-section, which acts as a 'textbook for the pupils'; perhaps based on Śaṅkara's own 'pedagogical experiences' (Mayeda 1992: xvii). The explicit need for a teacher to pass on the ultimate knowledge of the Vedas is also found throughout his commentaries and it is consistently to the Upaniṣads that he turns for authority, not to his own experience. That is why we should treat him primarily as an exegete.

The Upaniṣads are known as *śruti* (revealed text), which Śaṅkara typically treats as self-validating (B.S.Bh. I.iii.28). The *Bhagavad Gītā*, though an example of *smṛti* (remembered text), and thus one which ought to be interpreted through other texts (B.S.Bh. I.iii.28), is actually treated by Śaṅkara with the same authority as *śruti*.[3] This is no doubt because Śaṅkara takes it to be in agreement with the Upaniṣads (see B.S.Bh. II.i.1). Bādarāyaṇa's *Brahma Sūtra* is the most revered Vedāntic example of *nyāya* (logical treatise). Śaṅkara, in commenting on all these ancient texts, was involved in what Deutsch (in Larson and Deutsch 1988: 169)

---

1 Skoog (in Fort and Mumme 1996: 75) notes that the term '*jīvan-mukta*' appears nowhere in the Upaniṣads. Śaṅkara only used the actual term once (Bh.G.Bh. 6.27). Thus, Nelson (in Fort and Mumme 1996: 21) assumes that, for Śaṅkara, it had not yet become a 'technical term'. The *V.C.*, however, uses the term repeatedly (for example 428–40).

2 On the question of authentic works, see Hacker (in Halbfass 1995), Isayeva (1993: 92–8), Marcaurelle (2000: 12–13), Sundaresan (2002) and Suthren Hirst (2005: 19–25).

3 The *Gītā* is sometimes referred to as '*Gītopaniṣad*' (Theodor 2010: 36). The *Mahābhārata*, from which the *Gītā* was extracted, also calls itself the 'Fifth Veda' (Lipner 2010: 71).

has called the language of 'recovery'. However, Śaṅkara has sometimes been accused of forcing the texts into the service of his own doctrines (Otto 1957: xvii), or taking liberties with his interpretations (Isayeva 1993: 100). But as Deutsch (in Larson and Deutsch 1988: 170) more generally states with regard to Indian texts, the 'philosopher-commentator ... seeks to remain faithful to his authoritative sources, but in his own creative terms'. Śaṅkara was clearly a serious and creative thinker, endowed with 'too much creativity and reasoning power to remain a simple traditionalist' (Mayeda 1992: 48). Hence, the religious and historical significance of Śaṅkara's commentaries is immeasurable.

Now Śaṅkara is often spoken of as virtually the founder of Advaita. However, he did not truly found Advaita and writes as if he were following a tradition (*sampradāya*). Three ancient teachers are mentioned in the *Brahma Sūtra* itself (B.S. I.iv.20–22), but little is known about them except that they are claimed by both Advaita and Viśiṣṭādvaita (Potter 1981: 10–12). Other traditional teachers are also mentioned by Śaṅkara. However, no study of Śaṅkara would be complete without mentioning his huge indebtedness to the work of Gauḍapāda, who may well have been the teacher of his teacher (Govindapāda). Indeed, Śaṅkara refers to Gauḍapāda as '*parama-guru*' (G.K.Bh. Salutation), which translates as either 'teacher of the teacher' or 'great teacher'.[4] Aside from Bādarāyaṇa, the author of the *Brahma Sūtra*, the theoretical source of Vedānta, Gauḍapāda was possibly the most influential figure on Śaṅkara's philosophy.[5] His use of the Two-Truths doctrine and the notion of *māyā* can be traced back to Gauḍapāda's *Māṇḍūkya kārikā*, as well as his use of the term '*advaita*' to describe the highest reality.

Now, Gauḍapāda's text was 'undoubtedly composed under the direct impact of Buddhist ideas' (Isayeva 1993: 10). Even its use of *māyā* (as illusiveness of the phenomenal world) is a Buddhist rather than Vedāntin interpretation, traceable to Nāgārjuna's *MMK*. This has been confirmed by Richard King (1995: 2 and 126–7), amongst others (see Potter 1981: 78–9). Furthermore, Gauḍapāda's monism owes much to the Yogācāra. Dasgupta (1975) took this borrowing from both Madhyamaka and Yogācāra to be 'so obvious' that it was 'needless to attempt to prove it' (Vol.I: 429). Mayeda (1992: 13) thus speaks of the 'buddhification of the Vedānta tradition'. Due to a verse in the Kārikā (4.1) where Gauḍapāda apparently pays reverence to the Buddha, Dasgupta (1975, Vol.I: 423) even suggested that Gauḍapāda was 'possibly' a Buddhist. Hacker says that 'There cannot be any reasonable doubt that the person meant is the Buddha' (in Halbfass 1995: 36). However, Murti (1980: 13), amongst others (see O'Neil 1980: 54–6), believed Gauḍapāda remained a 'Vedāntist', despite the Buddhist influence. Personally, I feel that the more obvious conclusion to draw is that Buddhist and Brahmanical ideas are often *cross-cutting* and that their methodologies were *mutually borrowed*.

---

[4] On the ambiguity of this term, see King (1995: 16).

[5] Of course, the Vedas themselves are said to be authorless (*apauruṣeya*). For further commentarial influences on Śaṅkara, see Roodurmun (2002: 9–25).

I therefore see Malinar's (2007: 259) notion of 'floating concepts and practices' as a healthy one.

Śaṅkara does his best to distance Vedānta from Buddhism, attempting to explain away all the references to the Buddha. In a decisive passage, whilst admitting the similarities with Vijñānavāda doctrines and Vedānta, he insists on keeping them apart:

> Even though the view [of the Buddha], which rejects the existence of external objects and asserts the doctrine of consciousness-only, is said to be similar to the notion of non-duality; the ultimate non-dual reality is, however, only known through the Upaniṣads. This is the meaning (G.K.Bh. 4.99).

This is a critical statement, and supports the point made earlier that you simply cannot compare religions by comparing virtues like 'understanding'. An ultimate truth for one camp is but an approximation to it in another. Śaṅkara here refuses to acknowledge that the Buddha could have been enlightened *even though* they hold basically the same doctrine. Elsewhere, in his defining work, the *Brahma-Sūtra Bhāṣya*, he accuses the Buddha of 'incoherent prattling' (*asaṃbaddha pralāpita*). Buddhism is there declared to be 'nihilistic' (*vaināśika*) and 'untenable' (*anupapanna*). As such, Śaṅkara recommends that: 'The Buddhist religion should be totally renounced by those who desire the highest good' (B.S.Bh. II.ii.32).

Śaṅkara here calls for a complete break with Buddhism. In fact, as a good exegete, he ends the phrase with, 'that is the intended meaning'. In other words, he traces his position back to the *Brahma Sūtra* itself. Obviously, some change took place between Śaṅkara (the writer of the *Kārikā Bhāṣya*) and Śaṅkara (the writer of the *Brahma-Sūtra Bhāṣya*). Thus, Mayeda (1992: 7) claims that it was left to Śaṅkara to 'revedanticize' the Advaita tradition.

Hacker suggests that Śaṅkara moved on from Gauḍapāda into a more obvious 'Advaita period' developing a 'more independent way of thinking' (in Halbfass 1995: 108). We can certainly see that he moved away from the doctrine of 'mind-only' or 'consciousness-only', which he most certainly upholds in the *Kārikā Bhāṣya*. Here he states that an object (*artha*) perceived in the waking-state is as non-existent (*abhūta*) as those perceived in the dream-state. It is 'consciousness alone that appears as objects such as pots, just like in a dream' (G.K.Bh. 4.26). Śaṅkara here explicitly holds a 'consciousness-only' (*cittam-eva*) doctrine, in complete contradiction to his major works. Moreover, Śaṅkara admits that these doctrines are those of the Yogācāra Buddhist, and that they are accepted by 'the teacher', that is, Gauḍapāda (4.28). The reason they are accepted is that they 'refute the views of those who maintain the reality of external things'. He goes on to say that the only objection Gauḍapāda has to the Yogācāra thesis is the 'momentariness' (*kṣaṇikatva*) of consciousness (ibid.). For Advaita, consciousness is always steady and unchangeable in itself.

Two important points to notice here are: 1) Gauḍapāda is not simply accepting a particular Buddhist ontology without critique. He in fact denies part of their thesis; and 2) Śaṅkara, in this *Bhāṣya*, is happier to sit alongside an idealist Buddhist than be confused with the realists. Nor can we say that Śaṅkara was merely parroting the doctrines of Gauḍapāda here, for he says something very similar in the *Aitareya-Upaniṣad Bhāṣya*. Here, Śaṅkara likens the waking state to the dream state:

> In the waking state there is no consciousness of one's own self as the Absolute Truth, and one perceives unreal things as in a dream (Ait.U.Bh. I.iii.12).[6]

However, we should not too hastily assume that Śaṅkara's final position is that the 'world of everyday experience is a dream', as Phillips (in Deutsch and Bontekoe 1997: 326) does; for a whole different picture forms when we compare the following statement from his (later) *Bṛhadāraṇyaka-Upaniṣad Bhāṣya*:

> If no object distinct from consciousness were admitted, then the words 'cognition', 'pot', 'cloth', etc., having the same meaning, would all be synonymous (Bṛ.U.Bh. IV.iii.7).

A similar style of inquiry is found in his defining work, the *Brahma-Sūtra Bhāṣya*, where the following argument is offered to him by a realist opponent:

> It is quite obvious that there is a fundamental distinction between the subject of experience and that which is experienced; the subject being the embodied consciousness, the experience consisting of objects such as sound, etc. (B.S.Bh. II.i.13).

His answer is that: 'This distinction can indeed be upheld from our point of view, for it is seen to be so in the world' (ibid.).

In other words, Śaṅkara is agreeing with his opponent that the *pramāṇa* of perception (*pratyakṣa*) has the world of sensation as its valid domain.[7] But this does not mean that he accepts the opponent's claim that the Vedas only have 'validity in their own domain' and that direct perception is to be awarded priority in this provisional domain. It is rather that the Two Truths of the Vedas can equally allow for both domains. For Śaṅkara, the Vedas never simply leave this world to 'worldly' means of knowledge. Ram-Prasad (2002: 32) comments on this exchange with the realist:

[6] The *V.C.* (170–71) also explicitly holds a 'mind-only' (*mana-eva*) doctrine. It repeats the notion that sense objects perceived in the waking-state are as 'false' (*mithyā*) as those perceived in the dream-state (V.C. 252).

[7] Śaṅkara tends to focus on three *pramāṇas*: perception (*pratyakṣa*), inference (*anumāna*) and scriptural testimony (*śabda, śruti*). He typically places *smṛti* in the category of inference (B.S.Bh. I.iii.28). However, with regard to knowledge of the Self, he also seems to allow for experience (*anubhava*) as a further *pramāṇa* (B.S.Bh. I.i.2).

> It is from this experiential situation that the systematic nature of the *pramāṇas*, together with the requirement of a systematic order of objects (the extrinsic world), is derived. Objects have to be that way, or else experience could not be accounted for.

It is here worth comparing this to Śāntideva on the conventional status of objects and his defence of the Buddha's 'First Turning' pseudo-realist treatment of objects:

> The Protector [Buddha] taught of existents in order to guide people [gradually into the knowledge of emptiness]. If it is objected then that these ['entities'] are not really momentary, but only conventionally so, [the fact is that] there is no fault in a *yogi* adopting the conventional usage. He has a better understanding of reality than the worldly (BCA. 9.7–8a).

Before we compare this view on valid means of knowledge with Śaṅkara's, let us return to the latter's response (B.S.Bh. II.i.13) to his realist opponent:

> Thus, although foam, ripple, wave, bubble, etc. (which are different modifications of the sea) are non-different from that sea (being themselves water), they still demonstrate separate actions and reactions in the form of breaking up and coalescing. And yet, the foam, wave, etc, do not lose their individuality in relation to one another, even though they are modifications of the sea and non-different from it (being themselves water). To re-iterate, even though they do not lose their individuality in one another, they are never different from the point of view of their being the sea itself.[8]

We can see from the above that both Śaṅkara and Śāntideva struggle to find a place for external reality in their traditions' neither/nor models. They are thus both intent on creating a both/and model. A wave both *is* and *is not* the sea. Individuals both *do* and *do not* exist.[9] One way Śaṅkara does this is by claiming that the *pramāṇa* of direct perception (*pratyakṣa*) can be used to validate the *pramāṇa* of scriptural testimony (*śabda*, *śruti*). This makes him subject to normal conventions (*vyavahāra*) and a transcendental thesis. Śāntideva, however, maintains that the perception of a *yogi* is superior to normal perception. He therefore has no need to play ball with the conventional *pramāṇa* system. His ultimate *pramāṇa* then is the *yogi*'s superior understanding, which amounts to their 'privileged way' of describing reality. This is not so much a transcendental argument, but a gnoseological one.

---

8 This non-dual response could have been taken straight out of a Ch'an Buddhist text. But let us not forget that Śāntideva (unlike Chinese Madhyamaka) would not accept its metaphysical basis, there being no 'Absolute' ground in Indian Madhyamaka. Cf. *V.C.* (390 and 496).

9 Zaehner (1973: 187) saw a similar *both/and* model as a characteristic of the *Gītā*.

Now, Suthren Hirst (2005: 49) has claimed that Śaṅkara would not engage with the Mādhyamikas because they 'did not accept any *pramāṇas*'. And Matics (1971: 118) claims that Śāntideva 'accepts no criteria of valid knowledge'. However, this is simply not true. Śāntideva clearly accepts certain Buddhist scriptures as authoritative; the *Compendium* is almost entirely made up of such authoritative citations. He uses scripture as a means to prove the validity of the workings of *karma*, and even to justify his emptiness doctrine (BCA. 9.38–50). He also accepts the *yogi*'s 'superior understanding' as a form of knowledge (9.7–8) worthy of replacing the direct perception of common people (9.6). Furthermore, for Śaṅkara (see B.S.Bh. I.i.4 and II.i.14), ultimately, the *pramāṇas* 'fail to tell us about reality' (Potter 1981: 96), culminating in a neither/nor position, which arguably parallels that of Nāgārjuna. When *brahman*-knowledge is gained, the 'very conditions under which the system of knowledge operates cease to hold' (Ram-Prasad 2007: 128). Furthermore, Nāgārjuna did not say that he denied the *pramāṇas*, but that he neither affirmed nor denied them (Vv. 30). As pointed out by Westerhoff (2009: 179), it would be wrong to claim that, for Nāgārjuna, the *pramāṇas* and their objects do not exist at all. Rather, they have no independent existence. Nāgārjuna's assault was targeted at foundationalism, not epistemic instruments, *per se*. Thus, the apparent methodological difference between Śaṅkara and Śāntideva fails from both sides.

Śāntideva's *yogi-bodhisattva*, by flickering from ultimate to conventional reality, commands authority in both domains. Of course, to a certain degree, the same is true of Śaṅkara's *brahma-vid*, who will claim self-validating knowledge of ultimate reality. He will also claim to understand the true intent of the Vedas. But his knowledge seems not to extend to the point of claiming to know the truth about whether objects exist externally or not. He seems more concerned than the Buddhist as to whether his revisionary account will be 'dismissed out of hand' (Ram-Prasad 2001a: 180). But, more than fear of philosophical rejection is at stake. Both Śaṅkara and Śāntideva need the outside world for their traditions' ethics to function. They also need to remain sceptical of the world's 'solidity', as it were, in order for their world-transcending thesis to have full force. They must both make cognition central without falling into a mind-only position. Thus, we see a tension between the Two Truths.

Returning to the question of textual development; if we accept that the *Bṛ.U.Bh* and the *B.S.Bh* are his more 'mature' works, and if we also accept that the *Ch.U.Bh* was one of his two most important Upaniṣadic commentaries (see Suthren Hirst 2005: 19–25), then Hacker seems correct in his assessment that Śaṅkara moved away from Gauḍapāda. Dasgupta (1975, Vol.II: 28–9) also notes this change in Śaṅkara's attitude to external objects, feeling that his various statements would amount to 'contradictions' unless we accept a shift in thought between the time of writing the *G.K.Bh.* and the *B.S.Bh.* And any sympathetic reading of Śaṅkara should try to avoid such contradictions.

Certainly, if we examine the arguments that Śaṅkara offers against the Yogācāra in his mature texts, we have to agree with Ram-Prasad's (2002: 25–92) reading of Śaṅkara as offering a 'transcendental argument' with regard to externality. Put simply, the argument goes that we cannot prove external reality, but we have to take it, *a priori*, as given in order to tally the world with our experience. But we can neither prove that there is an external world, nor outright deny it. The world then, for Śaṅkara, has what Radhakrishnan (1989: 87) has called 'pragmatic justification'. Contrary to Thurman's (1976: 3) thesis of 'absolute' metaphysics, Śaṅkara does not impel us to 'negate our immediate reality'. The 'mature' Śaṅkara therefore sits closer to the Madhyamaka than to the Yogācāra. We might say that Śaṅkara moves from an idealistic/anti-realist position to a sceptical/non-realist position. This allows him to talk coherently about the world and its social structures without compromising the possibility of world-transcendence.

If we do accept this chronology, then it could be argued that at some point in his life, Śaṅkara no longer found idealism to be reasonable. But I would like to think that he also moved away from the mind-only position because he saw it as undermining the ethics of the Vedas and the *Gītā*. However, he maintained the Two Truths because that allowed him more scope to split the Vedas in two, creating two clear domains, the provisional and the ultimate. Keeping hold of the early Vedas allows for a more conservative traditional structure, and the *Bhagavad Gītā* provides him with the vehicle to express his views on class-based *Dharma*. Ram-Prasad (2007: 126) describes the Advaitin's position thus:

> Advaitins must reconcile a radical concept of liberation that rejects Vedic ritual by calling for it to be transcended with a conservative acknowledgement of the significance of Vedic orthopraxy.

On its Advaitin methodology, the *V.C.* states: 'Neither the method of complete rejection nor that of total retention is fitting. But a method based on both approaches should be adopted' (247).

It is this *tension* which comes of maintaining the Two-Truths hermeneutics along with an insistence on traditional ethics that makes Śaṅkara's both/and methodology appear so much like Śāntideva. But the doctrine he holds is not that of the Madhyamaka, only the methodology. When dealing with ethics, texts are explained in conventional terms, but when dealing with liberation, texts are explained in ultimate terms. Thus, in balancing the provisional with the ultimate, both Śaṅkara and Śāntideva manipulate the traditional texts to suit the context. For Śaṅkara, the wave is both wave *and* sea; for Śāntideva, the wave is both wave *and* empty. They share the '*and*', but not the ontology. And, of course, they disagree on the source of their provisional ethics. For Śaṅkara, the Vedic rituals must go on; for Śāntideva, they are futile. Thus, Śaṅkara's traditional Vedāntin stance remains intact despite the similarities with his Buddhist compatriots. And we might believe that he became more radically sectarian as a reaction to the obvious similarities.

As for Śaṅkara's dates, it seems that the first Western attempt was made by Tiele, who suggested 788–820. Hacker offers 680–720 (in Halbfass 1995: 27 and 192). Olivelle (1986) accepts Mayeda's dates of 700–750. The debate goes on (see Isayeva 1993: 83–7). Śaṅkara's dates have relied upon astrological charts, hagiographical materials, dating of contemporary polemics within his works, as well as the dating of his followers, none of which are particularly conclusive. Let us accept then, until proven otherwise, that Śaṅkara flourished around the 8th century.

In terms of caste and lineage, Śaṅkara seems to have a major task at hand if he wishes to: 1) link himself with the early Upaniṣads, and 2) see his own lineage as that of celibate monks. Even though the non-celibate life was ridiculed in the *Muṇḍaka Upaniṣad* (see Olivelle, in Olson 2008: 156–7), it is quite evident that the earlier Upaniṣads take the lineage of 'knowers' to be a lineage of householders. The *Chāndogya Upaniṣad*, for example, is quite explicit that its lineage is one of 'great-householders' (*mahā-śālāḥ*) (Ch.U. VI.iv.5). And Śaṅkara himself makes it explicit that by 'knowers' the Upaniṣad means 'knowers of *brahman*' (*brahma-vidāṃ*) (Ch.U.Bh. VI.iv.7). But in the very same commentary, Śaṅkara is quite insistent that 'the monk alone [*bhikṣuka eva*], having ceased rites, remains established in *brahman*' (II.xxiii.1). So insistent, in fact, that he repeats it with the paraphrased, 'only as a mendicant [*parivrājakasya eva*] who has completely given up difference can one remain established in *brahman*' (ibid.). He simply does not want to admit that householders could have knowledge of *brahman*. In fact, he goes one further, and claims that those who desire women cannot possibly have knowledge of the Self (VIII.v.4). This is because lust (*kāma*) supposedly arises from ignorance (*avidyā*) (U.S. Prose, 1.20). Elsewhere, he makes this explicit: 'Indeed, there can be no possibility of such defects as ignorance, craving, and the like, after the realization of the "fourth"[10] as one's Self' (Mā.U.Bh. 7). Moreover, 'The knower-of-*brahman* has already attained the desirable, an incomparable desire; so he cannot therefore have any more desires' (Bṛ.U.Bh. II.iv., intro).

The *Chāndogya Upaniṣad* thus speaks of a self-knower as 'one who has bliss in the self' (VII.xxv.2), and Śaṅkara comments that this bliss (*ānanda*) is 'without the need for union'. Furthermore, it comes to a man 'even while living' (*jīvann eva*)[11] (Ch.U.Bh. VII.xxv.2). Clearly, Śaṅkara is simply trying to trump the bliss of sexual union with the incomparably exalted bliss of realization. As in Buddhism, it is used as a sort of bait to persuade would-be renouncers, especially those who put more value on sensual-pleasure than on knowledge. Śaṅkara's style of argument, like Śāntideva's, was also persuasive, but also like Śāntideva, he found himself involved in persuading his followers in both ascetic terms and in more metaphysical terms. Thus, there is an inherent *tension* in his exegesis. On Śaṅkara's pure Advaitin terms, personal bliss is a faulty argument, for we see elsewhere that he denies that a *brahman*-knower could feel bliss as if it were something to be cognized (Bṛ.U.Bh. III.ix.28.7). That is why Indologists speak of Śaṅkara's 'reticence' (Potter 1981: 91) and 'reservations' (Hacker, in Halbfass 1995: 112) with regard to bliss. Śaṅkara is anxious to show that bliss of the self is not the object of a feeling. Hence:

---

10 The 'fourth' (*turīya*) state (that is, where one is neither awake, nor dreaming, nor asleep) (see Mā.U. 3–7).

11 This is Śaṅkara's typical way of referring to *jīvan-mukti*.

> Like a hand-full of water thrown into a lake, he does not retain a separate existence by which he could 'know' the blissful *brahman*. Hence, to say that the liberated man knows the blissful self is [ultimately] meaningless (Bṛ.U.Bh. III.ix.28.7).

More importantly, contra numerous claims for *jīvan-mukti*, Śaṅkara states that only 'absolute separation from the body amounts to final liberation' (ibid.). Thus, Śaṅkara's acceptance of *jīvan-mukti* appears less than wholehearted. And it may therefore appear that *mokṣa* 'belongs to *Ātman*, not to embodied existence' (Koller, in Deutsch and Bontekoe 1997: 289). The problem with this assessment, though, is that, if Śaṅkara wished to promote 'post-body liberation' (*videha-mukti*), then there are passages in the Upaniṣads that lend themselves to it, but Śaṅkara does *not* interpret them that way. For example, the *Chāndogya*'s 'This is *brahman*. After departing from here after death, I shall become that', which seems a classic case for *videha-mukti*, is taken by Śaṅkara to refer to a qualified (*saguṇa*) objective form of *brahman*, not the ultimate *nirguṇa-brahman* (Ch.U.Bh. III.xiv.4). Better then to see Śaṅkara as being left in a similar situation to the early Buddhists who devised the notion of two types of *nirvāṇa*, that is, 'with remainder' (*sopādhiśeṣa*), and 'without remainder' (*anupādhiśeṣa*) of the aggregates.[12] Whilst physically embodied, the *jīvan-mukta* can still be said to have attained 'immortality' (*amṛitatva*), in the sense that he has conquered death (Ch.U.Bh. VI.xiv.2) and has, as it were, become 'unembodied' (*aśarīra*) (Ch.U.Bh. VIII.xii.1). This makes sense when we realize that Śaṅkara defines embodiment in terms of the mistaken cognition (*mithyā-jñāna*) which identifies self with the body (B.S.Bh. I.i.4), and then defines bodilessness in terms of liberation (ibid.). The bodiless state is thus said to be eternal (*nitya*) and inherent in the Self (ibid.), as is immortality (Ken.U.Bh. 2.4). As Kuznetsova (2007: 35) points out, in Vedānta, liberation becomes the new immortality, a 'meta-ritual state' that usurps the privileged position of Vedic ritual sacrifice.

There is therefore another sense in which the *brahman*-knower can be said to be unembodied and/or immortal, for the *Saṃnyāsa Upaniṣads* speak of renunciation itself as the 'ritual death of the renouncer' (Olivelle 1992: 89). Thus, Dumont (1980: 184) speaks of the renouncer as being 'dead to the social world'. Likewise, the renouncing *bodhisattva* is said by Śāntideva to have 'already died to the world' (BCA. 8.36b). However, the *jīvan-mukta* cannot claim to have *complete* liberation – that which the Buddhists would call '*parinirvāṇa*' and Śaṅkara calls '*mokṣa ātyantika*' (Bṛ.U.Bh. III.ix.28.7) – for that would require *actual* disembodiment.

What we can tentatively conclude here is that, in order to promote the celibate life over the householder's life, Śaṅkara is willing to promote the notion of the pleasure that one derives from absorption in *brahman*. However, in order to save his non-dual interpretation of scripture he is willing to give up this notion of this superior pleasure. Furthermore, he is even willing to give up the notion of the

12 On notions of *nirvāṇa*, see Soonil Hwang (2006).

ultimate liberation of the *jīvan-mukta*, advancing instead a doctrine of *videha-mukti* (post-body liberation). The teacher thus seems to be one waiting for final liberation. This shows that when Śaṅkara shifts domains, from 'ascetic' discourse to metaphysics, the latter sublates the former. The teacher he is left with is thus a partially liberated one (see P.U.Bh., intro), who we may imagine to be alternating between dualistic and non-dualistic modes of consciousness.

Thus, we have an example of how Advaita tends to switch back and forth between ultimate and relative perspectives of the *jīvan-mukta*'s behaviour. Moreover, in order to save his fundamental Advaita doctrine of non-difference (*abheda*), Śaṅkara is willing to give up the *pramāṇa* of testimonial authority (*śabda*), even that of the Vedic scripture (*śruti*), which he is supposedly defending. In fact, he is even willing to claim that the 'Vedas contain contradictory statements' (Bṛ.U.Bh. III.ix.28.7). Like renunciation, scripture is merely a means to liberation, not liberation itself. In the final analysis, even scripture needs to be transcended, and, ultimately speaking, it is but another aspect of conventional reality. This may have been a lesson he learnt early on:

> The existence of such objects as scripture, etc. is but a conceptual convention. And this conventional reality is imagined as a means of attaining the ultimate reality; but anything that so exists has no real existence from the side of ultimate truth (G.K.Bh. 4.73).

What we see then, in Śaṅkara's work, is not so much contradiction, but *retraction*. Some of these retractions are due to the shift from conventional to ultimate truth, and might be more rightly called *sublation*. But others are due to an over-willingness to explain everything in absolute terms. Thus, *all* action is to be given up, rather than just ritual action, and *all karma* is burnt up by knowledge, rather than just some of it.[13] The *brahma-vid* is over-painted, as it were, to match the perfect image of *brahman*. But when Śaṅkara looks back at the world, he sees that he needs *karma* in order to have a body at all. He sees that the antics of the Upaniṣadic *brahman*-knowers fail to live up to the perfection of the absolute. Yet, the tradition's need for a teacher's liberating guidance, rather than the Lord's grace, forces Śaṅkara into a situation where an embodied knower is necessary.

Śaṅkara-the-exegete is also trapped by conflicting statements, such as the *Bhagavad Gītā*'s 'The fire of knowledge reduces all *karma* to ashes' (4.37) and 'the knowers, those who see true reality, will impart that knowledge' (4.34). And so Śaṅkara is left having to explain how the knower survives at all in order to teach. He does this by shifting to the *Chāndogya Upaniṣad* (VI.xiv.2), which speaks of a 'delay' before final liberation, and the *Brahma Sūtra* (IV.i.15 and 19), which, on Śaṅkara's reading, explains this delay in terms of types of *karma*, some being destroyed, some not. And from here, Śaṅkara develops his thesis of latent tendencies

[13] For an examination of 'weak' versus 'strong' subordination in Śaṅkara, see Ram-Prasad (2007).

and residual (*prārabdha*) *karma*. He must either give up the knower-cum-teacher, or he must give up *jīvan-mukti*. Yet he appears to opt for a middle ground, a teacher who flickers between absorption into thusness (*tattva*) and conventional modes of being. This also amounts to a retraction of the view that action (*karma*) and knowledge (*jñāna*) are contradictory, for the teacher must act. And so, by observing these major retractions, we can gain an insight into that which Śaṅkara will let go of, that which he will fight for and finally, his overall *both/and* position.

The only way of doing this is through cross-textual analysis. For example, in the *B.S.Bh*, just prior to admitting that ignorance continues even after knowledge, Śaṅkara uses the *Chāndogya* (VI.xiv.2) to prove that true and final liberation only comes *after* death (B.S.Bh. IV.i.15). Oddly enough, in the *Ch.U.Bh* itself (VI.xiv.2), while drawing on the distinction between the two types of *karma*, Śaṅkara makes no such denial of *jīvan-mukti*, but speaks of *prārabdha-karma* being destroyed by experience. It thus seems that in the *B.S.Bh* he is more concerned with saving the concept of *mukti* than *jīvan-mukti* specifically, even though he takes the *Brahma Sūtra* itself to be speaking of *jīvan-mukti*, when he interprets the phrase 'even of this world' (*api aihika*) as referring to living-liberation (B.S.Bh III.iv.51).

Another example is offered by the question of celibacy. Even though Śaṅkara is elsewhere insistent on celibacy as essential to liberation, when the text itself is found to be speaking of finding a wife and having children (for example T.U. I.xi.1), Śaṅkara accepts it. Furthermore, while claiming that a *brahma-vid* has no desire for women and sons, he accepts Uddālaka of the *Chāndogya Upaniṣad* and Yājñavalkya[14] the hero of the *Bṛhadāraṇyaka Upaniṣad* as ideal teachers, even though the former teaches the truth of *brahman* to his own son, while the latter has not one, but *two* wives. To reiterate, while Śaṅkara's ideal teacher is a celibate monk, most of his Upaniṣadic role models are in fact householders, but he is willing to accept this in order to promote the Upaniṣads and his non-dual interpretation.

However, as noted earlier, flickering consciousness, or temporary lapses, is one means of interpreting Śaṅkara's way of allowing for the behaviour of the enlightened householders. Seen in this light, it need not contradict Yājñavalkya's own claim that a knower of Self gives up the desire for sons, wealth and other worlds, and thus takes up the life of a mendicant (Bṛ.U. III.v.1). Certainly, it is as a realized mendicant that Śaṅkara salutes him (B.S.Bh. III.iv.9). The question would then be one of *delay* (cf. Ch.U. VI.xiv.1) and may fit either the life-stages or the life-choices model. Marcaurelle (2000: 138) suggests that Śaṅkara believed that the householder, once enlightened, would abandon his lifestyle 'spontaneously'.

The notion that an enlightened householder must spontaneously renounce is also found in Theravāda Buddhism in the form of the claim that a lay person who attains *arhatship* is obliged to ordain that very day, or else he will die (Miln. 264–6). And perhaps Śaṅkara would accept that the 'lofty nature of this state cannot be expressed

---

[14] Yājñavalkya has been called the 'first exponent of Advaita Vedānta' (Roodurmun 2002: 10).

in a lay context' (Harvey 2000: 92). Whether liberation is possible with or without physical renunciation, a subject on which both Śaṅkara and (his pupil) Sureśvara were truly ambiguous (Marcaurelle 2000: 174), the bottom line is that they both would have liked the scriptures to have unanimously and categorically stated that physical renunciation was a prerequisite of liberating knowledge.

None of this need affect Śaṅkara's main social claim that a knower of *brahman* is to give up ritual action, this being the principal use of the term '*saṃnyāsa*' (Olivelle 1992: 59). And Marcaurelle (2000) is surely correct in his emphasis on the 'inner' renunciation of doership as the key to understanding Śaṅkara's metaphysical take on renunciation. He also seems correct in indicating two types of renunciation, one for the enlightened and one for the seeker (p185). Perhaps, then, when Śaṅkara talks of 'renunciation of all actions prior to steadfastness in knowledge' (Bh.G.Bh. 18.66), he is talking about a potential *deepening* of the knowledge of Self.

Let us turn to the *Bṛhadāraṇyaka Upaniṣad* (IV.iv.22) and see how Śaṅkara deals with its famous statement on renunciation. The text says: 'Desiring the world [of the self] alone, those renouncers renounce' (*etam eva pravrājino lokam icchantaḥ pravrājanti*). This seems rather circular, a problem which has haunted many translators.[15] However, Śaṅkara does not take this as a description, but as a *prescription*. He thus claims that 'this [sentence] is an injunction' (Bṛ.U.Bh. IV.iv.22). Śaṅkara takes the meaning to be, 'Therefore, desiring the world of the self, those who are disposed to renunciation [should] renounce' (*tasmād ātmānaṃ lokam icchantaḥ pravrajanti pravrajeyuḥ*).[16] This rids the text of its circularity. Taber (1983: 15) therefore reads Śaṅkara as applying the passage to those who have '*already*, to a certain degree, achieved self-knowledge'. In other words, Śaṅkara is admitting the existence of *partial* knowers, those who appear qualified to take the next leap into external renunciation. Taber thus reads this back into the original passage, translating it as 'Aspiring to that world [of the self] alone, those who are disposed to renunciation renounce' (ibid.). Again, this rids the original passage of its circularity. Comparing Śaṅkara's historical situation with Śāntideva's, we see the latter (in *BCA* Chapter 8) attempting to establish or deepen inner renunciation in those who (in the majority) had already formally renounced. Śaṅkara, however, was more focused on *establishing* formal renunciation in Vedānta.

Thus, Śaṅkara's claim for a life of celibacy remains more controversial than his stance on renunciation, for he is turning it into an injunction. Olivelle (1992: 72) saw it as a 'key element in renunciation', and Śaṅkara certainly took it to be an aid to knowledge (T.U.Bh. I.xi.2–4). Yet the ambiguity in the Upaniṣads allows Olivelle (1992: 43) to insist that the 'householder is replaced by the celibate ascetic as the new religious ideal', while giving room for scholars like Coward (2008: 128–9) to

---

[15] See Mādhavānanda (trans. 2008: 520) and Olivelle (trans. 1998: 67). Cf. Lipner (2010: 54).

[16] Mādhavānanda (trans., 2008: 527) therefore seems correct in adding 'i.e. should renounce' to the *Bhāṣya*.

claim that 'only when the responsibilities and joys of the student and householder stages have been fully enjoyed' does one 'seek to be freed from a worldly and sensuous life'.[17] Doniger (2010: 194) memorably describes this tension as one of violent extremes of addiction versus abstinence. As for Śaṅkara's commentaries, they clearly tend to side with Olivelle rather than Coward, with abstinence over addiction.

With respect to the system of stages, Śaṅkara (selectively) quotes the *Jābāla Upaniṣad*'s suggestion that a man 'may even renounce directly from the stage of studentship' (Jā.U. 4; B.S.Bh. III.iv.17). However, having selected only this possibility out of a whole list of alternatives, Śaṅkara essentially turns the 'may' into a 'should', calling this renunciation an injunction (B.S.Bh. III.iv.18). Nevertheless, Śaṅkara does go on to quote the passage in full (III.iv.20), where he uses the text to prove the authenticity of the life of the celibate. The text now loses its imperative tone and Śaṅkara appears more cautious, which shows how Śaṅkara still felt that he needed to 'sell' celibacy as an alternative lifestyle to the *Brahmin* orthodoxy. And yet, with respect to the status of life's joys and sorrows, Ingalls (1954: 306) notes how, by the time of Śaṅkara, 'the Vedānta had left its early joyous acceptance of the whole of life', with the pessimism of Buddhism having seeped into Vedānta, which now saw the world as a 'sorry place' to be (ibid.). Thus it is that Śaṅkara presents a rather extreme world-renouncing view of Vedānta.

Yet there remained a tangible tension in Śaṅkara's work, an exegetic tension which comes from trying to apologise for the worldly actions of the protagonists of the Upaniṣads whilst putting forward his personal ascetic ideal. Unlike Śāntideva (Ś.S. 167), Śaṅkara would not call on the theory of skilful-means (*upāya-kauśalya*) to explain these actions. Rather, he had to retract the notion of complete enlightenment, replacing it with the notion of residual (*prārabdha*) *karma* (B.S.Bh. III.iii.32). Śaṅkara could find no external excuse for one who falls from celibacy (III.iv.43). For Śaṅkara, unlike Śāntideva (Ś.S. 168), it is the *protagonist* who acts wrongly, not we who *see him* wrongly.[18] He here shows himself to be more realistic than Śāntideva, which maps onto the 'realistic thrust' (Black 2008: 21) of the Upaniṣads.[19]

Turning to Śaṅkara's argument for renunciation of ritual action, we see that it relies on the notion of non-difference (*abheda*) of self (*jīvātman*) and Self (*brahman*). Ritual assumes that one is a *Brahmin*, that is, a member of a class. This assumes difference in nature from other castes. But one who is desirous of liberation should not associate one's self with caste (U.S. Prose, 1.10–15). How could there be castes when *all* is the nature of the single Self (Ch.U.Bh. II.xxiii.1)? Moreover, ritual assumes that you are down here and the gods are up there; but

[17] For a review of Coward's *The Perfectibility of Human Nature in Eastern and Western Thought*, see Todd (2011).

[18] The *V.C.* alternates between these possibilities. For example, contrast verses 442 and 548.

[19] Cf. Sutton (in Rosen 2002: 94) on the 'realistic' and 'pragmatic' nature of the *Gītā*.

'you are that' (Ch.U. VI.viii.7ff) and are, thus, non-different (*a-bheda*). The subject-object dichotomy, necessary for ritual, premised as it is on the distinction between the act and the actor, thus falls apart. Furthermore, ritual has as one of its goals the going from here to a divine realm in the after-life. But if you (as pure consciousness) are of the same nature as *brahman* right now, right here, then where would one need or wish to go? In the final analysis, it is knowledge of reality that leads to liberation, not correct ritual action. The concept of going to heavenly realms must be replaced by the concept of attaining knowledge of *brahman*. Thus, liberation is not a movement or activity, and *brahman* (as absolute consciousness) is to be reached epistemically. So a knower cannot sincerely take part in ritual, he cannot be a *Brahmin* householder with ritual duties (Ch.U.Bh. II.xxiii.1). Others may, however, continue to indulge in ritual, for they still see difference.

Therefore, we see how the Two Truths may act as a hermeneutical key to Śaṅkara's philosophy. There is the ultimate goal of liberation and there are the conventional social playing grounds. Goals related to a personal God, or to heavens, whilst being beyond mundane goals such as wealth and progeny, are still to be included in the conventional category. Knowledge is the only means to true liberation and the ultimate statements of the Upaniṣads are the only means to such 'saving' knowledge. Thus Śaṅkara states that '*brahman* is known from scripture alone' (B.S.Bh. I.i.4). An ultimate Upaniṣadic statement is thus taken to be one that points to the non-duality of the self and *brahman*. Therefore, any statement which seems to demand the need for ritual action or meditation on a symbol, and thus assumes a duality of subject and object, is taken to be a conventional statement. Vedic listeners are thus divided into: 1) those *Brahmin*s who are ready for ultimate statements; 2) those who are merely ready for meditation; and 3) those who are simply at the stage of ritual action. Thus, Śaṅkara accepts and extends Mīmāṃsā hermeneutical criteria:

> Having granted that the Vedic sentences are intended as injunctions, it stands to reason that, just as such means as the 'agnihotra' sacrifice are enjoined for one desiring heavens, so the knowledge of *brahman* is enjoined for one who longs for immortality (B.S.Bh. I.i.4).

In dealing with the quite lengthy *Chāndogya Upaniṣad*, Śaṅkara takes it as presenting a gradualist approach to truth, which means that non-dual (*advaita*) revelations take precedence over dualistic (*dvaita*) revelations (for example see Ch.U.Bh., intro and III.xiv.4). In the middle are those meditations on symbols, recitations and so on. These may give one a 'flash' (*avabhāsaka*) of reality, but they do not present total absorption in *brahman*. This technique allows Śaṅkara to interpret the text on the lines of ultimate and non-ultimate teachings. He returns to this gradualism at the end of Chapter VI, where he states that it is not instinctive to see oneself as a soul (*jīva*) apart from the body (like non-Advaita Brahmanical Schools), never mind to see oneself as pure consciousness (*ātman*) (as the Advaitins do). That is, to think that 'I am an individuated soul, separate [from the body and mind]' is not a 'naturally held view of beings' (Ch.U.Bh. VI.xvi.3). And so, people need to be led to the truth of selfhood in stages, from the self as body doctrine to self as soul (that is, Dvaita) to self as *brahman* (that is, Advaita) (ibid.).[20] Śaṅkara, therefore, seems to have set himself the task of systematizing the Upaniṣads, and the Two Truths and the notion of gradual enlightenment are fundamental to his methodology.

However, just as with the so-called 'Sudden Schools' of Buddhism, Śaṅkara distinguishes those who need to be led gradually to the truth from those (rare) sharp pupils (*nipuṇamatīnāṃ*) who can grasp it at once. Of the former, he says:

> The phrase 'you are that' cannot produce a sudden realization of its true meaning in those people to whom [self and *brahman*] remain obstructed by ignorance, doubt and confusion (for the meaning of a phrase is dependent upon the meaning of the words). For such people, it is necessary to resort repeatedly to the study of scripture. … In this sense, gradualism is admitted (B.S.Bh. IV.i.2).

Of the latter, he writes:

> For those of sharp intellect, however, who have no obstructions like ignorance, doubt and confusion, with regard to subject matter, they can realize the meaning of 'you are that' from the very first utterance. So a repetition in their case is pointless. For the ascertainment of the Self is capable of removing ignorance in one single instant, and no stages need be admitted in this case (ibid.).

Hence, Śaṅkara, like Śāntideva, accepts that the task of removing ignorance, doubt and confusion is, for most people, a gradual step-by-step assent. And again, as with the Madhyamaka, much of the ignorance and confusion and so on is taken up by the notion of *māyā* (illusion). Now, given that we have already traced both Śaṅkara's use of the Two-Truths doctrine and the notion of *māyā* to Gauḍapāda's *Māṇḍūkya kārikā*, and given the consensus that Gauḍapāda took this from the Madhyamaka School, we might reasonably trace much of Śaṅkara's language on *māyā* to Nāgārjuna's *Mūlamadhyamakakārikā*. Here, the phrase 'as an illusion, a dream' is used to describe the concepts of arising, enduring and ceasing (MMK. 7.34). Again, the phrase 'like a mirage or a dream' occurs with regard to afflictions, actions, bodies, agents and karmic fruits (17.33), along with the five senses and all existents (23.8). We might also trace these similes back to the '*Diamond*' *Sūtra*'s list of nine, which includes a dream, a bubble, an eye defect, magical illusions and so on (Vajracchedikā, 32). In fact, we might go even further back and trace the notion to the Pāli Canon (S.N.III.140–42), where the list of similes also includes foam, and the plantain tree. We will see that Śaṅkara adopts these very same similes throughout his works.

[20] Cf. the *V.C.* (160).

Turning to the Vedic literature, the term '*māyā*' (pre-Śaṅkara) had been used in a variety of ways, the enquiry into which would be a major study in itself.[21] Dasgupta (1975) thus states that Śaṅkara 'never tries to prove that the world is māyā, but accepts it as indisputable' (Vol.I: 435). Yet we can distinguish two strands of *māyā*-talk in Śaṅkara's work, one cosmological and the other epistemological. In the *B.S.Bh*, Śaṅkara claims that absolute consciousness (*vijñāna dhātu*) may appear diversely due to either *avidyā* or *māyā* (B.S.Bh. I.iii.19). Śaṅkara later states that, just like a magician who does not believe his own illusions to be real, so *brahman* is unaffected by this 'cyclic world of *māyā*' (B.S.Bh. II.i.9). He then quotes the following verse from Gauḍapāda's *Kārika* (1.16): 'When an individual sleeping under the influence of beginningless *māyā* is awakened, he then realizes the birthless, sleepless, dreamless non-dual' (B.S.Bh. II.i.9).

The theory of '*māyā*' clearly played a pivotal role in Śaṅkara's system, but our task is to explain what Śaṅkara meant by '*māyā*'. The problem, as just noted, is that there seem to be two distinct meanings of '*māyā*' in his work. One type of *māyā*-talk is that found particularly in the *Gītā Bhāṣya*. It refers to a kind of creative power which emanates from Kṛṣṇa-as-Viṣṇu (Bh.G.Bh. 7.13). It is made up of the three attributes (*tribhir-guṇa*) of being, and is sometimes used synonymously with '*prakṛti*'. When conceived negatively, mankind are said to be deluded by *māyā* (Bh.G.Bh. 7.13–15). Kṛṣṇa is said to 'move' beings through *māyā* (Bh.G. 18.61), to which Śaṅkara adds: 'through concealment' (*chadmanā*) (Bh.G.Bh. 18.61).[22] For the purposes of this comparison with Śāntideva, I propose to bracket this cosmological notion of *māyā*, focusing on the epistemological *māyā* (=*avidyā*), the version most adopted in his major works. Like others before me (Otto 1957: 104; Suthren Hirst 2005: 134), I find the *Gītā* to be a text least amenable to Śaṅkara's usual Advaitin metaphysics.

Now, some scholars (Otto 1957: 93; Torwesten 1991: 123) claim that, through the notion of *māyā*, Śaṅkara tried to explain the world away. However, Śaṅkara actually uses the concept of *māyā* in an attempt to explain the world in a way that would cohere with Advaita metaphysics. The notion that the world is dream-like or illusion-like is not to suggest that it is not real, it is to highlight that what we take to be real is in fact just a 'faint reflection of what is truly real' (Taber 1983: 1). We see the world as if through a mirror. Yet, like Śāntideva, Śaṅkara is not saying that such reflections are totally non-existent. Thus, Śaṅkara writes that 'An illusory image cannot exist without a substratum' (Mā.U.Bh. 7). That substratum is *brahman*.

The individuated self (*jīva*) is said to be a mere reflection of the true Self (*brahman*). This notion of 'reflection' (*chāyā*) is brought out by a number of analogies, including the reflection of one's face in a mirror (U.S. Metric, 12.6), the reflection of the sun (Ch.U.Bh. VI.iii.2) or moon (B.S.Bh. III.ii.19) in water. However, Śaṅkara's three favourite analogies, which crop up throughout his works, are all to be found in the following verse:

---

21 See O'Neil (1980).

22 This take on *māyā* is more typical of Rāmānuja and Madhva (Chari 2005: 81).

> As a magician is not himself affected at any time [past, present or future] by the magic he conjures up, it being unreal, so also the supreme Self is not affected by this cyclic world of *māyā*. As one who dreams is not affected by the illusion of dreaming, because that illusion does not persist in him during clear wakefulness, so also the one, unchanging witness of the three states is untouched by the three varying states. This appearance of the supreme Self in identity with the three states is mere *māyā*, as in the case of the rope appearing as a snake (B.S.Bh. II.i.9).

Thus, we have: 1) the illusion (*māyā*) created by the magician (*māyāvin*); 2) the dream (*svapna*) world; and 3) seeing a rope (*rajju*) as a snake (*sarpa*). What does Śaṅkara want us to understand from these examples? He wants us to see that although the world may seem manifold, everything is in fact grounded in *brahman*. This universe is ultimately reducible to 'mere conscious being' (U.S. Metric, 17.13). Now, when a magician creates an illusion, he knows it to be an illusion. Equally, when *brahman*-knowledge is gained, the manifold world of apparently individuated selves will be seen to be but one singular, non-dual consciousness. The *brahman*-knower is not fooled by the appearance of the world. Its illusory manifestations simply 'vanish away like apparitions in a dream' (B.S.Bh. III.ii.21).

When one is dreaming, one may imagine beings and objects to be in certain odd spatial relationships to each other. However, when one awakens, these visions are sublated by the awakened mind which knows the dream content to be false (see Ch.U.Bh. II.xxiii.1). In one sense, we might say that 'dreams are false and illusory whereas waking experience is veridical, having an external cause' (King 1995: 171). But we should not forget that this fact is not typically grasped by one while dreaming. Also, for Advaita, cognitions are 'considered innocent until proven guilty' (Deutsch 1973: 87), that is, they are *prima facie* justified. Dreams are real *to the dreamer*, and that experience, though illusory, is valid until later contradicted.

Therefore, Śaṅkara draws on this dream analogy to make the point that, just as a man who awakens from a dream knows it to be illusory, so a man who awakens to *brahman*-knowledge knows this world of multiplicity to be illusory. The world is *deceptive*, but not false. After seeing through this deception, the old relationships he had with people, gods, rituals, desirable objects and so on no longer apply to the *brahman*-knower. In other words, Śaṅkara is not trying to deny the external reality of the world, but wants us to see the potential for its transcendence.

Third, we come to the famous Indian 'snake/rope' analogy. A person sees a coiled object in the corner of a dark room and imagines it to be a snake. As they get closer, they realize it is only a rope. Thus, perception can be sublated by a second perception. Just so, when a man realizes *brahman*-consciousness, his old view of the world is removed. Of course, his old perception was not entirely false, for there was in fact a rope there giving rise to the mistaken cognition of a snake. As such, the views of those yet to know *brahman* are provisionally true, merely awaiting sublation. In this sense, Śaṅkara's epistemology is 'realistic', for the cognition is said to point to an objective referent. This epistemic 'realism' is particularly brought out in his attack on the Mahāyāna Buddhists, and especially the Yogācāra.

Up until the ultimate Self is realized, objects are objects, and individuals are individuals. That, along with *karma*, is what makes rebirth and social interaction possible. That is why traditional ethics must remain in place. Śaṅkara wants to posit a transcendence of ritual, not a rejection of it:

> It is reasonable that their validity will continue with regard to a person who has not gotten rid of the conviction of separation; as in the case of dream experiences, etc. (which remain valid) before one awakens (Ch.U.Bh. II.xxiii.1).

Not only is it reasonable, it is necessary, because negative *karma* accrues to those who do not do their duty: 'The obligation remains for those whose conviction of separation has not been destroyed by knowledge' (Ch.U.Bh. II.xxiii.1).

Thus, Śaṅkara's goal is to 'assimilate ... ritual into his grand metaphysical project' (Ram-Prasad 2007: 116). In this grand scheme, God may shape and maintain the world, and even guide those of inferior wisdom, but he has very little to offer those sharp-minded ones who can grasp the true (Advaitic) meaning of the Vedas. In terms of Śaṅkara's central project of gnoseological liberation, God plays no real part. Nor can he play any part, for 'God conforms to the limiting adjuncts of name and form created by nescience' (B.S.Bh. II.i.14). Bondage is said to be a result of the play (*līlā*) of Īśvara (B.S. II.i.33) in combination with our own lack of insight. While ritual action requires Īśvara's presence, liberation, for Śaṅkara, is a gnoseological project in which there is no room for subject-object duality. That is why Śaṅkara adopts the term '*avidyā*' much more frequently than '*māyā*'. There is little room here for a theistic soteriology. It would be yet another case of the blind leading the blind. Only an enlightened teacher can remove the 'blindfold' from one's eyes and help one grasp the truth.

Given that the world is illusion-like, and given that Īśvara is its primal cause, we may ask how the *māyā*-thesis affects Śaṅkara's ethics. Matilal (2004: 41) has claimed that it is the 'general belief' that Advaita would use this *māyā* argument to solve the problem of evil. However, Śaṅkara does not use it. Nor does he hold Īśvara at fault. Rather, in his passing remarks on the potential problem of Īśvara's injustice and cruelty (B.S. II.i.34), framed, by an opponent, as the problem of unequal distribution of suffering amongst beings (B.S.Bh. II.i.34), Śaṅkara blames the beings who have generated their own *karma* in past lives, and indeed in past world cycles, for 'the transmigratory state has no beginning' (B.S.Bh. II.i.35). Elsewhere, Śaṅkara suggests the wise student should reflect on rebirth thus:

> If he says 'I am different from the body. The body is born and dies, is eaten by birds, destroyed by weapons and fire, etc., subject to disease, etc. I have entered into this [body], like a bird its nest, on account of the merit and demerit of my own actions. Again and again as a result of merit and demerit, when the body is destroyed, I shall enter into different bodies, like a bird entering a different nest when the previous one is destroyed. Thus am I in this beginningless transmigratory existence, giving up old bodies and assuming new ones, in

> the realms of gods, men, animals and hells. On account of my own actions, I am forced to rotate in the endless cycle of birth and death as if on a water-wheel. In the course of time I have obtained this body. I am sick of this cycle of transmigration and have come to you, Sir, in order to put an end to this cycle of transmigration. Therefore, I am eternal and other than the body. Bodies come and go, like the clothes of a person' … [Then] the teacher should say 'You have spoken well, you see correctly. [So] why did you wrongly say "I am the son of a Brahmin, of such and such a family, I was a student (or householder) and now I am a wandering highest ascetic"' (U.S. Prose, 1.12–13).

This student here accepts that he has been to blame for his own suffering due to his clinging to the body. And so, while Īśvara sees to it that all beings get the fruits they deserve, he did not create those beings *ex nihilo* and is thus not to blame. [Incidentally, Śaṅkara does say that a Creator God who *did* create the world *ex nihilo* would be to blame (B.S.Bh. II.i.35)]. If Īśvara did not control their entrance into life, then he is equally powerless in preventing their exit from the field of play. Those who overcome their *karma* (through knowledge) have no need to turn up for the next round of games.

3.2 Approaching Śāntideva

As with Śaṅkara, I prefer not to see Śāntideva as an innovator in the usual sense of the word. For one thing, he never saw himself as one. Though perhaps written as a typical counter to pride, Śāntideva introduces the *BCA* (1.2a) with the modest claim that he has 'nothing novel whatsoever to say here'. He begins the *Compendium* (Ś.S. 1.22) in a similar manner. Sweet (1977: 15) thus concluded that Śāntideva was 'essentially a transmitter and not an original philosophical thinker'. Nevertheless, I wish to claim that there remains something quite *unique* about his work, especially the *BCA*. What I find most interesting in Śāntideva, just as we find in Śaṅkara, are the *dramatic extremities* of his expression, and the *tension* that this creates.

The tension arises through the equal need Śāntideva's Mahāyāna tradition has placed on him for the two necessary virtues of wisdom and compassion. The tension between the cognitive and the affective is found throughout his work. It is as if he stands on a metaphysical tight-rope between two worlds, one of transcendent wisdom, the other of active compassion in a provisional world. By wisdom (*prajñā*), the Mahāyāna, and especially the Madhyamaka School, can be taken to mean the insight into emptiness (*śūnyatā*). This includes the emptiness of all personhood (*pudgala śunyatā*) and the emptiness of all experiential elements (*sarva dharma śunyatā*), both claimed by Śāntideva to be essential to perfect wisdom (Ś.S. 242). Wisdom (*prajñā*) has been defined by Prajñākaramati as 'The discriminative understanding of the reality of dependently-arisen phenomena just as they are' (BCA. Pañjikā, 344). This wisdom can be seen as a response to the so-called heretical views of permanent objects and self-identity (*satkāya dṛṣṭi*) which Śāntideva condemns (Ś.S. 242). Compassion (*karuṇā, daya, kṛpā*) can be taken to mean the will to lead all beings to liberation from suffering. As with Mill's conception of the breadth of human sympathy (Util. V.20), the Mahāyāna Buddhist sees this as extending to all sentient beings.

Dayal (1970: 42–5) has made the claim that Śāntideva, in his stress on compassion, seems to ignore wisdom altogether. He says that the 'later' period of the Mahāyāna sees a shift in emphasis from wisdom to compassion, pointing to a parallel shift from the cult of Mañjuśrī to that of Avalokiteśvara (the two Great Bodhisattvas of Wisdom and Compassion, respectively). Kinnard confirms that, in India, Avalokiteśvara became more 'popular' than Mañjuśrī (in Keown and Prebish 2007: 82). Nevertheless, there are two difficulties with Dayal's thesis. First, Śāntideva took Mañjuśrī as his patron deity (BCA. 10.51–8 and Ś.S. 365). Second, Dayal has placed too much weight on the word *prajñā*, whilst ignoring the fact that emptiness (*śūnyatā*) and no-self (*anātman*) are particular cases of the wisdom aspect. In fact, Paul Williams (1998a) has argued that Śāntideva takes the doctrine of non-substantiality (*niḥsvabhāvatā*) to such a limit that he might have destroyed the *bodhisattva* path. That, in my eyes, he does not destroy the path is due to the extraordinary emphasis he places on compassion, which allows him to compromise wisdom. Here Dayal is quite correct in noting the heightened status that Śāntideva grants to compassion, but he is wrong to place too much faith in a single passage of the *Compendium* (Dayal 1970: 42), where Śāntideva seems to advocate the notion that compassion includes all the other perfections (Ś.S. 286), for, in the same *Compendium*, we also find the statement, 'All things … are wisdom' (Ś.S. 257). And in the *BCA*, it is said that 'It is for the sake of wisdom that the Buddha taught this entire collection' (BCA. 9.1a). The *Compendium*, in fact, sees wisdom and compassion as complementary. Thus, it says, 'From action whose essence is emptiness and compassion, there is the purification of karmic fruit' (Ś.S. 270). The Buddha is praised as 'the possessor of unequalled wisdom' and the 'most compassionate' (Ś.S. 319). Overall, Śāntideva places equal emphasis on compassionate activity and wisdom. Nevertheless, they are often found to be in dynamic tension.

A comment is due on two further aspects of Śāntideva's heritage: 1) tantra, and 2) the three-body thesis. Now we can agree with Vaidya (1961: viii) when he talks of Śāntideva representing an 'advanced stage of Mahāyāna Buddhism', yet is there really a 'slight tinge of Tāntrism' (ibid.) in his work? Sharma (1990: x) claims that Śāntideva studied both 'sutra and tantra'. This is important, for a tantric slant would most certainly affect Śāntideva's views on asceticism and women. Now it would be to the advantage of Tibetans if they could claim Śāntideva as a Tantrika, and in fact they do (Gyatso 1994: 368). However, even while claiming that the attribution of a number of Tantric texts to him is 'credible', the Padmakara Translation Group (1999: 179) state that 'there is no hint of tantric teachings' in either the *BCA* or the *Compendium*. For this reason, Western scholars have been reluctant to grant tantric status to Śāntideva (Clayton 2006: 33). In fact, it could be argued that his rhetoric on bodies (BCA. Chapter 8), especially women's, is particularly *non*-tantric. Indeed, Tribe even uses Śāntideva's *BCA* as *the* example of a non-tantric attitude (in Williams and Tribe 2000: 199 and 240). So even though, in the 8th century, tantric approaches 'dominated Buddhist practice in India' (p194), Śāntideva appears immune to it.[23]

As for the three-body (*tri-kāya*) thesis, we should consider Mrozik's (2007: 7) conclusion that there is 'not a single reference' to this doctrine in the entire *Compendium*. It is certainly true that there is no *thorough* discussion of the doctrine, and nowhere are the three bodies spoken of together, but there are hints of its inclusion (Ś.S. 24 and 159).[24] If we turn to the *BCA*, there is again no *explicit* reference to this doctrine. However, there is one possible linguistic pun on the *nirmāṇa-kāya* (BCA. 5.57), highlighted by Crosby and Skilton (1995: 159, n.5.57). Furthermore, Śāntideva opens the text (BCA. 1.1a) with a verse of praise to the 'Dharma-bodies of the Buddhas and their children'. So perhaps the three-body thesis is assumed, as Matics (1971: 125) suggests. On the other hand, whilst showing some minor influence from 'buddha-nature' (*tathāgata-garbha*) thought in the *Compendium* (Ś.S. 172),[25] there is no mention of it in the *BCA*. Also, while including a quote from the *Śrī-mālā Sūtra* in the *Compendium* (Ś.S. 42), he does not draw on its famous passage on the *tathāgata-garbha* and the *dharma-kāya*. So we may conclude that the *tri-kāya* doctrine and the *tathāgata-garbha* doctrine did not play a major role in his system.

Nevertheless, rather than say outright that there is *no* three-body doctrine in Śāntideva, it is preferable to say that Śāntideva's soteriology is 'upward' looking, not descending, and that his resolve to return to this world is a mundane one based on *karma* and what I have called a 'voluntary delusion'. It is not the result of the manifestation of physical (*nirmāṇa*) and mental experience (*sambhoga*) form-bodies (*rūpa-kāyas*), as is the case in Tibetan tantra, and indeed in Candrakīrti (MMA XI.14 ff). Hence, we must assume the '*avatāra*' in *Bodhi-caryā-avatāra* to mean 'undertaking' or 'entering' the path, rather than the more literal 'descending'.

Thus, Śāntideva's *bodhisattva* should not be compared with either Kṛṣṇa or the Hindu *avatāra* ideal. Likewise, the *yogi* of the *Gītā* has not attained his position

---

[23] Śaṅkara has also been linked with a number of tantric texts by the Advaita tradition, but none of these texts are taken to be authentic by the academic circle.

[24] I agree with Mrozik's (2007: 42–4) interpretation of the one reference to '*Dharma-kāya*' (Ś.S. 159) as most probably being a reference to a purified physical body, for the text speaks of the possibility of physically touching it. However, the reference to a '*Dharma-śarīra*' (Ś.S. 24) is a little more problematic, for it appears as a result of right knowledge, and is said to remain intact after the donation of body parts.

[25] Śāntideva quotes the *Tathāgatakoṣa Sūtra* here, including the notion that 'All things are originally pure' (*ādi śuddhān sarva dharmān*) (Ś.S. 172). Śāntideva uses it to show that any sin can be purified through right view. The *BCA* also claims that 'beings are pleasant by nature' (*sattvāḥ prakṛti peśalāḥ*) (6.40). Here the focus is on tolerance. Contrast this with other verses in the *BCA* (for example 8.22–4), where the aim at hand is renunciation. In other words, Śāntideva modifies his rhetoric depending on the purpose.

from the 'top-down' (Malinar 2007: 117), and Kṛṣṇa as *avatāra* (Bh.G. 4.6–8) is thus unique. It is therefore my contention that Śaṅkara has a right to take Kṛṣṇa's wilful manifestation as being unique to the Lord. Nelson (in Fort and Mumme 1996: 41–2) has examined the similarities between the idea of the *jīvan-mukta* and Kṛṣṇa, and feels that these concepts are 'very close', yet he also admits that Kṛṣṇa may be a 'special case'. Along with Brodbeck, I believe Kṛṣṇa is better seen as a 'cosmic archetype' (in Mascaró 2003: xxiii). So it would be unwise to overdraw the parallels between Kṛṣṇa and Śaṅkara's *brahman*-knower. In fact, the *Gītā* states that a knower of the Self is never born again (Bh.G. 5.17, 8.15 and 13.23). Even the very verses in which Kṛṣṇa's cyclic re-creation through *māyā* is explained (4.6–8) are followed by stating that one who knows this is never reborn (4.9). A knower, then, even in the *Gītā*, is not obliged to come back for the benefit of mankind, though Kṛṣṇa himself takes on that burden. So while later Advaitin devotees would worship Śaṅkara as an *avatāra* (see Cenkner 1983: 153), there is nothing in his writings to suggest he was such a figure or that he held any such aspiration to be one.

The exact dates of Śāntideva are as yet unknown. Clayton's is perhaps the most recent detailed attempt at placing a date on him. The dates she settles on are 'somewhere between the last half of the sixth and the first half of the seventh centuries' (2006: 31). However, Paul Williams (2009: 66) maintains the dates of 695–743. If we compare the dates Clayton gives for Śāntideva with those Williams (2009: 66) and Ruegg (1981: 71) give for Candrakīrti, 600–650, then Clayton would put Śāntideva before Candrakīrti. This she admits would 'contradict all traditional chronologies' (Clayton 2006: 31). The Padmakara Translation Group (2004: 356, n.4) offers the dates for Candrakīrti as the 'first part of the seventh' century. For Śāntideva, they offer the traditional dates of somewhere between 685 and 763 (trans. Padmakara 1999: 178), the ones found in Crosby and Skilton (1995: viii). This early limit then, based on the non-mention of Śāntideva by the Chinese pilgrims I-tsing and Hsüan-tsang[26] (who visited India in 671–695 and 630–645 respectively), and the later limit, based on the fact that Śāntarakṣita (d. circa. 790) quotes from the *BCA*, do seem quite convincing. I see nothing in Clayton's argument to make me want to shift Śāntideva back a century. It is probable that Śāntideva and Candrakīrti were more or less contemporaries. They both aim their attacks at their rival Mahāyāna school, the Yogācāra, and they both adopt a similar line of argument, the *reductio ad absurdum* (*prasaṅga*). I think we may continue to assume that Śāntideva lived in the first part of the eighth century.[27] That is enough for us to assert that Śaṅkara and Śāntideva appear to have lived more or less at the same time. We may also assume, until further studies prove otherwise, that they remained unaware of one another.[28]

---

[26] Also known (in Pinyin) as Yi-jing and Xuan-zang respectively.

[27] For a complete attempt at the chronology of the Madhyamaka School, see Ruegg (2010: 13–36).

[28] The earliest mention of the Advaita School (*darśana*) in a Buddhist treatise is in the 8th century *Pañjikā* (328) by Kamalaśīla (Ruegg 2010: 31).

Unfortunately, if we do question the link between Candrakīrti and Śāntideva, and even worse, if we place him pre-Candrakīrti (as Clayton does), we lose the right to assume that Śāntideva accepts the systematic structures of Candrakīrti, namely the ten-stage (*daśa-bhūmi*) *bodhisattva* path, explicitly adopted by Candrakīrti in his *Madhyamakāvatāra*.[29] This is problematic, for the stages allow the Mahāyāna to claim that, above a certain level, one can break the monastic rules through the doctrine of skilful-means (*upāya-kauśalya*). This doctrine became a 'guiding principle in the ethics' of *Mahāsattvas* (that is, high level *bodhisattvas*) (Tatz 1994: 2).

Before we examine this problem, we also need to question whether Śāntideva even accepts the complete path of the six perfections. This is important in its own right, for it would establish Śāntideva as a Mahāyāna gradualist. Moreover, it was the apparent use of this thematic structure which, according to Ruegg (1981: 82), constituted his 'significant contribution' to the Madhyamaka School. Now, Chapters 6 to 9 of the *BCA* do in fact follow the perfections of 'patience' (*kṣānti*), 'effort' (*vīrya*), 'meditation' (*dhyāna*) and 'wisdom' (*prajñā*). This leaves out the first two perfections, 'generosity' (*dāna*) and 'morality' (*śīla*), which is no minor omission. Even so, these are not neglected, as such, and it may be said that, in the *BCA*, 'Instruction has been given in all six perfections' (Crosby and Skilton 1995: 133). Tibetan commentators have struggled with this possible omission, proposing that generosity is dealt with in Chapter 10, or that morality is covered by Chapter 5 (for example Gyatso 1994: 6). Nevertheless, if we take seriously the challenge that this may not be the case, we might turn to the *Compendium* for support. We will also find proof there that Śāntideva did in fact accept the ten stages.

First, with regard to the six perfections, Śāntideva lists them all (Ś.S. 16), discusses their correct practice (61, 89–90, 187 and 219) and argues against the concept of a 'wisdom-only' stance, stressing the necessity of all six perfections (97). In fact, the *Compendium* defines the Mahāyāna as 'Those who course in the perfections, it is they that embrace the Mahāyāna' (Ś.S. 4). Hence, we can safely suppose that he accepts the traditional gradualist Mahāyāna path, and that he has rightly been taken as a source of inspiration for that gradualist path in Tibet.

Second, the *Compendium* quotes extensively from the *Daśabhūmika Sūtra*, which is not only the *locus classicus* of the ten *bodhisattva* stages; its very title means '*The Sūtra of Ten Stages*'. Śāntideva also refers to at least three of the stages: the first, the stage (*bhūmi*) of joy (*pramuditā*) (Ś.S. 10), the seventh, the stage of skilful-means (*upāya-kauśalya*) (167) and the eighth stage of immoveable (*acala*) resolve (Ś.S. 103). Finally, the *Compendium* distinguishes between those who have entered the stages and ordinary people (140).

There are also signs that Śāntideva draws a distinction between those *bodhisattvas* who have attained to stages and those who have not. So, reflecting on the *Upāyakauśalya Sūtra*, Śāntideva seemingly equates those who follow the six perfections with those who have *not* attained the stages. And while he claims to personally follow the six perfections, he feels he has no right to comment on

[29] I thank Roy Perrett for pointing this out (personal communication).

the behaviour of those who have attained to the stages (Ś.S. 168). This is no doubt because the *Upāyakauśalya Sūtra* (112) itself states that skill in means is the *outcome* of the perfection of wisdom (the sixth perfection). Thus, *pace* Clayton (2006: 95 and 105), we can assume that he places some importance on the ten *bodhisattva* stages. From this analysis, we know that Śāntideva accepts the traditional Mahāyāna doctrine that after a certain level, *mahā-sattvas* can break the monastic code without reproach, assuming their actions are performed altruistically. We can now place the following verses in their full context:

> Each of the perfections, beginning with generosity, is superior to its predecessor. One should not neglect a higher one for a lower one, unless because of an established rule of conduct. Realizing this, one should always be striving to benefit others. Even that which is [normally] prohibited is permitted for the compassionate who can foresee a benefit (BCA. 5.83–4).

Yet it may well be that, in many cases, it is *only* the *mahā-sattvas* who *can* foresee the benefit, and for the vast majority, rules of conduct dominate. This is the essence of Mahāyāna ethics.

Now many scholars have claimed that the Mahāyāna movement in India was not a sect (Gombrich 1988: 112; Williams 2009: 3), and that those monks who saw themselves as Mahāyāna would have adhered to the same *vinaya* or *prātimokṣa* (monastic code) as the other monks. It is claimed that no Mahāyāna *Vinaya* was produced in India (Gombrich 1988: 112; Williams 2009: 4). Chinese pilgrim, Fa-hsien, in the 5th century, while noting one town that had separate colleges for the Mahāyāna, did not distinguish an exclusive Mahāyāna sect (Cousins 1997: 386). Hsüan-tsang (Pinyin: Xuan-zang), writing in the mid-7th century, noted that Mahāyāna and Śrāvaka monks lived together at Nālanda University (Gombrich et al. 1991: 82a). Half a century later, I-tsing (Pinyin: Yi-jing) noted a similar situation, with the monks sharing a common *Vinaya* (I-tsing 2009: 14).

Nevertheless, there are indications in the *Compendium* that things may have changed somewhat by Śāntideva's time. For one thing, Śāntideva distinguishes between the *Śrāvaka-Vinaya* (Ś.S. 135 and 168) and his own *Compendium*, which he calls a *Bodhisattva-Vinaya* (Ś.S. 366). In the middle of the *Compendium* (190) he asks, 'What form of learning is praised in the *Bodhisattva-Vinaya*?'. Now it hardly seems logical that this could be referring to his own text, so he could either be talking about another *Vinaya* text, or he is talking about the *Bodhisattva Code* in general terms. He also quotes extensively from a so-called *Bodhisattva-Prātimokṣa*, as well as from the *Upāli-paripṛcchā* (see Prebish, in Powers and Prebish 2009: 99), which is surely enough for us to question the notion that the Mahāyāna never thought of themselves as a sect. The *Compendium* (11–12) also talks of taking the Vow of Discipline (*saṃvara*) in the presence of a 'guru' who follows the *Bodhisattva* precepts (*bodhisattva śikṣapada*). So the aspiring Mahāyāna novice (*śrāmaṇeraka*) would be unable to take his vows with a non-Mahāyāna teacher. Also, as Mitomo (1991: 17) points out, Śāntideva takes refuge in, what he calls, the 'assembly of *bodhisattvas*' (*bodhisattva gaṇa*) rather than the traditional *saṅgha* (BCA. 2.26). Despite these specifically Mahāyāna rituals, Śāntideva states (Ś.S. 61) that the third root transgression of a *bodhisattva* is to claim that he need not keep to the monastic ethical rules (*pratimokṣa-vinaya śila*). But the actual rules he has in mind are not obvious. Clearly, further historical research, which is outside the purview of this present work, is called for. What we can conclude is that Śāntideva was following more than one standardized mode of conduct.

Now, Prajñākaramati claims that Śāntideva was a member of the Madhyamaka School (in Vaidya 1960: XI) and all scholars accept this. The Madhyamaka School derives its name from the Sanskrit for 'middlemost', denoting a conceptual method, which vows never to fall into either of the extreme views of eternalism or annihilationism. The founding text of the tradition, from which the school's name can be gleaned, is the *Mūla-madhyamaka kārikā* by Nāgārjuna. Nāgārjuna is thus considered the 'source or originator' of the Madhyamaka School (Ruegg 1981: 4). Most scholars agree that Nāgārjuna can either be dated to the first or second century (Garfield 1995: 87 and 97) or the second or third (Williams 2009: 24). Ruegg (2010: 16) decided on 150–200. Westerhoff (2009: 5), citing recent research by Walser, also accepts the late second century. The central claims of the *Mūla-madhyamaka kārikā* (hereon *MMK*) are that all 'things' (*dharmas*) are empty of inherent existence; that is, no 'thing' has own-being (*sva-bhāva*).[30] It is suggested that to understand the Buddha's law of dependent-origination (*pratītyasamutpāda*) is to understand what the Madhyamaka means by emptiness (*śūnyatā*). There is no doubt that Śāntideva's main text, the *BCA*, accords with the basic tenets and methodology of the *MMK*, and can therefore be called a 'mainstream' Madhyamaka text (Ruegg 1981: 83).

However, Mrozik (2007: 16) claims that Śāntideva's *Compendium*, while clearly Mahāyāna, 'should not be read as an exemplar of Madhyamaka thought'. To some extent this is true. While there are clear Madhyamaka ideas to be found in the text, perhaps they are not quite as extensive as some suggest (for example Sweet 1977: 3). As neither scholar backs up their view, we might note a number of classic Madhyamaka themes: the denial of individuality (Ś.S. 242), the denial of an ultimate agent (253), the emptiness of the aggregates (238) and of all experiential elements (117 and 242), the non-reflexive nature of consciousness (235), the nirvanic state of all elements (251) and the two domains of discourse (244 and 250). But more importantly perhaps, I can find nothing in the *Compendium* that the Madhyamaka would outright reject.

Dayal (1970: 45) claims that the 'later Mahāyāna reverts to the old ideal of celibacy and forest-life'. Now there is indeed internal evidence in the *BCA* that Śāntideva favours the forest-life. He writes: 'before he is carried away by four [pall-bearers] with the worldly lamenting, he should depart for the forest' (BCA. 8.35). Again: 'one should recoil from the passions and generate delight in solitude, in tranquil forests, empty of strife and trouble' (8.85). Furthermore, Chapter XI of the *Compendium* is actually entitled 'In Praise of the Forest'. There is also some evidence

30 For a more detailed study of '*svabhāva*' in Nāgārjuna, see Westerhoff (2009: 19–52).

in the *Compendium* (Ś.S. 64 and 114) that Śāntideva favours the meditating monk over the monastery-bound scholar. The *Compendium* even talks of the *bodhisattva* never making the monastery (*vihāra*) into a home (Ś.S. 137). Nevertheless, the *Compendium* continually glorifies the study of religious texts, even claiming that a *bodhisattva* should be 'diligent in reading and reciting' (Ś.S. 16). Needless to say, Śāntideva was himself a great scholar who clearly had a huge library at his fingertips. He certainly did not write the *Compendium* in a forest. As with celibacy, the forest-life was part of Śāntideva's 'ascetic' discourse, meant for the commencing-*bodhisattva*, but not meant for the more active *bodhisattva*, and certainly not to be taken as indicative of his complete ethical system. This is consistent with the Buddha, who 'recommended forests and lonely places only as ideal sites for training in meditation, but never for living' (Dharmasiri 1989: 14).

Like Śaṅkara, Śāntideva was against pure book-learning, but he saw it as a necessary qualification to higher knowledge. And, as Śāntideva's *BCA* and Śaṅkara's *U.S.* demonstrate, a written text can be put at the service of both meditation and compassionate activity. And again, like Śaṅkara, Śāntideva takes renunciation of social duties as essential for the path of seeing. Nevertheless, both the *bodhisattva* and the *brahma-vid* return to social conventions in order to pass on their realization. Hence, for both Śaṅkara and Śāntideva, we need to think in terms of ethical domains.

With particular reference to ethics, Goodman (2009) has recently gone as far as to divide the Mahāyāna into pre-Śāntideva and post-Śāntideva. His logic seems to be based on the idea that Buddhism has tended to move from being a rule-consequentialism to an act-consequentialism, with Śāntideva being pivotal in this shift. If nothing else, it goes to prove just how relevant the study of Śāntideva is to Buddhist ethics. Goodman (2009: 89) sees him as 'the greatest of all Buddhist ethicists', and as the one who 'comes closest to a worked-out ethical theory' in the Western sense, rightly describing Śāntideva's ethics as 'radical altruism' (p90). Nevertheless, most of what Śāntideva wrote was based on earlier *sūtras*, so to divide Buddhism into pre- and post-Śāntideva is always going to beg the question.

With reference to metaphysics, like Śaṅkara, Śāntideva stresses the illusory nature of existence. He therefore holds a very similar *māyā*-thesis, though one without the double-meaning found in the Vedānta. Given that Śaṅkara borrowed from Gauḍapāda, who borrowed from Nāgārjuna, it is no surprise that Śāntideva should describe the illusory-like world in similar terms:

> This world is like an illusion, to be understood as like a theatre, a dream. There is no self, no being, no life; all 'things' are like a mirage, like the moon's reflection in water (Ś.S. 319).

Similarly, in the *BCA*:

> There is seeing and touching by a 'self', which is like a dream or illusion. Sensation is not 'perceived' by consciousness, for they are born together (BCA. 9.99).

And again:

> When analysed, the state of existence is dream-like, [insubstantial] like a plantain tree. Thus, there is no substantial difference between the liberated and the non-liberated (BCA. 9.150).

The similarities with Śaṅkara are obvious. When we dream, we see certain 'objects' and believe them to be real. On awakening, we realize that they were in fact a mental projection. Likewise, when we realize emptiness, we will see that our lives up until now have been a mental projection. Nothing is as solid as we believed; everything is but a reflection of what is truly real. As with Śaṅkara, this does not imply that there is no external reality whatsoever and that things merely appear to the mind. That is, Śāntideva does not proclaim that ordinary experience *really* is illusory. Rather, he advises us to take a sceptical approach to what we take to be truly existent. Things may or may not be out there, but they are never how we believe them to be. All we see are distortions of that reality.

It is important to understand, then, that for Śāntideva, things are not literally *created* by the mind; they are rather *warped* by the mind. It is in *this* sense that one's world could be said to be 'mind-only'. Burton (2001: 101) therefore seems wrong in claiming that, for the Madhyamaka School, 'dependent origination of all entities means that all entities originate in dependence upon the mind'.[31] In fact, Śāntideva specifically attacks this idea when he writes, 'At no time was there a single cause that produced everything' (BCA. 9.13a).

So, while an object's existence is linked with the interrelations between conceptual thought and perception, this is not a mind-only thesis. Thus, Śāntideva contends that, 'Conception and the conceived are mutually dependent' (BCA. 9.108a). He denounces the notion of mind-only (*citta-mātra*) (BCA. 9.29) and the idea that illusory objects are mind-created. He asks the Yogācāra, 'If illusion is really mind itself, what is seen by what?' (BCA. 9.17a). When Śāntideva claims that the lust for an illusory woman may still arise in the magician who created her (BCA. 9.30–31), he clearly believes that there are women *more real* than this illusory type. The issue is this:

> If consciousness is established on the strength of the cognized object, how does one arrive at the existence of the cognized object? If they depend on each other for existence, then neither [ultimately] exists (BCA. 9.112).

We can understand this better through the common notion of mutual relationships. To take Śāntideva's classic example:

> If there is no father without a son, how can there be an [independent] son? With no son, there is no father. Therefore, neither of them [consciousness or the object] exists [ultimately] (BCA. 9.113).

[31] For a critique of Burton's 'idealist reading', see Arnold (2005: 170–71).

But clearly, the Madhyamaka are not saying that there are no fathers and no sons in the world, they are merely pointing to a symmetric dependence relationship. And whilst denying the greatest Father of them all, God (Īśvara), Śāntideva actually accepts the elements (earth, water, fire and air) that make up the world. The dependence relationship here is one of their co-arising with their cognition. Thus, Śāntideva asks the *Brahmins*:

> If you say 'God is the cause of the world', please explain what God is. If it's the elements, so be it, but why all this fuss over a mere name? Moreover, earth, etc [i.e. water, fire and air], are not one; they are impermanent, inert and in no way divine. One can step on them, and thus they are impure. These are not God. Space cannot be God as it is inert. Nor can the 'self' [be God] for it was refuted earlier. And if creation belongs to that beyond conception, then what can be said of the inconceivable? What is it that he [God] wishes to create? If [you say] a 'self', then surely this [on your account] is eternal, as are earth, the other elements, and God [himself]. [As for] consciousness, it arises from the cognized object and is beginningless (BCA. 9.118–21).

In other words, awareness is always awareness of 'something' which is itself interdependent on other 'things' and so on, *ad infinitum*. We can thus conclude that Śāntideva is not denying the conventional reality of the physical world. Rather, he adopts a sceptical position towards what we intuitively take to be real. When Paul Williams (in Williams and Tribe 2000: 150) characterizes the Madhyamaka as supporting the thesis that 'Everything is foam which dissolves into nothing', we should not forget that foam is in fact *not* 'nothing'. So things are not 'merely appearances' that 'have no existence beyond this', as Burton (2004: 81) claims, for even mirages and dreams are actual phenomena, which actually appear and have actual consequences. Śāntideva clearly states:

> All experiential elements are selfless. On the other hand, they are connected with the fruit of action. All phenomena lack own-being. On the other hand, there is an experiential, empirical world (Ś.S. 244).

At the ultimate level, there are no elementary 'things' (*dharmas*), and *karma* is fundamentally empty. But at the conventional level, things function as things, and *karma* functions as a cause of action. Hence, empirical phenomena are to be accepted on the basis of their causal efficacy. Thus, a person is undeniably established as a being capable of performing functions. As we noted above, even the Buddha is not excluded from this law (BCA. 9.9a). The apparent contradiction between function and being is due to our own lack of insight into emptiness. The worldly equate functional capacity with own-being, but the *yogis* see into the non-substantiality and other-derived nature of those functioning objects. That is the basis of their dispute (BCA. 9.5).

If there is anything like a true innovation to be found in Śāntideva it must be found at the breaking point of this tension of how to reconcile the ultimate truth of insubstantiality with the conventional truth of suffering beings. As indicated above, I believe the key to understanding his thesis is located in verses 9.75–6 of the *BCA*, where he answers the doubt as to whom compassion ought to be shown if there are no ultimately existing beings. His response is critical: 'For anyone who [our voluntary] delusion projects for the sake of what must be done' (9.75b).

When the only delusion left in the *bodhisattva* is of this voluntary nature, it is also what keeps him in *saṃsāra*. It is thus worth noting that the Oliners, in *The Altruistic Personality*, see the 'voluntary' nature of an action as one of the four defining features of true altruism (Oliner and Oliner 1992: 6). Just as Śaṅkara claims that the *brahma-vid* is beyond injunctions, so the *bodhisattva* is under no coercion other than his own vow. And as to the question of the rationale of such an altruistic self-imposed duty, given the supposed ultimate lack of individuation, Śāntideva's response is equally critical: 'In order to bring about the end of suffering, the delusion which conceives the task is not restrained' (BCA. 9.76b).

As in the case of Śaṅkara, Śāntideva is willing to play the game of individuation so long as it benefits the other. Here Dayal's compassion-theory trumps Williams' insistence on reason and logic, and Avalokita trumps Mañjuśrī. We see that Śāntideva's verses are often primarily persuasive, 'emotional rather than argumentative' (Dayal 1970: 45), 'pragmatic, rather than systematic and philosophical' (Matics 1971: 26). We may glean that this is not enough for the Buddhologist, Paul Williams, who, whilst admitting the apparent 'triumph of rhetoric over reason' (1998a: 107), still insists on a rational ontology. All Śāntideva can offer is the Two Truths, the flickering between self and no-self. Whether this is 'rational' or not, I leave for the reader to decide. However, I will continue to give him a sympathetic reading.

Thus, along with fellow Mādhyamikas, Śāntideva's contention is not with the pragmatic interpretation of phenomena commonly accepted by the worldly. That is, the contention is not with the common-sense view of external objects, but with their ultimate status. In fact, Śāntideva ends his *BCA* with a rhetorical question that clearly acknowledges the central role of the conventional:

> When, with this merit accumulated, will I respectfully teach this emptiness, through conventions, without projection, to those whose views are characterized by projection? (BCA. 9.167).

By 'without projection', he means the ability to teach without believing there to be a teacher and without becoming attached to the hearer or the conventional words one uses. Only when one can give without a sense of a giver can one be a true *bodhisattva* (Ś.S. 275). Also, to believe in an individuated self is to be bound to its longings, 'If one does not let go of self, one cannot free oneself from suffering' (BCA. 8.135a). So how could one free another? But remember that Śāntideva has allowed a certain amount of 'voluntary delusion' about other beings, thus reconstructing a receiver of the giving. But if this compassionate outpouring begins to seep back into one's own sense of selfhood, and one forgets how this self is constructed, then one must resort to its antidote, to 'meditate on not-self' (BCA. 9.77b).

So while compassionate acts must be performed, they must be performed without a sense of one's own self. Better to sit in solitude and drop the sense of self than to act with the sense of self. This partially justifies Arnold's (2005: 118) claim that '*selflessness* … is arguably what all Buddhist philosophy concerns in the end'. Yet one cannot act for others without a sense of *their* self. This is at the very heart of the 'tension' and 'flickering' models I have proposed. If the *bodhisattva* has the ability to flicker between relative and ultimate domains, then he is free to act as he likes; but as soon as he starts to believe that he has a self, in the sense of a fixed owner of his actions, those very actions will be tainted.

Śāntideva's version of compatibilism suggests that we are free to act on our choices, but we are only truly free to choose when we have a consciousness which flickers between seeing emptiness and being caught by false illusions, and by clearly seeing the possibility that the latter can be negated. The *bodhisattva* thus makes a deliberate choice regarding the notion of self. It is not so much the case that the maintenance of the no-self position is more essential than compassion, but that 'true' compassion cannot be maintained without the no-self position. But as we have seen, neither can it be maintained without the notion of self. Hence, we have a tension within awareness itself.

When we compare Śāntideva with Śaṅkara, it is vital that we do not get confused here with the notion of 'I' that needs to be denounced in order for true compassion to arise. It is not the ultimate *ātman* of Advaita that needs denouncing; it is egoism (*ahaṃkāra*). And this denouncement is as applicable to Śaṅkara as to Śāntideva. Olson (1997: 169) writes that 'the renouncer tries to destroy all traces of the ego, the false notion of self'. Ram-Prasad (2001a: 166–8) has spoken of *ahaṃkāra* as the 'sense of self which is ego', and that it is *jīva* that has this 'I'-sense, not *ātman*. More recently, he further confirmed that 'many brahmanical thinkers' speak out against this 'fraudulent (*sopadha*) sense of selfhood' (Ram-Prasad, in Siderits et al. 2011: 228). Śaṅkara associates *ahaṃkāra* with ignorance (Bh.G.Bh. 7.4). In the *Viveka Cūḍāmaṇi*, it is called 'one's enemy' (307). In the *Gītā*, Kṛṣṇa continually teaches Arjuna the means to be free of false ego. The 'absence of egoism' (*anahaṃkāra*) is praised along with 'non-attachment' and a list of other virtues (Bh.G. 13.8). Thus, the 'I', according to the *Gītā*, 'denotes no metaphysical entity' (Brodbeck, in Mascaró 2003: xx). The ego, as false centre is therefore to be eliminated. Ego's absence is deemed possible, as *ahaṃkāra* is but the 'defining mode of awareness of the individuated, unliberated self' (Ram-Prasad 2001a: 169); and as such, cannot survive liberating knowledge.

The *V.C.* states that 'Even though completely uprooted, this gross egoism, if attended to by the mind for even a moment, returns to life' (309). The *V.C.* then hammers home the need to return to absorption (*samādhi*) (310–55). Thus, in the *V.C.* there is an *explicit* acknowledgement of oscillating between states of egoistic and non-egoistic modes of consciousness. Nevertheless, the *V.C.* also defines a *jīvan-mukta* as 'one who never has the idea of "I"' (438). And it is worth repeating what Śaṅkara wrote on the difference between self and egoism:

> It must be accepted that [the self] is 'self-evident', which is synonymous with 'self-knowable'. And the experience of one's [true] Self is established along with the cessation of the [false] notion of 'I' (U.S. Metric, 18.200/203).

At this universal level, *ātman* comes to signify the complete opposite of ego. It is thus the false notion of self as a separate, independent being that is being attacked in both Advaita and Madhyamaka. Nevertheless, Śāntideva does go further, when he writes:

> However, egoism, which is the cause of suffering, increases from the delusion that there is a self. If this [particular delusion] cannot be avoided, better to meditate on not-self (BCA. 9.77).

This is where the *anātman* doctrine has its force. It is indeed egoism (*ahaṃkāra*) that causes suffering (*duḥkha*), but the belief that one has a permanent centre, a true self (*ātman*), according to the Buddhist, increases the delusion, which itself causes egoism. Here Śāntideva would agree with Metzinger (2010: 208) that 'there is no essence within us that stays the same across time'. So we need always to distinguish between the denouncement of the ego (*ahaṃkāra*) with the absolute denial of the self (*ātman*).

This is why Harvey has recently made the point that *anātman* should not be rendered 'egoless' (in Keown and Prebish 2007: 572). All Indian schools argue the case for being egoless. Moreover, it could be further argued that the *ātman* Śāntideva has in mind here is of the individuated kind, what Śaṅkara calls *jīva* or *jīvātman*. As such, they might still agree with each other. As just mentioned, the false notion of *jīva* falls away when one realizes *brahman*-consciousness, thus *jīva* is not an irreducible entity. To re-iterate Śaṅkara's position on liberation, the false self must be dropped in order to gain the true Self. But then, when we come to the notion of a 'true' Self, there is no way of reconciling this position with the Buddhist. The following attack by Śāntideva seems capable of applying to all senses of *ātman*:

> If the Self is eternal and without thought, then it is evidently inactive, like space. Even in contact with other conditioning factors, what activity could there be of something which is unchanging? (BCA. 6.29).

Again: 'If the self is in fact unchanged, what is achieved by it having consciousness? We might say that selfhood is like space, unconscious and inert' (BCA. 9.69).

Rather than seeing this immutable self as an obstacle to compassion, Śāntideva merely sees it as an unnecessary postulate. Naturally, there is still much we could say here about modes of consciousness. If consciousness is indeed local, or an occurrence within a local complex, as the Buddhist accepts, then there is indeed no need, philosophically, for this *ātman*. However, if, ultimately, there is no other conscious being apart from this pure consciousness, as Śaṅkara claims (Bh.G.Bh. 9.10), then its purpose is indispensable. Now some, along with Ram-Prasad (2007: 125), may feel that this is an 'astonishing' claim. And given Śāntideva's response to the Sāṃkhya School on the notion of an ultimate reality, it would seem he would agree:

> If the different natures are not its true being, then explain what its own nature is. If [you say] it is the nature of consciousness, then it follows that all people have the very same singular consciousness! (BCA. 9.66).

While of major interest to the study of Indian epistemology, this argument need not be taken up here.[32] All we need note is that the metaphysical and epistemological impasse between Advaita and Madhyamaka has been met. Nevertheless, despite this impasse, so many commonalities remain.

[32] For further discussion, see Ram-Prasad (2001a, 2002 and 2007), Siderits et al. (2011) and Kuznetsova et al. (2012).

Chapter 4
Their Common Approach to the World

In this section I wish to propose that Śāntideva and Śaṅkara, while apparently sitting at polar ends of the Self-spectrum, will nevertheless go on to assume almost identical positions with regard to key doctrines. It will be argued that their philosophical means and their gnoseological and ethical goals are so similar that they are able to take on a common opponent, defend a similar model of agency and finally call for a form of conduct which is equally 'provisional'.

This chapter is thus divided into three parts:

1. Their common denial of the Yogācāra idealistic worldview
2. Their common denial of the ultimacy of the individuated self
3. Their common response to tradition-based conduct

4.1 Their Common Denial of the Yogācāra Idealistic Worldview

Indian Mahāyāna is typically divided by scholars into two philosophical schools, the Madhyamaka and the Yogācāra. As such, Huntington (1989: 62) has referred to the Madhyamaka as the Yogācāra's 'most vehement opponent'. However, perhaps we will find, at least in his 'major' works, that Śaṅkara was even more vehemently against the Yogācāra than either Śāntideva or Candrakīrti. Before we look at Śaṅkara's and Śāntideva's critique of the so-called 'Idealistic' views of the Yogācāra/Vijñānavāda School, it is worth heeding Huntington's warning that we should not judge the Yogācāra solely on the basis of those accounts given by their opponents (ibid.)

So let me start by saying that they may well not have been 'Idealistic' in the Western sense of reducing all phenomena to mere ideas, to mental constructs. First of all, it is clearly possible to coherently talk of our private mental representation of the world as merely-mind. All we need mean by this is that we can never know the world directly, and must always rely on the mind for interpretation of perceptual data. This is not idealism, but phenomenalism. Yet the Yogācāra has often been labelled as the 'Mind-Only' School. Most importantly, for our study, Śāntideva (BCA. 9.29b) refers to their doctrine as 'mind-only' (*citta-mātra*), and Śaṅkara (B.S.Bh. II.ii.18) labels them the 'Followers of the theory that Only-Consciousness-Exists' (*vijñānāsti-mātra vādinaḥ*). What such commentators have in mind here is that the Yogācāra are claiming that all experiential elements are in fact products of the mind, *and* that the mind is all that ultimately exists, that is, 'metaphysical idealism' (Lusthaus 2002: 5).

Of course, a mind devoid of ideas, a pure awareness, which seems to constitute the ultimate goal of the Yogācāra (Mahāyāna-saṃgraha, III.9), would have no place in the Western category of idealism. In fact, one only reaches enlightenment when the so-called 'mind' (*citta*) is utterly destroyed (III.18; Triṃśika, 5 and 29). This ultimate status amounts to the very opposite of a mind-created universe. We should not forget that Western Ideal-ism bases itself on 'ideas', not 'ideals', which is why Nuttall (2002: 43) suggested that Bishop George Berkeley's (1685–1753) idealistic metaphysics might be better labelled 'Idea-ism'. But a state of mind which contained no such ideas or conceptual constructs would simply stand as pure consciousness, or perhaps flickering moments of cognition *sans* object. This sounds very much like what Harvey (1995: 223) has called 'Nibbānic discernment' in his interpretation of the final state of an *arhat*; a thesis which he admits is similar to that of the Yogācārin's (p250). Such an idea-free state cannot coherently be called Idealism.

There is however a second problem. If we analyse the Sanskrit phrase '*vijñapti-mātra*', a term the Yogācārins used to describe their own thesis, and indeed the opening words of Vasubandhu's *Viṃśikā*, we find that it could provide a variety of English translations. For example, '*vijñapti*' means 'information' (Monier-Williams 2002) or 'perceptions' (Grimes 1996) or 'representation' (Keown 2003). So to hold a theory of '*vijñapti-mātra*' need not bind one to the thesis that the world itself is mind-only. Furthermore, given that the word '*mātra*' may be equally translated as 'mere', we might in fact translate '*vijñapti-mātra*' as 'mere-representation', a rendering suggested by Kochumuttom's (1989: 257) translation of Vasubandhu's *Triṃśikā*, verse 17.

Arnold (2005: 23) has noted that scholars continue to be split on the question of whether Yogācārins, like Vasubandhu and Dignāga, were presenting an 'idealist metaphysics' or a 'representationalist epistemology'. Kochumuttom's (1989: 5) thesis is that the Yogācāra are really talking about mental construction, and any claim that this was idealism would be a 'gross misunderstanding'. Cook (1999: 374) also denies that Vasubandhu's work was idealistic, and suggests that the argument is one that claims that 'any cognitive experience is distorted as soon as it occurs'. Thus, Lusthaus (2002: 6) states that '*vijñapti-mātra*' should be seen as an 'epistemic caution' and not as an 'ontological pronouncement'. Anacker (1998: 159) also denies that Vasubandhu was really denying the existence of objects, claiming that what Vasubandhu is really getting at is that external phenomena are 'only inferable'. We may compare Hume here, who states that 'external objects become known to us only by those perceptions they occasion', and thus, 'we never really advance a step beyond ourselves' (Treatise, I.ii.6), and again, 'philosophy informs us, that every thing, which appears to the mind, is nothing but a perception', and it is only the 'vulgar' who 'confound perceptions and objects, and attribute a distinct continued existence to the very things they feel or see' (I.iv.2). Such a stance is often labelled 'scepticism', not 'idealism'. On such a reading of the Yogācāra, they would sit very close to Advaita's 'non-realism' in which there is 'no way of establishing that the world is external to cognition' (Ram-Prasad 2002: 14), as all phenomenal content is determined locally.

The subsequent difference would then boil down to whether one then *looks back* from this intuition at the world and assumes its (external) reality, or whether one moves on to transcend it. So framed, it is not an entirely ontological debate, but one framed within a larger soteriological project. If the Madhyamaka cannot be properly understood when extracted from its soteriological aims, then nor can the Yogācāra. They may well be accused of setting up an 'idealist epistemology', but their rationale may simply be to provide the practitioner with a platform for liberation from the world. If this were the case, their 'idealism' parallels the soteriological thesis of both Advaita and Madhyamaka, in that all of them wish to cast doubt on what we commonly take to be the constitution and the limits of reality, thus leaving room for the possibility of transcendence and an ideal (that is, perfect) form of living liberation.

Now that we have given the defenders of Yogācāra a fair hearing, we also need to be fair to Śāntideva and Śaṅkara, who both took the Yogācāra as idealistic. So in their defence, we can cite, for example, the following line from the opening verse of Vasubandhu's *Viṃśikā*: 'All this is mere representation because of the appearance of non-existent objects' (1a). This goes beyond Hume, who, due to the coherence and constancy of appearances, found himself 'naturally led to regard the world, as something real and durable' (Treatise, I.iv.2). From here, it is quite easy to see why Śaṅkara might also refer to them as the 'Followers of the theory that Only-Consciousness-Exists' (B.S.Bh. II.ii.18) and why Śāntideva might label their doctrine 'Mind-Only' (BCA. 9.29b).

Śaṅkara also referred to the Yogācārins as '*vijñāna-vādī*' (Followers of the theory of Consciousness) (B.S.Bh. II.ii.28). Now '*vijñāna*' had a technical meaning in early Buddhism, that of 'consciousness', being one of the five aggregates (*skandhas*). The early Buddhists also talked of the five sense consciousnesses as types of *vijñāna*, with intellect acting as a sixth. The Yogācāra School distinguished itself by proposing that there were in fact eight types of consciousness, including a store-house consciousness (*ālaya-vijñāna*).[1] Matilal (in Ames 1994: 287) suggests that this was the Yogācāra's 'substitute for the self'. Yet, it should be emphasized that the Yogācāra claimed that it was the error of the seventh consciousness, the 'tainted mind' (*kliṣṭa-manas*) to grasp at the *ālaya* as if it were a self.

We need to understand what it is that drives such an impassioned denial of their thesis by both Śāntideva and Śaṅkara. It may well have been that the Yogācāra simply constituted a formidable opponent to these schools. They may have had either political or scholastic reasons for attacking one another. Perhaps the Madhyamaka were responding to the claim that the Yogācāra was the third and final turning of the wheel, the Buddha's definitive teaching.[2] Ultimately, however, it will be argued here that, while the issue for Candrakīrti may well have been linguistic (Huntington 1989: 66), the common motivator for Śaṅkara and Śāntideva is *ethical conduct*, and that neither of them could imagine how ethics could function within a mind-only paradigm.

---

1 Like the Pāli texts, Śāntideva speaks of only six consciousnesses (BCA. 9.59).

2 See the *Saṃdhinirmocana Sūtra* (trans. Powers 1995: 139–41).

Nevertheless, our starting point continues on from the question of self. The methodology here is to focus on Śaṅkara's critique, whilst noting how similar Śāntideva's critique is to it. The reason for this is that Śaṅkara allotted significantly more space to the Yogācāra than did Śāntideva.

Before we analyse Śaṅkara's critique of the Yogācāra, it is worth noting a point made by Alston (2004), that Śaṅkara was 'more concerned with protecting the students of Advaita from the seductions of a non-Vedic path than with an objective statement of what the opponents actually said' (Vol. 4: 281). Indeed, we may note two passages in the commentaries that do seem to point to this conclusion. In one, Śaṅkara states that any teaching that opposes the Vedas was surely contradictory (B.S.Bh. II.ii.18). In another *Bhāṣya*, he states that any theory that denies a self (*ātman*) over and above the body and intellect contradicts the Vedic path (Bṛ.U.Bh. IV. iii.7). However, such dogmatic claims aside, it seems to me that Śaṅkara did in fact offer a fairly reasonable depiction of certain strands of the Yogācāra.

While it is true that any system that denies the Vedas is a system to be denounced by an Advaitin, it is my contention that there are deeper reasons for the sheer volume of attention that Śaṅkara gave to the Vijñānavādins. One reason, of course, is that he was well aware of just how close his own cognitive theory sat to theirs. For example, Śaṅkara admits that their theory of the self-luminosity (*sva-prakāśa*) of cognitions, at least on the surface, looks very similar to his theory that the Self-as-witness is self-established, self-reflexive and that it thus illumines cognitions (B.S.Bh. II.ii.28). Śaṅkara points out though, that if there is no Self behind the cognitions, throwing light on them, then what you have is tantamount to a fire burning itself (ibid.).

Śāntideva uses two such metaphors to make exactly the same point in his criticism of the Yogācāra. He states that 'Just as a blade cannot cut itself, so it is with mind' (BCA. 9.18a). He goes on to state that a 'lamp is not so illumined [by itself]' (9.19a).[3] He later goes on to say that whether the mind is luminous or not, it 'cannot be seen', so its discussion is 'futile' (9.22).[4] But for Śaṅkara, it is far from futile, for the luminous *brahman* is established by the Vedas, and is thus known on authority. He will therefore argue for its existence on the basis of an analogy with a lamp, which, though illuminating other objects, still needs an external agent to perceive it, as does consciousness (Bṛ.U.Bh. IV.iii.7).

There is much that could be said here regarding the nature of cognition, however it would lead us away from our central theme. All I wish to show here is that Śāntideva and Śaṅkara have already found themselves a common opponent in the Yogācāra. So far they have argued against them on sectarian grounds. For Śāntideva, there is no ultimate mind lying behind the momentary cognitions. For

[3] A similar argument appears in the *Vigrahavyāvartanī* (34), where Nāgārjuna states that 'Fire does not illuminate itself'. Matilal (2004: 60) traces the related 'light analogy' back to the *Nyāya Sūtra* II.i.9.

[4] For those who do not see it as futile, see Williams (1998b), Siderits et al. (2011) and Kuznetsova et al. (2012).

Śaṅkara, it is not mind or personal consciousness, but *brahman*-consciousness that lies behind those cognitions.[5] At this point then, the two philosophers remain divided essentially along *ātman/anātman* lines. But this is all about to change as they come to share the same ethical concerns.

The next stage of the debate is the question of subjects and objects, and their relationship to each other. We need to bear in mind here that while a pot or a snake is merely an object, a person is potentially both a subject and an object. What is meant by 'person' here has nothing to do with the question of *ātman*. The 'person', in the Indian context, is that who is stood before me, a man with a name and a family and a caste, born in such-and-such a village, holding such-and-such a trade. There is nothing metaphysical about this. Neither Śāntideva nor Śaṅkara wish to deny the person as an object. Neither of them wishes to say that 'you' are not *physically* there. Neither of them wishes to say that your family never *physically* existed, that your birth was not a physical occurrence within space and time.

Now it may well be that the Yogācārins never wished to be taken this way either. Perhaps all they wished to suggest was that a world out there could never be verified without recourse to consciousness. Perhaps we should not see them as proposing a world of cognition-only, but of representation-only. Be that as it may, historically they *were* taken to be denying an external world both by Śāntideva and Śaṅkara. Indeed they continue to be taken this way by the Tibetan Mādhyamikas, and there is certainly enough in the writings of the likes of Vasubandhu which would allow for this interpretation.[6] Again, whatever the historical or textual fact of the matter is, the work we need to do here is to understand why both Śāntideva and Śaṅkara would want to argue against such idealism. For our purposes, we can ignore the name Yogācāra and focus only on the construction of their project as described to us by Śāntideva and Śaṅkara. The key question to ask is: in what way does this project oppose what they wish to say about the world and our place in it?

Beginning with Śaṅkara again, we need to realize just how close his ontology looks, on the surface, to that of the Yogācāra. And this is so even in his post-Gauḍapāda period. Let us take for example the famous Indian 'snake/rope' analogy. First, let us examine it from a psychological perspective. A person, through fear or whatever, imagines they see a snake. As they get closer, they realize it is only a rope. What are we to take from this? All that is being pointed out here is that what we take to be the world (through perception) might not be the *actual* world. The world that we see passes through mental filters which distort its reality. In other words, the world is different from the way we perceive it. Up to here, the *Brahmins* and the Buddhists would agree. If we take this analogy of the 'snake/

---

5 That the 'I' (*ahaṃ*) is momentary (*kṣaṇikatva*) is also stated in the *V.C.* (293), where it is contrasted with the 'witness' (*sakṣī*) which is 'constant' (*nitya*) (294).

6 The Dalai Lama (2002: 102) states: 'although the Mind-only School rejects the reality of a self and rejects the reality of an external, objective material reality, it nonetheless maintains that subjective experience – that is to say, the mind – does have substantial reality'. Also see Hopkins (1996: 365ff).

rope' one step further, what Śaṅkara is accusing the Vijñānavādin of doing is reducing the object to an 'idea', to cognition:

> If no object distinct from consciousness were admitted, then the words 'cognition', 'pot', 'cloth', etc., having the same meaning, would all be synonymous (Bṛ.U.Bh. IV.iii.7).

On this account, a pot, or a cloth or a snake would all be equal in being mere ideas within a subject's consciousness.[7] He goes on to state that we could not function in society if we did not assume that other beings were external to consciousness. For example, to have a debate with an opponent, but to assume that this was all taking place at the level of cognition-only would 'put an end to all human interaction' (ibid.). This is an *explicit* reference to human conduct, that is, to social ethics. Human interaction, as we know it, simply could not take place if I assumed that 'others' were merely a figment of my imagination, an aspect of my own consciousness. What would it mean to be ethical if I did not feel that I was interacting with other distinct beings? Moreover, Śaṅkara points out that the teachings of the Buddhist path itself, which presuppose a distinction between means and the result, would be rendered useless. In full:

> Likewise, [if] the means [were taken as] being identical with the result, your scriptures, which assume a difference between them, would be useless, and the author [i.e. the Buddha] might well be charged with ignorance (Bṛ.U.Bh. IV.iii.7).

The conclusion could not be any clearer: *where there is no posited world of beings, there is no place for ethics*. No matter how much we seek to reduce existence to pure consciousness, in the final analysis, the 'way to liberation lies in and goes through unliberated life' (Ram-Prasad 2000: 184). Furthermore, and this is vital, the Yogācāra are being accused of putting the Buddha's ethical teachings at risk!

Naturally, it could be argued that Śaṅkara's own theory of *brahman*-consciousness as ground of all being, with 'things' being mere shapes of this Being (*sat*), is open to the same attack. Ingalls (1954), even while limiting himself to the two 'major' and 'mature' works of Śaṅkara (p291), admits that, 'If we are to adopt a metaphysical and static view of philosophy, there is little difference between Śaṅkara and Vijñānavāda Buddhism' (p304). Even though Śaṅkara may have left idealism behind, he still continues to claim that everything is a manifestation of the one ground, *Being* itself. For example, 'All things named … are Being-only' (Ch.U.Bh. VI.ii.1–3). Snakes, pots, whatever: 'all these are but different shapes of Being'. There is no snake (*sarpa*), only 'rope', not as '*rajju*', but as '*Sat*', Being itself. Further on in the text (VI.iii.2), forms are said to be ultimately non-existent

[7] The positive side of this doctrine, of course, is that one could never be scared by a snake, or be seduced by an object if one saw it as mind-created. This potential benefit of the Yogācāra view has in fact been pointed out by the current Dalai Lama (2002: 102).

(*anṛta*). Thus, Śaṅkara pushes the 'snake/rope' analogy beyond psychology into epistemology, and arguably into ontology. It is no longer due to fear that one sees a 'snake', it is (more directly) due to ignorance:

> All concepts of non-*brahman* are mere ignorance, like the notion of a snake superimposed upon a rope. *Brahman* alone is the ultimate truth (Mu.U.Bh. II.ii.11).

But then this is all that the Yogācāra (as painted by Śaṅkara) are saying; 'things' are verily non-other than ground (*ālaya*). So what is new in Śaṅkara is not that there are snakes or people out there, but that we must *pretend* that the snakes and people are real, that is real in the provisional sense of taking them seriously. There are snakes and people, as it were, but, to the enlightened, they are really just modifications of the one true Being, never to be grasped at. Nevertheless, for the sake of the majority, in everyday life, we must go along with the delusion that these 'things' are in fact real, and persons do in fact own their own lives and property. So while 'illusion cannot last when the truth is known' (Dasgupta 1975, Vol.I: 441), the illusory game can still be played. In other words, when discussing ethics, we must accept the provisional playing field, for that is where most people sport.

In the *Upadeśa Sāhasrī*, Śaṅkara also points out that before one realized that the 'snake' was in fact a 'rope', the 'snake' did in fact have an underlying existence, namely, the rope (Metric, 18.46). Thus, there is a real basis even for illusory existence. So even if all phenomena were taken to be illusory, there would still be an underlying reality, *brahman*. It might help to recall the analogy of the waves falling back into the sea (B.S.Bh. II.i.13). The waves are transitory, but the sea still underlies them, just as the earth underlies a temporary pot. Elsewhere, Śaṅkara offers the similar analogy of foam and bubbles on top of pure water; the elements of the body and the so-called individual self are like foam and bubbles of water which upon realization disappear into pure *brahman* (Bṛ.U.Bh. II.iv.12).[8]

The trick he plays with the reader then is to attack the Yogācāra's (ultimate) soteriological discourse with a (provisional) ethical argument. The Yogācāra are in fact right to see things as illusory, as dream-like, but they are wrong in not taking this provisional world seriously.[9] And the world, according to Advaita, *is* to be taken seriously. Dreams prove only that cognitions may be sublated and thus point to the possibility that the world of name-and-form may be transcended, not that the world has no relative existence. As such, Śaṅkara, without proving the externality of the world, merely assumes it. For this 'pseudo-realist' move, Bhāskara (8th to 9th century) charges Śaṅkara with hypocrisy, for it appears to contradict his Buddhist-looking *māyā*-thesis (see Ingalls 1954: 303–4). But the move is only hypocritical if we maintain an either/or discourse. But Śaṅkara's discourse, like Śāntideva's, is *both/and*. My contention is that Śaṅkara, like Śāntideva, wants

8 Cf. S.N. III.140–42.

9 Actually, as Ram-Prasad (2002: 45) rightly points out, ordinary experience (especially suffering) *is* of 'the utmost moral seriousness' to the Yogācārin.

us to see the illusion of the cake *and* eat it. It is this move that will allow him to defend the ethics of the *Bhagavad Gītā*. All we need do is assume that the world is out there, and hence *Dharma* can run its course. True, with regard to such things as caste, gender, renunciation and celibacy, he will place certain boundaries around human interaction, leaving room for a transcendent domain for the few. But there is nothing hypocritical about that. If Śaṅkara can be accused of anything, it is elitism, not hypocrisy.

Naturally, along with elitism comes a certain degree of arrogance. In one single line of the *Bṛ.U.Bh*, Śaṅkara dismisses the followers of the Madhyamaka School, to whom he refers to as the 'Followers of the Empty Doctrine' (IV.iii.7), on the grounds that their doctrine 'contradicts all means of valid knowledge'. Unfortunately, he offers no explanation. He says a little bit more in his *B.S.Bh*, where he implies that they refuse to accept the provisional reality which he finds essential for human interaction (II.ii.31). Needless to say, I do not believe that this critique can stand up against Śāntideva. For one thing, in the *BCA* (9.8a), Śāntideva states that there is no fault in the wise adopting conventional views. Furthermore, he later categorically denies that conventional ways of knowing are being denied:

> The [ordinary] way of seeing, hearing or knowing is not here being refuted. It is the reification of reality that is here refuted, as that is the cause of suffering (BCA. 9.25).

I will return to this subject later. But for now, allow me to show just how similar Śāntideva's views are to Śaṅkara's on this and related subjects. Like Śaṅkara, Śāntideva finds the Yogācāra's theory of non-externality as unreasonable as their theory of the luminosity of mind:

> [We ask] If, for you, the illusion does not exist [externally], what is there to be perceived? Even if [you say] it is an expression of mind itself, [we object] that in reality it is something other [than mind]. [We ask] If illusion is really mind itself, what is seen by what? Moreover, it was said by the World Protector [Buddha] that mind does not perceive mind (BCA. 9.16–17).

It is quite evident here that Śāntideva wishes to distinguish between the Madhyamaka theory of illusion-like objects and the mind-only theory of the Yogācāra. He wants to say that things (which will naturally include human beings), although they are lacking in permanence and independent existence, do nonetheless stand out there, external to consciousness. He further wants to say that the mind is not to be taken as being self-luminous. And herein follows a lengthy discussion on why this cannot be so. I do not wish to enter into this debate, other than to note that his analogy of a knife not being capable of cutting itself (BCA. 9.18) is parallel to Śaṅkara's claim that fire does not burn itself (B.S.Bh. II.ii.28). Of course, the reasons why they wish to deny the luminosity theory of the Yogācāra are totally opposed. Śaṅkara wishes to establish a necessary witness (*brahman*) behind the workings of mind, whereas Śāntideva wishes to say that all is inter-dependent and that nothing is self-standing. In other words, one attacks the Yogācāra in order to prove there is a self, and the other attacks it to prove there is no self.

Here, as we might well have predicted, they will meet a metaphysical impasse. On one side of the river, Śāntideva stands open to Śaṅkara's attack that the Śūnyavādin's doctrine 'collapses like a well in sand' (B.S.Bh. II.ii.32). On the other side, Śaṅkara stands open to Śāntideva's attack on those who would posit a more solid ground of existence. And here the Yogācāra appear to be standing on the bridge being fired at from both sides. Śāntideva would no doubt take Śaṅkara's attack on the chin, for he not only admits that his theory lacks any essential support; he even prays that all mankind adopt a view of things as being like space: 'Would that all mankind understood that all things are like space. But they delight in festivals and get angry in disputes' (BCA. 9.154).

In the following exchange, we again see just how closely the Yogācāra stood metaphysically to the Advaitin, as Śāntideva responds to the former's attack on his supportless universe:

> Just as the illusion which is perceived lacks [ultimate] existence, so it is with the seer, the mind. If [you think] cyclic existence must be supported by something truly existent, otherwise it would be like space ... [We reply] For you, the mind has been reduced to isolation, accompanied by non-existents. How could the activity of the unreal [objects] proceed, even if supported by a real existent [i.e. pure mind]? (BCA. 9.27–8).

While it is difficult to see just how this answers the question put forth, we can easily see how the final attack could apply to Śaṅkara. Both Śāntideva and Śaṅkara are admitting that the illusion exists, but only the former is willing to say that there is no ground to which the illusion refers. Indeed, Śāntideva will throw the accusation of a 'space-like' ground in the face of the Brahmanical schools, likening *ātman* (BCA. 6.29 and 9.69) and Īśvara (9.120) to space, and asking how this so-called God would add anything to our inter-dependent universe. Like the Yogācāra's luminous mind, it appears to Śāntideva as a barren concept. The metaphysical impasse seems to defy common ground, but the ethical consequences of their positions most certainly do not.

Notice here that we have a Buddhist school attacking another Buddhist school along with certain Brahmanical schools for holding to a metaphysical thesis that feels the need to posit an essential ground. At the same time, we have a Buddhist and a *Brahmin* firing the same accusation at a second Buddhist school, that of denying the provisional ground for ethics. The *cross-cutting* nature of Indian philosophy has thus been established. Furthermore, the fact that one's ultimate view on selfhood, though influential, is no give-away sign of one's ethical project has been proven. Thus, I will call on scholars to reflect further on how they distinguish Buddhism from Hinduism at the provisional level.

Having established these philosophical and disciplinary positions, a deeper investigation into their ethical projects will now follow (Chapter 4.3). This will attempt to establish further *historiographical* claims as to their focus on traditional ethics and lineage at the price of their ultimate metaphysics. But first we need to briefly sketch out the lack-of-agency thesis that underlies them.

4.2 Their Common Denial of the Ultimacy of the Individuated Self

Of all the topics under discussion, this is the key *metaphysical* similarity between Madhyamaka and Advaita. Remember, the Madhyamaka School has said that there is no selfhood anywhere to be found. Remember also that the Advaitin has said that all is but the one Self. The former is saying that 'you', under ultimate analysis, are not to be found; the latter is saying that 'you' *are* to be found, but only as 'that'. Hence, both are forced into the counter-intuitive position of denying that there is any individual unified self. This further means that both must target the 'I-making' mechanism (*ahaṃkāra*) that leads most people to believe that they do in fact have a permanent centre, a lasting individuated essence. We are never told that this *sense* of I-ness does not exist; rather, it is claimed to be a *mistake*, a mistake that blocks liberation.

It is easy to see, in Buddhist terms, that in order to become selfless, one must drop the notion of self. But it is less obvious, but equally crucial, that in Advaitic terms, in order to become Self (that is, *brahman*) one must likewise drop the notion of self (*jīva*). When we grasp this truth, we are faced with the fact that the whole question of self in Western philosophy has a whole different meaning to that in Indian philosophy. But equally, when a Buddhist realizes that the Advaitin is also denying the individuated self, he is faced with rethinking what it means to distinguish Hinduism and Buddhism on the grounds of self and non-self.

Nowhere in the Pāli Canon does the Buddha deny *brahman* (as absolute); in fact, it goes unmentioned. From this, I do not wish to suggest that the Buddha left open the possibility of a Self, as some have suggested (see Harvey 1995: 8). Rather, I wish to suggest that the not-self of the Pāli Canon is a psychological thesis, a means of denying the inclination to claim possession of things, of clinging to the categories of 'me' and 'mine'. In Harvey's words, it is a 'tool to cut off identifying with and clinging to things, including views' (in Keown and Prebish 2007: 570). I then wish to show that Śaṅkara uses the denial of self in a very similar psychological fashion.

Indeed, some scholars have hinted at this parallel before, but its implications have never been fully drawn out. For example, Saddhatissa (1997: 133) has noted that the *ātman* of the Upaniṣads 'signified the nonself rather than the self'. More recently, Ram-Prasad (in Siderits et al. 2011: 230) writes:

> If by the use of the word 'self' we mean necessarily an individuated locus of consciousness idiosyncratically designated by the 'I', then the *ātman* of the Advaitins is not a self at all.

For similar reasons, Grether (2007: 231) has called on scholars to simply stop translating *ātman* as 'self'. Unfortunately, we have yet to find a more suitable word, but that does not mean we cannot see the problem. Clearly, along with the *Bṛhadāraṇyaka Upaniṣad*, both Śaṅkara and the Buddha are saying 'not this, not this' or, as Harvey puts it, 'this, this, this … is *not* Self' (in Keown and Prebish 2007: 571). The *V.C.* states that 'The body, consisting of arms, legs, etc. cannot be the Self' (156). Śāntideva offers a similar meditation (BCA. 9.78–87), beginning with 'The body is not the feet, not the calves, not the thighs, and the body is not the hips'. The only thing these texts disagree on is what is left at the end of the process. Śaṅkara's Advaita will insist that we are left with *brahman*, an absolute ground, a singular Self. The Buddha refused to speculate, and modern scholars are left to debate his silence.

On the other hand, Śāntideva categorically denies the ultimate ground of the universe. He therefore denies both the self (writ small) and the Self (writ large). The so-called ultimate Self is dismissed as 'imagined' (BCA. 6.27). And even if it did exist conventionally, it would be dependent on something other (6.31), and thus ultimately non-existent. As for the individuated self:

> All the misfortunes in the world, the hardships and the fears, many as there are; they all result from clinging to this 'self'. So for what is this clinging of mine? (BCA. 8.134).

These are strong words indeed, attacking not so much the Brahmanical Self, but the more deeply ingrained conception of self. Nevertheless, Śāntideva insists on acting towards the world *as if* it were inhabited by multiple selves. This creates problems for a purely psychological interpretation of selfhood. As stated above, there is definitely a certain advantage to be gained in taking Buddhism to be essentially psychologically driven; however, the Mādhyamikas tend to see *anātman* in philosophical terms. Even if Garfield (1995: 88) is right that the *MMK* of Nāgārjuna is 'aimed primarily against philosophy', the Mādhyamikas have certainly offered a lot of philosophising in its defence!

In the case of Śāntideva, I will attempt to show that he adopts both a psychological deconstruction *and* a philosophical deconstruction. This lines up with de Silva's (2000: 2) claim that the Buddha's psychological analysis was 'interlocked' with the philosophical facets of his doctrine. Thus, in the *BCA*, we find such psychological language as: 'the body is not the feet' (9.78) and 'the equality of self and other' (8.90) and the accepting of another's body as 'myself' (8.112). Here we can agree with Pickering (1997: 160) when he suggests that the Buddhist analysis of self lies somewhere between the 'highly personalised' analysis of suffering and the 'depersonalised' analysis of impermanence. However, we also find Śāntideva using more philosophical language, such as this 'bundle devoid of self' (BCA. 9.101), along with his metaphysical critique of the 'imagined' and 'inactive' 'Self' (6.27–30). In this sense, the Mādhyamikas go one step further into the metaphysics of self than does early Buddhism. As suggested by Hayes, post-

Nāgārjuna, *anātman* becomes a 'thoroughgoing metaphysical doctrine' (in Keown and Prebish 2007: 29); there is literally 'no self' to be found.

Thus, *anātman* may rightly be translated as 'not-self' or as 'no-self' depending on whether it is a psychological or a philosophical claim. So Harvey's (1995: 7) argument about whether *anātman* is to be translated as 'no-self' or 'not-self', at least within the Sanskritic context, is largely irrelevant, because neither of these positions is held with any consistency. Furthermore, if Harvey is correct in claiming that the *anātman* doctrine should not generate the view, 'there is no Self' (in Keown and Prebish 2007: 570), then perhaps the Madhyamaka (including Śāntideva) are at fault. In no uncertain terms, the *Compendium* states that, ultimately speaking, there is no individuated self (*jīva*), or essential person (*pudgala*) or independent being (*sattva*) (Ś.S. 172). Moreover, the *BCA* not only claims that ultimately there is no self, but adds 'I' (*aham*) and 'body' to the list of negations (9.56 and 9.83).[10]

On the other hand, Śāntideva would certainly agree with Harvey that this view of no-self 'should not be clung to' (Keown and Prebish 2007: 570). For, according to the Madhyamaka, neither of the Two Truths exists ultimately. So while Śāntideva (BCA. 9.53) speaks of the validity of the doctrine of emptiness, he also notes that: 'For, if the being of an entity is deceptive, clearly its negation [i.e. emptiness] is equally deceptive' (BCA. 9.139b).

So we learn that, in line with Nāgārjuna's 'emptiness is the relinquishing of all views' (MMK. 13.8), Śāntideva teaches that even 'emptiness' is empty of existence. He sums up his understanding of the Madhyamaka position thus:

> The influence of phenomena is removed by employing the influence of emptiness. And even that emptiness is later eradicated by bringing to mind that 'nothing [truly] exists' (BCA. 9.32).[11]

Nevertheless, when Śāntideva reinstates the world as inhabited by multiple selves, he does it from a volitional, rather than a metaphysical, standpoint. To be sure, his metaphysics could not logically maintain such a reconstruction, either ontologically or motivationally, for he even denies that suffering (*duḥkha*) ultimately exists (BCA. 9.88ff). In other words, in the Madhyamaka context, we need to approach selfhood from a different direction depending on whether it is being philosophically/psychologically deconstructed or voluntarily/affectively reconstructed.

Summarising Metzinger's work; Ram-Prasad notes that it may well be impossible to *both* preserve a sense of 'real self' *and* become convinced that intuitively there is 'no such self' (in Siderits et al. 2011: 224). However, one can certainly convince oneself into accepting the delusion that *others* have a real (to them) self, to voluntarily reconstruct the 'other' for ethical purposes. Deluded beings continue to live in the conventional, and so the conventional world exists

---

[10] All of which, barring *brahman*'s 'Being', Śaṅkara would agree to.

[11] Emptiness is like the soapy water we use to wash the dirt off our hands. But we must still wipe off the soapy water! (Tsoknyi Rinpoche, personal communication).

for them. As Śāntideva puts it, 'In fact, the conventional does exist from the other's perspective' (BCA. 9.106b). As such, the immediate relevance of experience is from the point of view of the other, and the agent need not fully ascribe to it. Therefore, ethics are more fundamental to Śāntideva than teachings about emptiness.

Naturally, one might assume that it takes an act of a 'concrete' self to reconstruct the social world. However, we can imagine the impetus of this reconstruction deriving its force from the Bodhisattva Vow. By that I mean that the Vow is taken by one cluster of mental processes, while another cluster of mental processes (deeply affected by that Vow) is now causing the current reconstruction. In Śāntideva's terminology, it is due to the power of the preceding causes (BCA. 9.117). The repeated reviewing of the Vow by a given continuum creates a certain mindset, a mind-of-compassion or concern (BCA. 8.110), which constantly seeks the opportunity to act for the benefit of others. So while Garfield (2002: 192) may have a point in claiming that 'We act compassionately … precisely when we act not from duty', my contention here is that the *bodhisattva* takes it as a 'duty' to become and thus *be* compassionate. That is, the duty is surely of a different order than that which Garfield has in mind. It is this compassion-as-duty which imposes the reconstruction of the world and the will to embodied activity:

> Those whose continuum is so developed, for whom the suffering of others is as dear to them [as their own], plunge into hell like swans into a lotus lake (BCA. 8.107).

What I wish to highlight here is the use of the notion of a developed 'continuum' (*saṃtāna*), which demonstrates how Śāntideva wishes to avoid the notion of a *bodhisattva* as a substantial self. There is no substantial self or person who gets developed; there is just development. Even in the face of the notion of rebirth, he will ask, 'Why should it be that a being counts as ultimately existing simply on account of its long-lasting continuum?' (BCA. 9.10b). Long-lasting is still impermanent, and an impermanent 'thing' cannot be an ultimate existent.

It is also interesting how Śāntideva uses the term 'swans' (*haṃsāḥ*) to describe the actions of the *bodhisattva*, with Śaṅkara calling his monks '*parama-haṃsāḥ*' (U.S. Prose, 1.2), literally 'supreme-swans'.[12] Of much greater interest, at least metaphysically, is how Śāntideva also urges the *bodhisattva* to develop the 'great-self of a Buddha' (Ś.S. 145) and to preach it (330). Similarly, inner peace is spoken of as the 'tranquillity of the great-self' (119). Śāntideva defines this in gnoseological terms, stating that it is 'The capacity to produce the knowledge of reality as-it-is' (ibid.). But it would also seem to indicate a state of virtue with a predisposition to compassion. Śāntideva writes that, 'the *bodhisattva* who thus sees reality as-it-is feels a profound compassion for all beings' (ibid.). Likewise, such *bodhisattvas* are later described as 'great men' who 'with the Buddha's virtues, work for the good of the world' (330). As such, in denying their small self, the *bodhisattvas* are said to become great or immeasurable, selfless selves.

[12] For the origin and prevalence of the term *haṃsa*, see Olson (1997: 19–22).

Nevertheless, in the *BCA*, Śāntideva makes a conscious effort to remain true to the metaphysics of person-as-continuum, 'great' though that continuum may be.

For Śaṅkara, there is only one Supreme Self (*paramātman*), and that is *brahman*. It is unique, 'only one without a second' (Ch.U.Bh. VI.ii.1). Thus, Kasulis' (in Schweiker 2005: 298) translation of *ānatman* as 'no-I' hardly helps in distinguishing Buddhism from Hinduism, for Śaṅkara also denies the ultimacy of the 'I' (*aham*). But what is it, then, for Śaṅkara, that transmigrates? Who is it that acts?

Let us begin with a summary quote from Alston (2004, Vol.3: v):

> Considered as a finite conscious being, the soul, for Śaṅkara, belongs to the realm of appearance. In its true nature, it is the infinite non-dual Consciousness that is the sole reality underlying all appearance.

This line of thought is to be found throughout Śaṅkara's work and we could quote endless passages on this central subject of non-duality. Let us focus then on his central work, the *Brahma-Sūtra Bhāṣya*, and on how this position feeds into his ethical project. First of all, Śaṅkara tells us that *brahman*, merely 'appears to exist as an individuated self due to its association with limiting adjuncts' (B.S.Bh. II.iii.18). In other words, it is purely due to our physical and mental make-up that we imagine there to be individuation of the Self. Consciousness is mistakenly taken to be local by the mind (*manas*), or intellect (*buddhi*), and thus one's own fluctuating desires, joys and sorrows (which are mind-created) are mistakenly associated with consciousness, when in fact consciousness is immutable. It is this error that causes transmigration. Śaṅkara tells us that 'without these modes of intellect, there can be no transmigration of the pure Self' (II.iii.29). Here then lies the key to liberation: stop functioning through the limited intellect. And we might recall that Śāntideva (BCA. 9.2b) also proclaimed that the intellect (*buddhi*) is incapable of understanding reality, for it is grounded in the conventional.

Of greater interest here is that it must now follow that the apparent locus of individual agency and experience must be an illusion caused by this intellect. Śaṅkara continues:

> Though the Self is not an agent or an experiencer, and though it never itself transmigrates and is eternally free; it takes on the state of being an agent and an experiencer due to the superimposed nature of the intellect as adjunct (B.S.Bh. II.iii.29).

This gives Śaṅkara the platform he requires in order to make a number of important claims. He can claim that (provisionally) there is an agent, and as such, whilst in and of this world, one has a responsibility to act in accordance with traditional Law (*Dharma*). From here, it can also be claimed that (ultimately) there is no such agent, and thus one can transcend this world of transmigration. Using this Two-Truths strategy, Śaṅkara therefore concludes that:

> Ultimately speaking, there is no such distinctive thing as an individuated self apart from that imaginary appearance created under the influence of the intellect acting as limiting adjunct (B.S.Bh. II.iii.30).

And turning briefly to a more 'minor' text, Śaṅkara writes:

> There can be no agentship, no enjoyership, nor any ritual action, means, or result, where all is reduced to non-duality (P.U.Bh. 6.3).

This truth opens up the possibility of a person who has been taught and understood the fallacy of the intellect and the truth of *brahman*, a person who can act outside the normal restrictions of agent-based morality. This is the world of the *brahma-vid* or *jīvan-mukta*, to be examined in Chapter 6. For now, let us concentrate on how and why Śaṅkara and Śāntideva both defend a traditional ethics. While so focused, let us not lose sight of the fact, emphasised by French philosopher, Paul Ricoeur (1994: 18), and more recently echoed by phenomenologist, Dan Zahavi, that the 'identity of the self is only fully revealed the moment we include the *ethical dimension*' (Zahavi 2008: 113).

4.3 Their Common Response to Tradition-based Conduct

The person before you is not an ultimate being. Their apparent status as an individuated self is an illusion. Their personal sense of self is based on a cognitive error. Your view of them as a role-playing individual within a given social structure is based upon a socially constructed delusion. Society is a mere designation, an aggregation of persons who have no ultimacy. Thus far, Śaṅkara and Śāntideva appear to be in full agreement. Hence, tradition-based conduct, which takes social categories as given, would seemingly be swept away by an insight into the ultimate nature of being. There can be no class, no caste system, no nation and no rightful kingships. There can be no monks, no laity, no men and no women. And yet, given all of this, which flows so naturally from their revisionary metaphysics; both will make a space for their traditions. Not only that. Both will *insist* on their traditions. This insistence on tradition has three major impacts:

1. It highlights how both philosophers stand on a doctrinal tight-rope, pointing upwards, away from the world, whilst looking downwards at the world, condoning their respective tradition's values.
2. It emphasizes the point that ethics are central to both schools of thought, and that the idea of a world without ethics is repugnant to both. Even in vowing to renounce the world, they cannot forget the world. Renunciation, then does not involve ceasing to have any actual relationship with society. Rather, it points to a reorientation of that relationship.

3. It sets limits on my thesis. For, even though their metaphysics on individual agency *should* lead to the collapse of the distinctions between their forms of Buddhism and Hinduism, in fact they do not, because both insist on maintaining that distinction at the provisional level. The most we can say, then, is that once we accept that the individuated self is being denied on both sides, we need to re-assess *how* we distinguish the two religions, not whether we *should* distinguish them.

There is no doubt that both Śaṅkara and Śāntideva will say that the person needs to be transcended for the sake of liberation. This agent comes to the respective tradition as a socially constructed being; made up of class, caste, family and duty. They have an expected mode of conduct. Both Śaṅkara and Śāntideva will say that this expectation is provisional. It may generally be claimed that, in India, 'proper conduct has counted for more than ideological purity' (Olivelle 1992: 12), but would a revisionary philosopher agree with this? What is 'proper conduct' for one who has seen through our social realities? Also, given that the Mahāyāna had introduced the notion of skilful means, and given that Śaṅkara was intent on creating a Brahmanical monastic order, what are the implications for the notion that, in India, 'orthodoxy is less important than orthopraxy' (Gombrich 1988: 112)?

In reading their response to traditional texts, the question is perhaps this: how much of a role does knowledge play in deciding on the right way to act? Just *who* do the traditional rules apply to? But there is also the more nagging question: why do these philosophers of non-individuation even *care* about the ethics of illusory individuals?

Case 1: Śaṅkara

As a champion of renunciation, Śaṅkara is faced in the Upaniṣads with the householder's claim to knowledge. Likewise, he had to answer for their desire for women. I have argued that Śaṅkara can allow for this 'lapse' in character by admitting that a knower may flicker between *brahman*-consciousness and habitual consciousness. His thesis is thus a practical one, based on the concept of latent tendencies (*saṃskāras*).

Even though Śaṅkara speaks of the knower's actions as non-actions, the notion that the knower was having sex without *really* having sex, or the notion that he was having sex purely for the sake of the other, did not occur to Śaṅkara. Or if it did, he rejected it. Unlike Śāntideva, Śaṅkara has no skill-in-means thesis to offer. His ethical evaluation of the Upaniṣads is thus based on levels of knowledge and the lingering strength of past tendencies. Just as Śāntideva was faced with late tradition texts and re-evaluations of renunciation, so was Śaṅkara. Written some centuries after the first Upaniṣads, the *Bhagavad Gītā*'s emphasis on a life of selfless action (that is, *karma-yoga*) arguably confronts Śaṅkara-the-exegete with his greatest challenge. How Śaṅkara reacts to this text is of supreme interest.

Śaṅkara saw himself as a renouncer. However, if we take this as our starting point, assuming that renunciation is the only option in Advaita, we run the risk of misunderstanding his position on conduct, that is, *Dharma*. In particular, I wish to argue that Śaṅkara holds a definite view on the actions of a *brahman*-knower (*brahma-vid*) within the world. So rather than start with Śaṅkara-the-renouncer, we might start with a *hypothetical ideal type* which Śaṅkara would have respected. That is, we are searching to privilege the male, *Brahmin*, who lives a celibate life with his mind fixed on attaining the highest good, *brahman*-knowledge. This hypothetical ideal will help us to unravel the apparent contradictions in his works. We need not take Śaṅkara himself as being a *brahman*-knower, merely as one advocating its attainment. But we should also keep in mind that the attainment of knowledge is a gradual affair, and so other provisional options remain.

With regard to literary methodology, we need to take account of all of Śaṅkara's authentic works. Nevertheless, it will bear fruit if we focus here on his commentary on the classic text on Hindu *Dharma*, the *Bhagavad Gītā*. The reason for this choice is five-fold: 1) it is here where Śaṅkara faces his strongest exegetical challenge; 2) it is steeped in ethical language; 3) it presents an ethics within what many Indians see as 'the illusory human drama' (Tripurari, in Rosen 2002: 207); 4) it is open to multiple interpretations,[13] some of which challenge Śaṅkara's own project; and 5) the story is a familiar one.

Theodor (2010: 21–2) has also suggested that Vedānta would be 'impoverished' without the *Gītā*. At the provisional level of discourse, this is certainly true. And it may also be true to say that our understanding of Śaṅkara would likewise be impoverished if we ignored his views on the ethics of the *Gītā*.

The scene we have in mind finds the great warrior Arjuna overcome by compassion (*kṛpayā*), caught between his caste-bound duty to fight (*kṣatriya-dharma*), his duty to his family (*kula-dharma*) and the desire to flee the war and renounce. What follows this moral dilemma is an 'ethical and metaphysical answer to the question of renunciation' (Marcaurelle 2000: 4). We all know the story. I request that, in addition to the usual battle scene, simply imagine Śaṅkara, the *champion of renunciation*, there alongside Kṛṣṇa. Arjuna is begging them for counsel. Now what would be the expected advice? We all know Kṛṣṇa advises Arjuna to fight:

> Therefore, without attachment, always perform the obligatory duty, for by performing one's duty without attachment, a person attains the Highest (Bh.G. 3.19).

Renunciation then, for Kṛṣṇa, is not about giving up action and going off to find God in the forest. Rather, Kṛṣṇa redefines renunciation. Kṛṣṇa reserves his highest praise, not for the renouncer who withdraws and abstains from worldly action, the type of renouncer we typically associate with Śaṅkara's Advaita, but for the

[13] For how the three main Vedāntin commentaries differ, see Chari (2005).

new type of 'renouncer' who continues to fulfil his traditional role in society. Renunciation, then, is *karma yoga itself*, which involves, not the renunciation of all action, but only the renunciation of the fruit of action. Kṛṣṇa becomes the 'only place for renunciation and attachment' (Malinar 2007: 189). Renunciation is thus 'rendered compatible with activism' (Perrett 1998: 16), making it compatible with being a householder.

This would all appear to come as a major challenge to Śaṅkara. His ideal type, the ascetic (*yati*), is indeed one that gives up all ritual action, and is thus contrasted with the 'man of action' (*karmī*) (Bh.G.Bh. 14.26). According to Śaṅkara, only the former is worthy of the 'highest'. Thus Śaṅkara needs to find a way of interpreting the text that will allow him to maintain that the 'highest' is the sole right of the ascetic renouncer, and that Arjuna-as-warrior is not qualified for it.

From a 'modern' point of view, it might be assumed that Śaṅkara would object to the life of the warrior as being 'antithetical to the renunciatory ideal of nonviolence' (Johnson 2004: xiii), and that he might beg Arjuna to renounce war. Along with Gandhi (2009: xxiv), we might expect Śaṅkara to claim that 'perfect renunciation is impossible without perfect observation of *ahimsa*'. But this is not the route he takes. If this 'existential tension is the axial core of the *Gītā*' (Schweig, in Rosen 2002: viii), it bypasses Śaṅkara. One might also expect a rejection of social norms and values, but there is no such rejection. Rather than making overtly moral or social judgements of the situation, Śaṅkara makes a gnoseological one.

Before we consider Śaṅkara's response, let us zoom in on the language of the above verse (Bh.G. 3.19). It is most significant that this verse begins with the word 'Therefore' (*tasmād*). If we look back at the previous verse(s), we might expect to find a *reason* why Arjuna should not renounce his *kṣatriya-dharma*. However, it is not (explicitly) there. The text states:

> But for a man who rejoices in the Self, is satisfied with the Self, and is content only in the Self, there is no duty to perform. For him, there is no concern with performance or non-performance of action in this world, and he has no kind of dependence at all on any objectives of beings (Bh.G. 3.17–18).

In fact, not only do these verses not explicitly supply the reason we were expecting, but they seem to be saying the complete opposite! These two verses interrupt the argument, highlighting the tension between *Dharma* and *mokṣa*. Zaehner (1973: 169) even suggests that we might regard these two verses as a 'later interpolation', but surely one needs to make such claims with care. Perhaps Davis (in Neusner and Chilton 2005: 174) could be accused of ignoring these verses when he stated that 'Renunciation of worldly actions', according to Kṛṣṇa, was 'not a legitimate option'. However, the issue may come down to how we interpret the 'Therefore' of verse 3.19. What Kṛṣṇa might be saying is this: 'You, Arjuna, have now been told, not whether to fight or not fight, but *how* to fight. That is, fight, not with a goal in mind, not with a personal concept of the fruit, not even with a notion of the objectives of your family, but fight selflessly'. And to fight 'selflessly' is to fight with no concept of individuality, but with a concept of one 'Self', who is verily the Lord Kṛṣṇa. On this interpretation, Davis appears correct.

However, Śaṅkara does not see it this way. For him, the 'Therefore' has a totally different meaning. Arjuna is not being told how to renounce, but *not* to renounce. He is being told that he is not ready for total renunciation. To make this point, Śaṅkara needs to insert the explicit reason which he feels Kṛṣṇa made implicitly. So just before verse 3.19, Śaṅkara (Bh.G.Bh. 3.18) inserts: 'You [Arjuna] are not established in this perfect realization'. In other words, the interpretation he gives of Kṛṣṇa's advice is something like: 'If you, Arjuna, were established in the Self, then renunciation would indeed be the most reasonable option open to you, but you are *not* so established. Therefore, go and fight'. That is, Śaṅkara wants to say that renunciation is for those who have already renounced *internally* and are tired of cyclic existence (Bh.G.Bh. 15, intro). Arjuna has not renounced in his heart; he is not trying to end cyclic existence. Nor has he seen through the delusion of his own agency. This interpretation seems consistent with the *Gītā* (18.59), where Kṛṣṇa accuses Arjuna of acting out of egoism (*ahaṃkāra*). That is, 'Arjuna measures the legitimacy of action according to what it means to him' (Malinar 2007: 72).

As noted earlier, Śaṅkara links *ahaṃkāra* to basic ignorance (Bh.G.Bh. 7.4). As such, one with *ahaṃkāra* could not be established in *brahman*. Śaṅkara had already hinted at such a conclusion in an earlier verse:

> [By his statement] 'Therefore,[14] undertake action', [the Lord] will show how Arjuna is to be excluded from steadfastness in knowledge (Bh.G.Bh. 3, intro).

And again:

> Before one has acquired eligibility for steadfastness in the knowledge of the Self, it is the duty of one who does not know the Self, to undertake *karma-yoga* for that purpose (Bh.G.Bh.3.16).

In other words, Śaṅkara seems to be saying that Arjuna would need to be enlightened *before* he could externally renounce. In fact, he later states that an unenlightened person is incapable of totally renouncing (Bh.G.Bh. 18.48). This agrees with the thesis that '*Jñāna* … goes hand in hand with *Saṁnyāsa*' (Tiwari 1977: 10), and disagrees with the thesis that, 'For the ideal *kṣatriya*, the sacrifice of battle becomes a form of total renunciation' (Rosen 2002: 20). For Śaṅkara, worldly action is always going to involve nescience, and the only true renunciation is the total renunciation of caste-based *Dharma*. And for that, one needs to renounce one's sense of 'I'. Action is said to be something 'superimposed on the Self through ignorance' (Bh.G.Bh. 18.48), and so the call to duty is meant only for the 'ignorant' (18.66 and 3.25) and they should never relinquish it (18.48).

---

[14] Gambhīrānanda (trans., 1984: 131) rightly notes that this verse comes from the *Gītā* 4.15, but the logic of 'Therefore …' could equally apply to verse 3.19.

Thus, Śaṅkara does not demand renunciation for everyone, but is selective, and prefers that those who are less than ready for renouncing the world continue to act in accordance with their *Dharma*.

Now, while Arjuna may have been going through a genuine dilemma, he also appears to be wavering between the larger *Dharmic* concern and egoistic concerns (Bh.G. 18.59). In the *Bṛ.U.Bh*, Śaṅkara makes a number of concessions to the need for means other than knowledge (I.iv.7), and there speaks of the need to 'mature one's knowledge of the Self' (IV.iv.7). As knowledge of the Self must be continually re-established, outer renunciation is the most favourable lifestyle (III.v.1). Therefore, in Arjuna's case, one might expect Śaṅkara to recommend total renunciation.

However, there is something else going on in Śaṅkara's ethics. The renouncer in the *Bṛ.U.* is also a *Brahmin*, whereas Arjuna is a *Kṣatriya* (warrior prince).[15] Within the context of the *Gītā*'s ethics, it is therefore Arjuna's duty to fight (Bh.G. 2.31), even if that duty is faulty (18.48). In fact, it is part of his 'own nature' (*sva-bhāva*) to fight (18.43), and it is futile to resist your 'nature' (18.59). But the notion of a caste-defining *sva-bhāva* seems to be in conflict with Śaṅkara's non-dualism. In fact, Śaṅkara immediately follows his acceptance of the *Gītā*'s caste theory (Bh.G.Bh. 2.11) with the remark that there is no multiplicity of selves (Bh.G.Bh. 2.12).

Śaṅkara thus accepts the provisional ethics as presented herein, whist ultimately denying the multiplicity theory that underlies it.[16] But elsewhere, Śaṅkara claims that one's caste or one's species is a result of past *karma* (B.S.Bh. II.i.34), which is beginningless (II.i.35–6), and nothing to do with Īśvara and/or *ātman*. It is for this reason also that Śāntideva (and Buddhism in general), whilst denying the ultimacy of Gods and selves, can maintain a karmic discourse which includes caste notions.

We can summarise Śaṅkara's position as: 1) Arjuna is not established in *brahman*-consciousness; 2) Arjuna has not realized inner renunciation; 3) Arjuna is a warrior by caste; and 4) Arjuna must act as a warrior so long as he has failed to internally renounce his sense of 'I'.

Śaṅkara thus distinguishes two types of renunciation. First, there is the (*Gītā*'s) renunciation of the *karma-yogī*, which incorporates 'dedication to the Lord without hope of results [for oneself]' (Bh.G.Bh. 5.6). For Śaṅkara, this is renunciation in a 'secondary' (*guṇavṛtti*) or 'figurative' (*gauṇa*) sense (Bh.G.Bh. 6.1). Then, there is the 'ultimate renunciation' for those 'steadfast in the knowledge of the Supreme Self' (Bh.G.Bh. 5.6). According to Śaṅkara, Arjuna is qualified for the former, but not for the latter.

The extension of this is that: 1) traditional ethics have their place for those who have not realized *brahman* as self; 2) the *varṇa* system supports such provisional ethics; and 3) this system cannot be violated by any individual unless that so-called individual has realized that he has no ultimate individuality.

---

[15] Both the Buddha and Śāntideva were of this class.

[16] The Viśiṣṭādvaitin, Rāmānuja and the Dvaitin, Madhva both deny that the individuated *jīva* is one with *paramātman*; both seeing them as distinct real ontological entities (Chari 2005: xxii).

And we can further judge that such an individual would be quite exceptional. This is the gist of Śaṅkara's insistence on provisional ethics. In the *Bṛ.U.Bh*, he writes:

> Nor do we deny the validity, for those without discriminating knowledge, of actions with their factors and results while the relative world of name and form exists (III.v.1).

Again, in his *B.S.Bh*:

> For worldly behaviour, conforming as it does to all right means of valid knowledge, can only be denied when a different eternal order of reality is attained, such an exception aside, tradition should prevail (II.ii.31).

Individual doubt about self and ethical conduct is thus to be resolved through the denial of one's individuality and the realization of a higher truth. In one interpretation of the *Gītā*, this amounts to selflessly acting for the sake of God, becoming his 'instrument'. Where Olivelle (1992: 42) sees the Upaniṣads as considering individuals as 'complete in themselves', in the *Gītā*, these so-called individuals are given a mere role in this new socio-cosmic theology. Their completeness ultimately lies in their true nature as *ātman*, but conventionally speaking, their completeness lies in their fulfilment of their duty to the Lord. That is, 'Kṛṣṇa proposes to eliminate the phenomenal person by making … his goal impersonal' (Kuznetsova 2007: 111). Arjuna is merely granted a 'brief indulgence in individualism' (Olivelle, in Rosen 2002: 115) before returning to his warrior nature.

In Śaṅkara's interpretation, the *Gītā* is consistent with the Upaniṣads in calling for the person to see the delusion of individuality and hence renounce society. In this sense, we might say that one 'still has a fair amount of free will' (Theodor 2010: 11). Yet, those who do not see through this delusion are provisionally advised to continue to act as if they were an agent within a *Dharmic* social structure. They are in fact compelled to act. For Śaṅkara, this is how it ought to be. That is, Śaṅkara wanted the 'vedic presumptions of varṇa and āśrama to be the foundation of lay life' (Tambiah, in Madan 1988: 318). Ultimately speaking, Kṛṣṇa is the personification of *brahman*, announcing his awareness of his own non-dual consciousness, and as such, for Śaṅkara, he is the great teacher of Advaita metaphysics. Provisionally, Kṛṣṇa stands as a personal God, to whom one devotes one's actions, thus rendering them dependent on his Being. At this provisional level, Śaṅkara might accept that Kṛṣṇa is involved in a relationship with embodied selves. This exclusive devotion is thought to weaken one's attachment to selfish concerns. It is an act of purification. However, for Śaṅkara, such devotion could only serve as a step towards seeing the non-dual nature of *brahman*-consciousness and realizing that worldly action is merely instrumental:

> Impurities are removed by dutiful actions, while knowledge is the supreme movement. When actions have burnt up impurities, knowledge emerges (B.S.Bh. III.iv.26).

Provisional reality is therefore a necessary 'playing ground' for the vast majority of beings and ideally acts as a stepping stone to the realization of the ultimate. Within this provisional reality, Śaṅkara simply assumes the validity of the Hindu *varṇa* system. Although such social categories have no meaning in ultimate terms, Arjuna is unquestionably treated as a *Kṣatriya*. Beyond the gnoseological response he gives in the *Gītā*, Śaṅkara is unwilling to allow for a non-*Brahmin* to (externally) renounce, for only the male *Brahmin* is to be released from duty. This is clearly stated in the *Bṛ.U.Bh* (IV.v.15) where both warriors and merchants are excluded from the path of the wandering mendicant. Thus, being a *Kṣatriya*, 'Arjuna is not qualified for steadfastness in Knowledge through monasticism in the primary sense' (Gambhīrānanda 1984: 739).

Again, in his non-commentarial work, Śaṅkara's exclusions are made clear, where the pupil is defined as a pure *Brahmin*. Śaṅkara writes:

> The means to liberation is knowledge. It should be repeatedly explained to the pupil until firmly grasped, to one who is indifferent to everything transitory, achievable through means, and who has no desire for sons, wealth, this world or the next, who has adopted the way of the highest ascetics, who is endowed with tranquillity, self-control, compassion, etc., possessed of the qualities of a pupil, well-known from the scriptures, if he is a pure *Brahmin*, who approaches the teacher in the prescribed manner, and if his birth, deeds, conduct, knowledge and family have been examined (U.S. Prose, 1.2).

There is a clear social tension here. For Śaṅkara, the *Brahmin* male is unique in his (albeit temporary) claim to individuality, and thus only he may follow his own will in renouncing worldly activities which include so-called ritual and reproductive duties. And it is this decision to renounce duty (with non-individuality in mind) that Śaṅkara denies Arjuna. It does not, however, follow from this that Śaṅkara has 'restricted enlightenment and even the aspiration to enlightenment to Brahmins', as Olivelle (1993: 197) claims. For, as we have seen in the case of Arjuna, one can still remain on the path of *karma-yoga*, with the intention of 'purifying the mind' and 'acquiring knowledge'; only later, 'renouncing all ritual action', and aspiring towards 'steadfastness in knowledge' (Bh.G.Bh. 5.12).[17]

Even where Śaṅkara claims that 'knowledge of the Self' is 'exclusively the cause of the highest good', and that 'steadfastness in knowledge combined with [ritual] action is illogical' (Bh.G.Bh. 18.66); he goes on to say that the Vedic injunctions have relative validity in that they 'create the tendency of movement towards the indwelling Self' (ibid.). That is, 'Actions and attitudes contribute in

---

[17] This is confirmed in the *V.C.* (11).

changing the quality of the subject's epistemic grasp' (Ram-Prasad 2007: 114). Hence, Śaṅkara shows himself to be one of those renouncers who 'does not deny the religion of the man-in-the-world' (Dumont 1980: 275). The worst we can say of Śaṅkara, then, is that he 'presupposes a certain state of purification as a prerequisite' (Taber 1983: 55) for receiving and achieving *brahman*-knowledge. Whether this can be achieved in this life is an open question, but it is certainly open to future incarnations.

In what way, then, does Śaṅkara deviate from tradition-based ethics? Action, for Śaṅkara, is not only secondary to knowledge, but can get in its way. He therefore reads Kṛṣṇa's call to 'Abandon all duties' as a call to total renunciation of all actions (Bh.G.Bh. 18.66). And for sure, if there is one verse in the *Gītā* that favours such a renunciatory interpretation, it is this one, even though it would 'negate the entire preceding teaching' (Kuznetsova 2007: 146). In the *Upadeśa Sāhasrī*, this renunciation of all ritual actions (*karma sādhana*) is a sign of a *brahma-vid* (Prose, 1.6). For Śaṅkara, a renouncer is only a renouncer if he focuses all his attention on knowing *brahman*, if he renounces all sense of doership; that is, if he is the highest form of renouncer, the so-called *parama-haṃsa*. And, according to Śaṅkara, it is only the *parama-haṃsa* who can achieve knowledge of *brahman* (Ch.U.Bh. VIII.xii.1).

Renunciation, then, is not an end in itself. It is not simply renunciation *from*, but renunciation *to*, that matters. Renunciation, for Arjuna, would simply have been a way of refusing to deal with the situation, and Śaṅkara would no doubt agree with Olivelle (1992: 79) that a 'renouncer who does not pursue knowledge is a false renouncer'. This is confirmed by Deutsch, who interprets Śaṅkara's fourth pre-requisite for the search of *brahman* (B.S.Bh. I.i.1), that of '*mumukṣutva*', as a 'positive longing for freedom and wisdom' (Deutsch 1973 105).[18] It thus seems reasonable to believe that Śaṅkara senses that Arjuna did not have the pursuit of knowledge as his motivation for renunciation.

Needless to say, Śaṅkara's principal aim is not to exclude Arjuna from qualification, but to send a louder message, that only *total* renunciation of this life is sufficient for true liberation. Gambhīrānanda (1984: 739), as a modern Advaitin, thus interprets the *Gītā* verse 18.66 as generally advocating monasticism, even though Arjuna would himself be excluded by his caste. In other words, the *Gītā*'s words are not necessarily meant for Arjuna's ears.[19] But this relies on a translation of '*saṃnyāsena*' as 'through monasticism', the validity of which is questionable. Again, the sectarian conflict that Gambhīrānanda faces could be overcome by simply allowing the sense of renunciation to have inner meaning. Thus, Arjuna is indeed qualified to renounce all his past notions of duty, giving them up for a new form of non-attached action, grounded in steadfast devotion to Kṛṣṇa. And as Kṛṣṇa

[18] The four prerequisites are: 1) discrimination between the eternal and the non-eternal; 2) dispassion for the enjoyment of fruits [of work]; 3) control of the mind; and 4) a longing for liberation.

[19] This follows the interpretation of Ānandagiri. For a debate between Śaṅkara's commentators, Madhusūdana and Ānandagiri, on this issue, see Marcaurelle (2000: 198–202).

warns, only one so devoted to him can so renounce his past duties (Bh.G. 18.67). This is how Madhusūdana (16th-century Advaitin) interprets the *Gītā*; hence, overtly disagreeing with Śaṅkara (see Marcaurelle 2000: 199).

There is one further factor we need to consider. Why is it that Śaṅkara, in his non-commentarial work, allows for a student (*brahmacārin*) to be taught the truth of *brahman* (U.S. Prose, 2.45), even though he is not a *parama-haṃsa*? My contention is, if we focus on the ideal type, rather than on renunciation, we will see that this student is in fact a male, *Brahmin*, celibate, intent on *brahman*-knowledge. He is already one sick of transmigratory existence. Compare:

> Realizing that there is not the least trace of happiness in cyclic existence, one should withdraw the organs from the objects which are comparable to a mirage (Bh.G.Bh. 5.22).

It is this total renunciation of worldly existence that Śaṅkara admires. Thus, in allowing room for such a student in his non-commentarial work, Śaṅkara is not showing the same 'liberality' as the Upaniṣads (Marcaurelle 2000: 37; Cenkner 1983: 49), but is simply admitting that renunciation may be an inner state rather than an outer one.[20] A celibate student with the sole desire for becoming *brahman* need not necessarily pass through the ritual of abandoning the way of action. He already has renunciation in his heart, especially if he is the 'constant' type of celibate student, living in the teacher's house for his whole life, that Śaṅkara champions (Ch.U.Bh. II.xxiii.1). Elsewhere, Śaṅkara states that knowledge can be acquired by one who has been under the vow of *brahmacarya* for a year (P.U.Bh., intro), and later highlights that celibacy is an especially important factor (1.2). Competent men are thus listed as celibates, forest-dwellers and monks (1.16).

In contrast to such competent men, Arjuna possesses neither this inner state nor the ideal outer state of being a celibate *Brahmin*. To borrow Marcaurelle's (2000: 91) terms, he fails both from the 'end perspective' and the 'start perspective'. Without this inner renunciation of the self, actions, even those undertaken after formal renunciation, would still have consequences. A person does not avoid incurring *karma* by (merely) abstaining from action (Bh.G. 3.4). One should therefore never become attached to either results of action or to inaction (2.47). But action is certainly superior to inaction (3.8a). In any case, it is a physical impossibility *not* to act, for even basic bodily sustenance requires action (3.8b). For Kṛṣṇa, what is called for is a devotional response to action in which the self is handed over to

[20] If Upaniṣadic 'liberality' implies 'egalitarianism', then we need to read this against Brian Black's (2008: 27) assessment that the 'Upanishadic self is largely restricted to Brahmins'. As for the illegitimacy of reading modern concerns back into Śaṅkara, Suthren Hirst (2005: 44) rightly states that to 'foist feminist and egalitarian concerns upon him would be to misconstrue his social context'. For a critique of the inclusivist and egalitarian claims of Neo-Vedānta, see Halbfass (1983: 85–94) and Fort (1998: 172–85).

Kṛṣṇa (3.30) or *brahman* (5.10).[21] This kind of action is 'obligatory action' (*niyataṃ karma*) combining the two traditional paths (3.3 and 3.7) of action (*karma-yoga*) and knowledge (*jñāna-yoga*). Outer renunciation is ruled out as hypocritical (3.6), whilst action is sanctioned in that it originates from *brahman* (3.15). Actions maintain the world (3.20), and the best action, even if done badly, is the one that follows your own inherent duty (*sva-dharma*) (3.35), determined by your class (*varṇa*) (18.41–8), which Kṛṣṇa himself created (4.13).

For Śaṅkara, 'true renunciation' is accompanied by enlightenment. More specifically, with world transcendence as its goal, true renunciation implies an ultimate understanding of self as *brahman*. As such, without the doer, caste-based duty is unnecessary, and there is the knowledge that there is no *jīva* to hand over. Outer renunciation and inner renunciation are inter-linked. Kṛṣṇa, in rejecting the Brahmanical way of the renouncer, opens the door to devotion (*bhakti*). In denying the ultimacy of *jīva*, Śaṅkara makes *bhakti* a provisional mode of operation for those unestablished in the Self.[22] The *V.C.* went on to give *bhakti* an Advaitin gloss, by claiming that 'The seeking after one's own true nature is what is meant by devotion' (31). But Śaṅkara seems to accept the *bhakti* of the *Gītā* as a stepping-stone to dropping the false sense of 'I'. As such, neither Śaṅkara nor later Advaita were ever in true conflict with India's most influential ethical text.

What we have shown, by analysing his response to the *Gītā*, is that, despite all his talk of ultimate truth, Śaṅkara still falls back on the concept of class, of duty, of *Dharma*. Even so, he never willingly embraces this new type of 'renouncer' that Kṛṣṇa so glorifies. Whilst the *Gītā* claims that the devotee 'attains the highest' through unattached action (Bh.G. 3.19), Śaṅkara maintains that 'Knowledge of the Self' is 'exclusively the cause of the highest good' (Bh.G.Bh. 18.66), the Advaitin view he holds in his Upaniṣadic commentaries (for example T.U.Bh. II.i.1 and II.viii.5).

Nevertheless, the partial alignment of Advaita with the ethics of the *Gītā* has continued right up until the modern age, with Śaṅkarācārya Jayendra (b. 1935) stating that a Śaṅkarācārya must care for the 'welfare of the world', whilst a 'mere' *jīvan-mukta*, like Ramana Maharshi (1879–1950), need not (Fort 1998: 167). According to Fort (ibid.), Śaṅkarācārya Bharati Tirtha (b. 1951) specifically relates his ethical outlook with the *Gītā*, especially where Kṛṣṇa states that though he has no need for action he still acts for the benefit of the world (Bh.G. 3.22–4). My argument is that Śaṅkara exclusively offers the *brahman*-knower as a teacher, which is of course the origin of the title, Śaṅkarācārya.

While it is true that Śaṅkara argues that 'injunctions of *dharma* have no force' on the *saṃnyāsin* (Perrett 1998: 57) and that he is 'beyond the life-stages' (Ch.U.Bh. II.xxiii.1), it is not so obvious, when it comes to the need for a teacher, whether '*mokṣa* precludes action, and hence *dharma*', as Perrett (1998: 56) believes. In

---

21 Kṛṣṇa goes on to explain that He is *brahman*.

22 For the Viśiṣṭādvaitin, Rāmānuja, *bhakti-yoga* is the main theme of the *Gītā* (Chari 2005: xx).

my opinion, the passing on of knowledge might well be seen as acting within the framework of *Dharma*. Thus Olivelle's (1986: 18) assertion that a *jīvan-mukta* is 'beyond *dharma*' may also need re-assessing. I would argue that Śaṅkara, though little concerned with 'universal responsibility', was most concerned with the continuation of the lineage of *brahman*-knowers. As with the Buddha, this passing on of salvific knowledge became his *sva-dharma*:

> For when knowledge is firmly grasped it is conducive to one's own welfare and to continuity. And the continuity of knowledge is helpful to beings, like a boat to one wishing to cross a river (U.S. Prose, 1.3).

As such, just as the Buddhist monk need not become socially isolated, so Śaṅkara was no isolationist. Nevertheless, Śaṅkara's mission, like the Buddha's, was soteriological rather than social. He therefore asks that his lineage and teaching mission be continued by a certain type of person. This is in line with the Upaniṣads, where the teachings ought only to be given to the eldest son or to a 'worthy disciple' (C.U. III.xi.5). Brian Black (2008: 53) has noticed that in the early Upaniṣads, the 'lineages from teacher to student became as important as family pedigrees'. Thus, we might need to qualify Olson's (1997: 65) assertion that the renouncer is 'unconcerned with social lineage', for it is the renouncer-cum-teacher who verily 'sustains and transmits lineage' (Cenkner 1983: 37–8). But if this is so, might we not question why Cenkner also claims that Śaṅkara has 'renounced normal society' (p38). The thing is, the student comes to the teacher from that 'normal society' and the teacher is therefore obliged to be involved in social correctness. For, according to Śaṅkara (U.S. Prose, 1.2), among the things that a teacher must check before giving the teachings to a potential pupil are his birth, his profession and his family. The student is also assumed to come to the teacher with a keen sense of caste and lineage (1.16). This does not sound like someone who is oblivious to social norms. Śaṅkara is well aware of Indian social norms. His additional move then is to shift the teaching away from hereditary concerns, thus making way for a lineage, not just of Advaitin teachers, but of *celibate* Advaitin teachers. We might note then that in the *V.C.* the guru tells the pupil that he has revealed the secret of *brahman* to him 'as to one's own son' (575). The Advaitin teacher essentially usurps the seeker's real father, and may also rightly be called 'father' (*pitā*). This is so, because 'through knowledge, he produces a [new] birth in *brahman*' (P.U.Bh. 6.8).

Having given up the false sense of individuality, the teacher, in passing on his knowledge to a worthy pupil, truly acts selflessly. This specific form of altruistic action does not go against Śaṅkara's claim that action does not lead to liberation, for here the liberation in question is not the teacher's and the action involved is both an ethically selfless *and* metaphysically self-less one. Proceeding, as it does, from a self-less person, it is therefore a *non*-activity. As Śaṅkara states:

> Ultimately speaking, actions done by a man of knowledge are in fact non-actions, since he is endowed with the realization of the actionless Self (Bh.G.Bh. 4.20).

Thus, Śaṅkara need not be taken as contradicting his own thesis that 'steadfastness in knowledge combined with [ritual] action is illogical' (18.66). However, we can question Śaṅkara's insistence that 'the renouncer acts merely for survival purposes' (4.19), for this takes no account of his other-regarding activities, a necessary facet of the teacher's life. Thus, Mādhavānanda (trans. 2003: 167) notes two external activities of the *brahman*-knower: 'satisfying the physical needs' and 'teaching enquirers'. Majithia (2007: 245) thus predicts that Śaṅkara would not have denied that a *brahman*-knower 'lives, breathes, eats, and even helps others attain enlightenment'. It is my contention that the latter of these activities is a case of what I call 'constructive altruism'.

Despite claiming that the renouncer 'does not engage in actions' (Bh.G.Bh. 4.19), Śaṅkara, like Śāntideva, could not avoid the notion of a paternal pedagogue, acting solely for the benefit of others. Thus, he follows his claim to inactivity with this admission:

> But if, for some reason, it becomes impossible to abandon action, and he, for the sake of preventing people from going astray, and without attachment to the results due to the absence of any personal desire, were to engage in actions as he did before [realization], he surely does nothing at all. His actions are 'non-actions' because of his [past] *karma* having been burnt up by the fire of wisdom (B.G.Bh. 4.19).

To give people spiritual guidance and thus help 'prevent people from going astray' is Śaṅkara's way of upholding Kṛṣṇa's *Dharma*. Thus, Cenkner (1983: 72) is wrong to claim that, 'Altruistic and selfless activity is merely a prerequisite for knowledge'. In fact, I would say that, for Śaṅkara, altruistic and selfless activity only truly starts when one has the supreme knowledge. For, while knowledge may 'destroy the notion of doership' (U.S. Metric, 1.14), it does not and cannot prevent the doing. It is simply that this doing is done by one who has *completely* seen through the delusion of self-agency. In this sense, knowledge does indeed affect action. Yet, this action of the *brahma-vid* is hardly done to contribute to the maintenance of cosmic order. Rather, it is aimed at the liberation from that very cosmos.

This selfless person of Śaṅkara's is more than just 'one who sees inaction in action, and action in inaction' (Bh.G. 4.18a), he is a type unto himself. He is a type drawn by equating the *Gītā*'s *sthita-prajña* (man of steady wisdom) with a *saṃnyāsin* (Bh.G.Bh. 2.55–6), and the *saṃnyāsin* with the *brahma-vid* (2.59), and the *brahma-vid* with the *jīvan-mukta* (5.24 and 6.27; B.S.Bh. I.i.4). He is thus one who has attained 'identification with *brahman*' in the autumn years of this very life (Bh.G.Bh. 2.72). This *brahma-vid* is a pure *Brahmin* male, a celibate, *parama-haṃsa* ascetic (U.S. Prose, 1.2), and 'with the sole aim of helping others, he wishes to make use of knowledge' (1.6). Yet, like the *bodhisattva* (BCA. 1.35), he does all of this effortlessly, 'without attachment to the results' (Bh.G.Bh. 4.19). By passing on the knowledge of *brahman* to others, and by reconstructing their selfhood for soteriological purposes, his actions may rightly be called 'constructive altruism'. Nevertheless, his vision is transcendental rather than social, his sole objective, to bring his disciples to the vision of *brahman*.

Case 2: Śāntideva

Both Śaṅkara and Śāntideva see themselves as monks. Both come from traditions where renunciation was seen as a viable option. In fact, Buddhism began as the renunciatory religion *par excellence*. Nevertheless, by the 8th century, the Mahāyāna's stress on the validity of lay practice would clearly be imposing itself on the tradition. Celibacy would no longer express the 'totality' of the monk's life. Yet, Harvey (2000: 92) has noted that 'while the *Bodhisattva*-path gives an increased scope for lay practice, the monastic life is still highly regarded', citing Śāntideva in his defence. But the argument should not be seen as simply one between monks and laity. In response to Lamotte's theory that the Mahāyāna arose amongst the laity, Paul Williams (2009: 26) has argued that 'Doctrinal innovation in Indian Buddhism was almost entirely the concern of monks'. He also argues that, in India, most religious change was initiated by *Brahmins* and renouncers (p24).

Unlike Śaṅkara (and Nāgārjuna), Śāntideva was not a *Brahmin*, but he *was* a renouncer. Yet he was a renouncer who had taken a vow to benefit all beings, and most beings, humans anyway, were not to be found in the forest. Now, we have already commented that Śāntideva did not write the *Compendium* in a forest, and have qualified Dayal's (1970) claim about the later Mahāyāna reverting to the old ideal of celibacy and forest-life. Nevertheless, Śāntideva can at times appear quite radical in his asceticism, which includes not only chastity, but vegetarianism (Ś.S. 131–4). He tells us that one must give up the society of householders and make one's home in the forest (Ś.S. 46 and 106–7). What we need to do now then is to see how Śāntideva, the renouncer, deals with the question of lay ethics. We need to see how he reacts to the Mahāyāna ideal of maintaining close contact with the masses.

Let us begin with the (2nd century) *Vimalakīrti-Nirdeśa Sūtra*, which Sponberg described as a 'proto-Madhyamaka' text (in Keown and Prebish 2007: 802). This 'early' Mahāyāna *sūtra* prides itself on its radical break with Śrāvaka Buddhism, and is severely critical of monasticism. The hero is provocatively portrayed as a lay practitioner (*upāsaka*) who practices his skilful-means (*upāya-kauśalya*) in bars and brothels. Surprisingly, Śāntideva does not shy away from the *Vimala*, acknowledging that male *bodhisattvas* 'practice enjoyment among the sexual' (Ś.S. 325) and female *bodhisattvas* 'become a courtesan to draw men' (326). The theory that sex may be used as a skilful means to benefit others is also found in his discussion of the *Upāyakauśalya* (Skill in Means) *Sūtra* (Ś.S. 167), where a seventh-stage *bodhisattva*, the youthful Jyotis, (compassionately) allows a woman to ravish him after 42,000 years of celibacy! So Śāntideva appears willing to condone such activities and to accept the authority of such *sūtras* even though he equally stresses the monastic life. It seems that he would agree with Siderits (in Bilimoria et al. 2007: 294) that the wisdom of the likes of Vimalakīrti makes 'rules of thumb unnecessary'. But it is plainly the case that such teachings are not for everyone. And here we need also pay attention to Clayton's (2006: 104) twist on virtue ethics, whereby she states that it is the 'character of the virtuous person that generates the norm'. This would amount to the claim that it is because Vimalakīrti *is* Vimalakīrti that he can do as he pleases.

Nevertheless, we should not conclude from this that desire (*rāga*) is spoken of as a 'virtue' by Śāntideva, as Keown (2001: 226) claims. In fact, Śāntideva takes *rāga* to be a transgression (*āpatti*), just a lesser one than hatred (*dveṣa*) (Ś.S. 164). That being said, ethical ambiguities do abound in the *Compendium*. For example, while acknowledging the higher ethics of householders like Vimalakīrti, it also states that the *bodhisattva*'s objective is to release the whole world from the 'bonds and cravings of the household life' (Ś.S. 330). Such an exemplary one is described as desireless (*niṣkama*) and a follower of the 'ten ways of [right] conduct' (*daśa carya*). It is uncertain whether this refers to the ten novice vows (*daśa śīlāni*) or the ten wholesome actions (*daśa kuśalāḥ karmapathāḥ*). To my knowledge, he only mentions the former once, referring to them as '*daśa śikṣāpadāni*' (Ś.S. 174) and comparing followers of these to those who follow either the five precepts (*pañca śikṣāpadāni*) or the 400 *bodhisattva* precepts (*bodhisattva saṃvaraṃ caturvaraśikṣāpadaśata*). In contrast, references to the *daśa kuśalāḥ karmapathāḥ* are found throughout the *Compendium*. Now while he states elsewhere (Ś.S. 13) that following the ten wholesome actions leads to Buddhahood, he also describes the benefits of supporting lay disciples who follow this path (Ś.S. 87). So it is clear that one need not denounce the household life to follow this path. Whichever way we read '*daśa carya*', the *bodhisattva* contradicts it by manifesting as a dancer, a musician, a king, even a thief (Ś.S. 330–31). For example, theft is second in the list of both the novice vows[23] and the classic list of ten unwholesome actions.[24] And in fact, Śāntideva not only cites this latter list (Ś.S. 60, 170 and 173), he explains in explicit detail the dire consequences of each unwholesome act (69–75) as well as offering a worst case version of the list (171–2). Furthermore, enjoying music and dance goes against the seventh of the ten precepts of a novice monk. Not to mention that the *Compendium* advises the *bodhisattva* to shun all interaction with kings (47), with dancers (48), indeed with *all* householders (52). We are putting it mildly then, when we say that Śāntideva maintains an *ambiguous* position with regard to society and right conduct.

There are two hermeneutical strategies we could adopt to explain this phenomenon. Either he does not agree with all the scriptures he quotes in the

---

[23] The ten vows are to refrain from: 1) killing, 2) theft, 3) sexual misconduct, 4) lying, 5) intoxication, 6) eating after midday, 7) singing, dancing, playing music or attending entertainment programs, 8) wearing perfume, cosmetics and decorative accessories, 9) sitting on high chairs and sleeping on luxurious beds and 10) accepting money.

[24] The ten unwholesome actions are: 1) killing, 2) theft, 3) sexual misconduct, 4) lying, 5) slander, 6) harsh speech, 7) gossip, 8) covetousness, 9) malevolence and 10) wrong views (Ś.S. 69–75).

Compendium, or else he suits his ethics according to the relative level of the practitioner. Considering that we can also observe such opposing domains of discourse in his *BCA*, we can safely assume he is doing the latter.[25] So, on the one hand, we have the commencing-*bodhisattva* who requires an ascetic ethic and should live a solitary existence; on the other hand, we have an advanced *bodhisattva* who ought to use his skilful means to their fullest, mingling with all levels of society. It is due to the acceptance of such gradualism that Śāntideva condones the teaching that:

> Those *bodhisattvas* who lack skilful means are afraid of transgressing through desire, but those in possession of skilful means fear transgressing through hatred, not through desire (Ś.S. 164–5).

The '*sine qua non* of enlightenment', then, is not *rāga*, *per se* (see Keown 2001: 226), but non-fear of acting on it, or the ability to remain undisturbed by it. The lifestyle of the commencing-*bodhisattva* is summed up thus: 'He should keep to the domain of conduct of non-union and purity' (Ś.S. 47). This beautifully brings together both the Indian etymology of 'celibate' (*brahmacarya*), as relating to the student (*brahmacārin*), and the Western etymology, as relating to being alone (Lat. *caelebs*) (see Olson 2008: 5). The fact that this domain should not be kept up indefinitely is immediately confirmed in the *Compendium*, where a 'false' or 'evil' 'friend' is said to be one who tells the *bodhisattva* to work when he should be meditating and to meditate when he should be involved in action (Ś.S. 50). In order to indicate Śāntideva's ascetic views on the passions, Powers (in Olson 2008: 213) offers the following verses from the *BCA* (translation mine):

> No sword, no poison, no fire, no precipice, no enemies can compare with passions when one remembers the torments of hell, etc. Thus, one should recoil from the passions and generate delight in solitude, in tranquil forests, empty of strife and trouble (that is, BCA. 8.84–5).

However, this only gives half the story. It is in the *Compendium* where we find the other half, where we see just how influential the understanding of ultimate truth is to the ethics of the *bodhisattva*. It comes midway through Chapter 8 on the purification of misdeeds and follows a lengthy discussion of the ten unwholesome actions. Here, the ethical thesis suddenly takes a radical turn (Ś.S. 167ff). Śāntideva here tells us that advanced *bodhisattvas* 'may neglect the rules of conduct' if they should see greater advantage for beings. This gains an epistemological basis when he claims that 'misdeeds can be purified through a conviction of emptiness' (Ś.S. 171).

---

[25] Of course, this does not exclude the possibility that he does disagree with some sections of some of the scriptures he quotes. However, as a working premise, I have assumed that Śāntideva's two texts do in fact represent his ideals.

So while forest-life and seclusion are certainly praised (BCA. 8.85–8), one should not get too comfortable in this life-style. One should not become indifferent to learning, nor to compassionate activity (Ś.S. 50). Hence, Śāntideva's ethics are not simply gradualist; they also contain over-lapping realms of discourse. The *bodhisattva*'s vow to save all beings is there even at the ascetic stage. The non-self doctrine is there even at the stage of activity. In other words, the valid reasons to be active and the valid reasons to be passive are in constant tension.

But what then of the divisions and distinctions that all of these moves imply? How can they be maintained by a Mādhyamika who claims that all is empty? For example, the Pāli Abhidhamma speaks of two types of sexual material phenomena: the faculty of maleness and the faculty of femaleness (Vm. 14.58). Whilst it also claims that the terms 'man' and 'woman' are only conventionally valid (Bodhi 2006: 26), the Buddha is said to have established a four-fold assembly, made up of male and female monastics and a male and female laity. The *Vinaya* (monastic code) was drawn up under such an assumed categorization. This assumption of conventional categories is based on the further assumption of the aggregates of form and consciousness. Not only does Śāntideva follow traditional Buddhist metaphysics in denying ultimacy to the terms 'man' and 'woman', he also claims that all aggregates are unreal (*avastu*) (BCA. 9.96b). Men, women and aggregates are equal in being empty. As such, he appears to leave himself no basis whatsoever for the categories which the *Vinaya* takes as its starting point. I will deal with the issue of gender in Chapter 7.2. Here, I will focus on the issue of conventional ethics.

Śāntideva is well aware of the ethical problem posed by the denial of the aggregates. In the mouth of a Buddhist 'realist', Śāntideva poses himself the problem: 'If consciousness does not exist, there's no evil in killing an illusory-person' (BCA. 9.11a). If there are no aggregates, there is no consciousness. If there is no consciousness, then rebirth would be impossible. If rebirth is impossible, this form belongs to no one. And, anyway, if there are no aggregates, then form is also an illusion. Thus, killing this person would not be of any account. It would be like 'killing' a man created by a magician.[26]

In his Madhyamaka defence, Śāntideva turns the doubter's challenge around. For him, believing that you are a person, with your own consciousness, is the *cause* of 'morality' and 'immorality'. He thus replies: 'Rather, merit and demerit arise with the illusory consciousness' (9.11b). A similar quote from the *Compendium* may help here: 'Where there is mind, there is virtue and vice. Where mind is not, there is no virtue or vice' (Ś.S. 122). This would seem to put to death any notion that Mahāyāna Buddhism could be called a Virtue Ethics. However, it would also seem to imply a classic 'transcendency' thesis.

There is an inherent tension in this view. According to Śāntideva, those who amass merit (*puṇya*) are those possessed of knowledge (Ś.S. 4). Also, the *bodhisattva* needs a mass of merit in order to benefit all beings. He prays:

---

26 The likeness to the ethical problem of the *Bhagavad Gītā*, presented by Kapstein (2001: 41) as 'to slay a body is not to slay a person', should not go unnoticed.

> When, with this merit accumulated, will I respectfully teach this emptiness, through conventions, without projection, to those whose views are characterized by projection? (BCA. 9.167).

That is, the *bodhisattva* 'must try to eliminate factors of reification without destroying confidence in persons, karma, and so forth' (Newland 1999: 13). But if the *bodhisattva* is to gain merit without projection or reification, then he must do it with a non-deluded consciousness. But if this non-deluded consciousness is not *their* consciousness, then how does it accrue to *them*? Indeed, when faced with such a question (from a virtual Yogācārin), Śāntideva simply reverses the question. The question is this: 'When even false perception no longer exists, by what is illusion perceived?' (BCA. 9.15b). This question makes more sense when placed alongside a later verse, where we find Śāntideva debating with the Sāṃkhya School. Here he argues that consciousness is not a 'thing', but more like a moment:

> If the non-perception of something is 'consciousness', then it follows that a piece of wood is [equally] consciousness. This proves that there is no [independent] consciousness in the absence of something to be perceived (BCA. 9.61).

That is, on the Madhyamaka account, consciousness can only arise when there is something there to be conscious of. So the Yogācārin's question (above) can now be read as asking the Madhyamaka: when a *bodhisattva* no longer has a deluded consciousness, and if consciousness only arises in dependence on (illusory) objects, how does he perceive at all?

As we have already noted, Śāntideva will get around this issue by demanding an occasional *voluntary* entrance into a slightly delusional mode of consciousness, whilst denying the ultimacy of that consciousness. In other words, he demands that the *bodhisattva* flicker between domains, deliberately accepting the illusion to be real. Basically speaking, Śāntideva advises the *bodhisattva* to maintain a provisional view of the world which includes a provisional view of objects and *karma*. Hence, in this world, 'happiness and suffering are the result of action' (BCA. 9.122a). This is in line with classical Hindu and Buddhist ethics and resists the 'transcendency' thesis.

In context, the ethical compromise allows him to share common ground with the Hindu virtual debater. But the compromise stretches much further when a voluntary delusion is taken on, allowing him to remain in *saṃsāra*, and thus providing the basis for the continuation of a traditional ethics. For Śāntideva, in denying that external objects exist at all (BCA. 9.16), the Yogācāra leave no ground for ethics to take place (BCA. 9.28). Likewise, Śāntideva will be forced into admitting that if beings are ultimately non-existent, then there are in fact no players within the ethical sphere (BCA. 9.75). We should therefore take Clayton's (2006: 97) claim that the need for morality, for Śāntideva, is 'ultimately an illusion' in its total context, which, on my reading, includes the need for a voluntary delusion (BCA. 9.75–6). And, as already conceded, this delusion also opens the way to demerit (*pāpa*) and vice (*doṣa*). Thus, *karma* continues to be accumulated by the continuum (BCA. 9.72).

This means that the renunciation stage of the commencing-*bodhisattva* is paramount, a practice which sees morality (*śīla*) and meditation (*samādhi*) go hand in hand (Ś.S. 121), culminating in the view of emptiness. Hence, one should realize the emptiness of all existents, but 'without giving up the practical morality' of the *bodhisattva* (Ś.S. 117). Hence, the *bodhisattva* is in a position to choose when to act and when to remain aloof.

Now Goodman (2009: 89ff), as part of his consequentialist thesis, thus talks of Śāntideva's ethics as 'balancing' the pros and the cons of an action. But I am not convinced that 'choosing' requires 'balancing'. The only time I have noticed true balancing in the *Compendium* is when the question of whether to give to another *bodhisattva* is raised (Ś.S. 144), whereby the giver is 'supposed to measure the relative level of skilfulness of himself and the recipient, and their respective capacities to help others' (Clayton 2006: 144). A clearer explanation is given in the *BCA* on the question of bodily sacrifice:

> The body is the servant of the True *Dharma*. One should not harm it for an insignificant benefit. For it is the only means available for one to quickly fulfil the needs of sentient beings. Therefore, one should not sacrifice one's life for someone whose compassion is not as pure. But for someone whose compassion is comparable, one should relinquish it. That way, there is no loss (BCA. 5.86–7).

A commencing-*bodhisattva* then, according to Śāntideva's rule, *should not*, for example, give his body to save a starving animal (Ś.S. 51), despite apparent teachings to the contrary. So, in reading the following verse, we need to keep in mind that this is not for all *bodhisattvas*:

> Though acting in this way for the good of others, there is neither exhilaration nor pride. Even when giving oneself [to animals] as food, the desire for [karmic] reward does not arise (BCA. 8.116).

A commencing-*bodhisattva* will not have seen deeply enough into emptiness, having yet to reach the first *bhūmi*. They have yet to understand the dream-like quality of all phenomena. Nor have they developed the wisdom that fully understands the consequences of their actions. So the so-called 'frightening extremism of Buddhist ethics' (Goodman 2009: 52) may only find expression on very rare occasions. The gradualism of Mahāyāna ethics is perfectly brought out by Śāntideva:

> At the beginning [of the path] the guide encourages the giving away of vegetables and the like. Later on, by degrees, one is even able to give away one's flesh (BCA. 7.25).

Of course, in verses 5.86–7 (above), there is the implication that the commencing-*bodhisattva* may well give his life for another *bodhisattva* who happens to possess even greater compassion. It is thus problematic to take Śāntideva's ethics as being 'agent-neutral' or as a general ethics of 'balancing' (see Goodman 2009: 97–8). First, Śāntideva is explicitly against any act of balancing where he himself would bring harm to somebody else. He writes: 'May I never be the cause of harm to another' (BCA. 3.14b). One must assume that the personal tone of this verse is due to the fact that he never saw himself as someone who could do the kind of 'balancing' calculations necessary for pure act-consequentialism. Śāntideva tells us that the essential meaning (*piṇḍārtha*) of the *Compendium*, that which should 'always be kept in the heart-mind of the *bodhisattva*', is that one should not harm others (Ś.S. 127). This follows the admonition that a *bodhisattva* must not conduct himself 'like those who kill' (Ś.S. 125). Remember, even *bodhisattvas* of skilful-means still fear breaking the *Vinaya* code through acts which pertain to hatred (Ś.S. 164–5).

Second, verses *BCA*. 5.86–7 are quite the opposite of a universal ethics. A *bodhisattva* is a type apart, he is not 'merely one individual among many' (see Nagel below), but has a worth based on his relative compassion. This is confirmed by the statement that a *bodhisattva* 'can only be brought to ruin by the sin of defaming another *bodhisattva*' (Ś.S. 85). To borrow Gethin's (1998: 29) phrase regarding the Buddha, the *bodhisattva* is '*sui generis*'. Indeed, it is from the *bodhisattvas* that Buddhas arise (Ś.S. 86). Now, the notion that a *bodhisattva* may give his life for a more advanced *bodhisattva* may appear at first glance to be a virtue ethics, but even Clayton (2006: 109) admits that this logic, although based on the relative virtues of compassion, is in fact consequentialist. The logic seems to be that a *bodhisattva* with greater compassion can (and will) do greater good, and therefore has more 'right' to survive. This is certainly a form of 'weighing consequences' (Clayton 2006: 109), but they are consequences that only involve harm to one's own body, not to another. To repeat:

> If the suffering of many disappears through the suffering of one, then that suffering must definitely be made to arise by one with compassion for oneself and for others (BCA. 8.105).

On this altruistic account, the body is to be simultaneously protected *and* forsaken:

> Therefore, disregarding myself, I forsake this body for the benefit of the world. For this reason, though it has many faults, I endure it as an instrument of work (BCA. 8.184).

Yet one should never forget the explicit gradualism in Buddhist ethics, which means that there are few guidelines which apply to all subjects. So this ethical discourse should not be allowed to spill over into domains which do not involve other *bodhisattvas*. Hence, if Buddhism ever truly 'universalized' *karma* (Gombrich

2009: 44), the *bodhisattva*-ideal reversed it to a form of agent-dependency. And this, despite the fact that they claim the agent has no ultimate existence.

Interestingly, apart from the actions of a *bodhisattva*, Śāntideva has very little to say about conventional ethics. This is surprising given that he offers his *Compendium* (Ś.S. 1) to all those of 'like elements' (*sama dhātu*). Despite this apparent universality, his focus is almost exclusively on either: 1) the compassionate activity of the *bodhisattva*, or 2) the renunciation stage as a necessary means to such activity. Thus, Paul Williams' 'like-minded friends' (in Crosby and Skilton 1995: xxvi) gives a more accurate characterization of his target audience. His main contribution to lay ethics comes under the umbrella of faith (*śraddhā*). He thus makes the overtly religious claim that 'In a faithless man, pure conduct does not arise' (Ś.S. 5). This is even less inclusive than it sounds, for he also makes the more controversial claim that one without devotion specifically to the Buddha is of 'evil mind' (Ś.S. 54). It would seem then, that for Śāntideva, one who does not follow Buddhist conduct is simply immoral by default. A discussion of non-Buddhist ethics is therefore futile.

Buddhist monastic ethics receive rather more coverage. It should be noted then that the *Vinaya* should not be disregarded by a *bodhisattva* just because he is following the Mahāyāna (Ś.S. 61 and 67). Most of the discussion on monastic ethics surrounds what we might call etiquette, especially that of alms-collection (Ś.S. 127–35). This includes the condemnation of meat-eating (131–5), a *Mahāyāna* innovation which Śāntideva traces back to the (4th century?) *Laṅkāvatāra Sūtra* (Ś.S. 131).[27] This is followed by a discussion of the correct use of medicine, robes, accommodation and protective charms (134–43). Elsewhere, there is also a special section on the conduct code of the so-called 'serving monk' who acts as a kind of errand-boy and door-keeper for other monks, as well as dealing with the *saṅgha*'s finances (Ś.S. 55–6). The frightening consequences of their misdeeds are listed herein (56–9).

Of course, monastic servants were 'taken for granted' even in the Buddha's time (Gombrich 1988: 102), and in Sri Lanka, 'monastic slaves' were bought with donations specific to that cause (p162). This seems to argue against Thapar's (in Madan 1988: 279) notion of a monastery as an 'egalitarian sanctuary'. Overall, there is enough evidence in Buddhist institutions to show that Gombrich's (2009: 15) suggestion that the 'only true criterion of ranking people is moral' is simply false. For one thing, Buddhism has clearly never valued nuns as highly as monks. And as Dharmasiri (1989: 66) notes, 'the Buddha never thought of the possibility of a classless society' and a 'class structure' was always evident in the monastery. And, of course, legal slavery was found in Aśoka's India and even in pre-20th-century Thailand (Harvey 2000: 188–9). And needless to say, Buddhist monasticism has always survived on the back of lay donations and the theory that merit is thus gained. Maybe this is one area where Buddhism and Aristotle truly

[27] Vegetarianism can also be found in the *Mahābhārata* (see Chapple, in Rosen 2002: 149ff), which Chapple puts down to possible 'Jaina influence' (p159).

meet. As Stalley put it, 'not everyone' can achieve the 'good life', and the 'rest of us are best off serving those who can' (in Aristotle 2009: xiv). I will return to this question of so-called Buddhist egalitarianism in Chapter 7.

Returning to the *Compendium*, following a short discussion of faith, Śāntideva moves on to discuss the importance of *bodhicitta* (the thought of enlightenment) and the will to liberate all beings (Ś.S. 5). This is the crux of his ethics. In the *BCA* (1.15) he divides *bodhicitta* into 'aspiring' and 'proceeding', the former being a form of resolve towards enlightenment, the latter being actual engagement. In the *Compendium*, Śāntideva describes the first in terms of an inner pledge, 'I must become a Buddha' (Ś.S. 8). In the *BCA*, he compares the difference between the two stages with the difference between thinking 'I really should go to x' and *actually* going (BCA. 1.16).

In the *Compendium* (Ś.S. 103), he gives a list of four stages of *bodhisattva* development: 1) the thought of enlightenment (*bodhicitta*), 2) compassion (*kṛpā*), 3) an immovable (*acala*) resolve, which seems to point to one who has reached the eighth *bhūmi*, and 4) enlightenment (*buddhi*). The ideal *bodhisattva* is then described as being 'intent on the liberation of the whole world' (Ś.S. 104). We will analyse the enlightened activity of such a *bodhisattva* in Chapter 6.1. But let us turn now to the ethics of the commencing-*bodhisattva*, starting with renunciation.

As with Śaṅkara, we may divide renunciation here into inner and outer. According to Śāntideva, 'No mendicant is truly a follower of the Buddha's religion who has not given up on existence' (Ś.S. 8). This is his inner renunciation. As for outer renunciation, Chapter 8 of the *BCA* describes how the *bodhisattva* leaves for the forest in order to meditate on the insubstantiality of self and things. This includes the renunciation of thoughts: 'With body and mind aware, distractions do not arise. Thus, having renounced this world, one should avoid conjecture' (BCA. 8.2).

He goes on to deny society, his longing for a wife, his will to status and power, confronting and hopefully 'dissolving' the *karma* that got him where he is. To aid him in his renunciation, he mocks society, mocks the value of family and relationships, mocks the notion of beauty and basically derides people in general. This seems a far cry from the other-regarding ethics of a *bodhisattva*, and must therefore be treated as a means rather than an end. It is a mental exercise undertaken in solitude, and should not be projected onto actual people. In fact, Śāntideva asks the monk to be civil to those he happens to meet. His ambivalent attitude is perfectly portrayed in the following verse: 'One should steer clear of the immature. On meeting, one should be pleasant, not intimate. Be kind but indifferent' (BCA. 8.15).

I will try to demonstrate how this ethical oddity functions in Chapter 6.1. For now, let us continue on our road to renunciation. With the aid of meditation, the renouncer denies the objective world. We might say that he enters into a mind-only world. As such, he sits very close to the Yogācārin, whom Śāntideva would normally see as a metaphysical opponent. His temporary aim is to develop what we might (following Hume) call 'monkish virtues'; that is: solitude, detachment, self-denial, self-chastisement, humility and celibacy. Like Śaṅkara, Śāntideva strictly imposes celibacy on his audience, with *BCA* verses 8.5–8 most likely being aimed at monks who have not come to terms with celibacy. His focus here is on one of the three marks of Early Buddhism, the impermanence of worldly objects and relationships:

> How can an impermanent being have attachment for impermanent beings, when a loved one may not be seen again for one thousand lives? Not seeing [them] one becomes disturbed and cannot remain in meditation. And even on seeing them one is not satisfied. As before, one is afflicted with longing. One does not see reality as-it-is. One loses drive. One is consumed by grief, longing for contact with one's beloved. While uselessly preoccupied with these people, life gets shorter by the minute. For the sake of a transient companion, the ever-lasting *Dharma* is lost (BCA. 8.5–8).

Virtues like detachment and chastity, however, are mere preliminaries; they are means to the renunciation of selfish desires. Ultimately, this is not a virtue ethics. Through such renunciation, the monk is able to get a glimpse of emptiness, he understands impermanence, and he realizes the selflessness of all beings. For the Madhyamaka, only through an understanding of emptiness can awakening take place. Thus, Śāntideva addresses the Śrāvaka monk, when he says:

> [You say] Liberation comes from understanding the [Noble] Truths. What then is the point of seeing emptiness? [We reply] Because [Mahāyāna] scriptures say that there is no awakening without this path (BCA. 9.40).

Through glimpses of emptiness and the loosening of personal identity, one is able to meditate on exchanging self for the self of others:

> Whoever wishes to quickly save himself and others, should practice the supreme mystery, and exchange 'self' and 'other' (BCA. 8.120).

Now we might wonder how a Buddhist, who is denying the existence of the self, could then go on to advocate a practice of exchanging one's 'self' for the self of another. First of all, we might note that the trainee *bodhisattva* still has a *sense* of self. While the monk knows the self to be ultimately illusory, this sense of self is still quite real.[28] Śāntideva writes:

> If, due to over-attachment to this self, even the slightest thing causes fear, should I not detest this self in the manner I hate the fearsome enemy? (BCA. 8.121)

In other words, it is the denial of self that is at stake. And second, this is no Lockean transference of consciousness (Locke, Essay: II.xxvii.15); rather it is to be seen

[28] Cf. Albahari (2006: 16–17).

as a mental exercise of putting oneself in another's shoes, that is, it is a program of imagination aimed at undermining the self. One puts oneself in the place of the onlooker and looks back at one's own mannerisms. And so:

> Taking an inferior, then a superior, and then an equal as 'oneself', and taking oneself as the 'other'; with a mind free of conceptions, experience envy and pride (BCA. 8.140).

In this way, the monk overcomes envy and competitiveness, and goes on to generate compassion for all beings. We might note that 'moral maturity' to this day is often measured by the degree to which one can 'take the perspective of the other' (Scott and Seglow 2007: 71). However, at this point in the *bodhisattva*'s training, it is still a mental program, and the field must now shift to a more practical level. Now the practical world the *bodhisattva* enters is one much different from the forest setting and the monastery setting which he is used to. His monastic vows may well be compromised. Śāntideva is aware of this, and allows for the breaking of the Pratimokṣa vows under certain conditions (BCA. 5.84). For example, 'At the time of giving, one may overlook such things as the moral code' (Ś.S. 11).

With the *bodhisattva* leaving the monastery, the distinction between the monk and the lay practitioner is potentially broken. However, there still remains the distinction between the homeless monk and the householder. Like Śaṅkara, Śāntideva clearly gives preference to the life of the former (Ś.S. 14), suggesting that, while both the lay disciple (*upāsaka*) and the monastic (*bhikṣu*) are worthy of gifts, the monastic is infinitely more worthy (87).[29] This forms part of the 'dialectic of attachment and non-attachment to worldly life' as described by Thapar (in Madan 1988: 274). But the fact that the *bodhisattva* may also be a householder complicates Thapar's model of the householder as being 'the source of dāna' (p283). In the Mahāyāna, the lay *bodhisattva* had a wider religious role to play. Nevertheless, when giving (especially *Dharma*), the monk is said to gain infinitely more merit than the householder (Ś.S. 144).[30] When it comes to the householder, Śāntideva is just as biased as Śaṅkara ever was. In fact, the refrain 'He has no yearning for wife, sons and daughters' (Ś.S. 14) might as easily have come from Śaṅkara's pen. Still, being a householder does not exclude one from being a *bodhisattva* (19 and 144), even if the household life does have 'innumerable faults' (196). While adultery is culpable by nature, having sex with one's own wife is only culpable by convention (192). One should therefore regard her with misgiving (78). In other words, one must become as unattached as is reasonably possible within one's social domain.

---

[29] On the practice of giving (*dāna*) and the notion of worthy recipients in Indian ethics, see Heim (in Bilimoria et al. 2007). Also see Harvey (2000: 21–3).

[30] Thapar (in Madan 1988: 289) notes that there is inscriptive evidence that monks and nuns also gave donations to the *Saṅgha*, thus further complicating the division of donor and receiver.

Mrozik (2007: 35) thus talks of the 'asceticized laity'. Still, a *bodhisattva* must give this household life up at some stage, for a householder can never become a Buddha (Ś.S. 193), asceticized or not.

Interestingly, whereas the *Gītā* (3.6) describes the (external) renouncer as a 'self-deluded hypocrite', Śāntideva states that one who leaves the household life is 'free from deceit and hypocrisy' (Ś.S. 196). One can imagine Śaṅkara nodding in agreement. Once again, it seems that the ethics of Śāntideva and Śaṅkara *cut across religious boundaries* and often pose more of a challenge to their *own tradition* than to each other. This is why a comparison of their ethics bears so much fruit for the study of Comparative Religion.

In short, we have seen that both Śaṅkara and Śāntideva see the world through renouncer's glasses, and yet both agree to play ball according to traditional rules. That is, traditional ethics survive both their ultimate discourses. These traditional ethics are lineage-specific, which prevents Hinduism and Buddhism from collapsing into a single path. We have also come to understand that both Śaṅkara and Śāntideva feel that those very rules can be side-stepped by the liberated few. We will now attempt to discover exactly what it means to be liberated on their gnoseological terms, and how such liberating knowledge may be developed.

Chapter 5
Knowledge and Liberation

Here I will show that both Śaṅkara and Śāntideva wish to insist that liberating knowledge, that is, enlightenment, is made possible through a certain insight, a realization. Both will link this realization to their textual tradition, and both will claim that this realization leads to the liberation from conditioned consciousness. As we have seen, both have claimed that the average person inhabits a world we fail to know. While it is normal to think of knowledge in terms of distinctions and categorizations, both Śaṅkara and Śāntideva will insist that the intellect which makes such mundane distinctions is not only incapable of grasping the ultimate truth, but, in the final moments, actually stands as an obstacle to its dawning. Our cognitive error is therefore self-imposed, and so we need to remove that 'self'.

From what we have heard about their respective metaphysics, it comes as no surprise that the final realization they have in mind is different. Writing about philosophers in general, Lehrer (2000: 1) opens his account of knowledge with the claim that 'All agree that knowledge is valuable, but agreement about knowledge tends to end there'. And Śaṅkara can confirm that the same was true of philosophers in 8th-century India (B.S.Bh. II.i.11). True, Śaṅkara also wants to say that 'true realization has no diversity' (ibid.), and that 'in liberation there can be no superiority' (III.iv.52). But then, as we have already mentioned, he would argue that the Mādhyamikas had taken hold of a mistaken view and that their search for liberation was incomplete. And of course Śāntideva would say the same of the Vedāntin's grasp of truth and their mistaken view of the self. Hence, we see a strong structural similarity between the two thinkers, whilst noting that 'realization' or 'liberating knowledge' has a different meaning for each tradition based on their conflicting metaphysics.

For Śaṅkara, liberating knowledge can be restricted to the understanding of the non-duality of consciousness in terms of the tropes of self and *brahman*. Thus he will claim that enlightenment comes about when one realizes that all is indeed *brahman*. For Śāntideva, necessary knowledge is derivative of the understanding that all phenomena are inter-dependent and thus empty of inherent existence. Thus he will claim that enlightenment comes about when one realizes that all is empty of independent existence. But while the content claimed of the insight differs, we might note that if knowledge be taken as that which 'rests on our capacity to distinguish truth from error' (Lehrer 2000: 7), then both Śaṅkara and Śāntideva are clearly coaching us in the same direction. For both agree that it is through this capacity to distinguish truth from error that one is said to be liberated from ignorance once and for all. But 'truth' here is not to be taken as an objective fact about the state of things in the world, but rather as a conscious state which is free from error. Such a liberated one is henceforth a teacher of men.

5.1 Śaṅkara: Liberation through Knowledge of *Brahman*

The Vedic corpus is commonly divided into two categories, the section on rites (*karma-kāṇḍa*) and the section on knowledge (*jñāna-kāṇḍa*), where '*jñāna*' indicates a state of consciousness which directly 'knows' *brahman*. The latter section of the Vedas is referred to as the *Upaniṣads*. The 'Vedānta', which literally means the end (*anta*) of the Vedas, and thus essentially equivalent to the Upaniṣads, came to be seen by many as the summit of the Vedas. Śaṅkara was a leading figure in the promotion of this line of thought, and worked tirelessly to strengthen its non-dual interpretation, typically, but not exclusively, against his Mīmāṃsā opponents.[1] Śaṅkara thus distinguishes two types of knowledge, and claims that:

> Understanding determined by action and the 'state of knowing' are opposed to one another … This 'state of knowing', in the form of realization (born of scriptural understanding) cannot arise without demolishing the common notion regarding the differences between actions, accessories and results, which is the cause of rites and injunctions, because the two philosophies of difference and non-difference are contradictory (Ch.U.Bh. II.xxiii.1).

Knowledge of *brahman* is clearly unlike other forms of knowledge. It is said to be a 'knowledge that is different from the known' (Ken.U. 1.4). That is, it is neither factual nor empirical knowledge, nor the acquired experiential knowledge or instrumental knowledge required for action. It is also said to be 'beyond the unknown' (Ken.U. 1.4). It is a 'higher knowledge' (Mu.U. I.i.4), *brahman* itself. It is 'totally ineffable' (V.C. 482), for '*brahman* is inexpressible' (Bh.G.Bh. 13.12). Elsewhere, Śaṅkara explains, 'For nothing which lacks genus, etc. can ever be described in words' (U.S. Metric, 18.30). And turning to scripture, Śaṅkara writes:

> For in all the Upaniṣads, the knowable, *brahman* has only been indicated by negation of all attributes, such as 'Not this, not this', or 'Neither gross nor subtle'; but never as 'That is this', for it is beyond speech (Bh.G.Bh. 13.12).

Hence, *brahman*-knowledge is a knowledge which cannot be owned by an agent, for 'the two contradictory notions, "I am *brahman*" and "I am an agent", cannot co-exist' (U.S. Metric, 18.225). In fact, Śaṅkara explicitly denies that *brahman* (B.S.Bh. I.i.4) is an object of knowledge. So when Olson (2011: 249) calls *nirguṇa-brahman* an 'object of knowledge', what he must mean is that *nirguṇa-brahman* belongs to the realm of *vidyā* as opposed to *avidyā* (the realm of ignorance). In other words, it is a worthy subject of inquiry, all else being inferior, ultimately worthless. Put bluntly, 'inferior knowledge is no knowledge' (B.S.Bh. III.iv.52).

---

[1] On the debate between Advaita and Mīmāṃsa, see Ram-Prasad (2007: 101–31). See also, Halbfass (1983).

True knowledge, then, is that which remains after all inquiries are done, when the 'desire to know ceases' (III.ii.22).

Considering all that Śaṅkara says it is, and even more that which he says it is not, it would appear that this state of knowing *brahman* is really more of a *sense of conviction* than of knowing *about* something. *Brahman* is not 'known' representationally, but experientially. This is no doubt a special type of experience, one which arguably parallels the *as-it-is-ness* of the Buddhist. In other words, it is an enlightening knowledge which illuminates the situation for what it really is. It is not that one has a self with the quality of consciousness which grasps *brahman* in a cognitive event; for it is said to be beyond the propositional knowledge of beings (Mu.U. II.ii.1). Strictly speaking, the 'knower cannot be known by the knower' (Ken.U.Bh. 2.1). Hence, realization is not *of* the ultimate, but is itself the ultimate. So even firm conviction that one knows *brahman*, though desirable, is equally questionable, for one might not fully know (Ken.U.Bh. 2.1).

This state of knowing (*pratyaya*) therefore sits somewhat outside of the *pramāṇa* system and should not be equated with, say, the Nyāya's valid presentational knowledge (*pramā*), which for Advaita, means uncontradicted (*abādhita*) cognition. Rather, this state of knowing falls into that category of which the 'genuineness of the experience' is determined by an 'external reference' (see Flew 2005: 145). In contrast to external objects, *brahman* 'possesses an inherent unknowability by normal faculties of knowledge' (Olson 2011: 251). Yet, experience of it sublates all past knowledge. Furthermore, it cannot be a (conventional) form of experiential knowledge, because the 'object' is non-different from the 'subject'. It takes a skilful teacher to know whether the pupil has attained knowledge or not, and the rule-of-thumb seems to be, if he thinks he has, he has not (Ken.U.Bh. 2.2–3).

So even the 'all-knowingness' of the *yogi*, who has perfected his *sattva*-quality,[2] does not touch *brahman*-knowledge, because the truth that is *brahman* is of a different order, being eternal knowledge (B.S.Bh. I.i.5). To know *brahman* is to share in the knowing that *is brahman*, it is to 'become' *brahman* (Mu.U. III.ii.9). The truth is that the Self *is* reflexive-consciousness and this singular consciousness *is brahman*. This state of knowing is therefore immediate and direct (Bṛ.U. III.iv.1). It is a state which permits of no doubts (B.S.Bh. IV.i.15). It cannot be attained through works, for as Śaṅkara tells us, work assumes the dualistic notion that there is a difference between agent and results gained (Ch.U.Bh. II.xxiii.1). Nor is *brahman*-knowledge to be gained through argumentation (Ka.U. I.ii.8–9), as it lies beyond the intellect.

This higher knowledge is not the result of any active work, then, but dawns when physical and intellectual effort stop, when the individual rejects the adjuncts which separate him from *brahman*. One gains knowledge of *brahman* through truly *listening* to one's teacher (Ka.U.Bh. I.ii.8–9). All other instruments are ultimately

2 According to Sāṃkhya, nature (*prakṛti*) is made up of three qualities (*guṇas*): *sattva* (purity), *rajas* (activity) and *tamas* (inertia). The *yogi* becomes perfect by becoming pure-*sattva*. The *Bhagavad Gītā* defends this view (Chapter 14), as does the *V.C.* (119).

impediments to knowledge. Hence, Śaṅkara concludes that *brahman* is to be known by the Vedas alone and not from reasoning (B.S.Bh. II.i.31). Thus, authoritative word (*śabda*) from scripture (*śruti*) via teacher (*ācārya*, *guru*) is the only valid means (*pramāṇa*) for the final attainment of *brahman* knowledge. That is, according to Śaṅkara, it takes a qualified teacher to advise whether one knows or not:

> The scriptures also say 'Even if one were to give him this [world] surrounded by oceans, filled with riches … this truly is more than that'. Since knowledge is obtained in no other way. For the Śrutis say 'He with a teacher knows', 'Knowledge learnt from a teacher …', 'The teacher is a boatman', 'His right knowledge is said to be a boat', etc. The Smṛti also says 'Knowledge will be imparted to you', etc. (U.S. Prose, 1.3).

So on the question of whether conviction equals knowledge, or whether there is such a thing as self-authenticating experience, Śaṅkara may not appear quite consistent. Compare the above with this statement, quoted earlier: 'For when somebody feels in his heart that he has realized *brahman*, and yet bears a body, how can this be contested by anyone else?' (B.S.Bh. IV.i.15). However, I think we can reasonably take him to mean 'anyone' *except his teacher*.

Unfortunately, the addition of the teacher does not overcome the metaphysical problem of the need for an individual 'experiencer' who has an 'experience' which either does or does not require external validation. If anything, we are now faced with a further individual. And it would seem that a teacher fully absorbed in *brahman* simply could not validate whether or not another was so absorbed. My notion of flickering would however solve both these issues. First, on my account, the teacher at the time of teaching would not be absorbed; but would be voluntarily within the provisional world. Second, while the individuated self of the student may get lost in the 'experience' of *brahman*-consciousness; due to past tendencies, it inevitably returns.

Such a state of *brahman*-consciousness is impossible for one who relies solely on the intellect in his search for knowledge. On the limits of intellect, Śaṅkara writes:

> As long as the contact between the self and the intellect necessarily follows, so the self is subject to transmigratory existence. So long as there is no right seeing, so long as there is connection with this intellect, there will be no end to cyclic existence. And this individuality and this transmigratory state will last as long as there is this connection with the intellect as adjunct (B.S.Bh. II.iii.30).

So while no stranger to pure philosophizing, it would appear that Śaṅkara is warning us that this state of knowing will forever elude one who limits himself to such modes of inquiry and dispute, the so-called 'big-talker' (Mu.U. III.i.4). Śaṅkara clearly wants to lead us to experience, not to argumentation, for it is in experience that we transcend this world.

Nevertheless, he does so through what Forsthoefel (2002: 320) has called 'intellectual therapy'. Along with other more spiritual virtues, it is one's intellectual work that gets one to the place where the intellect may be dropped. In the *Chāndogya Upaniṣad*, Nārada, who begs Sanatkumāra to teach him about the Self (Ch.U. VII.i.3), is described as a 'mere knower of the textual tradition', but he *is* a knower of it. Again, the man who has his 'blindfold' removed by the teacher is said to be intelligent (VI.xiv.1). In the *Upadeśa Sāhasrī* (Prose, 1.2), the student is possessed of many excellent qualities, which include both 'conduct' and 'learning'. Śaṅkara tells us that the Vedas assume that the person seeking a teacher is an intelligent man (B.S.Bh. I.i.2). Thus, the worthy seeker must show himself to have intellectual acumen. It is due to the intellectual search and the student's own exertions that he now stands before the teacher. This imposes upon the teacher the need for a 'superlative degree of intellectual acumen' (Cenkner 1983: 41). Reflecting on the teacher's words is the active counterpart to hearing, and there is no doubt that hearing is 'enriched by what the hearer brings to it' (Ram-Prasad 2001a: 201).[3]

True, Śaṅkara critiques those 'self-styled scholars', the 'logicians' who use reason as a substitute for the Vedas (Bṛ.U.Bh. II.i.20). Yet, despite citing the *Kaṭha Upaniṣad*'s (I.ii.8–9) claim that knowledge cannot be reached 'through reason' (Bṛ.U.Bh. II.i.20), in the very same *Bhāṣya*, Śaṅkara still adds 'reasoning' to the Upaniṣad's classic statement on the matter (Br.U.Bh. II.iv.5). In fact, it has been claimed that reason is 'paramount' in Śaṅkara's system of liberation (Cenkner 1983: 33). His concern is really with the *misuse*, rather than the use of reason.[4] Reasoning is only acceptable when it is in accordance with the Vedas. Śaṅkara, like other Hindu thinkers, thus warns against 'rationalistic self-sufficiency' (Radhakrishnan 1989: 23) or 'dry' reasoning (Chakrabarti, in Deutsch and Bontekoe 1997: 264).

Nevertheless, Olson's (1997: 168) claim that *brahman*-knowledge is 'independent of man' needs qualifying. Śaṅkara tells us that '*brahman*-knowledge is independent of man's actions' (B.S.Bh. I.i.4). He also says that the 'realization of *brahman* is not determined by human effort' (Ken.U.Bh., intro), in that *brahman*-knowledge depends on *brahman* itself (B.S.Bh. I.i.4). It is the Self revealing itself. Conventionally speaking, however, it is within the embodied human mind that knowledge dawns. It is simply that, once at the threshold of knowledge, the mental apparatus should be silenced. Śaṅkara states:

> Moreover, this connection of the self with the adjunct of intellect has forever been associated with misunderstanding and misunderstanding cannot come to an end except through right knowledge. Hence, so long as there is no realization

[3] The classic Advaitin methodological trio is hearing (*śravaṇa*), reflection (*manana*) and contemplation (*nididhyāsana*) (Bṛ.U. II.iv.5). Also see the *V.C.* (70). On varying interpretations of the 'three methods' in Vedānta, see Ram-Prasad (2001a: 198–209), Cenkner (1983: 21–8 and 65ff), and Roodurmun (2002: 212ff). Cf. the Theravāda's *D.N.* iii.219.

[4] See Halbfass (1991: 131–204).

> of the Self as *brahman*, so long does the connection with the intellect persist (B.S.Bh. II.iii.30).

The world of the intellect, like caste duties and associations, must be left behind. Only by renouncing all, even one's own 'personality' (caste, family history, beliefs and so on), is the knowledge of *brahman* attained. Of course, even the teacher must be 'versed in the Vedas' (Mu.U. I.ii.12), and the teachings he gives must include the 'great sayings' (*mahāvākyas*) of the Vedas. Śaṅkara suggests the following format:

> He should first teach the Śrutis which primarily present the oneness of Self, such as: 'In the beginning, my child, this [universe] was existence only, one alone, without a second …', 'Where one sees nothing else …', 'All this is the Self', 'In the beginning, all this was but the Self', 'Indeed all this is but brahman'. After teaching these, he should help him, by means of the Śrutis, to grasp the marks of brahman, for example: 'The Self is free from evil …', 'That brahman which is manifest and directly known', 'That which is beyond hunger and thirst', 'Not this! Not this!', 'Neither gross nor subtle', 'This self is not this', 'It is the unseen seer', 'Knowledge, bliss', 'Real, knowledge, infinite', 'Invisible, bodiless', 'That great unborn Self', 'Breathless, mindless', 'Without and within unborn', 'Consisting of knowledge only', 'Without interior or exterior', 'It is indeed beyond the known and the unknown', 'Called space …' (U.S. Prose, 1.6–7).

And so it is ultimately to Vedic revelation that reason is subordinated. The *V.C.* (58–62) appears at variance on this point with the authentic works of Śaṅkara, even suggesting that the study of scripture is useless (58). However, even here (33), the 'guru' is said to be 'versed in the Vedas'. Despite all the rhetoric to the contrary, scripture is still seen as the 'ultimate instrument to fashion the transformation of the mind' (Forsthoefel 2002: 320).

This intimate knowing of *brahman*, that results from such understanding of the Vedic teachings, does not lead to worldly gain, or even other-worldly gain. Śaṅkara tells us that it is the way of a man who has 'renounced' all 'seen' and 'unseen' results (Ken.U.Bh., intro), meaning that even the wish for heavenly realms or bliss is to be denounced. This amounts to an essentially negative liberation, a 'freedom from', what has been called the 'minimal account of *mokṣa*' (Perrett 1985: 345). 'Knowledge' then, in Advaitic terms, is really the removal of the apparatus of individuation. There is nothing added. One who knows simply becomes 'identified with the eternal and unborn *brahman*' (Ch.U.Bh. III.xi.3).

Throughout his works, we see Śaṅkara's goal as being that of a final state of *brahman*-consciousness with the simultaneous release from the suffering of existence (for example B.S.Bh. I.iv.6 and IV.i.2). As the Upaniṣads say, 'a knower of the Self goes beyond sorrow' (Ch.U. VII.i.3). In Śaṅkara's interpretation, this knowledge of Self is achieved, not in the after-life, but 'right here while alive'

(Ch.U.Bh. III.xii.9). And subsequently, the renouncer overcomes sorrow even while alive (Ken.U.Bh., intro). The soteriological goal then, for Śaṅkara, is to become such a *jīvan-mukta* (Mu.U.Bh. III.ii.9), apparently resting in the ultimate peace of *brahmanhood* (Bh.G.Bh. 2.72).

As we shall see below, this essentially negative thesis only presents itself as positive, as 'freedom to', when the *jīvan-mukta* is given the role of teacher.[5] This knowledge, when passed on from teacher to pupil, may rightly be called 'saving' knowledge (Deutsch 1973: 47), if by that we mean a knowledge which *saves* one from further rounds of suffering. It is therefore interesting to note that, in the *V.C.* (35), the student's supplication to the guru includes the phrase 'save me'. When used in this pedagogical sense, the Buddha's knowledge has also been called 'saving knowledge' (Bastow, in Deutsch and Bontekoe 1997: 412). As Gombrich (2009: 78) states, 'The nearest thing to a saviour that the karma doctrine allows is a teacher'. And this seems as applicable to Advaita as to Buddhism. Thus, Cenkner (1983: 15) is justified in speaking of a 'salvific relationship between teacher and pupil'.

But in truth, nothing is passed on, for *brahman* was already there in both teacher and pupil. What takes place is therefore an epistemic switch to precognitive knowledge. It is like the boy who knew his group had started out as ten boys, but could now only count nine. A passing man points out to him that *he* is the tenth boy and an 'a-haa' experience takes place (T.U.Bh. II.i.1 and U.S. Metric, 12.3). Nothing new has been added to the situation; only the ignorance of the boy has been removed. Śaṅkara writes:

> Unlike the attainment of things that are not-self, the attainment of the Self does not involve the obtaining of something not previously obtained, because there is no difference between the attainer and what is to be attained … Therefore, the attainment of [the Self] is simply the removal of that [ignorance] through knowledge (Br.U.Bh. I.iv.7).

So it would seem that, just as with Śāntideva above (BCA. 9.150), there is, in fact, no difference between being liberated and not being liberated. Elsewhere, Śaṅkara confirms this in remarkably similar language:

> There is actually no difference between liberation and bondage. For, indeed, the Self is always the same. However, ignorance of this matter is removed by the knowledge that arises from the teachings of the scriptures. But until one receives these, the effort put into attaining liberation is perfectly reasonable (Bṛ.U.Bh. IV.iv.6).

---

[5] When Mumme asks whether the *jīvan-mukta*'s status is marked by 'freedom from' or 'freedom to' (Fort and Mumme 1996: 264–7), she is questioning whether or not the *jīvan-mukta* is free 'from' the law (*Dharma*), or free 'to' follow it. My concern here is more with the *brahma-vid*'s parallel with Śāntideva who wishes to be free in order that he may liberate others.

Śaṅkara's '*na hi vastuto muktāmuktatva viśeṣo 'sti*' (There is actually no difference between liberation and bondage) looks so much like Śāntideva's '*nirvṛtānirvṛtānāṃ ca viśeṣo nāsti vastu taḥ*' (thus, there is no substantial difference between the liberated and the non-liberated) (BCA. 9.150) it is almost eerie. Perhaps both are traceable to Nāgārjuna's '*na nirvāṇasya saṃsārāt kiṃcid asti viśeṣaṇaṃ*' (there is no difference whatsoever between *nirvāṇa* and *saṃsāra*) (MMK. 25.19b). All three lend themselves to the same translation. The link between Śāntideva and Nāgārjuna is of course established, with Śāntideva recommending that one should consult Nāgārjuna's work (BCA. 5.106). As for Śaṅkara, we can only speculate. Ram-Prasad (2001a: 210) wrote that Śaṅkara may have 'deliberately or unwittingly' copied from Nāgārjuna. But the evidence here shows an even closer relationship to Śāntideva's wording. It is indeed ironic that Otto (1957: 150) claimed that the doctrine that 'Nirvāna and Samsāra are one and the same' would be 'sheer madness on the basis of Śaṅkara's teaching'.

On the basis that Śaṅkara accepts the notion of effort in attaining liberation, Taber (1983: 19) has spoken of Śaṅkara holding a 'threefold scheme for liberation', which involves preparation, insight and consolidation. This is further evidence that the commonly held thesis that Śaṅkara denounces action is essentially false, as I will later demonstrate. And as we saw in Chapter 4.3, Śaṅkara is further compromised by the fact that the *Bhagavad Gītā* went to great length in its glorification of action. And so Śaṅkara, in accepting the *Gītā*'s authority, must allow for the notion of 'non-attached' action as a form of renunciation. It is thus accepted as a means to purifying the mind to make it ready for the realization of *brahman*. This does not strictly mean that religious practices 'cause' knowledge, as Taber (1983: 23) suggests; rather they prepare the ground, providing an opportunity to purify the mind, making it ready to receive the teachings which will cause knowledge to dawn (B.S.Bh. III.iv.26).

Renunciation, then, is not necessarily physical renunciation, but more essentially involves an 'inner' renunciation; the letting go of the notion that one is the ultimate agent of one's actions. But whether one remains embedded in the provisional world or (epistemically) rises up to the heights of the true world, one's actions must be conducted selflessly. That is Śaṅkara's central ethic. And such an ethic, at all levels, requires a certain degree of understanding. At the highest level of understanding, where one sees the lack of individuated self, where one has gone beyond attachment to results, but even so continues to act towards others *as if* they had an individuated self, that is what I call 'constructive altruism'.

Clearly, if knowledge (*vidyā*) is the key to liberation, then nescience (*a-vidyā*) is its enemy. Śaṅkara writes: 'Knowledge and ignorance cannot co-exist in the very same person, for they are contradictory like light and dark' (Bṛ.U.Bh. III.v.1). He continues, 'Thus, the knower of Self must not be supposed to have any relationship with the sphere of ignorance' (ibid.). Elsewhere, he writes: 'This enlightened man ... does not see anything, does not hear anything, does not cognize anything other than the Self' (Mu.U.Bh. II.i.4). He asks:

> How could there be [flickering between] seeing and not-seeing in me who is forever of the nature of [pure] seeing? No experience, therefore, other than [the self] can be accepted (U.S. Metric, 12.9).

Śaṅkara thus appears to be asserting a constant 'context-free state of consciousness' (Ram-Prasad 2001a: 171), which is permanently opposed to ignorance. This is in direct opposition to my notion of flickering. If this were his final word on the matter, then we would be faced with the same problem that has faced those scholars who have pondered the Mādhyamika's thesis that the Buddha's pure mind is so non-conceptual that it would contain no cognitive images at all (see Arnold 2005: 184, and Williams, in Powers and Prebish 2009: 115). That is, pure consciousness would be indistinguishable from unconsciousness. Clearly, 'life requires a richness of quality which neutral consciousness' could not explain (Ram-Prasad 2001a: 167). It is this richness of quality that my flickering model provides.

As noted earlier, Śāntideva's voluntary delusion saves us from such an investigation into the contents of a transparent consciousness. And thankfully, as was mentioned earlier, Śaṅkara's final word on the subject will save us again (at least with regard to the pre-death scenario), for it is in a sense another *retraction* of the above statements; for there is still the matter of past tendencies. Let us remind ourselves then of the following admission: 'However, mistaken cognition, even when annulled, continues for a while owing to the influence of past tendencies' (B.S.Bh. IV.i.15). Furthermore, Śaṅkara quite remarkably accepts that these past tendencies are *stronger* than this knowledge. Hence: 'The operation of [pure] knowing, being weaker than they, is only one possible mode' (Bṛ.U.Bh. I.iv.7).

Thus, we are surely justified in imagining the *brahman*-knower flickering between moments of 'light' and moments of 'darkness', or periods of right-cognition (*samyag-jñāna*) and wrong-cognition (*mithyā-jñāna*). It would seem that light and dark *can* co-exist in the very same person, but not at the same time. Or we might say that the one 'person' flickers between imagining himself to be an individuated self and being in a non-individuated state of *brahman*. In his *brahman*-moments, the imaginary individuated self disappears, and with it, desire for objects. The *V.C.* confirms our suspicions that the early Advaitins acknowledged this flickering:

> Even after knowledge has been attained, there remains that beginningless, strong, obstinate impression that one is an agent and an experiencer; the cause of transmigration (V.C. 267a).

It is due to this instability that renunciation is paramount, allowing time for full establishment in *brahman*. Śaṅkara states that renunciation merely serves to mature Self-knowledge (Bṛ.U.Bh. IV.iv.7). Thus, the world is not only there from the side of conventional truth, but may also act as a bridge, for liberation verily comes from within this world. Individuation must therefore be provisionally retained in order to pass on that knowledge to the next generation of seekers. But, while knowledge should be repeatedly explained to the pupil until firmly grasped (U.S. Prose, 1.2), it should also be consolidated by the teacher himself.

The teacher must therefore flicker between teaching others and absorption in *brahman*. This is implicit in Śaṅkara's notion that 'total consummation in *brahman*', or being 'steadfast in *brahman*', denotes the 'absence of any other preoccupation' (B.S.Bh. III.iv.20). For it is clear that, in teaching others, one must assume an additional preoccupation. Also, if the 'Vedas are no Vedas' in such a state of awakened consciousness (B.S.Bh. IV.i.3), then surely the teacher must come out of this state in order to teach from them. Hence, the only way the enlightened can help the unenlightened is by occasionally coming out of this state of absorption in order to share in the student's distorted vision of reality. Through such flickering, the knower is potentially fit for both domains. And through such a *theory* of flickering, we save Śaṅkara from the charge of contradiction.

5.2 Śāntideva: Liberation through Seeing into Emptiness

We have seen that liberation had a double meaning for Śaṅkara, being: 1) an end to nescience, and 2) an end to rebirth and suffering. For Śāntideva, enlightenment does not naturally lead to liberation from cyclic existence (*saṃsāra*), for the *bodhisattva* has already denounced such liberation, both ultimately and conventionally. Ultimately speaking, there can be no ceasing of that which did not arise. Conventionally speaking, the Bodhisattva Vow will keep him in the round of rebirths, not through bondage, but through an act of will, through choice. Unlike Śaṅkara, Śāntideva has no problem with action, for the *bodhisattva* does not resist the results of *karma* and may even risk some negative *karma* if the overall benefit is thought to outweigh the cost. As such, Śāntideva can focus on putting an end to nescience in all beings without over-worrying about the possibility of gaining a karmic result, especially as accumulation of merit (*puṇya*) is simultaneously the elimination of demerit (*pāpa*). The commencing-*bodhisattva* should even be willing to suffer a little in order to remove the suffering of others. Śāntideva writes:

> You may argue, 'If compassion brings [us] so much pain, why force it to arise?' But having determined the degree of suffering in the world; is the suffering from compassion so great? (BCA. 8.104).

For Indian Buddhists, like Śāntideva, knowledge is not an end in itself. It is not so much knowledge that is at stake, but the subsequent reduction in suffering which is said to follow from such knowledge. Whether this distinguishes Śaṅkara from his Buddhist contemporaries, as claimed by Ram-Prasad (2001a: 186–8), is open to debate, though I personally feel the question is perhaps one of emphasis rather than substance. Ram-Prasad argues that Śaṅkara's emphasis is on ending 'epistemic failure' rather than suffering. However, near the close of the *B.S.Bh* (IV. iv.2), Śaṅkara states that 'liberation is nothing but the cessation of bondage', and in the *U.S.* (Prose, 2.45), we are told that the seeker of liberation ought to be 'tired of the cycle of birth and death', not tired of being ignorant. Moreover, Śaṅkara goes far beyond the source text in his description of the suffering inherent in the act of birth (Ch.U.Bh. V.ix.1). Saha (2009: 28) therefore appears wrong to suggest that, for Śaṅkara, 'Suffering is not a matter for [sic] experiencing any physical discomfort'.

Furthermore, we should not forget that, in India, *re*-birth implies *re*-death, and this may well be seen as the greater of the two evils. And Śaṅkara tells us that 'One who sees diversity [in brahman] goes from death to death' (U.S. Prose, 1.26), whereas liberation puts an end to re-death (Bṛ.U.Bh. III.ii.10). As such, Karl Potter (1981: 6) appears justified in claiming that the 'purpose of philosophy' for Advaita is to 'point the way to liberation (*mokṣa*) from the bondage of rebirth'. In that case, I see no substantial difference with the Buddhist view of philosophy's primary role.

So while it is ignorance which binds the seeker, existentially, it is suffering which inspires the wish for knowledge. Śāntideva makes this incredibly explicit when he writes, 'Therefore, with the desire to end suffering, one should develop wisdom' (BCA. 9.1b). Thus, he demonstrates the fact that 'Buddhist ethics is based on the ultimate good, the liberation from suffering' (de Silva, in Bilimoria et al. 2007: 233). Here, he appears to sit comfortably alongside the Śrāvaka Buddhist. However, it is because this desire to end suffering extends to all other beings that, unlike the Śrāvaka, an end to rebirth plays no part in Śāntideva's soteriology.

Unlike the Śrāvaka, and indeed Śaṅkara, the *bodhisattva* is willing to be reborn in order to help other sentient beings. The path he walks is one of accumulation of merit, through virtuous practice and meditation, finally leading to wisdom (*prajñā*) and higher knowledge (*jñāna*). That is, he walks the traditional *bodhisattva-yāna*. The path is thought to naturally lead to an insight into emptiness, a true cognition of how the world is. Meditation leads to seeing. Such a virtuous seer is henceforth possessed of the enlightened freedom to act for the benefit of all. Śaṅkara thus sits closer to the historical Buddha here than does Śāntideva, for it was an innovation of the Mahāyāna to denounce the final liberation of *nirvāṇa*, and to see *nirvāṇa* in non-ultimate terms.

Like Śaṅkara, one of Śāntideva's first moves is to denounce the intellect (*buddhi*). Hence, as we saw earlier, reality (*tattva*) is said to be beyond the scope of the intellect (BCA. 9.2b). He also went on to tell us that the mistake made by the common man is to imagine the objects within the world to be real, when they are in fact illusion-like (BCA. 9.5). Therefore, he adds that 'It is the reification of reality that is here refuted, as that is the cause of suffering' (9.25b).

The only way that this reification can be annulled is through an insight into emptiness (*śūnyatā*), which, according to Nāgārjuna, corresponds with the cessation of discursiveness (MMK, Dedication). Thus, we saw Śāntideva addressing the Śrāvaka monk:

> [You say] Liberation comes from understanding the [Noble] Truths. What then is the point of seeing emptiness? [We reply] Because [Mahāyāna] scriptures say that there is no awakening without this path (BCA. 9.40).

We see here that Śāntideva does not try to justify emptiness in terms of a self-validating experience, but gives a testimonial argument for its efficacy. Of course, it is a testimony that his opponent, the Śrāvaka, will reject. He therefore tries another tack, an assault on outward behaviour (that might as easily apply to the *brahman*-knower):

> If liberation results from the destruction of the defilements, [as you say], it ought to follow immediately after. Yet the influence of *karma* can still be seen in those ['arhats'] who are free of defilements (BCA. 9.45).

The mind might well have moments of purity without the realization of emptiness, but it will continually return to normal states of ignorance; that is, it will oscillate. This oscillation, however, is no voluntary flickering, for it is beyond the monk's control. And so he tells the Śrāvaka monk:

> Without emptiness, the fettered mind arises again, as in the case of the meditative state of non-perception; therefore one must cultivate emptiness (BCA. 9.48).

In other words, it is not enough to settle on the ability to enter into certain higher states of consciousness. One must attain a higher degree of wisdom. Hence, we have to train ourselves out of the habit of projecting inherent existence onto a world that lacks it. In the words of Nāgārjuna: 'When ignorance ceases, mental formations will not arise' (MMK. 26.11a).

Śāntideva argues that the potential benefits of realizing emptiness are two-fold; firstly, the power it gives one to act compassionately, and secondly, the guaranteed removal of both the defilements *and* the obscurations to omniscience. While the *arhat* may have removed the defilements, they are still left with certain mental obscurations which prevent omniscience, and only the *bodhisattva*'s path of emptiness and skilful means can remove them:

> Being able to remain in cyclic existence, free from attachment and fear, for the benefit of those suffering through their delusion – such is the fruit of emptiness (BCA. 9.52).

> Since emptiness is the antidote to the veil of afflictions and to obscurations of knowledge, how is it that one desirous of omniscience [i.e. Buddhahood] does not hasten to meditate on it? (BCA. 9.54).

While Śāntideva goes to some length to explain what he means by emptiness, a more succinct definition was given by Nāgārjuna, said to contain the 'entire Mādhyamika system in embryo' (Garfield 1995: 304). It runs, 'Whatever is dependently arisen, that we call emptiness' (MMK. 24.18a). In other words, because everything arises dependent on prior causes and conditions, there is no 'thing' which may be said to exist inherently without the need for such causes and conditions. This lack of inherent existence is called their emptiness. And the Mādhyamika assumes that everything, including one's mental states, is dependently arisen. To understand this truth is to be liberated from the reification of imagined, self-standing 'objects', including the Yogācāra's *citta* and the *Brahmin*'s *puruṣa*. And as we have seen, to teach this ultimate truth without projection to those people whose views are characterized by projection is Śāntideva's ultimate aim (BCA. 9.167). As for the view of emptiness itself, Śāntideva advises the Śrāvaka that they should: 1) accept its validity as a teaching of the Buddha, and 2) meditate on it:

> As such, there is no valid objection to the emptiness doctrine. Therefore one should meditate on emptiness without hesitation (BCA. 9.53).

Buddhism has traditionally divided meditation practice into calm-abiding (*śamatha*) and insight (*vipaśyanā*). The contrast is sometimes explained in terms of states of absorption (*dhyāna*) and modes of analysis. Now, given that Śāntideva claims that even the higher absorptions do not guarantee insight into emptiness (BCA. 9.48), it would seem that what is required is some form of insight meditation. In fact, we may reasonably assume that the practitioner alternates between analytical and stabilizing meditation. Thus, Śāntideva writes:

> With body and mind aware, distractions do not arise. Thus, having renounced this world, one should avoid conjecture (BCA. 8.2).

> Knowing that one of well-attuned insight through tranquillity destroys the defilements, one must first seek tranquillity; and *that* by first becoming indifferent to one's delight in this world (8.4).

Thus, Śāntideva calls for a state of inner-renunciation which will then allow the mind to settle. From this state of tranquillity it is deemed possible to begin the analysis into the nature of consciousness and its relation to the world of 'objects'. We can then read much of the ninth chapter of the *BCA* itself as a form of analytical insight meditation. The main analytical conundrum is that of the illusory nature of pseudo-reality and its causes:

> What is created by illusion and what by causes? From whence do they come and where do they go? This we must examine (BCA. 9.143).

Relying on what he calls the 'Mādhyamika style of reasoning' (Gyatso 1975: 42), the Dalai Lama writes, 'Once the referent object of the conception of inherent existence is known to be non-existent, one can easily ascertain emptiness' (ibid.). The Dalai Lama then confirms Śāntideva's assertion that the intellect is incapable of such a grasp on reality, but reminds us that this is a two-stage process which includes the intellect. Thus, the Dalai Lama continues:

> With respect to a non-conceptual wisdom that apprehends a profound emptiness, one first cultivates a conceptual consciousness that apprehends an emptiness, and when a clear perception of the object of meditation arises, this becomes a non-conceptual wisdom (p55).[6]

Śāntideva muses:

> When one considers that the entity does not truly exist, and nothing is perceived, how could a baseless non-entity stand before the mind? (BCA. 9. 33).

His response, taken by Ruegg (1981: 83) to be a 'summing up of the central idea of the Middle Way', runs:

> When neither entity nor non-entity stands before the mind, because there is no other mode, the mind, without support, becomes tranquil (BCA. 9.34).

This process of 'self-critical rationality' (Ganeri 2001: 47) is one of shaking oneself out of habitual patterns of thought. One must 'eradicate the innate non-analytical intellect that misconceives the nature of the person and other phenomena' as having inherent existence (Hopkins 1996: 30). Hence, one analyses the object of meditation until the 'cognition of unfindability' arises with sufficient force (p64).[7] And, according to Śāntideva, we can be sure that we have come to the end of this process when there is no basis left for analysis:

> [Objection] But when analysis is itself analysed by analysis, there is no end, since that analysis may also be analysed. [We reply] But when the thing to be analysed has been [truly] analysed, there is no basis left for analysis. Without basis, it ends. That is said to be *nirvāṇa* (BCA. 9.109–10).[8]

At this point, the *yogi* is unable to find any 'thing' to call an object. One has here reached the limit of analysis. However, even when this emptiness has become a direct realization, flickering still occurs. This is said to continue up until the eighth *bhūmi*; for, until that stage of the path, the *yogi* is said to be incapable of consistently remaining in that direct realization of emptiness during the actual perception of phenomena (see Hopkins 1996: 103–4).

Now Śāntideva is well aware that he cannot help himself to the standard Indian 'means of knowledge' (*pramāṇa*) system in order to justify emptiness, but he seems unconcerned by this:

[6] For a comprehensive study of emptiness meditation techniques in Tibetan Prāsaṅgika-Madhyamaka, see Hopkins (1996). For a brief resume of Hopkins, see Williams (2009: 79–81).

[7] On the notion of unfindablity (*anupalabdhi*) of self, see Kapstein (2001: 77ff).

[8] Cf. *MMK*. 18.4–5

> [Objection] If a means of knowledge is [in fact] not [ultimately] a means of knowledge [for you], then surely all gained by that means is falsely established. Therefore the emptiness of phenomena is not truly ascertained [by a valid cognition]. [We reply] Where there is no contact with an imaginary existent there is no grasping at its non-existence. For, if the being of an entity is deceptive, clearly its negation [i.e. emptiness] is equally deceptive (BCA. 9.138–9).

In other words, as the 'object' under analysis is not truly existent, so its emptiness is not truly existent. And so, when one's insight into the illusory nature of phenomena is so strong that there is no expectation of contact between an individuated consciousness and a self-standing object, then emptiness is fully established. There is no need for a positive perception of emptiness itself as there is no such self-standing emptiness. It is not the case that an Absolute appears when the conventional ceases. Rather, in order to understand the non-substantial nature of a conventional 'existent' it is of value to first examine its imagined nature and then to remove one's false perception of it as being a self-standing 'object'. The subsequent view of emptiness is thus free of reification.

Beyond this point of realization, one would need to voluntarily assume persons as self-standing individuals in order to fulfil the Bodhisattva Vow. While it may be true that one might eventually reach such a level of clarity that one's epistemic transparency would lead to a state where the 'two cognitions [conventional and ultimate] no longer function alternatively or separately', but 'simultaneously' (Thakchöe, in Cowherds 2011: 49), Śāntideva's solution appears a more realistic one. Śāntideva reminds his *bodhisattvas* that they are not buddhas, but humans who must know their level of development. Thus, Śāntideva's is a traditional Mahāyāna cultivation of insight through tranquillity, with altruistic intent, with the addition of a voluntary delusion. Therefore, Śāntideva's 'emptiness-based altruism' (Clayton 2006: 63) is one that involves an implicit flickering between the Two Truths.[9]

One question that remains unanswered is how wisdom should lead one to selfless action. Is it that such wisdom makes one automatically moral? Is it that without belief in a self, egoism naturally turns into altruism? I have been able to glean at least four possible responses in Śāntideva's works: 1) the weakening of craving, attachment and fear, along with an insight into non-self, makes one less self-centred, redefining one's boundaries, leaving one more open to others; 2) an understanding of the inter-dependence of karmic relationships leads one to view others as being profoundly relevant to one's own path; 3) when one has become free of the shackles of *saṃsāra*, one gains a deep sympathy for those that remain caught in it; and 4) one feels duty-bound via the Bodhisattva Vow to save others from suffering and to continue the Buddha's lineage. This seems to amount to a complete reorientation in one's view of the world. Śāntideva writes:

---

[9] All of these steps depend on the previous perfections, for which one may read the *BCA* itself. Also refer to Huntington (1989: 69–104), an excellent guide to the *bodhisattva* path, mainly based on Candrakīrti's presentation.

> Suffering has a further quality in that it inspires the desire for liberation. One feels compassion for those in cyclic existence, a fear of demerit, and a yearning for Buddhahood (BCA. 6.21).

But we should not forget that a certain degree of *bodhicitta* was already present long before the view of emptiness. And so throughout this chapter on patience (*kṣānti*), we find references to compassion. Another quote shows how compassion appears as the antidote to anger and intolerance:

> Driven mad by their defilements they resort to killing themselves. How is it that you show no compassion, but become angry? (BCA. 6.38).

Finnigan and Tanaka (in Cowherds 2011: 229) have also highlighted how, for Candrakīrti, 'compassion is the root of both the aspiration for enlightenment and nondualistic wisdom'. So it might be suggested that 'selfless concern' is in fact needed in order to 'actualize the concept of emptiness' (Huntington 1989: 84). In other words, selfless action is partly the result of a selfless attitude previously developed which has already sensitized one to the suffering of others. Thus, the Dalai Lama (1994: 114) suggests that while one may not need the first five *pāramitās* in order to realize emptiness, one certainly needs them if one wishes to benefit others. One might therefore speak of the monk or the *bodhisattva* as having an 'ethicized consciousness' (Gombrich 2009: 83). Such an internalized compassion 'imperatively compels us to act selflessly' (Thurman 1976: 4), making one feel 'obliged to go out and help others' (Dharmasiri 1989: 50). That is why we sometimes need to think of Buddhist ethics in terms of a *duty* to act compassionately.

It is the heightening of this sensitivity through the realization of the truth of interdependence (Ś.S. 119) along with the constant reaffirmation of the Bodhisattva Vow which finally leads to a complete reorientation in one's lifestyle. Compassion is then in 'profound accord with the knowledge gained through philosophical analysis' (Huntington 1989: 102). It thus becomes 'effortless' (BCA. 1.35). And it should by now be clear that there is no obvious 'means/end distinction' (Siderits 2003: 111, note c) in Śāntideva's *bodhisattva* path and that compassion runs right the way through. The mind must return to *bodhicitta* over and over again, for wavering (*dolāyamāna*) is inevitable (BCA. 4.11).

Given that the virtues of the *jīvan-mukta* are also said to run right through (Fort and Mumme 1996: 144), and given that Śaṅkara explicitly endorses such a thesis (U.S. Prose, 1.2–6), then it comes as no surprise that we can glean parallel responses in Śaṅkara on the link between *brahman*-knowledge and compassion. This is so, even if Śaṅkara does claim that the *jīvan-mukta*'s 'knowledge cannot supply any impulsion to action' (B.S.Bh. III.iv.8), for it is clear from the context that it is ritual action that is being denied. Thus, we may still find: 1) a similar weakening of craving and attachment, along with an insight into the non-self of the *jīva*-trope giving rise to an unbounded view of reality; 2) a conviction in the one basic ground of being (*sat*) which leads one to view others as manifestations of the one source; 3) a similar sense of freedom from the shackles of *saṃsāra*, leading to a sympathetic attitude to the seeker of liberation; and 4) a feeling of being duty-bound to protect others, along with a simultaneous need to continue the Vedāntin lineage of *brahman*-knowers.

So once again, we see how close Śāntideva and Śaṅkara stand in both aim and method. Both wish to be rid of reification, of false understanding. Both describe this as a form of realization that is beyond the intellect. Both ground their views almost exclusively within their own textual tradition, in what Forsthoefel (2002: 320) has called the 'external circuitry' of 'text, tradition and teacher'. While Śāntideva informs us that the Buddha's word is to be taken as 'truth' (*bhūta*) (BCA. 8.156), Śaṅkara states that any teaching that opposes the Vedas is contradictory by default (B.S.Bh. II.ii.18). Moreover, both form hierarchies of knowledge within their tradition, claiming that certain practitioners know better than others and that certain textual statements are more definitive than others. Both see the aim of their texts and the result of the eventual realization as a reversal of the egoistic attitude, though both suggest that a hint of this non-egoistic attitude is in fact necessary for the path. Both claim that realization removes ignorance (*avidyā*) and leads to an end of suffering (*duḥkha*). Both insist that renunciation is a necessary preliminary to insight, and that some form of inquiry into reality is necessary. Both then claim that this inquiry must eventually cease, and both surprisingly devalue the rewarding bliss (*ānanda*) that their traditions assert arises at this juncture. And finally, both will place their knowers-of-reality in the role of teacher, whose 'job' it is to show others that there is in fact no individuated self. That is, both would agree with Dharmasiri (1989: 52) that 'The most important expression of the monks' sympathy is their teaching'. Thus, both Śāntideva and Śaṅkara advocate what Cooper and James (2005: 82) have called an 'ethically charged form of knowledge'.

Chapter 6
A Selfless Response to the World

We have just drawn a distinction between the forms of liberation espoused by Śaṅkara and Śāntideva. Both are now faced with the issue of the life that the 'liberated' person lives before their physical death. Both have nominated the life of teaching others as the perfect occupation. Yet, due to their radically revisionary metaphysics, both are faced with a critical ethical question: how should such a 'person' respond to a world which is like an illusion? In fact, we may well ask the deeper motivational question: *why* should they respond to a world that is like an illusion?

The question is perhaps more complex for Śaṅkara than for Śāntideva. While it is true that both share the notion that we are kept in gnoseological bondage due to ignorance, they do not agree on what keeps us in the world. For Śāntideva, it is the will to benefit other beings, the voluntary accumulation of merit (and thus positive *karma*) that keeps one in the world. For Śaṅkara, the liberated person has gone beyond *karma*, and so no such accumulation could take place. As a consequence of this metaphysics, it is only past *karma* that could keep one here. Now, if knowing *brahman* is going to put an end to rebirth, and if rebirth is caused by *karma*, then the knowledge of *brahman* must also put an end to *karma*. But if *karma* were to end with knowledge, then this body (which is the result of *karma*) must also (instantaneously) end. The question thus arises, how does one who knows *brahman* continue to live? And so we will see that Śaṅkara is forced into denying that all *karma* is ended with knowledge of *brahman*. Rather, some is and some is not. This will amount to a theory of three types of *karma* (that is, *saṃcita*, *āgāmi* and *prārabdha*).

We therefore need to be careful of the assertion that, for Advaita, *karma* is a 'convenient fiction' (Deutsch 1973: 69). Deutsch clearly overstates his case, for if *karma* was indeed some sort of heuristic device, then it was a sticky one, one which refused to go away after it had surpassed its usefulness. Better to say that it was a meaningful notion which helped the Advaitins explain certain phenomena; such as bondage, class status, justice, morality, purification and liberation; but a notion that only holds true for provisional reality.

According to certain texts, all *karma* is reportedly burnt up when ultimate knowledge dawns (Mu.U. II.ii.8 and Bh.G. IV.37). Nevertheless, the fact that the body of the seeker (which is the result of past *karma*) evidently remains intact even after *brahman*-knowledge has dawned forces Śaṅkara-the-exegete into a compromise whereby *karma* crosses over (as it were) into the terrain of the ultimate, with the *jīvan-mukta*'s mind flickering between absolute and provisional states. In other words, the ultimate gnoseological life kicks in prior to the ultimacy of *karma*-less, incorporeal liberation (*videha-mukti*). According to Śaṅkara, the liberated being (*jīvan-mukta*) must still live out a certain type of residual (*prārabdha*) *karma*, after which he will 'fall', as it were (Ch.U.Bh. VI.xiv.2).

But, at this level of explanation, the concept of *karma* actually becomes *inconvenient*. As Śaṅkara's own 'objector' states: why doesn't the knower fall immediately on the attainment of knowledge? How can one be sure that the knower's *karma* will end at death? How does one know that rebirth will come to an end? (Ch.U.Bh. VI.xiv.2). Śaṅkara's response is that knowledge of *brahman* has eliminated past *karma* which has yet to bear fruit (*saṃcita-karma*), but the knower is still subject to past *karma* that has already begun to bear fruit (*prārabdha-karma*). This *karma* does not affect his conduct, and for the rest of his existence, his conduct is said to be 'beyond good and evil' (Deutsch 1973: 100). This does not mean that he may act as he likes; rather, he has gone beyond the making of merit (*puṇya*) and demerit (*pāpa*), and will thus produce no future (*āgāmi*) *karma*.[1]

His *prārabdha-karma* will naturally wear out with the passing of time, just as an arrow which has left the bow must travel and then come to a stop (Ch.U.Bh. VI.xiv.2). But the problem of the 'delay' will not go away so easily, and even Śaṅkara, who claims that it is 'illogical' that one who has put an end to ignorance should take rebirth (B.S.Bh. III.ii.9), is later forced to admit that rebirth may be necessary if the knower is given a 'mission' by the gods (III.iii.32). In order to answer the question of how long this mission will last, Śaṅkara again turns to the analogy of the arrow (ibid.), whereby the end of the mission means the falling of the man. But the question of how long it takes for *prārabdha-karma* to end is never made clear, for it seems to be at the mercy of the gods.[2] In other words, the 'liberated' being does not as yet have the total freedom of action or self-rulership (*sva-raj*) mentioned in the *Ch.Up.* (VII.xxv.2). This sits in contrast to the *bodhisattva*, who makes it his own mission to return for the sake of other beings. But in order to have his 'own' mission, he must remain an 'agent', so the selflessness of the *bodhisattva* is again brought into question.

For Śaṅkara, the teacher's passing on of the knowledge of *brahman* produces no positive *karma* whatsoever for himself, for none of the knower's actions bear any personal fruit (Ch.U.Bh.VI.xiv.2). Of course, it will help the pupil toward removing past *karma*. This act of teaching is not to be seen as an obligatory duty, but as selfless, spontaneous action, arising from within the *jīvan-mukta*'s very nature. This spontaneity is indicated in the Upaniṣads by the notion of child-like behaviour, whereby the *mukta* acts 'howsoever he may' (Bṛ.U. III.v.1). According to the *V.C.*, this includes a form of altruism: 'It is the very nature of those of great-self to labour of their own accord in order to dispel the troubles of others' (V.C. 38).

---

[1] Cf. the Buddha's description of a true monk (Dhp. 267) and a true *Brahmin* (Dhp. 412).

[2] Śaṅkara discusses divine missions here on his opponent's terms. There is no hint in Śaṅkara's ethical philosophy that the *brahman*-knower awaits these missions; quite the opposite.

And Śaṅkara seems to reinstate the notion of *Dharma* and duty, stating that the enlightened (*vidvān*) should act according to the laws of scripture (*smṛti*). He seems rather cautious about the interpretation of the Upaniṣads, insisting that 'howsoever he may' does not imply 'disrespectful' behaviour (Bṛ.U.Bh. III.v.1). Rather, the teacher needs to act with a certain level of modesty, and so Śaṅkara reads 'child-like' to mean free from haughtiness (B.S.Bh. III.iv.50). As this teaching will necessarily include the use of the 'great sayings' (*mahāvākyas*), we should also be cautious about such statements as, 'The need for sacred texts loses its validity only for the adept' (Isayeva 1993: 197). Such language of transcendence, if limited to injunctions, may well be appropriate. However, it is problematic once the *brahman*-knower takes on the 'job' of teacher (*ācarya*), and as such turns around to face the world. It is with *language* that he turns around, and it is the language of scripture. Thus, while the *jīvan-mukta* is beyond being directed by the scripture (B.S.Bh. II.iii.48), it is still his instrumental means of directing others. Therefore, the 'deep-rooted reliance upon the language of *śruti*' (Isayeva 1993: 237) is a trait that the Advaitin adept never shrugs off, and its authoritative validity is demonstrated in Advaita's insistence on the *śruti* as enlightening device *par excellence*. In fact, Śaṅkara explicitly rejects the idea that the Vedas become invalid after one has let go of the false sense of agency, for they remain meaningful with regard to knowledge of *brahman* (Bh.G.Bh. 18.66). Thus, the need for sacred texts never loses its validity. When the Upaniṣads themselves speak of the Vedas as no Vedas, Śaṅkara glosses it as 'Since he transcends those rites, the Vedas are not the Vedas' (Bṛ.U.Bh. IV.iii.22). In other words, he takes it to apply only to the *pūrva* section on rites, and the Upaniṣads are left untouched.

For Śāntideva, it would seem to be a case of business as usual, for the *bodhisattva* has already been involved in selfless activity, and is now simply capable of more of the same. From the early stages of the path, his actions have been motivated by the desire to liberate all beings. But given that his vision of this world has so radically changed, that he has now attained to the level of 'seeing' (the first *bhūmi*), we may well ask what it is like to see the world from the (subjective) position of emptiness. For if one sees one's non-self, who is it that acts, and whose intentions are carried out?

Here I wish to introduce a hermeneutic device (Figures 6.1 and 6.2), a new way of describing the vision of the metaphysical and ethical worlds of both Śaṅkara and Śāntideva. I argue for a model which is more complex than the 'either/or' model of Western philosophy, a model which may take us beyond the *either-self-or-no-self* parameters. In doing this, we will be forced into re-evaluating just where the borders lie between a tradition which supposedly believes in a 'self' and one which supposedly rejects it. When we combine both the ultimate world of metaphysics with the conventional world of ethics, that is, when we take the Two Truths together, we are forced into acknowledging the relocations of self which take place in both Hinduism's and Buddhism's most revisionary exponents. This relocation will lead to a model which is best described, not as 'either/or', but as 'both/and'.

Moreover, we need to enter into a debate, begun by Paul Williams (1998a), which questions Śāntideva's insistence on the no-self position, even at the cost of the *bodhisattva* path becoming unjustified. I argue for a model which is more complex than the *either-self-or-no-self* model that Williams assumes. This will take into consideration the context of each chapter of the *BCA* as well as the *Compendium*. The intention is to make use of the aforementioned hermeneutic device, a schematic diagram, to both challenge Williams' dualistic approach, and provide the reader with a new point of entry into Śāntideva's personal vision of the *bodhisattva*. We have seen that, in order to attain ultimate realization, according to Śaṅkara and Śāntideva, one must become cognizant of one's selflessness. It is not so much then that this selflessness is subsequently made central to their ethical systems; their ethics are rather embedded in this search for selflessness.

Now, the moral philosopher Thomas Nagel, in *The Possibility of Altruism* (1978: 100), states that 'Ethics is a struggle against a certain form of the egocentric predicament'. We can see that both Śaṅkara and Śāntideva tackle this issue head on, destroying the very notion of ego as a persisting centre of individualistic thinking. We have called their resultant activity 'constructive altruism'. According to Nagel (1978: 3), altruism depends on: 1) recognizing the reality of other persons, and 2) an equivalent capacity to regard oneself as merely one individual among many. But have we not just witnessed both Śaṅkara and Śāntideva denying the reality of persons? And can it be said that a *brahman*-knower or a *bodhisattva* are merely individuals among many individuals? Neither answer is a simple 'yes' or 'no'.

Both Śaṅkara and Śāntideva will deny that there is an ultimately individuated person to be recognized, but neither will deny that there is a 'conventional person' there in front of them, with a name, a caste, a gender and a relative qualification. As for whether they have the capacity to see themselves as 'one individual among many', we would then need to ask what an 'individual' is. For sure, they will both recognize that their bodies provisionally belong to a certain karmic history. As for the mind, Śaṅkara will claim that unenlightened beings have their own mind (*manas*) which interferes with the pure consciousness of *brahman*, whereas the *brahman*-knower's mind only minimally and infrequently interferes with *brahman*-consciousness. As such, the *jīvan-mukta* both is and is not an individual agent, with the emphasis on the latter. Now Śāntideva will have the *bodhisattva* recognize the Vow he took as *his* vow. That is, the 'Buddhist too requires an agent-oriented perspective to reach a more impersonal goal' (de Silva, in Bilimoria et al. 2007: 243). Nonetheless, it is this Vow which makes *bodhisattvas* different from other beings, in that they have a duty to be self-defacing. Furthermore, when the *bodhisattva* has seen the non-self of his own being, he does not allow that to be transferred onto other beings.

Therefore, by seeing themselves as empty of individuated self, and yet continuing to see others as having an individuated self, the *bodhisattva* and the *jīvan-mukta* quite deliberately adopt a view which sees others as of a different kind. In other words, they do not put their own self down, but rather emphasize the individuality of the other. This is not a simple 'other-regarding' ethics; it is an '*other-constructing*' ethics. The *bodhisattva* agrees to acknowledge the personal suffering of the other, whilst the *brahman*-knower agrees to acknowledge the qualifications of the potential student, allowing them their badge of caste where no castes ultimately exist. So, the manner by which they create what we might see from the outside as an 'altruistic situation' is done, not at the expense of their own self, but through the temporary elevation of the other, which is itself derived from a prior decision to see the world in conventional (and thus fabricated) terms. Hence, I have spoken of 'constructive altruism', and as such, I re-define altruism.

It could indeed be argued that altruism *demands* such an unbalanced view of oneself versus others. For one thing, 'self-sacrificial altruism would seem to entail a positive violation of principles of justice' (Krebs and van Hesteren 1994: 126), stemming from the fact that such actors do not see themselves as 'one individual among many'. That is, it might be said that the heroes of this world see themselves as having a particular duty to act heroically, a duty that they would not demand of others (see Urmson 1958). In fact, the philosopher and Utilitarian, J.J.C. Smart (in Smart and Williams 1973: 32) sees this as the distinguishing feature between altruism and utilitarianism. We see that 'Western altruism' demands a temporary 'sacrifice' of self rather than a complete over-coming of the very belief in self. The self is thus taken as being a thing which is normally constant, but which, under certain conditions, can be devalued. We now know that this is in sharp contrast to both Advaita and Madhyamaka assumptions. And with the emergence of non-self philosophies in the West, this surely has implications for the future discussion of Comparative Ethics.

6.1 Śāntideva: Wisdom and Compassion – a Complex Model

I would imagine that by this stage, Śāntideva's altruistic intent has already been established. He told us: 'May there be in me no root of good or knowledge of *Dharma* or skilfulness which is not of benefit to all beings' (Ś.S. 33). In the *BCA*, he resolves thus:

> So mind, make the resolve 'I am bound to others'. From now on, you must have no other concern than the welfare of all beings (BCA. 8.137).

Śāntideva's major task is the justification of this compassionate response towards all other beings despite their illusory nature. Specifically, he wishes to persuade others to take on the Bodhisattva Vow to liberate all beings from suffering and from false seeing. It would seem most likely that he is first and foremost appealing to Buddhist monks on the verge of taking the Bodhisattva Vow. He may also be appealing to certain 'Śrāvaka-oriented' monks whose primary intent is their own liberation. That is, Śāntideva sees both hesitancy and reluctance towards altruism within his own Buddhist camp.

What then would appeal to both of these groups? The first doctrine that would appeal to them would be the First Noble Truth of the Buddha (see S.N. V.421), which is that all beings subject to conventional reality are in a state of suffering. Because this audience would believe that all beings are subject to rebirth, they would envisage this suffering as endless. But the Third Noble Truth states that the truth of *nirvāṇa* is an end to suffering (ibid.). So Śāntideva's argument must appeal to a group of monks who perhaps regularly oscillate between meditational states of non-suffering and other more 'ordinary' states. If they do not so oscillate between states, they at least know that it is possible. Further, as these monks have yet to be fully convinced of the benefits of taking the Bodhisattva Vow, we must assume (from Śāntideva's perspective) that they have a tendency to be locked into durable states of self-interest. Put simply, his Buddhist audience wish to liberate themselves, and *only* themselves, from suffering. So Śāntideva begins, quite predictably, with the basic truths of suffering, self-love (*ātma-sneha*), and the wish for happiness:

> At first, one should meditate carefully on the equality of self and other. Thinking, 'All experience happiness and suffering, [so] I should take care of them as I do myself'. Just as the body with its many parts – divided into hands, etc. – is protected as one thing, so too should this [whole world of beings], which though divided, is undivided in its nature to experience suffering and happiness. Even though my pain does not torment the body of others, that pain on the other hand is unbearable for me based on the love for myself (BCA. 8.90–92).

His next move is to shift the focus onto the other:

> Although the suffering of another cannot be experienced by me personally, nevertheless, for him that pain is unbearable because of self-love (8.93).

We might note here that Śāntideva has actually helped himself to one of Nagel's conditions for altruism, which is the 'capacity to regard oneself as merely one individual among many' (see above). At this conventional level, persons are real indeed. If one has self-love, something which is said to subsist until the first *bhūmi* (Ś.S. 11), and if one accepts the general Buddhist truth that all beings (conventionally) suffer, then one must accept that others suffer. One does not need to feel their pain to know that they have it. All one needs to see is their self-love (which will show in their selfish behaviour) and their pain follows through inference. We might write this logically as follows: 1) I suffer, 2) I am a self-loving human, 3) they appear (from their behaviour) to be self-loving humans; therefore 4) they suffer. We have now created the ground for sympathy on purely logical grounds based on one's own experience.

This is not quite yet 'compassion', more a sense of sharing a common ground with others, an 'interpersonal framework' (Wetlesen 2002: 60). It seems comparable to Hume's notion of 'sympathy', which should not be confused with the sentiment of compassion, which is 'merely one of its products' (Penelhum 1993: 134). Naturally, Śāntideva wants to go beyond mere participation in the emotional life of others, and wishes for a more pro-active stance. While for Hume it might be enough to feel at one with others, for Śāntideva the goal is to become, not their equal, but their helper. His is the kind of sympathy born of 'unequal power', derived from both the suffering other and from asymmetrical levels of wisdom (cf. Ricoeur 1994: 191).

It is interesting to note how Śāntideva goes through these steps. For example, with regard to the fact that we all suffer, he could have just gone straight to the conclusion, on authoritative grounds, *viz.* the First Noble Truth; but this would not have involved the audience emotionally. However, he makes no attempt to prove that pain is undesirable. It is of course an accepted truth in Buddhism that suffering is not only felt, but is undesirable. It is the basic reason why the audience became Buddhist monks in the first place, the reason in which *nirvāṇa* finds its value. But we might also note that it defies a rational explanation. As Hume noted, if you ask a man why he hates pain, he cannot supply an answer (Enquiries, Appendix I, 244). Pain and suffering are (conventionally) basic facts, assumed (by most) to be undesirable. We can find statements to this effect scattered throughout the *BCA*. For example:

> If all sentient beings were to have their wish fulfilled, no one would suffer. No one wishes for [their own] suffering (BCA. 6.34).

He later extends this to give a more general account of the undesirability of pain itself, unrelated to the person who it happens to afflict:

> That suffering should be prevented, no one disputes. If any of it is to be prevented, then all of it is. If not, then that goes for me too (8.103).

Put simply, either pain is to be accepted, including my own, or pain is to be tackled head on, including that of others. And of course, no Buddhist can accept the first option. But must they accept the second? Logically they need not. Not that they could claim that they are justified in willing pain on those they dislike, for this would go against the Buddhist ethics of non-harming (*ahiṃsā*). What they might say is: 'I feel my pain, and wish to be free of it, but I do not feel his or her pain in the same way. I know they have pain, but what is that to me?'. In other words, they may stick with self-love and go no further. However, this response is unacceptable, for Nagel (1978: 86) is surely right when he says that 'in order to accept something as a goal for oneself, one must be able to regard its achievement by oneself as an *objective* good'. And in Buddhist terms, *nirvāṇa* (*viz.* the end of suffering) simply *must* be taken by these monks as an objective good. What they are more likely to say then, is: 'I feel my pain, I recognize that life is suffering and wish to be ultimately free of it. I know others have pain and are subject to all kinds of suffering, but how am I to free them of it?

I can only free myself'. That is, 'emotional empathy for pain, however intense, does not necessarily result in a helping response' (Oliner and Oliner 1992: 174). This may not be due to self-love, but more a sense of self-limitation. If someone comes to me complaining of lung cancer, I am not uncaring if I fail to perform an operation on them. The monks might therefore reasonably claim that 'ought' implies 'can'. As the *Compendium* states, 'There is no fault concerning matters beyond one's powers' (Ś.S. 15). Hence, it is reasonable to accept that others suffer whilst maintaining the view that one lacks the means to put an end to this. Of course, I could drive someone to a hospital, or even put bandages on their wounds, but this will only *reduce* their suffering, it will not put an end to it, and will certainly not put an end to the cycle of suffering (*saṃsāra*). They may also say, along with the *Dhammapada*, that 'one cannot purify another', or that, 'one should not abandon one's own purpose for the purpose of another' (Dhp. 165–6).[3] Taken this way, it would seem to parallel Nagel's (1978: 129) point that there are 'certain ends and objects which one is in a *logically* better position to pursue for oneself than for others'.

The fact is that Śāntideva has still failed to establish a logical foundation for a life of selfless conduct. His first response to this failure is an attempt to shorten the gap between the way his audience see their own plight and that of others. He does this: 1) through a reiteration of the universality of pain, 2) by an appeal to sympathy, 3) by trying to weaken their self-love, and 4) by strengthening their compassion for others. Now, altruism, on Comte's (1798–1857) original account, involved the 'subordination of self-love to meeting the needs of others' (Scott and Seglow 2007: 16). But Śāntideva first wishes to demonstrate an equal ground for concern before going on to the more developed subordination of selfish concern. Thus:

> I should dispel the pain of others, just as I do my own, based on the fact that it is pain. And I should help others for they are beings like me. Since happiness is equally dear to me and others, what's special about me that I strive after my happiness alone? Since pain and fear are disliked by me and others, what's special about me that I protect myself and not the other? (BCA. 8.94–6).

At the conventional level of discourse, it would seem that he has gone as far as he can in his 'logical' approach to compassion. We have no need to qualify this with the metaphysics of non-self for he has yet to raise the issue. At this level of discourse, he is in fact talking to those who still hold to the sense of self, a self equally prone to pain as all other selves. With such rhetoric, he may well have convinced the more sentimental amongst the audience, but what of the hardened

---

[3] Naturally, the latter verse should not be taken as an outright rejection of compassion/altruism (see below), but rather seen in the soteriological context of *nirvāṇa*. It does not mean that 'the only real help is self-help', as Matics (1971: 19) implies. Nor should it be taken as proof of a transcendent self, as Pérez-Remón (1980: 28) suggests.

intellectuals? I believe he realizes that he needs a second approach, that is, the Two Truths.

Before we go any further though, I would like to introduce the first of my diagrams (see Figure 6.1 on p.149). With this diagram, I wish to introduce a new dimension into the debate, through which I hope to demonstrate that the Two Truths ought not to be seen in a dualistic manner. To believe that all Śāntideva has open to him is *either* conventional truth *or* ultimate truth is to miss a major dimension of his argument. It is not simply a question of asking whether there is a self (*ātman*) or not a self (*anātman*), but about asking when one should see one way or the other. That is, it is about *flickering* between these views. I have added arrows to the axes to further indicate the constant shifts involved. The upper section of the diagram maps the conventional world of the *bodhisattva*, a world where the 'I' exists on the *bodhisattva*'s side of the fence, and a world where other beings exist on the other side of the fence. This world is neither empty of inherent existence, nor mind-created. It is a world to be taken very seriously, a world run by karmic laws, where merit is accumulated and dispersed amongst the needy. The lower section of the diagram maps the ultimate world of the *bodhisattva*, a world which offers him a means to renunciation from the evil world of the other. It also offers him the opportunity to see the emptiness of his own self and the self of the other. This diagram helps to highlight that the 'other' for Śāntideva is to be contrasted with the 'me', not with the 'self'. Thus, there appear to be *four views* open to Śāntideva: 1) I have a self which suffers and so do others, 2) I have a self which suffers whilst others are empty of self, 3) I have no self and neither do others, and 4) I have no self and yet others have a self which suffers.

However, it is in fact even more complicated than that. For one thing, in order to renounce, one must focus on one's own suffering, whilst perhaps accusing the world of creating problems for oneself. It is not enough to say 'I suffer and they suffer'. To gain distance, one must *disparage* the other. That is, one must form a mind which rejects the world. And so, in his earlier ascetic mode, Śāntideva wrote:

> Self-aggrandizement, scorn for others, talk of the pleasures of life, etc. When two fools meet, all things disagreeable will certainly follow. In this way, contact with [a fool] brings harm [to myself] and to him. [So] I will dwell alone, happily, my mind undefiled (BCA. 8.13–14).

If one moves from this mind-state and assumes common sympathy for others, one will need to remind oneself that others will not listen to reason. People play deaf and dumb. They hardly deserve to be helped:

> One moment they are friends, the next moment enemies. In a pleasant situation they get angry. Common people are impossible to please (BCA. 8.10).

In fact, they are almost impossible to help:

> Beings are of varying character. Not even a Buddha could satisfy them. Let alone the ignorant like me. Thus why worry about the worldly? (BCA. 8.22).

So the 'Others/Not-self' quadrant includes a deconstruction process. People to whom we are emotionally attached are rejected as being a 'hindrance' to my liberation:

> Man is born alone and indeed he dies alone. No one else shares his suffering. So what's the use of these 'dear' ones, these hindrance-makers? (BCA. 8.33)

Clearly, where Śāntideva wants to have us, if we are to be selfless compassionate beings, is to see others as needy of our help, and to see our job as being that of the helper. But he cannot have us believing too much in our own existence, for then we will fall into the ancient habit of putting oneself first. Ideally then, the *bodhisattva* must see himself in terms of non-self whilst seeing others as suffering and of being worthy of his help. Thus, the Comtean subordination of self-love to meeting the needs of others is only a preliminary step in the process of becoming a *bodhisattva*, for it remains within the framework of an individualistic self-conception. So the above verses which depend on this self-love (BCA. 8.94–6) still position the monk firmly within conventional reality.

The *bodhisattva* must move on from this to see that there is in fact no self which requires subordination. The love of self must be replaced by the knowledge of no-self, but this knowledge of no-self must itself be over-ridden by the compassionate vow to liberate all other beings (who happen to believe they are selves).

We are thus required to read the question of self and no-self within a complex framework of contexts. While aware that there are other more social contexts within which Buddhism might allow for the notion of self, such as monastic/lay distinctions or king/subject relationships; here the term 'context' is being used more in the sense of *time* than role. In other words, though being a *bodhisattva* may indeed be seen as a role, it is one that depends on a progressive shift from right motivation through renunciation to selfless activity. One's view of self is therefore a function of one's level of wisdom rather than of one's social circumstance.

There are perhaps two exceptions to this: first, in that a *bodhisattva* may (theoretically) remain in a state of mind which sees all as non-self so long as he is not confronted by a living being; and second, when a *bodhisattva* meets with another *bodhisattva* and must ask about their relative level of attainment. The first instance implies that there are times when a *bodhisattva* will need to switch from seeing all as non-self to seeing the confronted being as taking themselves as having a self. The second instance demonstrates that even though a *bodhisattva* is said to have no self, that does not imply that all *bodhisattvas* are thus equal, and status does in fact play a part in their interaction (see below). Let us now turn to the diagrammatic representation of the *bodhisattva*'s life and see the domains available to him:

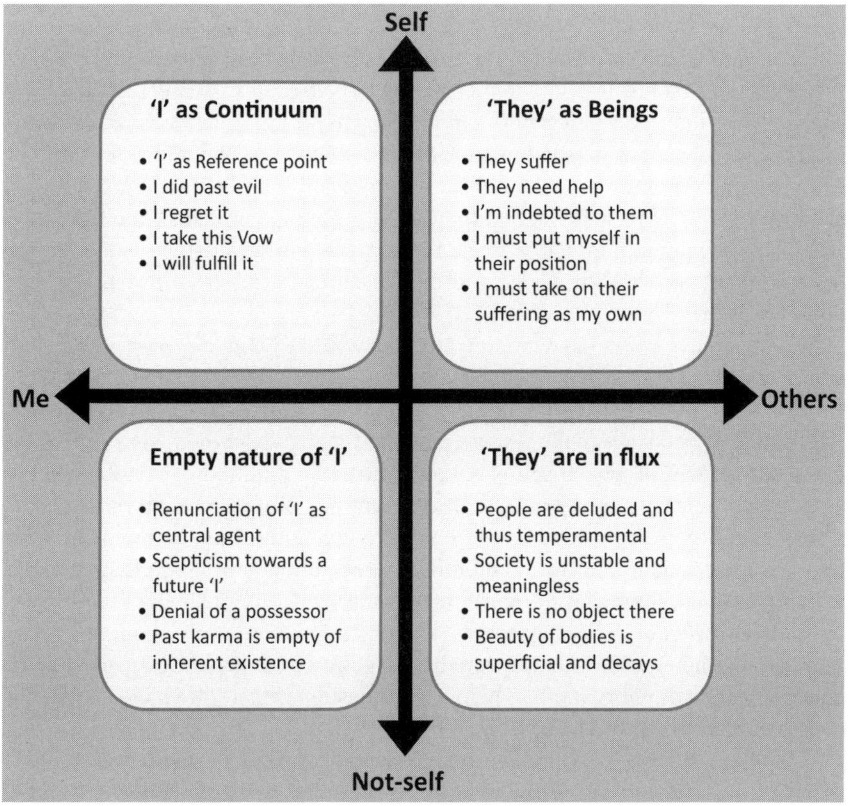

Figure 6.1 The Function of Domains in Śāntideva's Ethics

The above diagram represents a visual summary of the *BCA*. The key principle to grasp here is that Śāntideva is well aware that the would-be *bodhisattva* must have a keen sense of self-agency in order to take the Vow to benefit all beings and to ultimately deliver them from suffering. Likewise, he must see beings as existent in order to form the wish to benefit them. If I do not exist, how can I take the Vow? If suffering beings do not exist, how can one free them? Indeed, why would one bother? The active component of Buddhist ethics, then, cannot be based on the *anātman* principle, and the *anātman* principle should not be used to deny the conventional reality of persons. The one who takes the Vow is a person: me; and the ones I vow to help are persons: Peter, Paul and Mary. This is fundamental.

But let us not forget Śāntideva's predicament. He has just managed to convince some sentimental listeners to turn towards the path of selfless compassion. Perhaps this group has now gained 'aspiring' *bodhicitta* (see BCA. 1.15–16), that is, the wish to benefit all beings. But he is left with the hard-headed intellectual bunch. As we have already suggested, the only strategy left open to him is the ultimate side of the Two Truths. He needs to convince the audience that they are the same as all others, not only in their desire to be free of suffering (conventional truth), but in their non-being (ultimate truth). His solution then lies in his ability to prove to others (or persuade them into believing) that they have no ultimate selfhood *and* that they must help others who equally have no ultimate selfhood, but suffer from the false belief that they do. It is not that altruism directly follows from the insight into *anātman*; rather, one is made more available to others when one disregards one's own needs, and this is felt to follow from the insight into *anātman*.

He thus picks up on the everyday fact that we care about our own future. This caring about our future may not appear strange, especially if we adhere to Nagel's (1978: 38–9) premise that we all take our future as being part of our own *life*. But two Buddhist doctrines make it more peculiar than Nagel would admit. First, the idea that the present mental self is but a momentary cognition to be succeeded by another momentary cognition, with the present physical self being a momentary arrangement of elements and conditions. So your future 'self' is not 'you' (that is, your present bundle of form and mind-states), but another such bundle as yet to arise. Second, the belief in rebirth means that your 'life' is better seen as your 'continuum' (*saṃtāna*). In other words, it would seem that to care about this future bundle, whether in this life-span or the next life or ten lives down the line, is equivalent to caring for 'another' being. The question is therefore more subtle than a simple dilemma of prudence over altruism.

There are two ways a Buddhist can go from here. Either you see the stupidity of your ways and stop caring about yourself, or you make the sympathetic leap and see others as equally deserving of your care and attention. That is, you either give up prudence, or you take up altruism. In other words, Śāntideva's argument could just as well motivate apathy as compassion. Logically, of course, both options are open, but remember that the starting point was self-love. So it would seem to be an assumption of Śāntideva that the first option is blocked by a natural inclination to care for your own 'self':

> If I don't care about them because their pain does not afflict me, then why do I care about [my] future-body's suffering when it doesn't afflict [the current] me? The notion 'It is the same "me" even then' is false. Since it is one [person] who dies and quite another that is [re-] born. If you believe that pain should be protected by whoever it belongs to, [note that] a pain in the foot is not of the hand, so why does one protect the other? If it is argued that this is inappropriate as it proceeds from self-identity, then one ought to equally refrain from such 'inappropriateness' to do with oneself (BCA. 8.97–100).

The final point then is surely not a recommendation, but a sarcastic punch-line. Clayton (2006: 64), through her assessment of the *Compendium*, comes to the very same conclusion:

> [J]ust as it is natural to do things now to benefit yourself in the future, even though it is not the same person, you should work to benefit other beings besides yourself in the present.

Śāntideva has pointed out to his audience that the person they are to be in their next life is not the same person that they are now. It is indeed the same 'person-as-continuum', but not the same 'specific-person'. Thus, the 'person' who is reborn is 'neither the same nor different' from the one that died (see Collins 1982: 190). It is therefore not a total absurdity to care for the 'person' that you will be reborn as, just as it is not absurd for the hand to protect the foot. But if it is not absurd to care for this future person, why not care for other people as well? The response, of course, is that the person I will be in my next life is continuous with the person I am now in a way that other beings are not.

It should be noted that I have taken what Paul Williams (1998a: 31) calls the 'narrower' interpretation of Śāntideva's verses. The Sanskrit compound I have translated as 'future-body's suffering' (*āgāmikāyaduḥkhān*) (BCA. 8.97) might conceivably be translated as 'body's future suffering'. This 'wider' interpretation would be more problematic for Śāntideva, because he would then be implying that me (t_1) and me (t_2) are different persons. I do not think we need to take Śāntideva in this way, the reason being that he specifically mentions rebirth in the next verse.[4]

Nevertheless, it would seem that if the audience did understand him on this wider interpretation, he would have even less success in convincing them that caring for others is logically equivalent to caring for one's own self. After all, it would seem only rational to brush one's teeth at t_1 to prevent suffering toothache at t_2. I would therefore reject Pelden's (2007: 287) claim that it 'makes no sense' to protect oneself from future suffering. It clearly does make sense in the conventional world. It would seem that Śāntideva needs to go back to the drawing board. There is one move open to him, but it would seem to be based on a doctrine that his audience may not accept. He states that:

> All those who suffer in the world do so because of their desire for their own happiness. All those who are happy in the world are so because of their desire for the happiness of others (BCA. 8.129).

He seems to think that this wins the argument, for he asks us rhetorically 'Why say more?' (8.130a). But surely he does need to say more, for how, we may ask, could this doctrine possibly be proven? The first premise clearly follows from the Second Noble Truth, which states that suffering is the result of selfish desire or craving (see S.N. V.421). Thus all Buddhists ought to accept it. But the second premise seems to assume

[4] The Dalai Lama (1994: 102) seems to be working from a Tibetan text which suggests this 'wider' application, but still finds it justifiable. See Padmakara (2003: 124) translation from the Tibetan text, which speaks of 'my future pain'. However, I think that a defence of this 'wider' position would be much more problematic.

an altruistic context, which is the very thing the audience has yet to be convinced of. It assumes that happiness is the result of altruistic conduct, and that even the personal strife which this conduct generates is itself turned into a form of happiness. Śāntideva seems to be asking how one could possibly be content without a sense of concern for others. It is reminiscent of Ricoeur's (1994: 180) claim that 'self-esteem and solicitude cannot be experienced or reflected upon one without the other'. This is not to be taken in the Aristotelian sense that the happy man needs friends (p182), but in the sense of what Scott and Seglow (2007: 125) call that 'intrinsic satisfaction' of the 'saintly participation altruist'. This inner-satisfaction must be more fulfilling than the so-called bliss (*sukha*) of a private *nirvāṇa*. As Śāntideva puts it:

> Those who over-flow with joy when beings are being liberated; it's surely they that will be fulfilled. What's the point of 'tasteless' [individual] freedom? (BCA. 8.108).

One is reminded of Levinas' (1906–95) more overtly humanistic ethics of 'being for-the-other', described by Richard Cohen as taking precedence over, and being better than, being for-itself (in Levinas 2006: xxvi), with both the descriptive and prescriptive connotations this carries. While their cultural goals may vary, both are critical of those complacent ones who would neglect their moral responsibility. But the 'selfish' monk can still claim that his own liberation has a sweeter taste (for him) than the liberation of others. Or once again, he can claim that he is simply incapable of liberating others, so the 'tasteless' freedom will just have to do. In other words, he can respond to both description and prescription.

In fact, the debate would now appear to be over *types* of bliss, for even Śāntideva admits that the meditating monk is in bliss. The argument pretends to be one of 'bliss' versus 'higher bliss', though it is no mere hedonistic argument. If it were hedonistic, we could not make sense of the notion that the *bodhisattva* selflessly postpones his entrance into the bliss of *nirvāṇa* in order to be of benefit to others.[5] This issue is made more complex by the fact that Śāntideva will later claim that the Śrāvaka monk's *nirvāṇa* is 'poorly-established' (BCA. 9.44), and always will be unless he realizes the emptiness of phenomena (9.48). The debate then is not about bliss at all, but about the two pillars of Mahāyāna Buddhism, wisdom and compassion.

Nevertheless, bliss is critical to the argument for two reasons. First, it has become a resting place for those monks who falsely believe that they are liberated. The bliss or happiness (*su-kha*) they feel is of course the negation of the suffering (*duḥ-kha*) they had felt, and thus the fruit of the merit produced by following the Buddhist Path. It could therefore be seen as *the goal*. But Śāntideva sees bliss more as a means than as a goal. In the hands of a *bodhisattva*, bliss is turned into a store-house of merit to be donated to the needy. This is possible for the Mahāyāna tradition, for to them karmic fruitfulness is 'empty' and does not inherently 'belong' to any particular 'being'. In short, the bliss and non-abiding (*apratiṣṭha*) *nirvāṇa* Śāntideva has in mind trump the Śrāvaka bliss and private *nirvāṇa* through an inherent ability to benefit others. Thus:

[5] On the *bodhisattva*'s postponement of *nirvāṇa*, see Williams (2009: 58ff).

> When will I be able to bring relief to those in this hellish fire, with offerings of bliss flowing from the clouds of my merit? (9.166).

The 'cloud' metaphor is also found in the *Compendium* with reference to the *Gaṇḍavyūha Sūtra* (Ś.S. 122). The mind (*citta*) of the *bodhisattva* must be supported by roots of goodness. 'Clouds of Dharma' must flow from this mind.[6] Here in the *BCA*, we see that a further analogy takes place between *Dharma* and bliss (*sukha*), such that merit (*puṇya*) rains down from the *bodhisattva*'s compassionate mind in the form of bliss. And while the 'Śrāvaka-bliss' is to be enjoyed only by oneself, the 'Mahāyāna-bliss', like merit, is *transferable*. Clearly, this phenomenon of transfer of merit is central to understanding Mahāyāna ethics.[7] Therefore, Śāntideva's position on helping others may appear to be in direct opposition to the *Dhammapada*'s 'one cannot purify another' and that 'one should not abandon one's own purpose for the purpose of another' (Dhp. 165–6).

Of course, the Buddha also said, 'Go forth, oh monks, for the benefit of the many, for the happiness of the many, out of compassion for the world' (Vin.1.21).[8] This verse has been called an 'altruistic exhortation' (Lewis, in Neusner and Chilton 2005: 88), and is highlighted by such scholars as Collins (1982: 194), Cousins (1997: 388) and Goodman (2009: 49) in defence of the apparent lack of emphasis on compassion in early Buddhism.[9] Nevertheless, Śāntideva's final ethics do go beyond what is generally taken to be the Buddhist rationale for action, seeing the Śrāvaka emphasis on 'renunciation and ascetic self-restraint' (Collins 1982: 194) as a mere preliminary for selfless action in the world. This distinction still remains even if we take on Gombrich's (2009: 78–91) recent re-evaluation of the Buddha's teachings on the four 'boundless states'. For, even if the *bodhisattva*-path is indeed a 'restatement of the spirit of the *brahma-vihāras*' (N. Smart, in Deutsch and Bontekoe 1997: 87), and even if 'compassion is replete in all strands of the Buddhist tradition' (Carter, in Deutsch and Bontekoe 1997: 365), it is generally accepted that there remains a special emphasis on compassion and altruistic action in the Mahāyāna that went beyond that found in the early tradition. So when Collins (1982: 193) claims that Buddhism does not provide for either self-interest or 'self-denying altruism', he was talking from within the Theravāda (monastic) tradition. Contrast this with the following verses of Śāntideva:

---

6 Note that 'Cloud of Dharma' is also the name the *Daśabhūmika Sūtra* gives to the tenth *bhūmi*.

7 For an overview of the literature on merit transference, see Clayton (2006: 76–88).

8 Also found in the Sarvāstivādin *Catuṣpariṣat Sūtra* (see trans. Kloppenborg 1973).

9 The anomaly could be explained as: 'Do not put others before yourself *until* you have become an *arhat*'. This would fit both scriptural contexts. The *Dhammapada* speech, according to the commentarial story, was given to a single would-be *arhat* (see Narada 1993: 150); the *Vinaya* speech was given to the 60 enlightened *arhats* (Kloppenborg 1973: 43). Thus, the Buddha's philosophy may be interpreted as, 'One's own house must be put in order before busying oneself with other people's' (Cooper and James 2005: 56).

> 'If I give, what will I have?' – Such concern for oneself is demonic. 'If I have, what can I give?' – Such concern for others is divine. Oppressing others for one's own sake, one will roast in hell. But from oppressing oneself for the sake of others, one always meets with success. Distress, inferiority and stupidity are the result of desiring one's own promotion. By transferring that same desire onto others, one gains happiness, honour and intelligence. Putting others at the service of one's own aims will lead to your own servitude. Putting yourself at the service of others will lead to your own [true] lordship. All those who suffer in the world do so because of their desire for their own happiness. All those who are happy in the world are so because of their desire for the happiness of others (BCA. 8.125–9).

While true that 'oppressing oneself for the sake of others' is not Śāntideva's final position, it is an important step towards a life of pure selfless activity.

But returning to our blissful 'selfish' monk, he may still feel unmoved by Śāntideva's 'my bliss is better than your bliss' argument. And he is unlikely to accept that his liberation is poorly established. So Śāntideva now adopts yet another tactic, the rhetoric of shame and blame. He thus speaks to the 'lazy' and 'proud' monk in everyone present. Thus, 'We must cause him to fall from bliss, and continually appoint him distressful duties' (BCA. 8.154a); and again, more generally: 'Make yourself fall from bliss and involve yourself in the suffering of others' (8.161a). But such self-punishing rhetoric may still fail to arouse the listener into compassionate action, though it might lead to a feeling of guilt.

What Śāntideva seems to require then is a philosophical means of persuading the audience that their own self is ontologically equal to that of others. One method is the famous 'exchanging self and other' meditation (BCA. 8.140ff), mentioned above. Another method, which is more metaphysical in nature, is to offer a seemingly nihilistic evaluation of the person, whilst offering a universal view of pain:

> Continuities and aggregates, such as queues and armies are fictitious. There is no one who is suffering. Therefore, to whom will it belong? Without any exceptions, all sufferings are ownerless. As pain is pain, it should be warded off. Why put restrictions on this? (8.101–2).

The first line states that such wholes as 'queues' and 'armies' are fictitious, merely labels, placed on top of the separate parts to designate an object which is ultimately empty. The implication is that the momentary aggregates likewise do not go to make up a 'person'. In defence of a similar sceptical thesis by Hume (Treatise, I.iv.6), Penelhum (1993: 141) writes, the 'perceptions the mind has can well include perceptions of the series that constitute it, without there having also to be any supervenient subject beyond the series' successive members'. Pains are but perceptions, belonging to no one. Post-reduction, there is ultimately no 'person' or 'self' to whom pain belongs, no substance in which these sensations inhere. There is an obvious problem here, which Paul Williams (1998a: 104–76) has so ruthlessly exposed. Pain, on this account, appears to be free-floating. But how are we to make sense of a free-floating pain? Like Williams, I doubt that this is 'rationally' possible. But unlike Williams, I do not think Śāntideva is open to the charge.

While not the methodology I would normally condone; if we are going to hand-pick single verses for critique, then one text that may be open to the charge can be found in the Theravāda. One of its passages reads: 'For there is suffering, but none who suffers' (Vm. 16.90, trans. Ñāṇamoli). As Pérez-Remón (1980: 11) has noted, the 'moral self is utterly denied' here. Now, the reason this is open to the charge of a free-floating pain is that, for the Theravādin, pain is generally taken to be inherently real. Thus, Harvey (1990: 48) states that, 'suffering is inherent in the very fabric of life'. And Sarah Shaw (2008: 4) defines '*dukkha*' as 'an inherent, moving tension or dynamic that inheres in all existence'. Shaw goes on to claim that 'the cause of *dukkha* is the wish for things to be other than they are' (ibid.).

The problem here, from a Madhyamaka standpoint, is two-fold. First, *nothing* has inherent existence (*svabhāva*), so an inherent suffering is a conceptual construction. And second, if we were to accept that *dukkha* did inherently exist, then it quite evidently is *not* caused by desire, for it must pre-exist desire. Thus, to 'put suffering on the same level as impermanence and nonself', that is, as one of the three marks of existence, is an 'error' (Nhat Hanh 1998: 21). While the truth of suffering is thought by the Śrāvaka to be seen by a Noble's wisdom, the Mādhyamika sees it as a truth merely for 'conventional valid cognizers' (Hopkins 1996: 290). That is why the commentator of the *BCA*, Prajñākaramati, sees all but the Noble Truth of Cessation (*nirvāṇa*) as being conventional (*saṃvṛti*) truths, thus reducing the four truths to two (see Kapstein 2001: 217–18).

Śāntideva therefore asks the Śrāvaka, 'If suffering really exists, why does it not afflict people when they are cheerful?' (BCA. 9.88a). That is, for the Mādhyamikas, pleasure (*sukha*) and pain (*duḥkha*) are impermanent phenomena and mind-dependent; whereas, for the Śrāvakas, 'even happiness is to be seen as *dukkha*' (Harvey 1990: 48). So, just as Nāgārjuna did, Śāntideva distances himself from the Śrāvaka, for whom suffering truly exists.

Of course, if the Śrāvaka maintains that suffering is the end result of the various limbs of dependent origination (see Anderson 2001: 94–7), then they must give up the notion of its inherent existence. Likewise, if the Śrāvaka truly wishes to claim that the four Noble Truths 'do not have any permanent existence in the world' (p121), then once again they must give up the notion of *dukkha*'s inherent existence. Suffering, under Madhyamaka analysis, must lose its universal position in Buddhist ontology. However, it is never quite dislodged from its soteriology. While the 'fact of ill cannot maintain itself against the fact of emptiness' (Conze 2001: 111), the fact of emptiness must bend, as it were, to allow for the conventional truth of suffering in others.

The problem that Śāntideva faces is that he needs to keep the language of suffering at the conventional level for it has obvious soteriological value. Put simply, if there were no suffering in conventional reality, nobody would renounce. So, in denying suffering, Śāntideva does still seem to be committing a logical error. He has to answer two questions: 1) if suffering does not exist *conventionally*, then why do my knees hurt?, and 2) if suffering does not exist *ultimately*, then why should I care about the imaginary suffering of others?

Before we go any further, it is worth repeating that Śāntideva does not deny conventional reality. He writes quite explicitly that:

> All experiential elements are selfless. On the other hand, they are connected with the fruit of action. All phenomena lack own-being. On the other hand, there is an experiential, empirical world (Ś.S. 244).

Conventionally speaking, there is suffering and indeed, 'All those who suffer in the world do so because of their desire for their own happiness' (BCA. 8.129a). So, for this reason, we should renounce. Indeed, we should develop wisdom 'with the desire to end suffering' (BCA. 9.1b). In other words, not only does Śāntideva not deny pain conventionally, but, like any good Buddhist, he makes it the starting point of the quest for wisdom. And it is the 'person' that goes forth on this quest. With wisdom as the updated goal, he states that it is 'the reification of reality' that is the 'cause of suffering' (9.25). And so, he tells us that there is no 'I' whatsoever (9.56). We discover that 'the "I" has no existence under analytical investigation' (9.74b). When this becomes established, we are ready for the final altruistic both/and twist of his Two-Truth rhetoric. Henceforth, monks, 'Make yourself fall from bliss and involve yourself in the suffering of others' (8.161). Where is Śāntideva here if not in the midst of our conventional world of happiness and suffering?

This is not 'incoherent' rhetoric, as Williams (1998a: 160) claims; it is simply Śāntideva's both/and model at its most extreme. If you argue:

> 'For whom is compassion if no beings exist?' [We respond] For anyone who [our voluntary] delusion projects for the sake of what must be done (BCA. 9.75).

If there is a 'logical' incoherence here, then Śāntideva is saying 'so be it'. One needs to be able to flicker between these domains. One has to live with such 'tension'; that is the *bodhisattva*'s task. But if this flickering between seeing a self in others whilst maintaining the view of emptiness becomes problematic, and you start to imagine you have a self, then two paths open up. First, you could use this self-love as a device, and:

> … in the same way that one desires to protect oneself from pain and grief, etc., so one should develop a mind of compassion and concern towards the world (BCA. 8.117).

But if this prudence-cum-compassion method leads to one's self-love becoming so strong that you start to care more for your own happiness than for that of others, then 'better to meditate on not-self' (BCA. 9.77b). Thus, it would seem that there are methods available for those who have become selfless and for those who still have a trace of self. So Siderits (2003: 204) is not quite right when he says that 'one must become a truly empty person in order to effectively practice compassion'. This is an ideal, but it is not a pre-requirement.

Returning to our audience, they may still be hoping for a rational explanation, and may find this reductionism question-begging:

> Whose is the task to be done if there are no beings? [Response] True, the work is indeed delusional, but in order to bring about the end of suffering, the delusion which conceives the task is not restrained (BCA. 9.76).

As stated above, this voluntary delusion is the key to understanding Śāntideva's ethics, and indeed it must fail to pass the rationalist's criteria. For how can we make logical sense of a voluntary delusion? Nevertheless, that is how Śāntideva describes the move which one needs to make in order to admit a 'person' conventionally so as to avoid an ethical nihilism. That is, Śāntideva agrees that ethics needs people. So, while Wetlesen (2002) argues with Paul Williams over whether Śāntideva's conception of a person is reductive or non-reductive, the fact is, it is both. Śāntideva reduces himself to a complex set of inter-dependent conditions with no underlying self, but reconstructs the other to something more than that, that is, an individuated person with their own valid hopes and fears.

The question remains as to whether Śāntideva has gone off the Buddhist rails here, or whether he is in fact following a traditional view. Now Harvey (1990: 121) reads the *Diamond Sūtra* to be saying something quite similar, and so claims that the *bodhisattva* knows that there are no 'beings', but his skilful means 'enables him to reconcile this wisdom with his compassion'. In fact, the *Diamond Sūtra* is a *Prajñāpāramitā* text which completely rejects the notion of 'self', claiming that a *bodhisattva* is unworthy of the name (that is, 'wisdom-being') if he should hold such a notion (*Vajracchedikā*, Ch. 3). But, as we have seen, Śāntideva allows for the notion, if, and only if, it applies impersonally and conventionally. So Śāntideva appears even more conventional than the *Diamond Sūtra*. Paul Williams (2009: 61), for his part, draws on the *Aṣṭa*, another *Prajñāpāramitā* text, for what he calls the 'clever means and stratagems' of the *bodhisattva*. In this text, the *bodhisattva* refuses to realize the so-called 'reality-limit' (*bhūta-koṭi*), the (inferior) *nirvāṇa* of the *arhat* (*Aṣṭa*. 373). He does this through an intense focus on compassion, which prevents him from falling into complete emptiness, which would lead to the 'non-perception of any living being' (Streng 1982: 93).[10] According to Williams (2009: 61), the *bodhisattva* is thus 'able to combine simultaneously his direct meditative awareness of emptiness with awareness of others'. In other words, rather than attain the transparent mind of a Buddha, he opts for a flickering *both/and* mode of cognition.[11] Now, Śāntideva sits much closer to this *Aṣṭa*-model than to the *Vajracchedikā*, for he deliberately holds 'persons' as a support, so as never to fall into either the *nirvāṇa*

---

[10] Streng (1982) has listed four possible meanings of 'reality limit' in the *Aṣṭa*.

[11] The account of how he does this is rather complex. For the full text, see Conze (1973: 222–6).

of the *arhat* or into ethical nihilism. We thereby see that the move to re-instate the individuated person is not unique to Śāntideva, but has scriptural support.

Why Williams (1998a) picks out Śāntideva for particular attention is therefore puzzling. There has to be more to it than that 'unresolvable struggle between Reductionists and non-Reductionists' (Kapstein 2001: 44). It would seem that Williams assumes Śāntideva to be denying the person at both the ultimate and the conventional level. Yet, we have already shown that Śāntideva does in fact accept reality at the conventional level. Now Siderits (2000: 416) has stated that Śāntideva's arguments would indeed break down if he were denying the person at the conventional level, however, Siderits does not believe that he is so denying the person. He therefore, like me, disagrees with Williams' conclusions. But before we close the door on the debate, let us re-examine the particular verses which Williams selected for critique.

In the first set of verses selected by Williams (1998a: 29–51) (i.e. BCA. 8.97–8), Śāntideva is simply saying that the person when reborn is a different "specific" person than the current "specific" person which is "me". He wrote:

> If I don't care about them because their pain does not afflict me, then why do I care about [my] future-body's suffering when it doesn't afflict [the current] me? The notion "It is the same 'me' even then" is false. Since it is one [person] who dies and quite another that is [re-] born (BCA. 8.97–8).

He is not denying either of those persons conventionally here, nor is he is denying consciousness-as-continuum which links those two persons. In fact, verse 8.107 reads "those whose continuum is so developed". This continuum even survives the ultimate analysis of Chapter 9. Thus:

> "The cause is connected with the fruit" [you say]. But such an event is never seen. It is taught that there is an agent and an experiencer [of the fruit merely] in terms of a unity of the continuum (BCA. 9.72).

There is simply no way that Williams (1998a: 41) can maintain the claim that Śāntideva sees the relationship between my current life and my future lives as one of 'complete otherness'. It is 'other', in that I may not even be a human being in my next life, but it is not *unrelated* to my current continuum. So, rather than Williams' 'somewhat selective reading of the text' (Wetlesen 2002: 34), we need to pay attention to the context in order to understand Śāntideva's true meaning. For example, in verse 8.98 (above), Śāntideva is simply downplaying this continuum-aspect and focusing on the specific-person-aspect, because that has more persuasive force *in this stage* of the meditation. Williams fails to grasp the difference between these two. In a later work, Williams (2002, Appendix I) does seem to pay lip service to the true Buddhist position, but still claims that 'in terms of personal survival, being causally dependent upon the one that died is irrelevant' (2002: 200). But how is it irrelevant? To grasp Śāntideva's self-model, one needs to be quite flexible with regard to self and persons, but Williams appears rather one-dimensional. Of course, as already mentioned, Śāntideva's argument *would* have less force if he were talking about me (t_1) versus me (t_2) in this present life; but as Williams himself points out (1998a: 31–3), in the Sanskrit text, this is not the case.

In the second set of verses selected by Williams (1998a: 104–76) for critique (BCA. 8.101–3), Śāntideva is simply denying ultimate existence to the person, whilst admitting conventional existence to pain. People are like armies, made up of parts, with no ultimate status. Conventional pains are thus ultimately ownerless. In full:

> Continuities and aggregates, such as queues and armies are fictitious. There is no one who is suffering. Therefore, to whom will it belong? Without any exceptions, all sufferings are ownerless. As pain is pain, it should be warded off. Why put restrictions on this? That suffering should be prevented, no one disputes. If any of it is to be prevented, then all of it is. If not, then that goes for me too (BCA. 8.101–3).

The Dalai Lama (1994: 103) summarizes these verses thus: 'Although the "I" does not truly exist, in relative truth everyone wants to avoid suffering'. It is because Śāntideva's rhetoric flickers back and forth between domains that this is difficult to grasp. I therefore agree with Pettit (1999: 129–30) that Williams' critique of Śāntideva appears 'fundamentally misguided'. Nevertheless, I will respect Williams' issue with the notion of altruism as normally understood, and thus demand that from now on we call Śāntideva's ethics 'constructive altruism'.

Whether this is an altruism of 'complete rationality' (Williams 1998a: 29) is for the reader to decide. But note that Williams himself warns us that we ought to take such writings as the *BCA* as 'counselling' rather than as 'abstract statements about the universal way things actually are' (in Crosby and Skilton 1995: xv). Williams also, quite rightly, notes that the *BCA* is a 'meditation manual' (xxvi), a point he repeats in his own work (Williams 1998a: 29). So perhaps, as Pettit (1999: 134) suggests, we may need more than just 'philosophical reflection' to understand Śāntideva's ethics.[12] Perhaps Madhyamaka philosophy only makes real sense as an 'expression of an entire form of life' (Huntington 1989: 59). However, I believe that we have been able to save Śāntideva's ethics on the basis of the Two Truths without having to claim a need for 'meditative and moral practice' (Wetlesen 2002: 53), or being in a 'trance' of some kind (Matics 1971: 29). In other words, we might rightly claim to have a rational explanation for 'constructive altruism', so long as one understands that the 'person', for Śāntideva, is this embodied being, but that this 'person' is also empty, in the sense that me at t_3 is not exactly the same me as at t_1 or t_2, but is nevertheless conditioned by them.

In fact, when examined in its entirety, Śāntideva's ethics accept the conventional person in a fuller manner than some other Mādhyamika exponents. For example, Candrakīrti distinguishes between ordinary perfections and supramundane perfections (MMA. 1.16). A supramundane form of giving would have 'no conception of the fundamental real existence of the giver, gift or receiver' (Williams 2009: 51), the

[12] Paul Williams (2002: xiii) later confessed that his meditation was mainly on paper.

so-called 'three-fold purity' (Conze 2001: 18) of the *Prajñāpāramitā Sūtras* (see Conze 1975: 50). It is an 'unqualified rejection of any reified concept of giver, gift or recipient' (Huntington 1989: 70). This threatens to make the Levinasian 'face-to-face encounter' of giving (see Heim, in Bilimoria *et al* 2007: 192) rather *faceless*.

But, as argued throughout this book, Śāntideva's altruism is indeed a 'qualified' one. While the notion of 'altruism' is denied by Levinas (2006: 55) on the grounds that the impulse to give derives itself from the 'Other'; in Śāntideva, the 'Other' must first be constructed, deriving its force from the Bodhisattva Vow. Śāntideva's ethics of 'constructive altruism' thus appears as a Buddhist compromise on self, allowing for the qualified notion of a receiver, if not for a giver (which is non-existent) or a gift (which is illusory) (Ś.S. 270–75). Thus, an ultimately understanding giver gives an ultimately understood gift to a *constructed* receiver. The other person's face is given new life through the *bodhisattva*'s compassion. For Śāntideva, then, it is a clear case of the ends (the reduction in overall suffering) justifying the means (voluntarily adopting a fabricated view of the situation).

Note that by saying that the delusion is 'not restrained' (BCA. 9.76), there is the implication that the *bodhisattva* is indeed *free* to restrain it. This would mean that a superior *bodhisattva* could apply his wisdom to the delusion that saw the other person as real, but *chooses* not to. At this level, dualistic appearances would not interfere with his non-dualistic vision of emptiness unless he *forces* the interference. It is not the case that the *bodhisattva* maintains a slightly delusional mentality which allows for a mildly delusional view of beings as real, the kind of 'madness' that Burton (2004: 85) suggests. It is more a case of willing the subordination of wisdom to compassion. Again this highlights the advantage of taking the mind as flickering between seeing things as existent and non-existent, and then having the freedom to act accordingly, either on the basis of wisdom or on the basis of compassion.

If we now return to Figure 6.1 (on p.149), we see that we now have the entire picture of the path before us. The *bodhisattva*, in the Me/Self quadrant, sees the suffering of the provisional world. He sees the error of his ways, both ethical errors and cognitive errors. He regrets his ethical errors and prays for forgiveness of sins. This person-as-continuum thus vows to change his ways and to generate enough merit to liberate all beings. Misdeeds are 'dissolved' or 'purified' by a combination of prayer and the realization of emptiness. Merit is accumulated through the practice of the six perfections. The first steps to realizing emptiness are a certain form of moral conduct conducive to the denial of the egoistic self.

The *bodhisattva* thus shifts into the Me/Not-self quadrant. He works on renunciation of self. He wishes to be self-reliant, but without the notion of a self. Naturally, a denial of the self is itself an act of self, which demonstrates the preliminary nature of this stage of renunciation. In this quadrant, we find the *bodhisattva*'s denial of society, family and status, his renunciation of selfish desires. This is followed by the subsequent glimpses of emptiness, growing out of an inferential understanding of the teachings, and the realization of impermanence and the selflessness of all beings. Subsequently, 'The influence of phenomena is removed by employing the influence of emptiness' (BCA. 9.32a).

Through the loosening of his personal identity, he meditates on exchanging his self for others, a now standard popular method of generating empathy in Tibetan Buddhism. We can thus deduce that the term '*ātma*' in '*parātma*' (that is, '*para ātma*') (BCA. 8.120) has no metaphysical implication, but implies the taking up of a different view-point. In fact we can again relate Śāntideva's psychology with what Hume called 'sympathy'. Thomas' explanation of Hume captures this practice perfectly: 'I might imagine what it would be like to go through what you are undergoing and in some way I reproduce in myself what you are experiencing' (Thomas 1993: 57). Through such meditation, the *bodhisattva* overcomes envy and competitiveness, creating a basis for generating empathy and compassion for all beings.

At this point it is still a mental program, and the field must now shift to a more conventional worldly level. As stated by Oliner (2003: 210), 'just thinking empathetically is not in itself altruistic'. Thus, the altruistic impulse and the feeling of compassion and loving kindness are insufficient. We do not become virtuous by ourselves but are 'made virtuous through relationship with others' (Mrozik 2007: 10). In short, 'Altruism must entail action' (Monroe 1998: 6). But in shifting the field to the external world, in wishing the well-being of 'real' others, the *bodhisattva* has to re-instate them, reconstruct them. This is a move that may not so readily occur to most Western ethicists, and hopefully our explanation of Śāntideva will help future discussion of ethics within other forms of non-self metaphysics.

Returning to the diagram (on p.149), the *bodhisattva* thus moves out of the Others/Not-self quadrant and into the Others/Self quadrant. People suffer, they need help, they deserve help, and surely in the past they have helped 'me'. *Karma*, though empty, is meaningfully re-instated. We might recall that people 'may well behave at a high level in one domain and at a low level in another' (Krebs and van Hesteren 1994: 107). My quadrants can thus be seen as 'domains' in which shifts of cognitive maturity take place, sometimes through meditational progress, sometimes as a voluntary fall. The *bodhisattva* moves back to the Me/Self quadrant and reinforces the Vow to help all beings: 'So long as space remains, so long as the world remains, so will I remain, to dispel the suffering of the world' (BCA. 10.55).

If he acts on this vow, if his resolve remains steady, then he becomes a true *bodhisattva*. If his mind is still prone to wavering, and if he continues to choose to benefit others over himself, then he is surely a true altruist, even in the Comtean sense of the word. But once he firmly grasps that there is no self, and has the need to delude himself about the self of others, then his 'altruism' is of a different kind, it is 'constructive altruism', which relies on skilful means.

Yet an ethics that bases itself on such a tension between the ultimate and the conventional is bound to be unstable. It is an ethics which can be *explained*, but hardly *justified*. It may even be an ethics that we find difficult to accept, given our modern emphasis on the body and the rights of the individual. Moreover, it is a risky ethics. What happens if I spend so much time in the Others/Self quadrant that the conventional notions of their worldly reality start to filter back into the ultimate notions of my *bodhisattva* reality? If too much time is spent in one domain, could it be that one's cognitive level might fall irreparably into an old stage-structure? It is worth reminding ourselves of Śāntideva's solution:

> However, egoism, which is the cause of suffering, increases from the delusion that there is a self. If this [particular delusion] cannot be avoided, better to meditate on not-self (BCA. 9.77).

Egoism (*ahaṃkāra*) is to be stamped out because it is the biggest obstacle to liberation. But to see others as non-existent is the biggest obstacle to compassion. It is through flickering between these views (these quadrants) that one is able to remain on the *Bodhisattva* Path. If one becomes too deluded by compassion, one shifts the focus to not-self. If one becomes too wise, as it were, through an intense realization of emptiness, if one 'destroys the *bodhisattva* path', to use Williams' phrase, then one needs to re-instate beings through a 'voluntary' or 'deliberate' act of delusion. This deliberate act needs to become habitual:

> In the same way that, through habit, the idea of a 'self' arose about this, your own body, though it is without self, will not the 'selfhood' also arise through habit with regard to others? (BCA. 8.115).

He then turns this into an injunction:

> Therefore, just as you have formed the notion of individuality from the drops of [your parents'] sperm and blood, so you must develop the notion regarding others (BCA. 8.158).

There is still something to be said for Nagel's (1978: 88) point that 'recognotion of the reality of others depends on a conception of oneself'. Śāntideva accepts this view, but with a slight modification. The recognition of oneself as being real is applicable to the past, whereas the recognition of the reality of others is applicable to the future. It is through the memory of the former notion that the latter notion is to be constructed. But the former notion is then to be dropped. For example, the body is important to the other, but it must be transcended by a *bodhisattva*. It must be placed at the service of those others. Of course, one would still recognize a body and a need to eat, but its impermanence and inter-dependence would be a feature of that recognition. That is, the *bodhisattva* both experiences the conventional world whilst perceiving it as a fabrication. So when Nagel (1978: 101) states that 'it must be possible to say of other persons anything which one can say of oneself', we need to qualify this. For my purposes, I will qualify it here in terms of flickering, and note that the *bodhisattva* *could say* he exists or does not exist as a self, and *could say* that others exist or do not exist as selves, but *opts to say* that he does not exist as a self but others do.

If we were to place Śāntideva's *bodhisattva* into Bernard Williams' case study situation (see p.29 above), he might report that (ultimately speaking) he neither believed himself to be either A or B. He might therefore add an unexpected dimension to the case (though one that may become more and more familiar in Western thought). Yet one would imagine that (despite struggling with the non-altruistic response required of the test), he would posit B's mind to be the most relevant factor in the A-body-or-mind/B-body-or-mind enigma. We therefore see that it remains *possible* for Śāntideva's *bodhisattva* to speak of others as he speaks of himself, but he chooses not to do so. Rather, like the *jīvan-mukta*, he chooses to participate in the 'magic show'. The delusion is not restrained, allowing him to take the perspective of the suffering other.

6.2 Śaṅkara: Living Liberation – the True Place of Action

Much of the inspiration for this chapter comes from the following verses and the Advaitin concept of the 'living-liberated being' (*jīvan-mukta*). Here, Śaṅkara describes how such a person has apparently reached the final goal of life, wishing for nothing further, established as he is in *brahma-nirvāṇa*:

> That *yogi*, having attained the final state, even while living, absorbed in *brahman*, he is satisfied, liberated ... A living-liberated being [*jīvan-mukta*], having certitude that *brahman* is all, has become pure consciousness, taintless and free from merit and demerit ... It is said that he remains established in this state in the autumn years of his life, free, absorbed and satisfied in *brahman*. What need is there to say that he who has abided in *brahman* during his whole life, from celibate pupil to renunciate, alas attains the final peace of *brahmanhood* [*brahma-nirvāṇa*] (Bh.G.Bh. 5.24, 6.27 and 2.72).

But even more inspiring is the way in which Śaṅkara deals with the following verse from the *Chāndogya Upaniṣad*. In this commentary, we find Śaṅkara's theory of lineage and salvation. A man finds himself lost in this world. Not even God has shown mercy on him. He is anxious to find direction. Luckily for him, there are those who know reality, the ultimate and the provisional. They can guide him. Through their speech, the blindfold is gradually removed and the newly enlightened man can see the way. But unlike the picture painted above, we do not simply find our way and leave it at that. We do not sit in absorption longing for the final release of death. Rather, we stand at the side of the road and wait for those who may also want to find the promised land, and slowly-slowly, we remove their blindfold. Only then may the body fall off. Thus, we begin our interpretative journey, as Śaṅkara did, with the Upaniṣads, whose ethics of 'non-attachment and altruism' (Lipner 2010: 261) are here enriched even further by Śaṅkara's exegesis. The square brackets are included to express a number of Śaṅkara's separate comments which I find particularly poignant:

> If a [kind] person [a knower of Self, who is free from bondage] were [out of compassion] to remove the blindfold from the eyes of a man [lost in a forest]

> and say, 'The land of Gandhāra lies this way. Walk in this direction', and if he who received this instruction, being an intelligent man, by asking his way from village to village, verily reached the land of the Gandhāras [attaining peace and happiness]; so in the same way a man [who has been forced to inhabit this 'forest' of a body by the 'thieves' of merit and demerit, etc.] having [by some merit or other] met with a [preeminent] teacher [becomes dispassionate towards cyclic existence and when told 'you are not a transmigrating being' – 'you are that'] acquires knowledge in this world [attaining his own true self]. For him the delay lasts only until he becomes liberated [i.e. attains immortality when the body falls]. Then he will merge [with existence (*sat*)] (Ch.U.Bh. VI.xiv.1–2).

From the above comments, the picture painted by Śaṅkara is in near-perfect harmony with that painted by Śāntideva. There are two issues the latter could possibly have with this: one ethical, the other metaphysical.

First, the notion of a final resting place would be resisted by Śāntideva on the grounds of an apparent lack of compassion. But then Śāntideva has the same issue with the Buddhist 'Śrāvaka' monks. And note that Śaṅkara explicitly adds here that the teacher teaches 'out of compassion' (*kārūṇikena*), as he does elsewhere (U.S. Prose, 1.6). In other words, the removal of the blindfold is both an altruistic act and a duty. It simultaneously saves the seeker from further suffering, while continuing the Advaitin lineage of knowers. So the disagreement is really about commitment to rebirth rather than compassion *per se* (as it arguably is with the Śrāvaka). Thus, the altruistic nature of the *jīvan-mukta* remains intact despite the denial of rebirth.

The second issue would be that, while Śaṅkara finds non-duality in 'Being' (*sat*), Śāntideva would find his non-duality in Nāgārjuna's equation of *saṃsāra* and *nirvāṇa* (MMK. 25.19). However, as we saw in Chapter 5.1, perhaps even this can be overcome to some degree by Śaṅkara's assertion that 'There is actually no difference between liberation and bondage' (Bṛ.U.Bh. IV.iv.6). The difference, however, would re-appear in the line that follows: 'For, indeed, the Self is always the same' (ibid.). And so we are back to our polar Self/Not-Self metaphysical differences. But we have known that from the start.

What remains startling is just how close Śaṅkara and Śāntideva still stand given this enormous difference in metaphysical doctrine. Running through the above comments to the *Chāndogya*, one is simply amazed at the similarities. We have the teacher painted as an all-knowing, kind-hearted helper, who takes it upon himself to direct others out of compassion. The person that comes to him, even though intelligent, is in some sense lost. The allegorical scene of this compassionate response is a forest, just as it is in the Mahāyāna *Aṣṭa Sūtra* (see Conze 1973: 223). The lost person does not turn to God for help, but turns to a fellow human being. There is no grace or divine intervention here, there is only the teacher. If it were not for this fearless guide, we would all be lost in the wilderness.[13]

[13] Cf. *S.N.* I.137.

Śaṅkara here appears to share with the Buddhist what Collins (1982: 10) calls, a 'pragmatic agnosticism'. The first step in this pragmatism is to turn away from the world of sense pleasures. Therefore, in line with Śāntideva (BCA Chapter 8), Śaṅkara adds his signature doctrine of a prior need for renunciation of the physical world. Hence, we have the negative evaluation of the body, this so-called 'forest of a body', described in graphically foul terms. In fact, Suthren Hirst draws our attention to this very passage (and Ch.U.Bh. V.ix.1), under the sub-heading of 'Renunciation', where she states that these lists are 'reminiscent of … Buddhist cultivations of mindfulness' (Suthren Hirst 2005: 74): this list includes: phlegm, blood, fat, flesh, semen, worms, urine and faeces. And, of course, Śāntideva's meditation at *BCA* 8.40ff has this very intent of renunciation of the body. For example:

> If you [believe you] have no passion for what is foul, why then do you embrace another, a cage of bones bound by sinew, smeared with slime and flesh? (BCA. 8.52).

Śāntideva even describes people as 'moving skeletons' (BCA. 8.70), just as the *V.C.* likens the body to 'living corpses' (297).

Having dispensed with what the pupil is not, that is, this body, the Advaitin teacher then tells him what he is. Of course, Śāntideva adopts a similar meditation on the body and aggregates at *BCA* 9.56ff to demonstrate that no self can be found. Śaṅkara will use the same deconstruction of the provisional to show that 'you are that' (*tat tvam asi*), the ultimate.[14] Once again, it would seem that it is *only* the Self-doctrine that divides the two philosophers.

Finally, having had his blindfold removed, the seeker has succeeded in finding his way, and is no longer in a state of anxiety, but is content. But Śaṅkara's altruistic ethics prevents the ascetic from buying a one-way ticket to the forest. Rather, like the *bodhisattva*, he re-enters the social arena as a paternal guide.

And so we will discover that so much of what we have said about Śāntideva's ethics is also true of Śaṅkara. He too sees the world in negative terms, but ultimately grounds human suffering in our confusion about the world rather than the world itself. He too is motivated by the wish to liberate beings from *saṃsāra*, and so he too, if restricted to his ethics of liberation, might well be labelled a 'negative consequentialist'. Unfortunately, his arguments are far more scattered than Śāntideva's. This means that we are faced with having to reconcile conflicting textual accounts. With regard to Śaṅkara, then, it is perhaps asking too much of the

[14] Harvey (1995: 21) notes that, in India, 'the religious life was popularly equated with "seeking for Self"', and certain passages in the Buddhist Canon show the Buddha loosely using this notion in a non-metaphysical sense. For Conze, this 'hunt' for the 'true self' left room in Buddhism for the notion of an 'Absolute in man' (Conze 1973: xv). For a sustained argument for a 'transcendent' self in Buddhism, see Pérez-Remón (1980). For a critique of Conze's and Pérez-Remón's positions, see Harvey (1995: 17–19). For a model based on the useful distinction between self and the 'sense of self', see Albahari (2006).

reader to assess the validity of my schema in Figure 6.2 (below). I trust, however, that any reader convinced of the validity and/or utility of Figure 6.1 will now be willing to accept a parallel schema for Śaṅkara.

As with Śāntideva, I feel that the best way to avoid an either/or reading of Śaṅkara's work is to place it in schematic form, highlighting the shifts that he makes. The horizontal axis will remain the same as before, with the distinction between 'Me' and 'Others'. When discussing Śāntideva, we saw how this distinction allowed the *bodhisattva* to divide the world into those who had taken the Bodhisattva Vow and those who had not. Śaṅkara can similarly use the distinction to distinguish between those who are qualified (*adhikāra*) for *brahman*-knowledge and those who are not. In making this distinction, the focus is on the most extreme case, which is that the candidate must be a qualified male *Brahmin*. If this remains controversial, I qualify it by claiming the Provisional/Me quadrant to be representative of an 'ideal' personality. As argued in Chapter 4.3, this would include the celibate student. Allow me then to simply introduce the diagram with no further ado and to base my following account on the summary it offers:

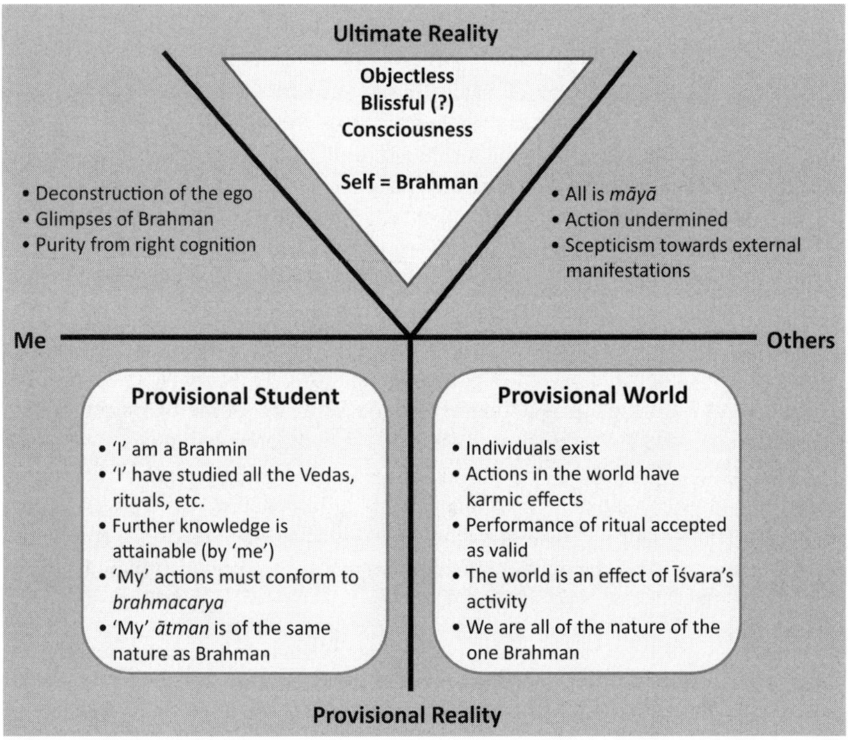

Figure 6.2 The Function of Domains in Śaṅkara's Ethics

The first thing one should notice about this diagram is that the vertical axis no longer represents 'Self' versus 'Non-self', but 'Ultimate Reality' versus 'Provisional Reality'. It should also be noted that 'Ultimate Reality' maps onto the realm of 'Self' as *brahman*. The notion of 'Ultimate Reality' went unstressed in my explanation of Śāntideva, because, unlike Śaṅkara, he offered no absolute transcendence thesis. In other words, placing these diagrams side by side, one might immediately notice the circularity of Śāntideva's model as opposed to the upwardly transcendent nature of Śaṅkara's model. I have therefore left out the arrows. Instead, 'Ultimate Reality' is shown as being a funnel-shaped space that one *visits* rather than being an absolute alternative to 'Provisional Reality'. This allows for my notion of flickering or oscillating between realities; the more one transcends, the wider the funnel, and the more time spent in 'Ultimate Reality', that being the (blissful?) consciousness of absolute being.

So while the commencing-*bodhisattva* entered the path at the level of 'self', the Advaitin pupil (*śiṣya*) enters the path at a level of 'not-Self'. His notion of 'My *ātman* is of the same nature as *brahman*' is in fact a lower level of understanding about *ātman*. He has yet to realize that his *jīvātman* and the *ātman* that is *brahman* are one and the same. That is, the 'Provisional Reality' of the pupil belongs to a worldview which assumes the self to be of the same nature as *brahman*, but still independent of *brahman*. The pupil still belongs to the provisional ethical world of *Dharma*, with its caste roles. That is why he continues to proudly see himself as a *Brahmin* male. He is one to whom the teacher might say:

> 'My child, you should not hold such a view, for it is forbidden to hold a doctrine of difference'. [If the student] then says 'Why is the doctrine of difference forbidden?', [the teacher quotes] 'He who thinks he is one and He [brahman] another, does not know', 'The Brahmins reject him who believes Brahmins to be other than Self', 'One who sees diversity [in brahman] goes from death to death' (U.S. Prose, 1.26).

This view of an individuated self with caste affiliations must now be transcended. Whilst the life of the *brahmacārin* has been one of outer-renunciation, the path now is one of inner-renunciation. This gradual path may take many years. Thus, we must imagine a mind that flickers between the provisional and the ultimate truth. The path which Śaṅkara lays out for the *Brahmin* male is one that requires both intellectual knowledge and direct knowledge. One begins the path as a student of the Vedas. One ends the path when one comes to understand that all is *brahman*. Hence, there is an obvious ascendency involved. It is for this reason that Figure 6.2 begins in the lower left quadrant, as opposed to the upper left in Figure 6.1. The person in this quadrant is a male *Brahmin* and a seeker of liberation. He is not as yet at the same stage as the *bodhisattva*, and need not have any altruistic motives. He is formally equivalent to a 'selfish' Buddhist monk, seeking liberation for himself.

It is only when he is established in *brahman*-consciousness that the knower turns round and offers this knowledge to those qualified to receive it. The student then becomes the teacher. These knowers of *brahman*, forever engaged in the practice of 'knowledge and absorption and so on' (*jñāna dhyānādi*) (Mu.U.Bh. III.i.4) are said by Śaṅkara to be the 'only true men of action in this world' (*eveha kriyāvān*) (ibid.). The action that Śaṅkara has in mind clearly includes the passing on of this knowledge to others. Action, then, does not stop when realization is attained; rather it *starts* when realization is attained.

This shows that knowers do not *literally* give up action, only the making of further *karma*, in the sense of that which creates positive or negative consequences and rebirths. When Śaṅkara speaks of the giving up of '*karma*' it is shorthand for '*karma-sādhana*' (ritual action). As pointed out by Kuznetsova (2007: 35), the 'most significant dimension of *karma* is the ritual act', and thus, for the renouncer movement, the 'elimination of *karma* means principally the elimination of rites' (ibid.). And so, as already mentioned, when Śaṅkara writes that 'steadfastness in knowledge combined with action is illogical' (Bh.G.Bh. 18.66), he is speaking of ritual action. Elsewhere, he makes this explicit:

> As the doctrine of difference is forbidden, so ritual actions which assume the domain of difference, and the sacred thread, etc., which are the means to their performance, are also forbidden. It should be known that the prohibition to undertake rites and their means derives from the knowledge of non-difference with the Supreme Self. For these rites and means to them, such as the wearing of threads, are at variance with the view of one's non-difference with the Supreme Self. Rituals and means, such as the sacred thread are indeed enjoined upon a transmigrator [but] not upon one who holds the view of non-difference with the Supreme Self. That one is other [than brahman] is due only to the [error of] accepting the doctrine of difference (U.S. Prose, 1.30).

Now it is evident that this prohibition of ritual action (*karma-sādhana*) is not a prohibition of *all* action, for it appears in a text used for teaching purposes, which is itself an action. Much confusion would be overcome if scholars were more careful about the distinction between these meanings of action.

So just like Śāntideva's *bodhisattva*, we can imagine the *jīvan-mukta* as 'acting nobly in the world' (Ś.S. 363), dedicated to his pupils. Indeed, this need for an enlightened teacher is much more explicit in Śaṅkara than in Śāntideva. True, Śāntideva (Ś.S. 34–42) speaks highly of the relationship with a '*kalyāṇa-mitra*' (lit. 'good-friend'), and thus all *bodhisattvas* are to be treated as one's 'instructor' (*śāstṛ*) (53). He also speaks of the advantage of taking the Vows with a '*guru*', namely the 'intense shame' that would follow if one broke them (11–12). He also laments at the difficulty in finding enlightened teachers (BCA. 9.162a). Nevertheless, he also allows for the taking of the Bodhisattva Vow in the 'absence of a good friend' (Ś.S. 12). Moreover, he follows his famous rendition of the

Bodhisattva Vow[15] (363) by vowing to become his own teacher (*ātmācarya*), forming a private student-teacher relationship with himself; becoming his own master.[16] And while, at the very end of the *BCA* (10.58) he thanks his 'good friends' for their '*prasāda*' (kindness, inspiration), nowhere does Śāntideva actually state that one *needs* a teacher in order to realize emptiness. So while this need not contradict Matics' (1971: 49) claim that, for Śāntideva, a 'Guru is indispensable', it does leave that possibility open.

In contrast, for Śaṅkara, knowledge of the Vedas *must be* imparted by a knower of the Vedas, and knowledge of *brahman must be* imparted by a knower of *brahman* (Ch.U.Bh. VI.xiv.2). In fact, Śaṅkara sees no other way to liberation, and therefore, until one is liberated, he urges constant reliance upon the guru:

> Since knowledge is obtained in no other way. For the *Śrutis* say 'He with a teacher knows', 'Knowledge learnt from a teacher …', 'The teacher is a boatman', 'His right knowledge is said to be a boat', etc. The *Smṛti* also says 'Knowledge will be imparted to you', etc. (U.S. Prose, 1.3).

The *Brahmin* pupil (*śiṣya*) must therefore search for his teacher (*ācārya*), who must subsequently assess his qualities:

> The means to liberation is knowledge. It should be repeatedly explained to the pupil until firmly grasped, to one who is indifferent to everything transitory, achievable through means, and who has no desire for sons, wealth, this world or the next, who has adopted the way of the highest ascetics, who is endowed with tranquillity, self-control, compassion, etc., possessed of the qualities of a pupil, well-known from the scriptures, if he is a pure *Brahmin*, who approaches the teacher in the prescribed manner, and if his birth, profession, conduct, knowledge and family have been examined (U.S. Prose, 1.2).

We see here that the pupil is explicitly restricted to the *Brahmin* class, and that his caste is also to be assessed based on family and profession. The pupil must have given up any wish for sons, which shows the stress that Śaṅkara placed on chastity. But it also highlights the one-pointed nature of Śaṅkara's view of renunciation. It is an all-or-nothing stance which explicitly rules out the life of the householder. It also rules out any desire for another 'world' (*loka*), by which he means heavenly realms. As with early Buddhism, Śaṅkara sees these realms as limited due to their impermanence, that is, one must someday fall from them. The only true liberation is total liberation, the complete merging with *brahman* (Ch.U. VI.xiv.2).

---

[15] This is a slightly modified version of the one found at BCA. 10.55. It runs: 'So long as space remains, so long as the world remains, so will I remain, acting nobly in the world, aiming towards enlightenment' (Ś.S. 363).

[16] Cf. *Dhammapada* (160).

Despite the seemingly world-denying tone of this verse from the *U.S.*, it is important to note that the pupil must have compassion (*daya*) as one of his chief characteristics, alongside the more renunciatory virtues of tranquillity (*śama*) and self-control (*dama*). And we have already seen how, in the *Ch.U.Bh*, Śaṅkara speaks of an auspicious meeting with a compassionate knower of the self who teaches the seeker the truth of non-duality (Ch.U.Bh. VI.xiv.2). We also find Śaṅkara advocating the need for compassion in *Bṛ.U.Bh* (V.ii.3), where *daya* is one of the so-called 'three Da's' that one must practice, the other two being 'self-control' (*dāmyata*) and 'generosity' (*datta*) (Bṛ.U. V.ii.1–3). But the virtues of compassion and generosity only have validity when they are applied. They become crucial when the pupil himself becomes a teacher, who must selflessly give his knowledge to others.

Indeed, Śaṅkara's *G.K.Bh.* ends (Salutation, 2) by thanking his *parama-guru* (great teacher, or teacher-of-my-teacher) for teaching the truth of the Vedas 'out of compassion' for the benefit of all beings. Also, in the *V.C.* (35), the guru is addressed as an 'ocean of compassion'. Written in these terms, these salutations might well have been addressed to a *bodhisattva*. Indeed, Śaṅkara demands all of the following qualities of his Advaitin teachers:

> Now the teacher is one who is able to grasp the pros and cons of an argument, who understands and remembers them, who has tranquillity, self-control, compassion, kindness, etc., versed in the scriptures, unattached to enjoyments (visible or invisible), having abandoned all ritual actions, he is a knower of *brahman*, he is established in *brahman*, breaking not the rules of conduct, free from faults such as: deceit, pride, trickery, wickedness, deception, envy, falsehood, egoism and selfishness. With the sole aim of helping others, he wishes to make use of knowledge (U.S. Prose, 1.6).

This verse is simply overflowing with information. We can immediately note how both the pupil and the teacher are to be possessed of tranquillity, self-control and compassion. The teacher is distinguished from the student by being a knower of *brahman*, established in *brahman*. In other words, his knowledge of *brahman* is immediate; he is literally one with *brahman* and has no other self but *brahman*. While he should remain detached from the world, the list of virtues makes it unlikely that he could be described as discarding social mores. In fact, on a virtue ethical account, he would seem like a model citizen.[17] Surely, his compassion need not be restricted to the teacher-student relationship.

Halbfass (1991: 384) speaks of the freedom of the *jīvan-mukta* as being 'carefully channelled' by conservative traditionalism. In more positive terms, Mumme claims that the Advaitin *jīvan-mukta* will 'naturally observe dharmic norms' (Fort and Mumme 1996: 266). Potter (1981: 37) also claims that the *mukta*'s ethical training

[17] Cf. the *V.C.* (33), where the guru 'demonstrates cardinal virtues' (Forsthoefel 2002: 319).

and liberation will guarantee an honest and helpful response from the liberated teacher. This accords with the Vedāntic mystical notion that, 'Inner perfection and outer conduct are two sides of one life' (Radhakrishnan 1989: 108). Established in *brahman*, having no further goals, the *jīvan-mukta* stands beyond egoism and selfishness. Such a *parama-haṃsa* is said to be selfless (*nirmama*) (Jā.U. 6).[18] And yet, according to Śaṅkara, this ideal renouncer 'does not transgress the limits of moral propriety' (Mu.U.Bh. III.i.4) (trans. Gambhīrānanda 1989, Vol. 1: 144), his behaviour is never 'disrespectful' (Bṛ.U.Bh. III.v.1).

Nevertheless, this selflessness does not imply an absence of activity. On the contrary, the teacher remains in society with 'the sole aim of helping others' (*kevala parānugraha prayojana*) (U.S. Prose, 1.6). This perfectly parallels the altruism of the *bodhisattva*. And although, unlike the *bodhisattva*, the *jīvan-mukta* does not vow to return to this world of suffering, his acceptance of the duty to pass on the knowledge of *brahman* ensures that beings will continue to be liberated by his pupils. The outcome is therefore the same, and can be compared to the Buddha's refusal to enter *parinirvāṇa* until he had disciples that could continue his work. And so, by claiming that the life of the *brahman*-knower is constructively altruistic, we must also question Perrett's (1998: 54) assertion that liberation (*mokṣa*) is the 'good life rather than the moral life'. For Śaṅkara, it is both.

We might also compare the *jīvan-mukta*'s 'constructive altruism' with Davis' treatment of the altruistic form of rulership as recommended in the *Mahābarata*. Davis (in Neusner and Chilton 2005: 167) suggests that 'The altruistic *dharma* of a king … lies in renouncing personal aims in favour of seeking to "benefit the world"'. The *jīvan-mukta*, by contrast, has already renounced everything, including this world and the next, and, as such, no longer has any personal aims. He need *do* nothing. His selfless following of the *Dharma* is therefore effortless. Yet, it is with *time and effort* that he teaches the truth of *brahman*. So while he *need* do nothing, he *does* do something. So he does not leave 'all activity and repose in oneness', as Otto (1957: 207) claims. Rather, he acts *from* that place of oneness, 'out of that consciousness' (Radhakrishnan 1989: 357). This constitutes his own form of altruistic *dharma*, where *dharma* stands more for conduct than duty. For if duty is a 'thing that can be *exacted* from a person, as one exacts a debt' (Util. 5.14), then his teaching is no duty. Better to see it as a spontaneous and compassionate gift. And as Mill noted: 'No one has a moral right to our generosity and beneficence' (5.15).[19]

It is quite interesting that according to Green's strict definition of altruism as 'intentional action for the welfare of others' which has 'only a neutral or negative consequence on the actor' (in Neusner and Chilton 2005: 191), Śaṅkara's *jīvan-mukta*, who is 'free from merit and demerit' (Bh.G.Bh. 6.27), would seem to pass

[18] While we have no commentary by Śaṅkara on the *Jābāla Upaniṣad*, Śaṅkara does quote from it (Ch.U.Bh. II.xxiii.1 and B.S.Bh. III.iv.17).

[19] Whether or not such generosity or compassion *should* be 'strictly optional' and whether or not liberalism is thus 'deficient' (Garfield 2002: 187–205) is open to debate.

the test where the *bodhisattva* might fail. The *bodhisattva* fails if he continues to accrue merit by his positive actions, and he will continue to accrue merit until he reaches the stage of an enlightened *arhat*. At such a time, the *arhat* is said to create no new *karma*, having passed beyond merit (*puṇya*) and demerit (*pāpa*), due to the destruction of the three roots of unwholesome action. However, they are still subject to past *karma*, and may still experience physical, if not mental, pain (Miln. 44–5). But as we know, Śāntideva has imposed a voluntary delusion on his *bodhisattva*, so *karma* and merit must still be functioning. Significantly, Śāntideva also argues that *karma* still functions in the *arhat* (BCA. 9.44–8), just as Śaṅkara admits that *karma* still functions in the *brahma-vid* (Ch.U.Bh. VI.xiv.2).

We might stop to question here whether Śāntideva, in dedicating all his merit to others (BCA. 9.166–7), has thereby transcended a 'eudaemonist interpretation' (Goodman 2009: 92). The only problem with this non-merit-making thesis is that the act of dedication traditionally forms part of a seven-limbed practice, as found in the *Gaṇḍavyūha Sūtra*. Śāntideva recommends this practice for the accumulation of merit. In fact, Chapters 2 and 3 of the *BCA* may well be seen as an extended version of this practice (Crosby and Skilton 1995: 9–13). But even so, whether merit is accumulated or not, this does not render it 'eudaemonistic' or selfish, for this accumulation is itself sought with the sole intention of fulfilling the Bodhisattva Vow. Śāntideva states that: 'In that merit which arises from the donating of merit, there is no ripening, except for another's benefit' (Ś.S. 147).

Thus, Śāntideva's ethics do indeed transcend a eudaemonist interpretation. The situation is much clearer for the *brahman*-knower, who is claimed by the Upaniṣads to be beyond the making of new *karma* (Mu.U. II.ii.8), a claim Śaṅkara explicitly endorses (Ch.U.Bh. VI.xiv.2). The *brahma-vid* is therefore a definite candidate for altruism according to Green's strict criteria. Unlike the *bodhisattva*, the *brahma-vid* has no need to 'generate' an altruistic motivation; he teaches spontaneously. Nevertheless, he still needs to *empathize* with the pupil. The pupil believes he is an individuated self. Even if he believes he has a relationship with *brahman*, it is still based on a notion of 'me' and 'Him'. So it would seem that the *brahman*-knower still needs to alternate between ultimate reality and provisional reality. But how is he to do this? The problem is similar to one we faced with regard to the fully enlightened Buddha. I therefore believe it better to understand the *brahman*-knower as flickering between these two realities. Like Śāntideva, Śaṅkara does not provide us with a positive theory of how such flickering would work. However, he does, reluctantly (Bṛ.U. Bh. I.iv.10) and unwittingly (U.S. Prose, 1.2), admit that it *must* so occur. Thus, the *brahma-vid* who also 'knows' his wife and the *brahma-vid* who sees fit to examine the pupil's credentials must rely on flickering cognition.

One thing worthy of note is that Śaṅkara's constructive altruism is mainly towards people who are overtly seeking the teacher's help. They come to him as 'seekers' of liberation. The *V.C.* thus speaks of the *brahman*-knower as acting 'through others' wishes' (539). Adopting Nagel's (1978: 81) words, the teacher's actions are 'motivated by reasons which the other person's interests provide'. The power structure is also quite clear, the pupil having already conceded a lack of knowledge. Of course, in this case it also happens that the interests of the teacher and pupil coincide, the teacher having once been a seeker himself. The teacher is simply one (admittedly profound) leap ahead of the pupil, and the pupil is potentially set to become a teacher himself. One is reminded of social theorist, Michel Foucault's (1926–84) notion of 'pastoral power' (Foucault 1982: 782–5), a power which concerns individuals rather than whole communities, a power which is "salvation oriented".

In contrast, the so-called other-regarding ethic of Śāntideva's advanced *bodhisattva* is aimed at all beings, whether they overtly realize that life is suffering or not. They thus vow to lead to *nirvāṇa* all those without refuge: the foolish, the ignorant and the blind (Ś.S. 287–9). He is therefore open to the criticism that some beings might not wish to be 'liberated' or 'perfected'. Of course, Śaṅkara may also help others who do not wish to be helped, but Śāntideva's ethics do seem to spread a wider net. Kantians may therefore point out that Śāntideva's ethics go beyond the 'duty of love'. They may insist, with Baron (1997: 14–15), that 'we are not to seek to perfect others', nor 'decide for them what their ends should be'. It could then be argued that this is not other-regarding at all, for the incentive to act comes from the *bodhisattva*'s projection of a Buddhist doctrine (that is, *duḥkha*, *nirvāṇa* and so on), not from the other person's overt interests. Furthermore, it would seem that the motivating factor is the *bodhisattva*'s own desire to liberate all beings. This appears to contradict the *bodhisattva*'s vow to work only if it is in the 'interests of others' (Ś.S. 117). It may also go against Śāntideva's own (Kant-like) claim that:

> It is not right for example to set the eyes of others onto your own goals. It is not right to use the hands and limbs of others for your own projects (BCA. 8.138).[20]

However, it would also seem rather perverse to treat this 'desire' for the happiness of others, or the 'desire' to end suffering on a par with egoistic desires. Levinas (2006: 30) asks himself if the 'Desire for Others' stems from appetite or generosity. Śāntideva writes:

> Actually, though acting for the good of others, he neither feels exhilaration nor pride, nor desire for the resulting [karmic] reward, with a thirst solely for the welfare of others (BCA. 8.109).

Śāntideva's other-regarding ethics, notably similar here to the ideal of the *Gītā*, are anything but 'egoistic'. And even Kantians would agree that 'We are very much obliged to try to alleviate suffering' (Baron 1997: 15). Following Nagel (1978: 121), we might see this desire of the *bodhisattva* in purely impersonal terms, re-writable as '*If only* all beings were liberated from suffering', a statement

[20] Cf. Kant's famous: 'Act in such a way that you always treat humanity … never simply as a means, but always at the same time as an end' (Kant 2005: 106–7).

which seems devoid of egoity. Sober and Wilson (1998: 230), drawing a distinction between 'ultimate' (that is, irreducible to other desires) and 'instrumental' desires, have claimed that 'altruists have ultimate desires concerning what they think will be good for others'. Foucault (1982) has also spoken of 'pastoral power' in terms of 'ultimate' soteriological aims, and has suggested that such power 'cannot be exercised without knowing the inside of people's minds' (p783). Sober and Wilson (1998: 230) further suggest that an 'altruist may want others to have what they actually want for themselves; alternatively, an altruist may want for others something they have never thought of'.

Consider again Śāntideva's position. On one side, there are those who are ignorant of their true state:

> Alas! – The extremely grievous condition of these beings that exist in this flood of suffering, not seeing their own state, while remaining in such wretchedness (BCA. 9.163).

> For people live on like this, pretending they will never grow old or die. Terrible misfortunes will be coming, with death the foremost of them (9.165).

On the other side, there are those *bodhisattvas*, 'in whom there is born a concern for the welfare of others beyond that which they have for themselves' (BCA. 1.25b). This may well be typical of the 'Well, *saṃsāra* is painful, though you do not feel it to be' attitude that Chakrabarti (1983: 168) claims the 'liberation-obsessed philosopher' throws at others. Yet we ought to remember that even Mill's idea of democracy was a decision-making process for 'the good of the people, not the will of the people' (Skorupski 1998: 25). Mill's society was one where the intellectual elite had an 'obligation to exercise moral and intellectual influence' (ibid. 1998: 29). Surely, no one would disagree that our modern forms of democratic government continue to abide by this principle.

And even if all this sounds rather paternalistic, then Śāntideva would say, so be it. In the *Compendium*, we see the *bodhisattva* appointing himself as a 'father to all beings' (Ś.S. 23). It could hardly be any more paternalistic, but it is a trait that Śaṅkara shares (Bh.G.Bh. 4.19). And assuming it to be of ultimate benefit to others, and so long as it honours a code of 'pastoral delicacy' (Matics 1971: 60), which we trust would involve both sensitivity and respect, it seems difficult to denounce; unless, of course, one has a very different definition of liberation. After all, even Freud (1856–1939), in *The Future of an Illusion*, suggested that we behave like an 'understanding teacher' (Freud 2008: 55), providing the other with 'a knowledge of the way things really are' (p57). Freud called this process '*education for reality*' (p63); but what else have we been talking about?

No doubt there is a glaring power gap here, and that may be worthy of further discussion, but the *bodhisattva* could simply argue that it is for the 'ignorant' that he is most called on to act. Just as Christ came to save the 'sick' and the 'sinners' (Mark, 2:17), so the *bodhisattva* returns to save the 'deluded'. Just as Kṛṣṇa acts in order to save the worlds from ruin (Bh.G. 3.22–4), so the *jīvan-mukta* acts 'for the sake of preventing people from going astray' (Bh.G.Bh. 4.19). Nobody would argue with the person who saved a blind man from falling off a railway platform, or persuaded the fool to stop hanging out of the carriage window, or prevented a child from crawling onto the tracks. Such interventions are accepted by all ethical parties. The argument is more about: 1) what constitutes 'blindness', being a 'fool' or a 'child', and 2) what the correct, wise and mature view of life ought to be. It is not a question of whether we ought to tolerate power relations or not, for a 'society without power relations can only be an abstraction' (Foucault 1982: 791). As such, modern ethicists would more likely start by criticizing the metaphysical bases of such power relations, rather than the use of power *per se*. And needless to say, both Madhyamaka and Advaita Vedānta would be equally open to attack on metaphysical grounds.

Focusing on Śaṅkara, we should note that not all seekers would be eligible for help, for not all would be of the right type, not all would qualify. When Śaṅkara talks of 'seekers of liberation' he has in mind a male *Brahmin* of a certain educational background. Of course, theoretically, when that student achieves self-realization, thereafter 'he and the teacher stand as equals' (Cenkner 1983: 17). As for everyone else, Śaṅkara simply assumes that they ought to be involved in worldly pursuits, hopefully generating the karmic merit to be reborn in a situation that will allow them to become true seekers.

For Śaṅkara, the final stretch of the path to liberation is grounded in the understanding of certain verses of the Upaniṣads. And, of course, he believes that only certain people are capable of such an understanding. This is not an agent-neutral theory. Rather, his ethics are explicitly hierarchical. For example, he writes, 'Owing to the gradation of duty, there is gradation of qualification' (B.S.Bh. I.i.4). His teaching is not for the 'guidance of mankind', as Tiwari (1977: 132) claims, but for the guidance of a select few. Not only are certain castes excluded from the renouncer's path to ultimate knowledge, but so are most women, at least in their present incarnation. It is true that in the *B.S.Bh.*, Śaṅkara states that Gārgī (a legendary female philosopher) was in fact a *brahman*-knower (III.iv.36–8), but his intention seems to be to make those not involved in ritual duty eligible for ultimate knowledge. That is, he wants to make room for himself and his monastic following, one which did not include women (see Cenkner 1983: 50). The logic is this: if a woman (who is ineligible for rites) can be a *brahman*-knower, then so can an ascetic who has renounced rites. In other words, ritual is irrelevant to knowledge.

Again, women can of course be reborn as men and can then go on to qualify for the path of renunciation. Just as all men have 'equal opportunities, but not in this life' (Weber 1958: 144), so it is with women. Śaṅkara's supporters could therefore claim that his apparent sexism is not entirely exclusivist. Like those of low caste, they are 'not doomed to be associated to any constant social label in different births', as Saha (2009: 72) puts it. Clearly, this concept of the temporary nature of one's present incarnation is one that may not satisfy the modern woman of today. It may also be small consolation to those of lower caste; nevertheless, it is a powerful concept, one which has been taken very seriously in India. And so the *V.C.* (2) states that, 'Liberation is not to be attained except through the well-earned merit of 100 million rebirths'. That Śaṅkara does not ultimately close the door on others, but merely tells them to 'come back later' is a fact that should not be lost on us, regardless of our politics and scepticism. After all, Śāntideva also talks of the immature and the unworthy as being disqualified from hearing the holy doctrine (Ś.S. 54). Taber (1983: 65) correctly notes that 'virtually all systems of Buddhism presuppose some spiritual conditioning which prepares one for the truth'. Śaṅkara's ethics then are not to be taken unquestionably as exclusive, just as Śāntideva's ethics ought not to be taken unquestionably as inclusive. Both throw out their doctrinal nets, yet both feel the need to scrutinize their takers. Yet, going back to our Figure 6.2 (p.166), we see that the knowers are those who see through the illusion (*māyā*) of difference and drop the individualistic notion of 'I'. They are therefore beyond the society whose divisions they condone.

Chapter 7
Marginal Cases

Here I wish to reflect on what we have gathered so far, and I particularly want to re-examine how the Two Truths are used with regard to the marginal cases of women and lower castes. In calling them 'marginal cases', I am thinking from the perspective of Śaṅkara and Śāntideva. I want to show that whatever they had to say about the level playing surface that an ultimate view theoretically provides, they nevertheless continued to play their social games on an inclined field. In other words, holding an ultimate view does not lead them to social egalitarianism. Rather, life is seen as a cultural and soteriological 'staircase' (Radhakrishnan 1989: 366). This ties in with Dumont's (1980: 108) claim that, in India, the 'language of religion is the language of hierarchy'. Now while this need not necessarily lead to actual temporal power and/or authority, I have argued that it does in fact lead to an assumed 'pastoral power'. Having established the nature of this hierarchy, through a number of examples, I will then be asking whether we still have the right to apply the word 'altruism' to their ethical views. Put another way, we need to ask whether egalitarianism or impartiality are essential components of altruism.

We have been searching for an approach to ethics which will allow us a direct comparison of the activities of a *bodhisattva* and a *brahma-vid*. The notion of a selfless response to the world has proven itself a useful tool, and this led us to believe that perhaps the Western notion of altruism could provide us with the final key which would offer up a fundamental category within which to discuss these ethical systems. However, we have come across a number of problems. First, we have been forced into noting that the standard Western notion of altruism assumes that the actor is fully aware that they have a self, one which needs protecting; and that this self is being momentarily denied attention. This notion is unacceptable to Śaṅkara, for his *brahman*-knower knows that he is one with *brahman*, and thus knows that he has no separate self which requires protection. His selfless acts are not altruistic in the sense that they put the self down in order to hold the other in higher esteem. There simply is no self to hold down. I have, however, argued that this notion is acceptable to Śāntideva, so long as the monk has yet to have a full insight into emptiness. Here, the monk is still subject to self-love and has yet to throw himself into the Bodhisattva Vow. A selfless act by such a monk would indeed be an altruistic one. But once the monk has had an insight into emptiness and has plunged into the life of a *bodhisattva*, he no longer acknowledges a self, and as such, his actions, though selfless, are not altruistic in the Comtean sense. In fact, we have noted how, instead of putting himself down, the *bodhisattva* actually voluntarily inflates the other, creating a self where there was no self. Thus, I have spoken of a 'constructive altruism'.

There are two more problems that our model of 'constructive altruism' would need to face, one of which has been mentioned already. This was the problem of doing things for others without their expressed consent and, moreover, possibly even against their will. That is, the *bodhisattva* can see suffering that you cannot see, and has taken it upon himself to remove that suffering from you. We tried to draw on Foucault's notion of 'pastoral power', but saw that this is too limited, for Śāntideva's 'flock' seems to stretch further afield, and could potentially cross both cultural and religious boundaries. For Śāntideva, so far considered, there are really only two categories of people, *bodhisattvas* and non-*bodhisattvas*, with the former having the responsibility to look after the latter.

This brings us to the second problem of our model of 'constructive altruism', the problem of partiality. It is probably fair to say that the problem is more acute for Śaṅkara, who explicitly accepts Hindu class and caste categories. Nevertheless, it is complicated by the fact that Śaṅkara holds that a *brahman*-knower does not see himself as being a *Brahmin*. In fact, he should not even see himself as male. Even so, when testing a student's qualifications, he must be aware that the student needs to be both a *Brahmin* and a male. This highlights two problems. First, Śaṅkara's ethics are clearly partial. Second, his ethics rely on an application of the Two Truths, and only work if the *brahman*-knower simultaneously denies his own family background, whilst taking extreme care in analysing the family background of the applicant. That is, the *brahman*-knower is selfless, but not just to anyone. Not only is he partial, but he is partial in a way that seems inherently paradoxical. The system only works because it relies on a Two-Truths philosophy embedded within a Hindu social context. It is altruistic only within this confined space. In other words, it threatens to fail the Comtean notion of altruism on two accounts, by denying the self on the subjective side of the equation and by denying the equality of the objects on the other.

Up to this point, it has been suggested that Śāntideva has only two ethical categories, the *bodhisattva* and the non-*bodhisattva*. However, this is not the whole story. Like the Buddha himself, he also discriminates between the lay and the monastic and between male and female. While class and gender should not matter to the Buddhist, in fact they were 'reinforced in institutionalized forms' (Kasulis, in Schweiker 2005: 303). However, we must hold Śāntideva more accountable than the Buddha, for the insight into emptiness that the Mādhyamikas posit as the turning point in one's view of the world ought to overcome any such discrimination. According to this account, all distinctions are unjustified. And yet, we see them being argued for. So while Huntington's (1989: 100) claim that the *bodhisattva* 'behaves in accordance with an ideal of impartiality' might only be intended to apply to those above the 7th stage, one may still wish to question its applicability *on the ground*. And perhaps Paul Williams (1998a: 144) is over-hasty in assuming that Śāntideva's arguments in the *BCA* are 'intended to lead to altruistic action which makes no distinction between different persons'.[1] While

[1] Wetlesen (2002: 39) claims to have found 'four different senses' of 'altruism' in Williams' work.

some of his verses may imply this, the context also plays a part in the actions of the *bodhisattva*. For example, while his argument at *BCA* 8.103 (see p.145 above) appears like a universal/egalitarian moral imperative, we have to remember that: 1) not everyone is a *bodhisattva*, 2) not all *bodhisattvas* have the same capacities and 3) not everyone is ready to let go of *duḥkha* and *saṃsāra*. So while it is a form of moral imperative, it has limited applicability. Hence, it could be argued that, in real terms, Śāntideva is just as partial as Śaṅkara.

Rather than go into the whole question of inequality in their relative systems, let us simplify things by allocating a single area of social context in each system. Let us compare how Śaṅkara handles the subject of class and caste with the way in which Śāntideva handles the subject of gender. Both will claim that these categories are *mere labels* to be left behind, yet both will confirm these labels within their ethical systems. To reiterate, ultimately speaking, according to both Advaita and Madhyamaka metaphysics, these categories cannot stand up to analysis. However, conventionally, they not only stand up, but Śaṅkara and Śāntideva continually *prop them up*. Through these means, I wish to demonstrate how the conventional, and thus moral-making, ground of each tradition consistently manages to survive the ultimate level of discourse. Needless to say, I am not simply trying to show how partial these thinkers were. They were no doubt no more or less partial than any other thinkers of their time. What I am trying to do is show how the doctrine of the Two Truths actually functions in practice.

7.1 Śaṅkara: The Reality and Non-reality of Class and Caste

Earlier, I had been trying to argue that Śaṅkara's teacher-student relationship could be seen as a particular manifestation of altruism. This had seemed to be beyond debate. Then we brought in the notion of self, and we were asked whether a *brahman*-knower, apparently having no self, could in fact be altruistic at all. It was decided that we would need to posit a more 'qualified' form of altruism, one in which the self of the other was projected solely for their sake. This we called 'constructive' altruism. We will now take this problem of altruism one step further.

It may seem too obvious to state, but the notion of ethics also involves the notion of morality, and some scholars have attempted to divide the altruistic from the moral. So while some scholars may be happy with me claiming that Śaṅkara's and Śāntideva's ethics are altruistic in some qualified manner, they may still propose that they are acting in ways that are less than moral. I have already mentioned the problem of doing for others things that they have not willed you to do. Here, however, I will focus on the debate from impartiality. In their recent book, *Altruism*, Scott and Seglow (2007) begin by offering two hypothetical cases, which they assume give us reasons to doubt whether an altruistic act need always be classed as a moral one. I wish to question this assumption. Not that I am suggesting that all altruistic acts are *de facto* moral. What I wish to question is the leap that Scott and Seglow make from partiality to immorality.

The first hypothetical case is one of a 'racist organ donor' (Scott and Seglow 2007: 2) who wishes to donate his organs, but only to those of his own race. This act is said to be 'altruistic, but hardly moral' (ibid.). A similar (actual) case, involving the deceased person's parents, is later claimed to be 'morally condemnable' (pp127–8). Personally, I cannot see why the donors here are not acting morally, and I believe most people would object to them being called *im*-moral. It certainly does not amount to a crime of any sort. Even radical humanists, like Peter Singer concede that 'Most people reserve their moral condemnation for those who violate some moral norm' (Singer 1972: 236). To condemn such an act is to deprive the donor of freedom of choice, and in the case of the family, may lead to them being less altruistic in the future. *To be openly partial when giving need not exclude one from being moral.* This is an essential point.

Let us put the partial-thus-immoral thesis to the test. Are parents being 'hardly moral' when they put their own children through school and college? I think not. And even Scott and Seglow (2007: 38) have to admit that it is a 'perfect duty' to look after one's own children. What about an elderly lady who leaves her house and wealth to her family on purely genetic grounds? Is she being hardly moral? I think the answer is once again negative. And remember, in the above cases, we are talking of the donor, not of the surgeon. If a white surgeon gave all available organs to white patients only, then that would indeed be condemnable. But here we are talking of a dying person's last wishes or a family in deep distress. So while I (and possibly all Buddhists) would agree with Scott and Seglow (2007: 127) that such forms of partiality follow from over-attachment, I feel that to publicly condemn such an act is both wrong and counter-productive. So how does this affect Śaṅkara and Śāntideva?

Well, if I am right about this, then an Advaitin teacher passing on Vedic knowledge exclusively to *Brahmins* is not immoral. In fact, his sense of exclusion is not based on over-attachment to the gift, but on a belief that the receiver needs to prove their worth before receiving such a valuable gift. As such, even a Buddhist must acknowledge this restriction for they too guard certain of their teachings. Śāntideva himself states that a *bodhisattva* commits one of the root downfalls 'if one communicates the doctrine of emptiness to those minds that are not as yet prepared' (Ś.S. 67); a rule that is still maintained in the (Tibetan) Bodhisattva Vow.[2]

Now the second hypothetical case, of an American citizen donating 'huge sums' to fellow Americans (Scott and Seglow 2007: 2), is even more controversial. In order to claim that it 'arguably offends the moral ideal of impartiality' on the grounds that these beneficiaries are 'quite well off' (ibid.), one would first have to *establish* such an 'ideal of impartiality'. Partiality only opposes the 'moral' within a certain negotiated ethics of justice, one which (arguably) few societies would accept. Mill suggested that impartiality was not to be seen as a duty, and that condemnation of partiality was 'rather the exception than the rule' (Util. 5.9). Modern day Europe and America, on the whole, clearly do not accept impartiality as a duty. And we can

---

[2] See Sonam Rinchen (2000: 129–30).

be quite certain that 8th-century India, with its own 'meritorian concept of justice' (Dissanayake, in Ames 1994: 275) did not accept it as a duty.

Most people, be they American or Indian, would rather buy their own child a large birthday present than buy them a small one and the next-door neighbour's child an equally small one. There is nothing immoral in this seemingly natural response. Recall Mill's 'No one has a moral right to our generosity or beneficence' (Util. 5.15). Hence, Singer's argument, which also uses the language of condemnation, is preferable to Scott and Seglow's on two accounts. First, in stating that 'If we accept any principle of impartiality ...' (Singer 1972: 232), he at least recognizes the *if-condition* of the argument. And second, his condemnation is of those who give *no money* to charitable causes (p235), not to those who give to the 'wrong' cause. While sympathetic to the possible egoistic nature of 'in-group altruism' (Scott and Seglow 2007: 4), I cannot accept that this makes such altruism 'incompatible with the impartial demands of morality' (ibid.), for no such 'impartial demands' have been established.

Moreover, as our discussion is one which involves religious values, we might ask just what is meant by the term 'well-off'. Although they only imply as much, I am assuming that Scott and Seglow's (2007: 2) criterion for being 'well off' is financial and that the 'huge sums' they speak of are dollars and cents. If so, it is a criterion that Buddhists and Advaitins would not accept, and clearly one that renouncers of any denomination, including the early Christians, would not accept. It might be noted here that what we in English call a 'renouncer', the Indians call a '*saṃnyāsin*', which in Sanskrit literally means 'one who has laid it all down'; and what we in English call a 'monk', the Buddha called a '*bhikku*', which in Pāli literally means 'beggar'. Now no one is financially worse off than a beggar who has laid all he had down. So the 'beggar you choose to give a few coins to in India' (Scott and Seglow 2007: 75) might well be a *bodhisattva*, and you might well receive a larger 'sum' in return. The currency of the 'renouncer', of course, is wisdom and merit, not dollars! In Śāntideva's words, 'The monks make virtue their object, not wealth' (Ś.S. 115). The wealth of a monk is measured in terms of his knowledge and his ability to teach. So, when we speak of the 'well off' or the 'affluent', we might pause to consider the scope of our definitions. And once again, we should not question the ethics of those religions which see teaching, rather than charity, as the highest of gifts. Whilst Śaṅkara and Śāntideva no doubt saw worldly pleasure as having a value of greater than zero, their central focus is clearly the highest good, that of ultimate knowledge.

Needless to say, Scott and Seglow, like Singer, do indeed raise important questions with regard to giving, inclusiveness and exclusiveness. Similarly, Nagel, who Scott and Seglow (2007: 35) take as a model 'impartialist', has many interesting comments to make on the matter of partiality with regard to family, clubs, businesses and nations (Nagel 1978: 130). His focus is not so much on their 'moral' nature, but on their subjective (versus impersonal) nature, which likewise puts limits on their altruistic force. Nagel is not about to say that caring more for one's own family is immoral. Rather, Nagel's interest is that while to speak of the act of helping one's family is objective, to actually help one's own family is essentially subjective, and is based on relationships rather than objective reasoning. It therefore sits outside his thesis that altruism follows from objective reasoning. By contrasting such acts with 'perfectly general altruism' (Nagel 1978: 130), it is not clear whether Nagel thus sees such acts as *non*-altruistic, though Scott and Seglow (2007: 37) appear to take him this way. It is particularly interesting, however, that Nagel (1978: 130, n.1) adds a short note that 'Religions present a more complex case', by which he must be taken to mean that religions are pre-disposed to partiality. This point has already been discussed above with regard to the larger problem of comparing religious and secular ethics. But to focus the discussion onto altruism, we might interpret Nagel's point here as being one with Neusner and Chilton's (2005: vii), that 'Each religious tradition frames altruism in its own context'. Let us then try to tease out the complexities of the religions under review.

There are two reasons why Śaṅkara's ethics may rightly be called 'altruism'. Oliner (2003: 15), in his interpretation of Comte's definition of altruism, highlights two phases: 1) the eradication of self-centred desire, and 2) a life devoted to the good of others. Both these phases are found in the path of the *brahman*-knower, whose task it is to drop the belief in the 'I' (*aham*) and then to remain in society with the 'sole aim of helping others' (U.S. Prose, 1.6). In fact, not only does the *brahman*-knower give up selfish desires, but in dropping the 'I', he even gives up *unselfish* ones. This shift in motivation involves the 'total de-identification from even the act of desiring itself' (Marcaurelle 2000: 20).

Naturally, as an Advaitin teacher, the main help that Śaṅkara has in mind is the giving of knowledge, and the 'others' he has in mind are male-only *Brahmin*s. It should by now be obvious that it is not just any knowledge given by anyone. It is a liberating knowledge given by one who has achieved all there is to achieve. It is a type of knowledge that Śaṅkara believes will put an end to the other's suffering. The worthiness of the task is obvious. The value of the gift is unmistakable. It is for these motivational and consequentialist reasons that such a life is worthy of the name 'constructive altruism'.

Now clearly, Śaṅkara cannot offer people of other religions the chance of liberation through knowledge of *brahman*. It would make no sense for him to offer this path to a Buddhist, for example, who denied the Self. Surely we can glean nothing of his moral character from such exclusion. Notably, the *Diamond Sūtra* excludes the hearing of its discourse from those who hold to the view of Self (Vajracchedikā, 15). This shows that even Mahāyāna Buddhism, despite its apparent universalism, must exclude others who hold conflicting beliefs. These are not merely cases of group loyalty. Such exclusion does not imply that an Advaitin cannot give food to a hungry Buddhist, or vice versa; but the giving of teachings, this most sacred of transmissions, must necessarily be guarded. This is simply a by-product of religious doctrine and has no moral content.

Nevertheless, while certain religious and inter-religious exclusions seem unquestionable, we may still want to question why Śaṅkara denies access to this path to fellow Hindus on the grounds of their *class, caste and gender*. After all, even the *Gītā* finds a privileged place for these groups, whereby, 'No devotee of Kṛṣṇa, regardless of social status or gender, is lost' (Johnson 2004: xvii). Thus, Kṛṣṇa permits 'each individual embodied self to reach the "highest self"' (Malinar 2007: 11). Certainly, on the basis of its metaphysics, Advaita seemingly offers the scope for transcending social and cultural boundaries. As already discussed, the logical implications of non-dualism should verily forbid distinctions. The central question thus remains unanswered: if knowledge and even existence reside in *brahman*, how can there be any distinction between classes and gender? In asking this question, I will focus on the issue of class (*varṇa*) and caste (*jāti*). My analysis will concentrate on Śaṅkara's use of the Two Truths, rather than on the question of 'discrimination' *per se*, which is, after all, a very complex and controversial matter. As such, my point can be made without referring to the issue of gender, an issue I will reserve for my discussion of Śāntideva.

Now Nagel (1978: 99) suggests that altruism need not rely on a 'mystical identification of oneself with other persons', or on a notion of a 'mass self consisting of all persons'. We can therefore assume that Nagel would agree that altruism *could* be based on such notions. And it would seem that Śaṅkara, at the ultimate level of discourse, can help himself to either of these conditions. We have already noted how Śaṅkara claims such a condition, when he quotes: 'When a man sees all beings in this Self, and the Self in all beings, he feels no hatred' (Īś.U. 6). The ethical point being made is that one who is fully satisfied can have neither desire nor hatred. The further point being proposed here is that when one realizes that there is only one Self, one literally becomes *brahman* (Mu.U. III.ii.9), that is quality-less (*nirguṇa*) *brahman*, and a quality-less *brahman* is incapable of hatred because there is nothing 'other' than the Self to either desire or hate. The problem Śaṅkara then faces is how to reconcile this with the relative level of discourse. Put simply, how can we all be the same, but different? If, at the level of consciousness, I am *brahman* and you are *brahman*, and *brahman* is quality-less, then I share your consciousness, and they are both quality-less. If the reply is that there is no 'I' and no 'you', then the question is: how can there be ground for a caste system?

The only way of penetrating this dilemma is through the Two Truths. On one hand, there is only *brahman*, and all beings share in being nothing but *brahman*. On the other hand, there is the provisional reality in which we must maintain the codes of *Dharma*. Where does this leave the question of class and caste? The class or caste into which you are born is the result of the *karma* accumulated in one's past lives. In the commentaries, we find that Śaṅkara holds a particularly negative view of lower castes, which, if taken at face value, is even shockingly violent. I am referring here to the pouring of lead into the ears of a *Śūdra* who accidently overhears the Vedas being taught, and the cutting off of his tongue should he repeat what he hears, and the cutting of his body into pieces should he dare commit any of it to memory (B.S.Bh. I.iii.38).[3] And while it may have scriptural backing

---

[3] *Śūdra*: the lowest of the four classes in India, as listed in the *Āpastamba Dharmasūtra* (1.4); the other three being: *Brahmins, Kṣatriyas and Vaiśyas*. These first three were known

(Gau.D.S. 12.4–6),[4] this is nothing short of barbaric. It is thus hard to accept that Śaṅkara possessed a 'critical attitude toward the Hindu caste system', as suggested by Cronk (2003: 10). Śaṅkara's ethics on caste seem a far cry from Vivekananda's (2009: 390) 'hurting anyone, you hurt yourself', the so-called Vedāntin 'basis of ethics' (pp384–5), written in what Lipner (2010: 81) calls 'the Age of the Śūdra'.

Now Marcaurelle (2000: 32) has suggested that the *Śūdras* were only to be denied access to the *Śrutis*, and not necessarily *brahman*-knowledge. This they could access through hearing the *Purāṇas* (Legendary Stories). He therefore feels that scholars such as Mayeda and Halbfass were wrong in claiming that the former restriction implied the latter (Marcaurelle 2000: 220, n.19). Similarly, Cenkner (1983: 49) has claimed that, 'Social status does not stand in the way'. Tiwari (1977: 132), writing about Advaita's monasteries (*maṭhas*),[5] claims that, 'There was hardly any scope for making a distinction between one caste or the other'. I am unconvinced. For one thing, as Taber (2003: 694) says, overhearing the *Purāṇas* does not constitute an 'established discipline of knowledge based on *smṛti*'. Second, Śaṅkara states that *Śūdras* lack scriptural ability (B.S.Bh. I.iii.34). Third, Śaṅkara categorically states that a born *Śūdra* has no right to knowledge (I.iii.34–8). And fourth, had Śaṅkara wanted to extend the eligibility of knowledge to *Śūdras*, then the story of Jānaśruti (Ch.U. 4) would have given him the ideal opportunity. However, in both the *Ch.U.Bh* (IV.ii.3) and the *B.S.Bh* (I.iii.35), Śaṅkara resorts to 'ingenious exegesis' (Suthren Hirst 2005: 43) to show that Jānaśruti is not really a *Śūdra* by caste or birth even though he is addressed as such. Finally, Śaṅkara is so stubbornly against a *Śūdra* gaining knowledge that he claims that even those that did gain it, did so due to tendencies acquired in a past (non-*Śūdra*) life (B.S.Bh. I.iii.38).

Now Marcaurelle (2000: 34) has also introduced *Ch.U.Bh* (V.xi.7) in order to show that Śaṅkara accepted that householders could receive the knowledge of *brahman*. Not only that, they receive it, not from a *Brahmin*, but from a king. But what message does Śaṅkara take from this? He tells us that, in requesting knowledge from one of 'inferior caste' (*jātito hīna*), the 'great householders', who incidentally were '*Brahmins*, deeply versed in the Vedas', 'abandoned their pride'. Hence, 'seekers after knowledge should behave in the same manner' (C.U.Bh. V.xi.7). He also tells us that the import of the story is that a teacher should only impart knowledge 'to competent persons' (ibid.). In other words, the pupil

---

as 'twice-born' (*dvija*), because the males of these classes underwent an initiation after which they were 'subject to the prescriptions of *dharma*', thus constituting a kind of 'second-birth' (Olivelle 1999: xxxv). *Śūdra* males, like the females of all classes, underwent no such initiation. The institution of Brahmanical renunciation therefore 'disregards' *Śūdras* and women (Olivelle 1992: 60).

4 See Olivelle (1999: 98).

5 Suthren Hirst (2005: 26) has recently said that there is 'no definite evidence' that Śaṅkara established any *maṭhas*. For a 'hypothetical construction' of their creation, see Hacker (in Halbfass 1995: 29).

must learn to be humble in front of the teacher, while the teacher must learn to discriminate between potential pupils. Both these morals are clearly expounded in the *Upadeśa Sāhasrī*. Thus, Śaṅkara states that the student 'should also be guided in humility, etc., the virtues which are means to knowledge' (U.S. Prose, 1.5). As to who was competent, when Śaṅkara is free to speak his own mind, it is a pure *Brahmin* (U.S. Prose, 1.2).

Now Marcaurelle (2000: 32) believes that such statements in Śaṅkara are exceptions to his normal inclusiveness. I am not convinced. For one thing, throughout the *Upadeśa Sāhasrī*, the teacher is explicitly told that he must use the 'great sayings' (*mahāvākyas*) from the Upaniṣads in order to enlighten the pupil. If this is so, even if certain non-*Brahmin*s were allowed a hearing, the *Śūdras* would hereby be *de facto* excluded from the lesson. Socio-religious circumstances 'stopped all but brahmin men from having access to the intellectual culture of the philosophical tradition' (Ram-Prasad 2001b: 378). To be fair to Marcaurelle, Śaṅkara was not particularly consistent, as is shown by his commentary of the *Taittirīya Upaniṣad* (I.xi.2–4), where he states that 'everyone has the right to knowledge'. Even here though, Śaṅkara's objective is not to open up access to knowledge to all and sundry. The main aim, as Marcaurelle (2000: 31) himself admits, is to establish acceptance of the monastic's right to knowledge without having to fulfil ritual duties.

Śaṅkara is thus abusing the notion of ultimate truth and its implied egalitarianism in order to gain an advantage for his group. However, he does not remain true to this universal position, preferring to keep the classes where they are. Whether Śaṅkara believed that *Śūdras* could have access to knowledge or not, the point still remains that he firmly accepted that class distinctions had validity and that people were far from being equal. In the *Ch.U.Bh*, he even claims that only *Brahmins* are straightforward by nature (IV.iv.5), and also implies that non-departure from truthfulness is a virtue solely belonging to the *Brahmin* (ibid.). So I will stand by Mayeda (in Larson and Deutsch 1988: 191) when he states that Śaṅkara was 'rather rigid and strict with respect to caste', and Halbfass (1991: 385) when he speaks of an 'uncompromising adherence to an unequal, caste-bound access' to liberation. Furthermore, no teaching on the ultimate truth changed this conventional view. Fort (1998: 174) thus states that 'traditional Advaitins find the nondual truth irrelevant to equality in everyday social relations'. So while Śaṅkara clearly believed that the Self was devoid of class distinctions (B.S. I.i.1), and that the *brahman* knower was thus beyond caste (Bṛ.U.Bh. II.iv.1), he still wanted the caste-system to remain in place (B.S.Bh. I.iii.34), even to the point of being violently imposed.

The most important point to take from this is that, relatively speaking, there are caste differences, but ultimately speaking, there can be no castes. Now Mayeda (in Larson and Deutsch 1988: 199) claims that Śaṅkara may not have been 'aware of any inconsistency', but I believe he was well aware of it. The Two-Truths strategy allowed Śaṅkara the possibility of holding both views and alternating between them depending on the context. That is why, in practice, he was able to adhere to caste distinctions. This is brought out quite vividly in the *Upadeśa Sāhasrī*, where the pupil (who must be a *Brahmin* in order to qualify as a pupil) is to understand that the Self is free of caste and so on if he is to become a *brahman*-knower:

> Because, by your statement 'I am the son of a *Brahmin* of such and such a family, and so on' you have identified the Self, which is free from caste, family and rites, with the body, which is subject to different caste, family and rites (U.S. Prose, 1.15).

Here we see a clear distinction being made between the body (which is subject to caste) and the Self (which is not subject to caste). But more importantly, we have a distinction between provisional reality, which must be upheld if we are to limit the gift of *brahman*-knowledge to male-only *Brahmin* pupils, and ultimate reality, which must be understood if this knowledge is to dawn on the pupil.

This leads to a vital point. It is misleading to think of Advaita as a non-dual philosophy, without being clear what they are being non-dual about. They are clearly not being non-dual about body versus Self. They are not being non-dual when it comes to the question of caste. They are not being non-dual with regard to gender. They are not being non-dual about other schools of thought. They are not being non-dual when comparing teacher and pupil. Hence, from the empirical point of view, we see that Advaita admits of numerous distinctions. Non-duality then, for Advaita, is of a very specific kind, it is the non-duality of the *ātman* and *brahman*, which, in a nutshell, means the non-duality of self-reflexive consciousness.

In Śaṅkara's Two-Truths model, castes and women can exist only in the conditioned domain (T.U.Bh. I.xi.2–4). It is because the majority of us move within the conditioned that the social norms must remain intact. In other words, it is our own ignorance which gives rise to empirical distinctions. However, it is my belief that we must see the *brahman*-knower's consciousness as flickering back and forth between domains. That is why there is no contradiction in the fact that a *brahman*-knower does not cognize women as women even though *they are* women. It is also why there is no contradiction in the historical fact that there has never been a female Śaṅkarācārya or an outcaste Śaṅkarācārya (see Knot 1998: 80 and 93). In fact, the Advaita order of renouncers, the Daśanāmi, does not accept women ascetics at all (Klostermaier 2007: 299). While this may be controversial, it is not contradictory.

On one side, there is the conditioned, provisional world of ethics, in which *Śūdras* are *Śūdras*, women are women, teachers are teachers, pupils are pupils and *Brahmin* males are *Brahmin* males. On the other, there is the ultimate, unconditioned, world of knowledge, 'where one does not see anything else, does not hear anything else, and does not cognize anything else' (Ch.U. VII.xxiv.1). In between, there is a door, open only to the *Brahmin* male, who paradoxically, once through it, must come to realize that he is *not* a *Brahmin* or a male. Holding the keys to the door is the *brahman*-knower who I believe flickers between the inner world of *brahman* and the outside world of caste, occupation and gender. If we understand these two domains, and the line that stands between them, we understand Śaṅkara's ethics.

7.2 Śāntideva: The Reality and Non-reality of Gender

Unlike Śaṅkara's system, there is no *explicitly* acknowledged class or caste system in Buddhism. I stress 'explicit', because caste clearly plays an important didactic role in Buddhism. For example, a virtuous Buddhist lay person may well expect to be born into a 'good family', which Keown (1996: 339) defines as one 'enjoying a privileged status in terms of caste and wealth'. Furthermore, the fact that the Buddha, in becoming an ascetic, gave up his rights to the throne, plays a major role in the story of Buddhist renunciation. It is no coincidence that the same story is repeated with regard to the hagiography of Śāntideva. It therefore comes as no real surprise that Śāntideva's *Compendium* should assume that 'Humans are superior to animals, high castes to low castes, men to women' (Mrozik 2007: 8).

Sweet (1977: 55) also points out how Śāntideva's statement that 'people are seen to be of two types, the ordinary and the *yogis*' (BCA. 9.3) should be seen as a Buddhist parallel to the 'pretensions to hereditary spiritual superiority' of the Hindu *Brahmin* class. And, needless to say, throughout the *Compendium*, Śāntideva explicitly accepts the hierarchy of the *bodhisattva* over the *Śrāvaka*. He also warns the *bodhisattva* about giving the Buddhist doctrine 'to those who are unworthy' (Ś.S. 54). He is told to 'live in a good caste' (106), which should not be one of the classic four (105). He speaks of the negative influence of 'inferior men' (161). Furthermore, the *bodhisattva* is specifically told to avoid the *Caṇḍāla* (outcaste) (48). And one of the warnings against acting immorally is that one may be reborn as a *Caṇḍāla* (69). Even an eater of meat is said to be reborn as a *Caṇḍāla*, whereas one who avoids meat is either 'born into a *Brahmin* family or into a practitioner's family' (133).

Such caste-related karmic consequences are no different than those found in the Hindu texts. So the *Chāndogya Upaniṣad* (V.x.7) likewise speaks of immoral behaviour leading to rebirth as a *Caṇḍāla*. And the *Bhagavad Gītā* (6.42) even includes the exact same phrase: 'into a practitioner's family' with relation to the positive consequences of *karma-yoga*. If nothing else, it shows that the 'Hindu' class categories may play similar ethical roles in Buddhist rhetoric. And such caste categories have survived in Buddhism for 2,500 years. In present day Sri Lanka, the monks hold an equivalent place to the *Brahmins* in India, and monastic communities favour certain castes to the extent that ordination may be refused to all other castes (Gombrich 1988: 143–75).

This is by no means a modern phenomenon. Thus, Mrozik (2007: 69) has argued that despite a recent change in attitude, 'premodern Buddhist literature indicates that social hierarchy was generally an accepted part of Buddhist life'. This is not to say that hierarchies are inherently wrong. Nor do I claim that the Indians held a principle *contrary* to our modern society, as Dumont (1980: 2) did. For surely the British that entered India had their own form of 'subtle and deeply entrenched social hierarchy', as Doniger (2010: 578) claims. And it would be foolish to argue that it is no longer present in our European society. My purpose then is simply to remove the notion that the Buddhists were somehow exempt from the concept of hierarchies and inequality. Hence, there are a number of easily over-looked passages in the Pāli Canon that make it clear that from earliest times the Buddhists wished to be seen as a class distinct from the *Brahmin*s. For example, at *D.N.*iii.84, there is a passage whose language 'echoes word for word' the creation myth of the Vedas (Gombrich 2009: 189).

Such examples indicate that even though the Buddhists ultimately claim that there is no abiding self, this does not prevent them from using conventional categories. As Gombrich (2009: 187) rightly claims, the Buddha clearly 'recognized the conventional nature of the caste system'. I would suggest then that the commonly spouted view that Buddhists believe in the equality of all people (for example Isayeva 1993: 22; Sen 2005: 10) may well need to be qualified. As these are complex issues embedded in the history of Indian culture, I prefer to focus on the example of gender categories as found in Śāntideva's texts.

Śāntideva could not deny the historical fact that women were allowed to join the *Saṅgha*. He speaks of those nuns who take 500 precepts (Ś.S. 174). While certain 'ill-behaved nuns' are to be shunned (48), this does not apply to all nuns. Women may also be allowed access to the *bodhisattva* path (116) and its moral code (60). Sometimes this inclusion has an edge to it, as when he says that 'even women', which Mrozik (2007: 35) reads as 'exceptional women', can follow the path (Ś.S. 11). But overall, women are certainly not excluded. Śāntideva thus includes quotes from scriptures which address women. For example, he quotes the *Gaṇḍavyūha*, which addresses its discourse on the cultivation of purity to a female (Ś.S. 180). Furthermore, Śāntideva quotes from the *Śrī-mālā Sūtra* (Ś.S. 42), a Mahāyāna text which supposedly recounts a discourse between the Buddha and a queen. In other words, Śāntideva does not hide the fact that women are very much part of Buddhist history.

Nevertheless, Śāntideva often talks as if his audience were male-only. The *Compendium*, 'primarily represents a male monastic perspective' (Mrozik 2007: 10). Similarly, the *BCA* was written for a 'monastic audience which without doubt would have been predominantly male, if not exclusively so' (Crosby and Skilton 1995: xxxv). Some of the bias may be due to the fact that Sanskrit uses masculine endings when both men and women may be implied. So when Śāntideva talks of 'men' or 'sons' he should not always be taken as excluding women. Some of the bias may also be due to the texts that Śāntideva is quoting from. For example, he quotes the *Saddharmasmṛtyupasthāna*, which claims that 'women are the root of ruin' (Ś.S. 72). He then quotes from the *Ugradatta-paripṛcchā*, which suggests that a wife is 'an obstacle to morality, meditation and wisdom' (Ś.S. 78), a common description of the eight-fold path. Of course, the act of editing is not restricted to the question of what to put in, but also what to leave out. So it might be just as telling to note that, while there are in fact Buddhist stories which depict female *bodhisattva*s as using their beauty to positive effect, for example, that of Vasumitrā (*Gaṇḍavyūha Sūtra*), Śāntideva chose not to include this story, even though he quotes extensively from this *sūtra*.[6]

[6] Mrozik (2007: 57–8), while noting the 'flagrantly misogynist' passages in the *Compendium*, also makes the valid point that Śāntideva may not have had the complete texts available to him.

Whether borrowed from other texts or not, there is no getting away from the abundance of sexism throughout the *Compendium*. For example, the *bodhisattva*'s generosity is shown in the giving away of his wife (Ś.S. 20 and 27), a gesture that would no doubt stir some modern controversy. And Śāntideva's stress on celibacy is made clear when he says that a true *bodhisattva* has no wife (115). Moreover, unspecified misdeeds of a householder are said to result in his rebirth as a woman (69). On the other hand, the passion of a woman, if directed towards a male *bodhisattva*, may lead to rebirth as a man (168). Similar gender bias can be found in his own *BCA*, where he warns that a woman comes at a price (BCA. 8.71), and that a man wastes his wealth on a woman (8.42). Moreover, when training oneself as a *bodhisattva*, one 'should be made to behave like a new bride; modest, timid and kept in order' (8.166). And when one becomes a true *yogi*, one will know for certain that a woman is '*aśuci*', that is, 'foul' or, more literally, 'impure' (9.8). In fact, this verse prevents us from claiming that his sexism can be put down to the culture he grew up in, for he actually claims that the 'worldly' disagree with the *yogi* on this one. So, let us not deny the blatant sexism in his work. Like Śaṅkara's ethics, Śāntideva's ethics were not egalitarian.

Having got this out in the open, let us get to the main issue, the philosophical problem with this rhetoric. The problem, as I frame it, with this conventional and often derogatory view of women, is that Śāntideva, in both the *Compendium* and the *BCA*, explicitly claims that there are no truly existing gender distinctions. And as with the case of Śaṅkara, it is this *manipulation* of the Two-Truths doctrine, rather than discrimination *per se*, that I wish to explore.[7]

Let us stay for a while with verse 9.8 of the *BCA*, for it does in fact highlight a number of interesting points. But to put it into philosophical context, we also need to remind ourselves of the three verses which came before. So we have:

> Ordinary people see existent things and imagine them to be real. They do not see them as illusion-like. This is where there is dispute between the worldly and the *yogis*. Even what we call perceptible objects, such as form, are only established by popular consensus, not by any valid means of knowledge. [However] such consensus is wrong, for example, when ordinary folk view the impure as pure.[8] The Protector [Buddha] taught of existents in order to guide people [gradually into the knowledge of emptiness]. If it is objected then that these ['entities'] are not really momentary, but only conventionally so, [the fact is that] there is no fault in a *yogi* adopting the conventional usage. He has a better understanding

[7] Those interested in a more 'feminist' discussion of Śāntideva can do no better than read the excellent (and balanced) study by Mrozik (2007).

[8] This is one of the four classic misconceptions of mankind as mentioned in the Pāli Canon (A.N. ii.52). Here, one takes the impure/foul (*asubha*) to be pure/desirable (*subha*). The other three misconceptions are: taking the impermanent to be permanent, the painful to be blissful and what is not-self to be self.

> of reality than the worldly. Otherwise, the objections of the worldly would invalidate the [*yogi*'s] determination of women as 'foul' (BCA. 9.5–8).

Now Arnold (2005: 202–3) has recently asked how the Buddha (see S.N. III.138) and Mādhyamikas, like Candrakīrti, can endorse the claim that 'the world disputes with me, I do not dispute with the world'. Arnold (2005: 203) offers what he believes to be a 'charitable reading', claiming that the Madhyamaka are really opposing the 'Ābhidharmika version of Buddhist thought' (ibid.). But as we can see from the above, Śāntideva is also arguing against conventional (that is, common) views about women, just as he and all Buddhists argue against certain commonly held views about the self. Arnold wants to say that the Buddhists are speaking purely at the ultimate level, and this saves them from falling into dispute with the worldly, and thus saves Arnold's thesis of the Madhyamaka offering 'transcendental arguments' (p139) rather than sceptical ones. With regard to the question of self, Arnold is no doubt correct. However, Śāntideva also feels that the common man gets the conventional truth wrong too, and explicitly states that 'common opinion' (*prasiddhi*) can be mistaken. The Buddhist therefore stands alongside Lehrer (2000: 72) when he cautions that 'common sense should not be allowed to run unbridled in the epistemic field'.

Mrozik (2007: 91) has rightly noticed how Śāntideva 'goes to great length to undermine the conventional view that women's bodies are desirable'. But further along, Mrozik seems to make the same mistake as Arnold by assuming that 'conventional view/perspective' must mean 'consensus' (p98). And Huntington's (1989: 48) linguistic notion of conventional truth as 'our shared sociolinguistic experience' does not help us here, for Śāntideva is attacking the use of verbal descriptions by the unenlightened. Mrozik (2007: 98) is therefore right in saying that the sexist remarks of Śāntideva cannot be wiped clear by an appeal to the Two Truths.

For Śāntideva, conventional truth (*saṃvṛti-satya*) is not synonymous with 'consensus' (*prasiddhi*). Here Śāntideva, contra Candrakīrti (?), does not 'let the mundane be just as it is seen' by the average person (see Arnold 2005: 192), and, contra Arnold's depiction of Madhyamaka, does in fact point to a 'privileged level of description', that of the *yogi*.[9] As Wallace notes, 'The insights of the enlightened few may invalidate the consensus of the masses' (in Dalai Lama 1988: 124, n.22).

Of course, Śāntideva is not interested in whether women really are, ontologically, foul or not; he simply wants men to renounce their lust for them. While I agree with Mrozik (2007: 98) that a Buddhist apologist cannot lean on the Two Truths to downplay such misogynistic statements, I contend that the 8th-century Śāntideva would offer no apology. Śāntideva, as promoter of asceticism, clearly needed such views as women being foul on a conventional level for his call for renunciation. The Buddhist needs to claim a privileged level of seeing for the *yogi* in order to add authority to their counter-intuitive claims. So this combined attitude of

[9] On Candrakīrti, see Huntington (1989) and Arnold (2005). On the notion of 'conventional' truth in Buddhist philosophy, see Cowherds (2011).

elitism and sexism would have been taken for granted in his cultural milieu. What allows the Mādhyamikas to 'keep *persons* in play' (Arnold 2005: 203), then, is not that they shy away from telling us how things really are, but by a voluntary delusion that (socially constructed) persons are indeed independently existent, and as such, open to conventional designation. And here I agree with Arnold that their motivation is both soteriologically (p176) and ethically (p203) grounded. It is in the conventional world where merit is accumulated and where people suffer. That is why the Buddha provisionally spoke of existents.

However, this decision to live in the conventional world does not mean that the Buddhist must *always* defer to 'ordinary intuitions', as Arnold (2005: 117) suggests. Even though the *bodhisattva* may accept much of what Nāgārjuna called 'worldly conventional truth' (MMK. 24.8), and might well participate in the established language games of his culture, the *yogi* sometimes has to step in and say 'I am sorry, but you are wrong here'. Thus, *yogis* are entitled to use conventional language, like 'pure' and 'impure', because they understand both the ultimate and the conventional better than ordinary folk. That is, on my interpretation, they can flicker between domains without misinterpreting either.

The ordinary person's misunderstanding of ultimate reality is shown in their grasping at impermanent objects as if they were ultimately real. And the ordinary man's misunderstanding of conventional reality is demonstrated by his belief that women are anything other than foul. The *yogi* is there to advise him that women are in fact foul, and that all objects are in fact illusion-like. Even the most beautiful of women will become a heap of bones. There is nothing inherent about her beauty, nothing permanent about the bliss she offers. We are all food for worms. Hence:

> They are nothing other than mere bones, independent [of you] and indifferent [to you]. Why don't you willingly embrace them [now] and feel bliss? That face, either you saw it as you tried to lift it up as it was lowered in modesty, or you never saw it as it was concealed by a veil. As if unable to bear your hardship, the vultures have now exposed that face. Look! Why do you now run away? (BCA. 8.43–5).

All this sits rather uncomfortably though with the contrary notion of the *bodhisattva* having a 'purified' (*viśuddha, pariśuddha*) body (Ś.S. 307, 151), and especially so alongside the story of the Bodhisattva Priyaṃkara (Pleasure-Maker!) who when gazed upon could lead a woman into rebirth as a man (Ś.S. 168). And if this privileging of *bodhisattva* bodies were not enough, we might introduce the story of the female *bodhisattva*, Candrottarā (Ś.S. 78–80), whose beauty, rather than being of benefit, actually has a 'deleterious effect on men' (Mrozik 2007: 56), by generating excessive lust in them. The contrasts between men and women and between *bodhisattvas* and non-*bodhisattvas* could not be more blatant.

Moreover, Mrozik (2007: 56) rightly highlights how Candrottarā's virtue is proven, not only by her physical beauty, but by her 'fine fragrance' (*atigandha*). She later (p68) contrasts this with the way one who eats meat is said by Śāntideva (Ś.S. 132) to 'stink' in their next life. However, the implication of the following verse from the *BCA* is that *all* lay people stink: 'Finding no pleasure in soft cotton-filled pillows, for they do not ooze a bad smell; lovers are infatuated by filth' (BCA. 8.50).

Even more informative, though, is the stress Śāntideva puts on the fact that the smell of perfume that a normal woman exudes is not inherently her own (BCA. 8.65). This seems to contrast with the scent of a *bodhisattva*, which does seem to be inherently their own. Moreover, he speaks of a woman's foul stench as being 'naturally her own' (*sva-bhāva*) (8.66). In full:

> Though applied to the body, this scent comes from the sandal-wood alone, not from anything else. Why are you attracted to one thing by the scent of something else? Rather it would be auspicious if its own natural smell prevented passion towards it. Why do the worldly take delight in worthless objects, anointing it with scent? (BCA. 8.65–6).

But how often have the Mādhyamikas claimed there to be *no svabhāva*? For Śāntideva, there just are no inherently existing 'things' with the power to exude inherently existing odours. So is this not an example of the *mistaken* 'belief in a real body' (*sat kāya dṛṣṭi*) that Buddhists accuse others of? If so, the question – 'Why are you attracted to one thing by the scent of something else?' (8.65b) – while persuasive, and mildly amusing, seems doctrinally contradictory. Even so, the seeming contradictions can be reconciled, by which I mean coherently explained.

One way would be to treat much of Śāntideva's argument as a sceptical one (which I believe it is). The attacks on women, for example, are there as a means of convincing men to renounce lay life, not because that is how Śāntideva actually views women (although it may be). As such, he does not have to actually believe his argument to be 'true'; he only needs to feel that it is convincing and potentially efficacious. As already noted, Śāntideva's verses are often primarily persuasive, and here we have just seen how irony plays a major part in that rhetoric. Thus, Mrozik (2007) speaks of two types of bodily discourse, the 'ascetic' and the 'physio-moral'.[10] In his 'ascetic' mode of discourse, Śāntideva claims that attachment to the body can only have negative results, whereas in the 'physio-moral' discourse, attachment to a *bodhisattva*'s body can in fact have positive results. And because Śāntideva is particularly set on producing celibate male monastics, the 'ascetic' mode sometimes trumps the 'physio-moral', thus allowing for the possibility of a positive (female) body directly leading to negative results. Of course, the effect is really 'indirect', and in the *BCA* we often find Śāntideva ridiculing the man for being taken in by the woman (e.g. 8.54–69). Mrozik (2007: 90–91) also notes this with regard to the *Compendium*; though she adds that Śāntideva sometimes

[10] I share the term 'ascetic discourse' with Mrozik, but for me it goes beyond the question of bodies, being a more general attack on society. It thus contrasts with a much wider ethical discourse on the need to help all beings. It is therefore about rejection versus embrace of the very same phenomena.

'blames women for male sexual misconduct', an attitude Sponberg (cited in Mrozik 2007: 91) has rightly called 'ascetic misogyny'.

A second way to reconcile the contradiction would be to rely on our old friends, the Two Truths. Now Mrozik (2007: 98) has claimed that the Two Truths 'will not help to reconcile the different discourses on women'. Her point is well taken; however, to reconcile is not necessarily to apologize for the discourse, but may simply be to coherently explain it. My whole thesis on the Two Truths has been modelled on the belief that there are two distinct modes of discourse at play, and that the writers alternate between them. This is another way of saying that there are two equally valid and valued approaches. Mrozik (2007: 99) asks if there are 'ways of upholding conventional and ultimate perspectives simultaneously'. The answer is 'yes'. What follows is my own explanation of the how.

What we have is a 'woman' (who does not ultimately exist) giving off a smell (which does not ultimately exist) which is cognized by a recipient (who does not ultimately exist) as being 'foul' (which is a mere conventional designation);[11] whereas a '*bodhisattva*' (who does not ultimately exist) gives off a smell (which does not ultimately exist) which is cognized by a recipient (who does not ultimately exist) as being 'pleasing' (another conventional designation). We would then expect a further argument from Śāntideva that would deconstruct this conventional situation, including the causal chain of sensation and the categories of 'womanhood' and 'manhood'. And this is indeed the route Śāntideva takes. If one believed that there was in fact an 'experiencer' of sensation, one should ponder on the following sceptical argument:

> Since there is no knower of sensation, nor any sensation, why 'oh craving', having seen this, are you not torn asunder? There is seeing and touching by a 'self', which is like a dream or illusion. Sensation is not 'perceived' by consciousness, for they are born together. What came earlier is remembered by what arises later, it is not 'experienced'. Sensation does not experience itself and is not experienced by another. There is no experiencer, and therefore in reality there is no sensation. So who, in this bundle devoid of self, can be afflicted by it? (BCA.9. 98–101).

Thus, a bad smell should not affect you any more than a good smell should. And what of the bodies from which these came? If you believe that a man or woman, *bodhisattva* or not, is their body, meditate as follows:

> The body is not the feet, not the calves, not the thighs, and the body is not the hips. It is not the belly, nor the back, nor is it the chest, nor the arms. It is not the hands, nor the sides, nor the arm-pit, nor the shoulder region. The body is not

[11] By conventional designation, I do not mean to imply that 'foul' is the conventional word used to describe women, it is not. What I mean is that 'foul' is a dualistic notion used as a convenient form of linguistic expression so that one may be understood.

> the neck, nor the head. What among these then is the body? If you argue that the body is partially present in all of these, [We reply that] it is only parts that are parts, so where is the body itself found? (BCA. 9.78–80).

Such a meditation should lead you to the conclusion that 'there is no body' (BCA. 9.83). Could it be then that there is difference at a more elemental level? Could a woman perhaps be made of different atoms? But, like Śaṅkara (B.S.Bh. I.iv.28, II.i.29 and II.ii.11ff), Śāntideva also denies the coherence of atoms:

> Even the parts can be broken down into atoms, and the atoms into directions. Being without parts, the directions are space. Therefore, the atom has no [ultimate] existence. Who, upon reflection, would take delight in this dream-like form? And since the body does not [ultimately] exist, what is 'woman', what is 'man'? (BCA. 9.86–7).

If there are no atoms, if atoms are but space, how can there be physical 'men' and physical 'women'? What would constitute them? That is the question Śāntideva poses. Now, if you say that men and women might have different types of consciousness, Śāntideva claims otherwise:

> The 'element' of consciousness is empty by its very nature; it is unestablished except by conventional designation. And even this conventionally [established consciousness] is neither 'female' nor 'male' (Ś.S. 250).

And if that were not clear enough, he repeats a little further along, 'And that which lacks own being can be neither "female" nor "male"' (Ś.S. 251). In other words, for a woman to really be a woman, she would have to have own-being (*sva-bhāva*), but nothing has own-being, everything is inter-dependent. Thus, a woman cannot be a woman.

If you are still unconvinced, and if, like the Advaitins, you distinguish between consciousness (*vijñāna*) and mind (*manas*), you might still wish to claim that men and women have different types of mind. If so, you need to meditate on these verses:

> The mind is not located in the sense faculties, nor in form, etc., nor in-between. The mind is found neither internally, nor externally, nor anywhere else. That which is not in the body, nor outside it, nor inter-mingled, nor separate; that is nothing whatsoever. Hence, beings are naturally liberated (BCA. 9.102–3).

Men and women then are equal in being empty of inherent existence and in being naturally liberated. This is so because: 'Neither the thought not the thinker exists. In woman there is no woman. In man there is no man' (Ś.S. 245).

But, you may ask, if the thinker does not exist, and if beings are naturally liberated, then what about the distinction between the ordinary beings and the *yogis*? The answer, as we know already, is that this distinction also breaks down:

> When analysed, the state of existence is dream-like, [insubstantial] like a plantain tree. Thus, there is no substantial difference between the liberated and the non-liberated (BCA. 9.150).

Once this distinction has been broken down, it also leaves the way open for the seemingly radical claim that the bodies of all beings are ultimately as equally non-defiled as the Buddha's (Ś.S. 230). Now Mrozik (2007: 110) states that such a claim only occurs once in the *Compendium*, but compare: 'All existents are originally pure' (Ś.S. 172). Both these quotes are used by Śāntideva to inspire the practitioner, making them believe that they can purify their bodies and their past *karma*, despite the apparent foulness of their bodies and the evil of their actions. Thus, in the *Compendium*, if not in the *BCA*, Śāntideva occasionally adopts 'buddha-nature' rhetoric for motivational purposes, which was probably the original intention of the *tathāgata-garbha* texts (see Williams 2009: 104). However, contra (?) the intention of the early texts (ibid.), it seems that Śāntideva did indeed draw ethical implications from this theory. Comparing Śaṅkara's argument in the *Īśā-Upaniṣad Bhāṣya* (5–6) [see p.10–11 above], it is tempting to see Advaitic influence here. However, Williams (2009: 109) believes the influence was possibly the other way round, with Gauḍapāda being influenced by *tathāgata-garbha* thought. Whatever the case may be, we continue to see the *cross-cutting* nature of Indian thought.

Nevertheless, as we can see from the following exchange with the Yogācāra, Śāntideva does not want his theory to collapse into their mind-only thesis:

> For you, the mind has been reduced to isolation, accompanied by non-existents. How could the activity of the unreal [objects] proceed, even if supported by a real existent [i.e. pure mind]? If the mind is free of objectivity, then everyone is a Buddha. And so, even if 'mind-only' were posited, what benefit is gained? (BCA. 9.28–9).

As we saw earlier, Śāntideva here argues against the Yogācāra's apparent denial of conventional reality (9.28). But the following verse also seems to want to deny the Yogācāra's thesis on account of its failure to distinguish the Buddha from others. But, at the ultimate level, once we allow for the doctrine of original purity, it is difficult to see how these two models differ.[12] At this level of realization, who could ridicule the ordinary man for being foolish, or the woman for being foul? Śāntideva certainly could not: 'When all things are thus empty, what can be gained or lost? Who can be honoured or humiliated by whom?' (BCA. 9.151)

In conclusion, men and women are different if and when we are caught in conventional reality. The more the mind is fed by desire, the more mistakes one makes at the conventional level of understanding. As soon as we get a glimpse of

---

[12] This is one reason why Loy (1988: 136) found such a 'remarkable similarity' between Śaṅkara's Advaita and the Zen of Dōgen.

emptiness, the attachment reduces, desire weakens, resolve strengthens and the illusion is deconstructed. When this view is made strong, women are no longer seen as desirable. Ultimately, 'women' do not exist as separate distinct objects. They are empty of inherent existence, mere labels added to a certain formation of conditions. The same, of course, is true of 'men'. They are conceptual fictions. There are no 'women' to be desired and no 'men' to desire them. Śāntideva uses provisional language because we are caught in the provisional realm. He uses it to deter monks from their desire for women. He uses it to dissuade the householder from having intercourse with his wife. He knows that those who have a weak grasp of emptiness are always prone to wavering. But that is not all his discourse is about. Celibacy is but a step towards selflessness.

Mrozik (2007: 97) has claimed that the 'primary goal' of the *Compendium* is 'the eradication of male sexual desire for women'. But that is only one third of the story, the other components being the realization of emptiness and the compassionate response to all beings. Thus: 'From action whose essence is emptiness and compassion, there is the purification of karmic fruit' (Ś.S. 270, Kārikā 21b). And a little further on, he writes: 'Here, in this world … the *bodhisattva* renounces the body and life, but he does not renounce the Good Law' (Ś.S. 274). When sitting, he thinks, 'May all beings sit on the thrown of wisdom'. When he lies down, he thinks, 'May every last being be led to final liberation' (348). Śāntideva thus uses provisional language to persuade us out of our state of self-serving ignorance into one of other-serving, selfless, compassionate action. This is the main teaching that Śāntideva wishes the monks to understand. Renunciation is but a prelude.

In brief, to get a man to see how he is caught in *saṃsāra*, Śāntideva has to borrow the voice of the perfected *yogi* in order to paint woman as an impure object, one that ultimately brings suffering. But to get a man to reach the threshold of transcendence, Śāntideva has to make him see that there are no men, no women, no self, no beings and so ultimately, no *yogis*. So the question arises: are there no *bodhisattvas* after all? Well, of course, a *bodhisattva* is only a *bodhisattva* when he knows that he is *not* a *bodhi-sattva* (Vajracchedikā, 3). Such a '*bodhisattva*' vows to save all 'beings', be they 'male' or 'female'. But upon liberation, he does not see them as male or female. As such, his 'qualified altruism' is untouched by the question of gender. Nevertheless, it becomes that much *more* qualified by the fact that he no longer sees *any self at all* before him. When he does happen to project such a self it is only for the benefit of that person. That is 'constructive altruism'. If he gets caught by his own projection, and starts to really see a self there, then he needs to return to meditation on not-self. That this projected person may (from their own side) not wish to be helped complicates the issue somewhat; but then, to save a man or woman from drowning (even if they are attempting suicide) is surely altruistic.

And so, after this rather complex diversion into the marginal areas of caste and gender in both Śaṅkara and Śāntideva, I wish to reaffirm the point I made at the outset that the issue here is not one of social discrimination *per se*. On the other hand, I refused to simply gloss over such discriminations, if only to discredit the appeal by their respective lineages to egalitarianism and universality. Nevertheless, the essential point to be grasped here is the manner in which they both adopt the Two Truths. What we have seen is that both admit that, ultimately speaking, there are no castes, no men, no women; indeed, no basis for distinction whatsoever. However, when it comes to provisional ethics, to the need for renunciation, to the need for class duties, to the need for monastic segregation and so on, then for sure, differences are not only condoned, they are promoted and sealed with approval. And yet, it has been argued that constructive altruism stands firm as the best way of characterizing their ethical projects, and while undoubtedly partial, their ethics are moral through and through.

Conclusion

We began our comparison with a warning. We prepared ourselves for the tensions and the ambiguities. We did our level best to clear the area of gods and magical powers. Our terrain was desolate rather than overgrown. The religious quest started to appear as a philosophical problem, a human dilemma. We were being faced with a number of particularly existential questions. How could the intuitive among us continue to participate in a social game that was no longer believable? How could one practice ethics amongst persons regarded as ignorant illusions? Why should one not simply turn away from society; transcend this world of name and form?

Then we met Śaṅkara, the Hindu, and Śāntideva, the Buddhist. One would tell us that, in reality, there was nothing but *brahman*, nothing else was worthy of the name 'real'. Even 'we' were unreal in our present state of being. And yet, with higher insight, we could change all of that. We were also that reality, *brahman*. We could be one in the knowing that is *brahman*, even whilst embodied. We could be truly liberated in this life, a *jīvan-mukta*. The other would tell us that all was in fact empty. There was no *brahman*; there was no self at all. True, we were ultimately unreal. Equally true, we could become liberated from nescience in this very life. But our reality would only be found in the *task* of living, not in any ground of being. Being was a state of acting, the way of the *bodhisattva*.

It became apparent that, on both accounts, we were currently in a state of delusion, but one that could be seen through. All we needed to do was recognize the truth. They both called it ultimate truth (*paramārtha-satya*). But despite their use of the same terminology, their ultimate metaphysics seemed to sit on opposite sides of the Self-spectrum. And yet, when limited to this life, the role they offered seemed surprisingly similar. Both would claim that the truth of non-individuation needed to be thoroughly grasped and subsequently spread to others. The life-style was that of the wise and caring teacher, the compassionate guru. The initial task was to deconstruct the self so as to become selfless. The further task was to then reconstruct the suffering other, so as to be capable of empathising with their confused condition. We were presented with two visions of the very same ethic, 'constructive altruism'. For Śaṅkara, it seemed largely limited to those who were willing and qualified to take the final epistemic leap into truth. Others were advised to follow their own social duty. For Śāntideva, the teaching of emptiness was equally reserved for the qualified few, though his compassion had the potential to include the helping of others in their quest for lesser goods than *nirvāṇa*.

Thankfully, we were invited here in order to compare, not to choose. And so, after flickering our way through two competing traditions, we have come to our comparative conclusions. Having already announced their metaphysical differences, we should now take stock of their similarities, and, given their ontological starting points, it is an astonishing list. A key feature for both writers was the need for renunciation of this world. Both painted it as one of suffering, a magical show of charming temptations just waiting to dupe us out of our strength, out of our money, out of our minds. Celibacy was seen as the key to liberating oneself from the bondage of family and home. Asceticism was central to letting go of the body's demands. And so women were to be seen as dangerous, their bodies described in foul terms, their impermanence brought forward to the now. They were walking corpses just waiting to rot. Nothing impermanent could have ultimate worth, and least of all the physical.

We were invited into the religious circle. But one could still go astray. Not all that was on offer was for the good. Śaṅkara would warn us against the way of action, which took knowledge as a mere means to ritual. Śāntideva tells us never to emulate those lazy, selfish monks, who sit all day delighting in their own private bliss. These paths were filled with subtle ignorance. One needed to be of sharp faculty to see the implications. Knowledge became the dominant quest. This knowledge was claimed to be beyond the grasp of the intellect, an intuitive knowledge. Nevertheless, it was a knowledge which gained its authority from scripture, its conscious experience merely confirming its validity. Both would admit to partial knowers, to glimpses of truth and backsliding. Thus, I proposed, we must imagine these partial knowers as flickering between ultimate and conventional modes of seeing.

Those who had come this far, who had purified the mind, who had distinguished themselves from the flock were now being invited to let go of all marks of difference. True liberation came when one understood that there was no ultimate difference between the liberated and the non-liberated. Only such an insight could truly count as liberation. Ultimately speaking, there was no duality between the ultimate and the conventional. One who had grasped this truth could find their place in either domain. This truth was so precious, that it simply had to be passed on. As Brahmā Sahampati once allegedly said to the Buddha (S.N. I.137), there would be those with little dust in their eyes.

And so, these knowers of reality were to take on the self-imposed duty of the compassionate teacher. Being almost exclusively male, their role would be that of the 'paternal pedagogue', guiding the other out of the forest of the body, beyond the magic show of the mind, into the pure light of knowledge. The path is a gradual one; it demands study, acumen, discipline, virtues. Such work demands self-control, fearlessness and a complete lack of selfish interest, a prime candidate for Urmson's (1958) category of 'Saints and Heroes'. But the rewards are boundless, an ineffable bliss, which is the bliss of knowing truth.

Given these startling commonalities, I would like to propose that this comparison has shown itself to have import in three distinct areas of scholarship. First, there is the *philosophical* conclusion, which shows how two very different – even radically opposite – views on cosmology of self and religious norms can generate strikingly similar accounts of the relationship between conduct and world in a 'selfless framework'. Despite their outright disagreement on the nature of the self, neither Śāntideva nor Śaṅkara required a view of the person as a stable individuated agent in order to posit a system of moral values that ought to be followed. In fact, both would conclude that the very belief in oneself as a unified moral agent was counter-productive to other-regarding moral thought. Second, there is the *historiographical* conclusion, which demonstrates the limits and power of doctrinal commitments to metaphysics and ethics. We showed just how committed these two thinkers were to the continuity of their lineages, both in terms of doctrinal commitments and normative conduct. We saw how the language of ultimate truth set the limits on these commitments, but also how the very force of tradition tended to balance the weight of any ultimate assertions. And third, there is the *disciplinary* conclusion, which highlights, not only the similarities between Buddhist and Brahmanical thinkers, but how their methodologies and aims, and even their inter-sectarian differences, are in fact *cross-cutting*. Thus, I proposed that the so-called *ātman/anātman* distinction between Hinduism and Buddhism needed further qualification. We have seen, both verbally and graphically, how Śāntideva and Śaṅkara shift between notions of self and not-self depending on the context. I thus presented a more nuanced approach to the question of self which took into consideration both the Two-Truths mode of discourse and the self-deluding form of emotive ethical rhetoric. Finally, I would like to propose that these medieval Indian models may well prove themselves to be a valuable source of both metaphysical and moral inspiration to those of us who continue to ask deeper and deeper questions about the self.

Bibliography

Primary Texts (Sanskrit Only)

De La Vallée Poussin, L. (1901), *Prajñākaramati's Commentary to the Bodhicharyāvatāra of Çāntideva*, Calcutta: Asiatic Society.

Mayeda, S. (1973), *Śaṅkara's Upadeśasāhasrī – Critically Edited with Introduction and Indices*, Tokyo: Hokuseido Press.

Śaṅkara (1983), *Complete Works of Sri Sankaracharya, Vol. 1–10*, Chennai: Samata Books.

Vaidya, P.L. (1960), *Bodhicaryāvatāra of Śāntideva – with the Commentary Pañjikā of Prajñākaramati*, Darbhanga: Mithila Institute.

Vaidya, P.L. (1961), *Śikṣāsamuccaya of Śāntideva*, Darbhanga: Mithila Institute.

Primary Texts (English Translations)

Anacker, S. (1998), *Seven Works of Vasubandhu – The Buddhist Psychological Doctor*, Delhi: Motilal Banarsidass.

Bendall, C. and Rouse, W.H.D. (1971), *Śikṣā Samuccaya – A Compendium of Buddhist Doctrine*, Delhi: Motilal Banarsidass.

Bhattacharya, K. (1998), *Vigrahavyāvartanī – The Dialectical Method of Nāgārjuna*, 4th Edition, Delhi: Motilal Banarsidass.

Bodhi, B. (2000), *The Connected Discourses of the Buddha – A Translation of the Saṃyutta Nikāya*, Boston: Wisdom.

Cleary, T. (1993), *The Flower Ornament Scripture – Translation of the Avatamsaka Sutra*, Boston: Shambhala.

Conze, E. (1973), *The Perfection of Wisdom in Eight Thousand Lines & Its Verse Summary*, San Francisco: Four Seasons Foundation.

Conze, E. (1975), *The Large Sutra on Perfect Wisdom*, Berkeley: University of California Press.

Conze, E. (2001), *Buddhist Wisdom – The Diamond Sutra and The Heart Sutra*, New York: Vintage Spiritual Classics.

Cook, F. (1999), *Three Texts of Consciousness Only*, Berkeley: Numata Center.

Crosby, K. and Skilton, A. (1995), *The Bodhicaryāvatāra*, Oxford: Oxford World's Classics.

Gambhīrānanda, S. (1972), *Brahma Sutra Bhasya of Shankaracharya*, Calcutta: Advaita Ashrama.

Gambhīrānanda, S. (1984), *Bhagavad-Gītā – with the commentary of Śaṅkarācārya*, Calcutta: Advaita Ashrama.

Gambhīrānanda, S. (1989), *Eight Upaniṣads – with the Commentary of Śaṅkarācārya, Vol. I & II*, Calcutta: Advaita Ashrama.

Gambhīrānanda, S. (1997), *Chāndogya Upaniṣad – with the Commentary of Śaṅkarācārya*, Calcutta: Advaita Ashrama.

Inada, K.K. (1993), *Nāgārjuna – A Translation of his Mūlamadhyamakakārikā*, Delhi: Sri Satguru.

Jagadānanda, S. (1941), *Upadeśa Sāhasrī of Śrī Śaṅkarācārya*, Madras: Sri Ramakrishna Math.

Johnson, W.J. (2004), *The Bhagavad Gita*, Oxford: Oxford World's Classics.

Keenan, J.P. (2003), *The Summary of the Great Vehicle*, revised 2nd edition, Berkeley: Numata Center for Buddhist Translation and Research.

Kloppenborg, R. (1973), *The Sūtra on the Foundation of the Buddhist Order (Catuṣpariṣat Sūtra)*, Leiden: Brill.

Kochumuttom, T.A. (1989), *A Buddhist Doctrine of Experience- A New Translation and Interpretation of the Works of Vasubandhu the Yogācārin*, Delhi: Motilal Banarsidass.

Luk, C. (2002), *Ordinary Enlightenment – A Translation of the Vimalakīrti Nirdeśa Sūtra*, Boston: Shambhala.

Mādhavānanda, S. (2003), *Śrī-Śaṅkarācārya's Vivekacūḍāmaṇi*, 17th Impression, Calcutta: Advaita Ashrama.

Mādhavānanda, S. (2008), *The Bṛhadāraṇyaka Upaniṣad – with the commentary of Śaṅkarācārya*, 11th Impression, Calcutta: Advaita Ashrama.

Mascaró, J. (2003), *The Bhagavad Gita*, London: Penguin Classics.

Matics, M. (1971), *Entering the Path of Enlightenment – The Bodhicayāvatāra of the Buddhist Poet Śāntideva*, London: Allen & Unwin.

Mayeda, S. (1992), *A Thousand Teachings – The Upadeśasāhasrī of Śaṅkara*, New York: State University Press.

Ñāṇamoli, B. (1999), *Visuddhimagga –the Path of Purification*, Seattle: BPS Pariyatti Edition.

Ñāṇamoli, B and Bodhi, B. (2001), *The Middle Length Discourses of the Buddha – A Translation of the Majjhima Nikāya*, 2nd Edition, Boston: Wisdom.

Narada, T. (1993), *The Dhammapada*, 4th Edition, Taipei: Buddha Educational Foundation.

Nyanaponika, T. and Bodhi, B. (1999), *Numerical Discourses of the Buddha – An Anthology of Suttas from the Aṅguttara Nikāya*, Creek Walnut: AltaMira.

Olivelle, P. (1992), *Saṃnyāsa Upaniṣads – Hindu Scriptures on Asceticism and Renunciation*, Oxford: Oxford University Press.

Olivelle, P. (1998), *Upaniṣads*, Oxford: Oxford University Press.

Olivelle, P. (1999), *The Dharmasūtras – The Law Codes of Ancient India*, Oxford: Oxford University Press.

Olivelle, P. (2004), *The Law Code of Manu*, Oxford: Oxford University Press.

Padmakara Translation Group (1999), *The Way of the Bodhisattva*, Boston: Shambhala.
Padmakara Translation Group (2004), *Introduction to the Middle Way – Chandrakirti's Madhyamakavatara with Commentary by Jamgon Mipham*, Boston: Shambhala.
Powers, J. (1995), *Wisdom of Buddha – The Saṁdhinirmocana Mahāyāna Sūtra*, Berkeley: Dharma Publishing.
Rhys Davids, T.W. (1963), *The Questions of King Milinda, Parts I & II*, New York: Dover.
Sharma, P. (1990), *Śāntideva's Bodhicharyāvatāra – Original Sanskrit Text with English Translation*, New Delhi: Aditya Prakashan.
Suzuki, D.T. (1999), *The Laṅkāvatāra Sūtra – A Mahāyāna Text*, Delhi: Motilal Banarsidass.
Tatz, M. (1994), *Upāyakauśalya – The Skill in Means Sūtra*, Delhi: Motilal Banarsidass.
Thurman, R.A.F. (1976), *The Holy Teaching of Vimalakīrti*, Pennsylvania: The Pennsylvania State University Press.
Wallace, B.A. and Wallace, V.A. (1997), *A Guide to the Bodhisattva Way of Life*, New York: Snow Lion.
Walshe, M. (1987), *The Long Discourses of the Buddha – A Translation of the Dīgha Nikāya*, Boston: Wisdom.
Wayman, A. and Wayman, H. (1990), *The Lion's Roar of Queen Śrīmālā*, Delhi: Motilal Banarsidass.
Westerhoff, J. (2010), *Nāgārjuna's Vigrahavyāvartanī – The Dispeller of Disputes*, Oxford: Oxford University Press.

Dictionaries

Grimes, J. (1996), *A Concise Dictionary of Indian Philosophy*, New York: State University of New York.
Keown, D. (2003), *Dictionary of Buddhism*, Oxford: Oxford University Press.
Monier-Williams, M. (2002), *A Sanskrit English Dictionary*, Delhi: Motilal Banarsidass.

Secondary Sources

Albahari, M. (2006), *Analytical Buddhism: The Two-Tiered Illusion of Self*, New York: Palgrave Macmillan.
Alston, A.J. (2004), *A Śaṅkara Source Book, Vol. 1–6*, 2nd Edition, London: Shanti Sadan.
Ames, T. (ed.) (1994), *Self as Person in Asian Theory and Practice*, Albany: University of New York Press.

Anderson, C.S. (2001), *Pain and Its Ending – The Four Noble Truths in the Theravāda Buddhist Canon*, Delhi: Motilal Banarsidass.

Aristotle (1998), *The Nicomachean Ethics*, Oxford: Oxford World's Classics.

Aristotle (2009), *The Politics*, Oxford: Oxford World's Classics.

Arnold, D. (2005), *Buddhists, Brahmins, and Belief – Epistemology in South Asian Philosophy of Religion*, New York: Columbia University Press.

Barnes, L.P. (2008), *Learning to Teach Religious Education in the Secondary School*, 2nd Edition, Abingdon: Routledge.

Baron, M.W. (1997), "Kantian Ethics", in Baron, et al., *Three Methods of Ethics*, Oxford: Blackwell, pp. 3–91.

Bilimoria, P., Prabhu, J. and Sharma, R. (ed.) (2007), *Indian Ethics – Classical Traditions and Contemporary Challenges – Vol. I*, Aldershot: Ashgate.

Black, B. (2008), *The Character of the Self in Ancient India – Priests, Kings, and Women in the Early Upaniṣads*, New York: State University of New York Press.

Bodhi, B. (2006), *A Comprehensive Manual of Abhidhamma*, Edited Edition, Onalaska: Pariyatti Press.

Brassard, F. (2000), *The Concept of Bodhicitta in Śāntideva's Bodhicaryāvatāra*, New York: State University of New York Press.

Burton, D. (2001), *Emptiness Appraised – A Critical Study of Nāgārjuna's Philosophy*, Delhi: Motilal Banarsidass.

Burton, D. (2004), *Buddhism, Knowledge and Liberation- A Philosophical Study*, Aldershot: Ashgate.

Cenkner, W. (1983), *A Tradition of Teachers - Śaṅkara and the Jagadgurus Today*, Delhi: Motilal Banarsidass.

Chakrabarti, A. (1983), Is Liberation (mokṣa) Pleasant?, *Philosophy East and West*, Vol. 33, No. 2, April 1983, pp. 167–82.

Chappell, D.W. (1996), Are there Seventeen Mahāyāna Ethics?, *Journal of Buddhist Ethics*, Vol. 3 (1996), pp. 44–65.

Chari, S.M.S. (2005), *The Philosophy of the Bhagavadgītā*, Delhi: Munshiram Manoharlal.

Clayton, B.R. (2006), *Moral Theory in Śāntideva's Śikṣāsamuccaya – Cultivating the fruits of virtue*, London: Routledge.

Collins, S. (1982), *Selfless Persons – Imagery and Thought in Theravāda Buddhism*, Cambridge: Cambridge University Press.

Conze, E. (1967), *Buddhist Thought in India*, Michigan: Ann Arbor Paperbacks – University of Michigan Press.

Cooper, D.E. and James, S.P. (2005), *Buddhism, Virtue and Environment*, Aldershot: Ashgate.

Cousins, L.S. (1997), "Buddhism" in *A New Handbook of Living Religions*, edited by J.R. Hinnells, Cambridge: Blackwell, pp. 369–444.

Coward, H. (2008), *The Perfectibility of Human Nature in Eastern and Western Thought*, Albany: State University of New York Press.

Cowherds, The (2011), *Moonshadows – Conventional Truth in Buddhist Philosophy*, Oxford: Oxford University Press.

Cronk, G. (2003), *On Shankara*, London: Wadsworth Philosophy Series.
Dalai Lama (1988), *Transcendent Wisdom – A Commentary on the Ninth Chapter of Shantideva's Guide to the Bodhisattva Way of Life*, New York: Snow Lion.
Dalai Lama (1994), *A Flash of Lightning in the Dark*, Boston: Shambhala.
Dalai Lama (2002), *Essence of the Heart Sutra*, Boston: Wisdom.
Dasgupta, S. (1975), *A History of Indian Philosophy Vol. I & II*, Delhi: Motilal Banarsidass.
Dayal, H. (1970), *The Bodhisattva Doctrine in Buddhist Sanskrit Literature*, Delhi: Motilal Banarsidass.
de Silva, P. (2000), *An Introduction to Buddhist Psychology*, 3rd Edition, New York: Rowman & Littlefield.
Deutsch, E. (1973), *Advaita Vedānta*, Honolulu: University of Hawaii Press.
Deutsch, E. and Bontekoe, R. (ed.) (1997), *A Companion to World Philosophies*, Oxford: Blackwell.
Dharmasiri, G. (1989), *Fundamentals of Buddhist Ethics*, Antioch: Golden Leaves.
Doniger, W. (2010), *The Hindus – an alternative history*, Oxford: Oxford University Press.
Dumont, L. (1980), *Homo Hierarchicus – The Caste System and Its Implications, Complete Revised English Edition*, Chicago: University of Chicago Press.
Flew, A. (2005), *God & Philosophy*, New York: Prometheus.
Forsthoefel, T.A. (2002), Retrieving the Vivekacūḍāmaṇi: The Poles of Religious Knowing, *Philosophy East and West*, Vol. 52, No. 3, July 2002, pp. 311–35.
Fort, A.O. and Mumme, P.Y. (ed.) (1996), *Living Liberation in Hindu Thought*, New York: State University of New York.
Fort, A.O. (1998), *Jīvanmukti in Transformation – Embodied Liberation in Advaita and Neo-Vedanta*, New York: State University of New York.
Foucault, M. (1982), The Subject of Power, *Critical Inquiry*, Vol. 8, No. 4, Summer 1982, University of Chicago, pp. 777–95.
Foucault, M. (1999), "Pastoral power and political reason", in *Religion and Culture by Michel Foucault*, edited by J.R. Carrette, Manchester: Manchester University Press, pp. 135–52.
Freud, S. (2008), *The Future of an Illusion*, London: Penguin.
Gandhi, M. (2009), *The Bhagavad Gita According to Gandhi*, Berkeley: North Atlantic Books.
Ganeri, J. (2001), *Philosophy in Classical India*, London: Routledge.
Ganeri, J. (2007), *The Concealed Art of the Soul – Theories of Self and Practices of Truth in Indian Ethics and Epistemology*, Oxford: Oxford University Press.
Garfield, J. (1995), *The Fundamental Wisdom of the Middle Way – Nāgārjuna's Mūlamadhyamakārikā*, Oxford: Oxford University Press.
Garfield, J. (2002), *Empty Words – Buddhist Philosophy and Cross-Cultural Interpretation*, Oxford: Oxford University Press.
Gethin, R. (1997), Review of 'The Selfless Mind', *Journal of Buddhist Ethics*, Vol. 4, 1997, pp. 73–8.

Gethin, R. (1998), *The Foundations of Buddhism*, Oxford: Oxford University Press.

Giles, J. (1993), The No-Self Theory: Hume, Buddhism, and Personal Identity, *Philosophy East and West*, Vol. 43, No. 2, April 1993, pp. 175–200.

Gombrich, R. (1988), *Theravada Buddhism – A Social History from Ancient Benares to Modern Colombo*, London: Routledge.

Gombrich, R. (2009), *What the Buddha Thought*, London: Equinox.

Gombrich, R. et al. (1991), *The World of Buddhism*, London: Thames and Hudson.

Goodman, C. (2008), Consequentialism, Agent-Neutrality, and Mahāyāna Ethics, *Philosophy East and West*, Vol. 58, No. 1 (Jan. 2008), pp. 17–35.

Goodman, C. (2009), *Consequences of Compassion – An Interpretation & Defense of Buddhist Ethics*, New York: Oxford.

Grether, H. (2007), Is There 'Self' Identity in Sāmkhya and Śankara?, *Theologica Xaverianna*, Vol. 57, No. 162, pp. 221–38.

Gyatso, K. (1994), *Meaningful to Behold – The Bodhisattva's Way of Life*, Ulverston: Tharpa.

Gyatso, T., the 14th Dalai Lama (1975), *The Buddhism of Tibet and the Key to the Middle Way*, London: George Allen & Unwin.

Halbfass, W. (1983), *Studies in Kumārila and Śaṅkara*, Reinbek: Verlag für Orientalistische Fachpublikationen.

Halbfass, W. (1991), *Tradition and Reflection – Explorations in Indian Thought*, New York: State University of New York.

Halbfass, W. (ed.) (1995), *Philology and Confrontation – Paul Hacker on Traditional and Modern Advaita*, New York: State University of New York.

Harris, S. (2011), Does Anātman Rationally Entail Altruism? – On Bodhicaryāvatāra 8:101–103, *Journal of Buddhist Ethics*, Vol. 18 (2011), pp. 93–123.

Harvey, P. (1987), The Buddhist Perspective on Respect for Persons, *Buddhist Studies Review*, Vol. 4, No. 1, pp. 31–46.

Harvey, P. (1990), *An Introduction to Buddhism – Teachings, history and practices*, Cambridge: Cambridge University Press.

Harvey, P. (1995), *The Selfless Mind*, London: RoutledgeCurzon.

Harvey, P. (2000), *An Introduction to Buddhist Ethics*, Cambridge: Cambridge University Press.

Hindery, R. (1996), *Comparative Ethics in Hindu and Buddhist Traditions*, Delhi: Motilal Banarsidass.

Hopkins, J. (1996), *Meditation on Emptiness*, Boston: Wisdom.

Hume, D. (1975), *Enquiries Concerning Human Understanding and Concerning the Principles of Morals*, 3rd Edition, Oxford: Clarendon.

Hume, D. (1978), *A Treatise of Human Nature*, 2nd Edition, Oxford: Clarendon.

Hume, D. (2007), *An Enquiry concerning Human Understanding*, Oxford: Oxford World's Classics.

Huntington, C.W., Jr (1989), *The Emptiness of Emptiness – An Introduction to Early Indian Mādhyamika*, Honolulu: University of Hawai'i Press.

Hwang, S. (2006), *Metaphor and Literalism in Buddhism – The doctrinal history of nirvana*, Abingdon: Routledge.

Ingalls, D.H.H. (1954), Śaṃkara's Arguments Against the Buddhists, *Philosophy East and West*, Vol. 3, No.4 (Jan. 1954), pp. 291–306.

Isayeva, N. (1993), *Shankara and Indian Philosophy*, New York: State University of New York Press.

I-tsing (2009), *A Record of the Buddhist Religion as Practised in India and the Malay Archipelago (A.D. 671–695)*, Milton Keynes: Bibliolife Reproduction.

Kant, I. (2005), *The Moral Law*, Abingdon: Routledge Classics.

Kapstein, M.T. (2001), *Reason's Traces – Identity and Interpretation in Indian and Tibetan Buddhist Thought*, Boston: Wisdom.

Keay, J. (2000), *India a History*, London: Harper Perennial.

Keown, D. (1996), Karma, Character, and Consequentialism, *Journal of Religious Ethics*, Vol. 24:2, pp. 329–50.

Keown, D. (2001), *The Nature of Buddhist Ethics*, New Edition, Basingstoke: Palgrave Macmillan.

Keown, D. (2005), *Buddhist Ethics – A Very Short Introduction*, Oxford: Oxford University Press.

Keown, D and Prebish, C.S. (ed.) (2007), *Encyclopedia of Buddhism*, London: Routledge.

King, R. (1995), *Early Advaita Vedānta and Buddhism The Mahāyāna Context of the Gaḍapādīya-Kārikā*, New York: State University of New York.

Klostermaier, K.K. (2007), *A Survey of Hinduism, Third Edition*, New York: State University of New York.

Knot, K. (1998), *Hinduism – A Very Short Introduction*, Oxford: Oxford University Press.

Kornfield, J. (1979), Intensive Insight Meditation: A Phenomenological Study, *The Journal of Transpersonal Psychology*, 1979, Vol. 11, No. 1, pp. 41–58.

Krebs, D.L. and van Hesteren, F. (1994), "The Development of Altruism: Toward an Integrative Model", *Developmental Review*, 14: pp. 103–58.

Kuznetsova, I. (2007), *Dharma in Ancient Indian Thought: Tracing the Continuity of Ideas from the Vedas to the Mahābhārata*, Aylesbeare: Hardinge Simpole.

Kuznetsova, I., Ganeri, J. and Ram-Prasad, Chakravarthi (ed.) (2012), *Hindu and Buddhist Ideas in Dialogue: Self and Non-Self*, Farnham: Ashgate.

Larson, G.J. and Deutsch, E. (ed.) (1988), *Interpreting Across Boundaries*, Princeton: Princeton University Press.

Lehrer, K. (2000), *Theory of Knowledge*, Boulder: Westview Press.

Levinas, E. (2006), *Humanism of the Other*, Chicago: University of Illinois Press.

Lipner, J. (2010), *Hindus – Their Religious Beliefs and Practices*, 2nd Edition, London: Routledge.

Little, D and Twiss, S.B. (1978), *Comparative Religious Ethics*, San Francisco: Harper & Row.

Locke, J. (1997), *An Essay Concerning Human Understanding*, London: Penguin.

Loy, D. (1988), The path of no-path: Śaṅkara and Dōgen on the paradox of practice, *Philosophy East and West*, Vol. 38, No. 2, April 1988, pp. 127–46.
Lusthaus, D. (2002), *Buddhist Phenomenology: A Philosophical Investigation of Yogācāra Buddhism and the Ch'eng Wei-shih lun*, Oxon: RoutledgeCurzon.
MacIntyre, A. (1966), *A Short History of Ethics – A history of moral philosophy from the Homeric age to the twentieth century*, London: Routledge & Kegan Paul.
Madan, T.N. (ed.) (1988), *Way of Life – King, Householder, Renouncer: Essays in honour of Louis Dumont*, Delhi: Motilal Banarsidass.
Majithia, R. (2007), Śaṅkara on Action and Liberation, *Journal of Asian Philosophy*, Vol. 17, No. 3, November 2007, pp. 231–49.
Malinar, A. (2007), *The Bhagavadgītā – Doctrines and Contexts*, Cambridge: Cambridge University Press.
Marcaurelle, R. (2000), *Freedom through Inner Renunciation - Śaṅkara's Philosophy in a New Light*, New York: State University of New York Press.
Matilal, B.K. (2004), *Logical and Ethical Issues – An Essay on Indian Philosophy of Religion*, New Delhi: Chronicle.
Metzinger, T. (2004), *Being No One: The Self-Model Theory of Subjectivity*, New Edition, London: MIT Press.
Metzinger, T. (2010), *The Ego Tunnel – The Science of the Mind and the Myth of the Self*, New York: Basic Books.
Meyers, K. (2010), *Virtues as Consequences*, Review of 'Consequences of Compassion', H-Buddhism. Available at: http://www.h-net.org/reviews.
Mill, J.S. and Bentham, J. (2004), *Utilitarianism and Other Essays*, London: Penguin Classics.
Mitomo, R. (1991), 'The Ethics of Mahāyāna Buddhism in the Bodhicaryāvatāra', in *Buddhist Ethics and Modern Society – An International Symposium*, edited by C.W. Fu and S.A. Wawrytko, Westport: Greenwood Press, pp. 15–26.
Monroe, K.R. (1998), *The Heart of Altruism: Perceptions of a Common Humanity*, Princeton: Princeton University Press.
Monroe, K.R. (2009), Review of '*Altruism*', *Political Psychology*, Vol. 30, Issue 3, June 2009, pp. 502–4.
Mrozik, S. (2007), *Virtuous Bodies – The Physical Dimensions of Morality in Buddhist Ethics*, Oxford: Oxford University Press.
Murti, T.R.V. (1980), *The Central Philosophy of Buddhism – A Study of the Mādhyamika System*, London: Unwin.
Nagel, T. (1978), *The Possibility of Altruism*, Princeton: Princeton University Press.
Neusner, J. and Chilton, B. (ed.) (2005), *Altruism in World Religions*, Washington: Georgetown University Press.
Newland, G. (1999), *Appearance & Reality – The Two Truths in the Four Buddhist Tenet Systems*, New York: Snow Lion.
Nhat Hanh, T. (1998), *The Heart of the Buddha's Teaching – Transforming Suffering into Peace, Joy, and Liberation*, New York: Broadway Books.
Nietzsche, F. (2001), *The Gay Science*, Cambridge: Cambridge University Press.

Nuttall, J. (2002), *An Introduction to Philosophy*, Oxford: Polity.

Oliner, S.P. and Oliner, P.M. (1992), *The Altruistic Personality: Rescuers of Jews in Nazi Europe*, New York: The Free Press.

Oliner, S.P. (2003), *Do Onto Others – Extraordinary Acts of Ordinary People*, Oxford: Westview Press.

Olivelle, P. (1986), *Renunciation in Hinduism – A Medieval Debate*, Vienna: Brill, Leiden, Gerold & co.

Olivelle, P. (1993), *The Āśrama System – The History and Hermeneutics of a Religious Institution*, Oxford: Oxford University Press.

Olson, C. (1997), *The Indian Renouncer and Postmodern Poison – A Cross-cultural Encounter*, New York: Peter Lang Publishing.

Olson, C. (ed.) (2008), *Celibacy and Religious Traditions*, Oxford: Oxford University Press.

Olson, C. (2011), The Différance That Makes All the Difference: A Comparison of Derrida and Śaṅkara, *Philosophy East and West*, Vol. 61, No. 2, April 2001, pp. 247–59.

O'Neil, L.T. (1980), *Māyā in Śaṅkara*, Delhi: Motilal Banarsidass.

Osto, D. (2008), Review of '*Moral Theory in Śāntideva's Śikṣāsamuccaya – Cultivating the fruits of virtue*', *Journal of Buddhist Ethics*, 15 (2008): pp. 63–7.

Otto, R. (1957), *Mysticism East and West – A Comparative Analysis of the Nature of Mysticism*, New York: Living Age Books.

Parfit, D. (1971), Personal Identity, *The Philosophical Review*, Vol. 80, No. 1, January 1971, pp. 3–27.

Parfit, D. (1984), *Reasons and Persons*, Oxford: Clarendon Press.

Pelden, K. (2007), *The Nectar of Manjushri's Speech – A Detailed Commentary on Shantideva's Way of the Bodhisattva*, Boston: Shambhala.

Penelhum, T. (1993), "Hume's Moral Psychology", in *The Cambridge Companion to Hume*, edited by D.F. Norton, Cambridge: Cambridge University Press, pp. 117–47.

Pérez-Remón, J. (1980), *Self and Non-self in Early Buddhism*, Hague: Mouton.

Perrett, R.W. (1985), Dualistic and nondualistic problems of immortality, *Philosophy East and West*, Vol. 35, No. 4, October 1985, pp. 333–50.

Perrett, R.W. (1998), *Hindu Ethics – A Philosophical Study*, Honolulu: University of Hawai'i Press.

Perrett, R.W. (2002), Personal Identity, Minimalism, and Madhyamaka, *Philosophy East and West*, Vol. 52, No. 3, July 2002, pp. 373–85.

Pettit, J.W. (1999), Review of 'Altruism and Reality – Studies in the Philosophy of the Bodhicaryāvatāra', *Journal of Buddhist Ethics*, 6 (1999): pp. 120–137.

Pickering, J. (1997), 'Selfhood is a Process', in *The Authority of Experience – Essays on Buddhism and Psychology*, edited by J. Pickering, Surrey: Curzon Press, pp. 152–69.

Potter, K.H. (1981), *Encyclopedia of Indian Philosophies, Vol.3*, Delhi: Motilal Banarsidass.

Powers, J. and Prebish, C.S. (ed.) (2009), *Destroying Māra Forever: Buddhist Ethics Essays in Honor of Damien Keown*, New York: Snow Lion.

Queen, C.S. and King, S.B. (1996), *Engaged Buddhism – Buddhist Liberation Movements in Asia*, New York: State University of New York Press.

Queen, C.S. (2000), *Engaged Buddhism in the West*, Boston: Wisdom.

Radhakrishnan, S. (1980), *The Hindu View of Life*, London: Unwin.

Radhakrishnan, S. (1989), *Eastern Religions & Western Thought*, Delhi: Oxford India Paperbacks.

Ram-Prasad, Chakravarthi (1993), Dreams and Reality: The Śaṅkarite Critique of Vijñānavāda, *Philosophy East & West*, Vol. 43, No. 3, pp. 405–55.

Ram-Prasad, Chakravarthi (2001a), *Knowledge and Liberation in Classical Indian Thought*, Basingstoke: Palgrave.

Ram-Prasad, Chakravarthi (2001b), Saving the Self? Classical Hindu Theories of Consciousness and Contemporary Physicalism, *Philosophy East and West*, Vol. 51, No. 3, July 2001, pp. 378–92.

Ram-Prasad, Chakravarthi (2002), *Advaita Epistemology and Metaphysics: An Outline of Indian Non-realism*, London: RoutledgeCurzon.

Ram-Prasad, Chakravarthi (2007), *Indian Philosophy and the Consequences of Knowledge – Themes in Ethics, Metaphysics and Soteriology*, Aldershot: Ashgate.

Ram-Prasad, Chakravarthi (2012), 'Self and Memory: Personal Identity and Unified Consciousness in Comparative Perspective', in *Hindu and Buddhist Ideas in Dialogue: Self and Non-Self*, edited by I. Kuznetsova et al., Farnham: Ashgate, pp. 129–46.

Ricoeur, P. (1994), *Oneself as Another*, Chicago: University of Chicago Press.

Roodurmun, P.S. (2002), *Bhāmatī and Vivaraṇa Schools of Advaita Vedānta*, Delhi: Motilal Banarsidass.

Rosen, S.J. (ed.) (2002), *Holy War – Violence in the Bhagavad Gita*, New York: Deepak Heritage.

Rosenthal, T.L. and Zimmerman, B.J. (1978), *Social Learning and Cognition*, London: Academic Press.

Ruegg, D.S. (1981), *A History of Indian Literature – The Literature of the Madhyamaka School of Philosophy in India*, Wiesbaden: Otto Harrassowitz.

Ruegg, D.S. (2010), *The Buddhist Philosophy of the Middle – Essays on Indian and Tibetan Madhyamaka*, Boston: Wisdom.

Rushton, J.P. (1980), *Altruism, Socialization & Society*, New Jersey: Prentice-Hall.

Saddhatissa, H. (1997), *Buddhist Ethics*, Boston: Wisdom.

Saha, S. (2009), *Socio-Religious Essays in Advaita Vedanta*, Calcutta: Jadavpur University.

Schweiker, W. (ed.) (2005), *The Blackwell Companion to Religious Ethics*, Oxford: Blackwell Publishing.

Scott, N. and Seglow, J. (2007), *Altruism*, Maidenhead: Open University Press.

Sen, A. (2000), Consequential Evaluation and Practical Reason, *The Journal of Philosophy*, Vol. XCVII, No. 9, Sept. 2000, pp. 477–502.

Sen, A. (2005), *The Argumentative Indian – Writings on Indian Culture, History and Identity*, London: Penguin.
Shaw, S. (2008), *Introduction to Buddhist Meditation*, London: Routledge.
Siderits, M. (1997), Buddhist Reductionism, *Philosophy East and West*, Vol. 47, No. 4, October 1997, pp. 455–78.
Siderits, M. (2000), The Reality of Altruism: Reconstructing Śāntideva, *Philosophy East and West*, Vol. 50, No. 3 (July 2000): pp. 412–24.
Siderits, M. (2003), *Empty Persons: Personal Identity and Buddhist Philosophy*, Aldershot: Ashgate.
Siderits, M. (2007), *Buddhism as Philosophy – An Introduction*, Aldershot: Ashgate.
Siderits, M., Thompson, E. and Zahavi, D. (ed.) (2011), *Self, No Self? – Perspectives from Analytical, Phenomenological, and Indian Traditions*, Oxford: Oxford University Press.
Singer, P. (1972), Famine, Affluence, and Morality, *Philosophy and Public Affairs*, Vol. 1, No. 3 (Spring, 1972), pp. 229–43.
Skorupski, J. (ed.) (1998), *The Cambridge Companion to Mill*, Cambridge: Cambridge University Press.
Smart, J.J.C. and Williams, B. (1973), *Utilitarianism For & Against*, Cambridge: Cambridge University Press.
Smart, N. (1964), *Doctrine and Argument in Indian Philosophy*, London: Allen & Unwin.
Sober, E. and Wilson, D.S. (1998), *Unto Others: The Evolution and Psychology of Unselfish Behavior*, Cambridge: Harvard University Press.
Sonam Rinchen (2000), *The Bodhisattva Vow*, New York: Snow Lion.
Sprung, M. (1973), *The Problem of Two Truths in Buddhism and Vedānta*, Dordrecht: Reidel.
Stone, J. (1988), *Parfit and the Buddha: Why There are No People*, Philosophy and Phenomenological Research, Vol. XLVIII, No. 3, March 1988, pp. 519–32.
Streng, F.J. (1982), Realization of Param Bhūtakoṭi (ultimate reality-limit) in the Aṣṭasāhasrikā Prajñāpāramitā Sutra, *Philosophy East and West*, Vol. 32, No. 1, January 1982, pp. 91–8.
Sundaresan, V. (2002), What Determines Śaṅkara's Authorship? – The Case of the Pañcīkaraṇa, *Philosophy East and West*, Vol. 52, No. 1, January 2002, pp. 1–35.
Suthren Hirst, J.G. (2005), *Śaṃkara's Advaita Vedānta – A Way of Teaching*, Oxon: RoutledgeCurzon.
Sweet, M.J. (1977), *Śāntideva and the Mādhyamika: The Prajñāparamitā – Pariccheda of the Bodhicaryāvatāra*, Michigan: UMI Dissertation Services.
Taber, J.A. (1983), *Transformative Philosophy – A Study of Śaṅkara, Fichte, and Heidegger*, Honolulu, University of Hawai'i.
Taber, J.A. (2003), Review of 'Freedom through Inner Renunciation - Śaṅkara's Philosophy in a New Light', *Journal of the American Oriental Society*, 123.3, pp. 692–5.
Thapar, R. (2003), *The Penguin History of Early India From the Origins to AD 1300*, London: Penguin.

Theodor, I. (2010), *Exploring the Bhagavad Gītā – Philosophy, Structure and Meaning*, Farnham: Ashgate.

Thomas, G. (1993), *An Introduction to Ethics – Five Central Problems of Moral Judgement*, London: Duckworth.

Tiwari, K.N. (1977), *Dimensions of Renunciation in Advaita Vedānta*, Delhi: Motilal Banarsidass.

Todd, W. (2011), Review of "The Perfectibility of Human Nature in Eastern and Western Thought", *Philosophy East and West*, Vol. 61, No. 3 (July 2011): pp. 568–72.

Torwesten, H. (1991), *Vedanta – Heart of Hinduism*, New York: Grove Weidenfeld.

Urmson, J.O. (1958), "Saints and Heroes", in *Essays in Moral Philosophy*, edited by A.I. Melden, Seattle: University of Washington Press, pp. 198–216.

Vivekananda, S. (2009), *The Complete Works, Vol.I*, 27th Impression, Calcutta: Advaita Ashrama.

Weber, M. (1958), *The Religion of India*, New York: The Free Press (Macmillan).

Westerhoff, J. (2009), *Nāgājuna's Madhyamaka – A Philosophical Introduction*, Oxford: Oxford University Press.

Wetlesen, J. (2002), Did Śāntideva Destroy the Bodhisattva Path?, *Journal of Buddhist Ethics*, No. 9, pp. 34–88.

Williams, B. (1976), *Problems of the Self*, Cambridge: Cambridge University Press.

Williams, P. (1998a), *Studies in the Philosophy of the Bodhicaryāvatāra – Altruism and Reality*, Richmond: Curzon.

Williams, P. (1998b), *The Reflexive Nature of Awareness: A Tibetan Madhyamaka Defence*, Richmond: Curzon.

Williams, P. (2002), *The Unexpected Way – On Converting from Buddhism to Catholicism*, Edinburgh: T&T Clark.

Williams, P. (2009), *Mahāyāna Buddhism- The Doctrinal Foundations*, 2nd Edition, Oxon: Routledge.

Williams, P. and Tribe, A. (2000), *Buddhist Thought*, London: Routledge.

Zaehner, R.C. (1973), *The Bhagavad-Gītā – with a commentary based on the original sources*, Oxford: Oxford University Press.

Zahavi, D. (2008), *Subjectivity and Selfhood – Investigating the First-Person Perspective*, Cambridge: MIT.

Index

abheda. *See* non-difference
Abhidharma / Abhidhamma 4, 111, 190
Absolute, the 1, 10, 18, 51–2, 54, 57, 61, 63, 90–91, 135, 139, 165, 167
act-consequentialist, Śāntideva as 31–4, 73, 113–14
act-utilitarianism 34
advaita. *See* non-dualism
Advaita Vedānta 2–3, 7–10, 12–13, 15, 17–18, 27, 34, 39–41, 47, 49–50, 57–8, 62–5, 68–9, 77–9, 82–4, 87, 90–91, 97, 101, 105, 122–3, 127, 131, 139, 141, 143, 175, 179, 183–6
 as non-substantialist 9–10
agency 4, 9, 13, 15, 17, 19, 22, 26, 30, 38, 43–4, 62, 72, 81, 84, 90, 93–6, 99, 101, 107, 114–15, 122–3, 128–9, 140–42, 149, 158, 175, 201
agnosticism 1–2, 165
ahaṃkāra. *See* egoism
ahiṃsā 34, 98, 114, 145
altruism (as defined in the West) 11, 25, 37–40, 76, 142–3, 146, 148, 160–61, 177–8, 182
 constructive 5, 40–41, 107–108, 128, 142–3, 159–61, 171–2, 177–9, 182, 196–7, 199
 monastically-informed 33–4
 and partiality 9–10, 177–82, 197
 qualified 40, 160, 179, 196
anātman. *See* non-self
anātmavādin 9, 17
arhat 27, 58, 82, 132, 153, 157–8, 172
Aristotle 30–31, 35–8, 115–16
Arjuna 11, 77, 97–104
as-it-is 19, 25, 29, 40, 42, 93, 117, 123
atheism 1, 7
ātman 4, 7–10, 13–14, 22, 42, 44, 47, 56, 59–61, 67, 77–9, 84–5, 89–92, 94, 100–101, 147, 166–7, 186, 201
ātmavādin 9, 17
avidyā. *See* ignorance

Bādarāyaṇa 48–9
Bhagavad-Gītā 7–8, 10–11, 22, 37, 39, 52, 54, 57, 60, 63, 68–9, 77, 88, 96–100, 104–107, 111, 119, 123, 128, 139, 173, 175, 183, 187
 as *smṛti* or *śruti* 48
bliss 36, 38, 55–6, 126, 137, 166–7, 189, 191, 200
 sensual versus spiritual 55
 Śrāvaka versus Mahāyāna 152–6
Bodhicaryāvatāra
 as BCA 19
 in diagrammatic form 149
 and the six perfections 20, 70–71, 135–6, 160
bodhicitta 36–7, 116, 136
 "aspiring" versus "proceeding" 116, 149
bodhisattva
 commencing 21, 32–3, 73, 110, 113–14, 116, 130, 167
 seventh-stage 108
Bodhisattva Path 31, 67, 70, 108, 135–6, 142, 162, 188
Bodhisattva Vow 14, 71, 76, 93, 108, 111, 130, 135–6, 142–4, 148–9, 160–61, 166, 168–9, 172–3, 177, 180, 196
both/and (models) 5, 25, 29, 52–4, 58, 87, 141–2, 156–7
Brahma Sūtra 48–50, 57–8
 as *nyāya* 48
brahma-jñānin. *See brahman*-knower
brahman
 nirguṇa 2, 8, 18, 56, 122, 183
 saguṇa 8, 56
brahman-knower 8, 15, 19, 22, 24, 38, 53, 55–8, 64, 69, 73, 76, 97, 103,

105–107, 127, 129, 132, 137, 140–43, 171–2, 175, 177–9, 182, 185–6
brahma-vid. See brahman-knower
Brahmin 7, 22, 24, 34, 60–61, 66, 75, 85, 89, 97, 100, 102, 104, 107–108, 133, 140, 166–7, 169, 175, 178, 180, 182–8
Bṛhadāraṇyaka Upaniṣad 11–12, 23, 58–9, 91, 100, 123, 125, 140–41, 170
buddha-nature 68, 195

Candrakīrti 23, 42, 68–70, 81, 83, 135–6, 159, 190
caste 11–12, 24, 44, 54–5, 60, 85, 88, 95–7, 99, 100–106, 126, 139, 142–3, 167, 169, 175–9, 182–8, 196–7
  in Buddhism 115, 187–8
Chāndogya Upaniṣad 6, 55–8, 61, 125–6, 131, 140, 163–4, 169, 184–7
Clayton, Barbra 26, 30–31, 33, 38, 67, 69–71, 109, 112–14, 135, 150, 153
compassion 2, 5, 7, 9, 15, 23, 25, 28, 31–2, 34–5, 37, 42–3, 48, 66–7, 71, 73, 76–8, 93, 97, 102, 108, 111, 113–18, 130, 132, 136, 143–57, 160–64, 169–71, 196, 199–200
Compendium, The
  as representing Śāntideva's own views 110
  as Ś.S. 21
Comte, Auguste 37, 146, 148, 161, 177–8, 182
consciousness-only. *See* mind-only
Consequentialist Ethics 30–34, 40, 73, 113–14, 165, 182
constructive altruism. *See* altruism, constructive
continuum, person as 6, 9, 12–14, 93–4, 106, 113, 150–51, 158, 160
conventional truth 3, 5–6, 8–9, 12–15, 19–20, 24–6, 28–9, 36–7, 40, 44–5, 47, 51–4, 57–8, 61, 64, 66, 75–7, 81, 87–97, 100–102, 105, 111–12, 124–5, 128–30, 135, 139, 141–51, 155–67, 172 179, 183, 185–6, 188–97, 200
  versus consensus 3, 19, 189–92

Dalai Lama 9, 21, 85–6, 133–4, 136, 151, 159
Daśabhūmika Sūtra 20, 28, 70, 153
deconstruction 4–5, 91, 148, 165
dependent origination 4, 13–14, 43, 53, 56, 72, 74–5, 88–9, 91, 121, 132–6, 155, 157–8, 162, 194
desire 5, 11, 13, 22–4, 37, 50, 55, 58, 94, 96, 102, 104, 107, 109–110, 113, 117, 123, 129, 131, 136, 141, 150–51, 154–6, 160, 169, 173–4, 182–3, 195–6
Deutsch, Eliot 25, 34, 41, 48–9, 64, 103, 127, 139–40
Dhammapada 28, 140, 169
  as apparently rejecting altruism 146, 153
Dharma 3, 11, 19, 31, 35, 42, 48, 54, 88, 94, 97–100, 105–107, 113, 117–18, 127, 141, 143, 153, 167, 171, 183–4
dharmas, as being empty 13, 66, 72, 75, 113, 121, 133–5, 152
domains 20, 27, 40, 51–54, 57, 72–3, 77, 88, 110–14, 118, 130, 148–9, 156, 159, 161–2, 166, 168, 186, 191, 200
duḥkha / dukkha 1–2, 5, 10, 12–13, 17, 23, 31, 33, 37–9, 42, 65–7, 76, 78, 87–8, 91–3, 112, 114, 126–7, 130–32, 135–7, 143–65, 171–4, 178–9, 182, 184, 189, 196, 199–200
  as inherent 155
  its value in Śaṅkara 126, 130–31
duty 33, 35, 37, 65, 76, 96–105, 135–7, 140–43, 164, 171, 173, 175, 180–81, 200
  Bodhisattva Vow as 93, 135–6
Dvaita Vedānta 8, 62, 100

egoism 2, 8, 10, 13, 25, 35, 40, 42, 77–8, 90, 99–100, 135, 137, 142, 160, 162, 166, 170–71, 173–4, 181
Eliminativism 5–6, 11, 15, 101
emptiness 4–5, 10, 13–16, 18, 21, 27–9, 37, 43, 47, 52–4, 66–7, 72–7, 88–9, 92–3, 110–13, 117, 121, 130–36, 141–2, 147, 149, 152–62, 169, 177–8, 180, 189, 194–6, 199

Engaged Buddhism 32–3

flickering 5, 15, 17, 20, 23–30, 53, 58, 76–7, 82, 96, 112, 124, 129–30, 134–5, 139, 147, 156–7, 159–60, 162, 167, 172, 186, 191, 200
versus oscillating 24, 28, 77, 132, 144, 167
versus wavering 28
voluntary versus non-voluntary 24, 132

Gauḍapāda 49–51, 53, 62, 73, 85, 195
as a possible Buddhist 49, 195
Gauḍapāda Kārikā 11, 36, 49–50, 62–3
gnoseology 1–2, 7–10, 15, 25, 29, 52, 65, 81, 93, 98, 102, 119, 139
Goodman, Charles 6, 32–3, 38, 42, 73, 113–14, 153, 172
gradualism 10, 20–21, 40, 61–2, 70, 97, 110–14, 163, 167, 200

Harvey, Peter 6, 9, 11–12, 27–8, 33, 59, 78, 82, 90–92, 108, 155, 157, 165
hatred 11, 13, 42, 109–10, 114, 183
highest good 35, 39, 50, 97, 102, 105, 181
Hume, David 15, 28–9, 36, 39, 82–3, 116, 144–5, 154, 161

idealism 14, 54, 81–6
metaphysical 81
ignorance 1–2, 9, 13–14, 20–22, 55, 58, 62–3, 65, 77, 86–7, 99, 121–2, 127–32, 137, 139–40, 148, 173–4, 186, 196, 199–200
illusion 2, 17, 22–6, 29, 49, 62–5, 69, 73–4, 77, 87–9, 94–5, 111–12, 131, 133, 139, 166, 176, 189, 191, 193, 196, 199
inherent existence 4, 29, 43, 67, 72, 75, 100, 121, 132–4, 147, 149, 155–6, 191–6
intellect. *See* reasoning
inter-dependence. *See* dependent origination
Īśvara 1–2, 7–8, 10, 75, 89, 100, 166
and problem of evil 65–6

jīva. *See* self, individuated
jīvan-mukta 8, 15, 39, 48, 56–7, 69, 78, 95, 105–7, 127, 136, 139–42, 163–4, 168–72, 175, 199
jīvan-mukti 1, 55–8, 126–7, 163
versus *videha-mukti* 56–7, 139–40
jīvātman. *See* self, individuated
jñāna. *See* knowledge

Kant, Immanuel 33, 173
karma
burnt up 57, 102, 107, 139
and continuity 12, 57, 65, 68, 100, 113, 130, 132, 139, 172, 183
as empty 149, 161, 195
as a form of realism 43
residual 9, 43, 58, 60, 139–40
as ritual action 47–8, 57, 103, 122, 168
three types of 139–40
yoga 22, 96–100, 102, 105, 187
karuṇā. *See* compassion
Keown, Damien 30–35, 42, 109–10, 187
knowledge 1–2, 7–8, 11, 14, 19–32, 35–7, 39, 41, 43–4, 47–8, 50, 53–69, 73, 81–2, 87, 93, 99, 101–2, 106–7, 111, 121–37, 142–3, 148, 157, 173–5, 180–82, 196, 200
of brahman (Self) 8, 11, 13, 20, 42, 44, 47, 51, 53, 55–61, 64–6, 77, 96–107, 121–8, 139–41, 163–71, 175, 177, 184–6, 199
and emptiness 14, 52, 131–5, 160, 162, 189, 195–6
partial 20–23, 28, 57, 59, 200
saving 1, 61, 106, 127, 164
and suffering 130–31
via the Vedas 47–8, 84, 102, 124–6, 141, 169
Kṛṣṇa 7–8, 22, 63, 68–9, 77, 97–107, 174, 183

liberation 1–2, 14–16, 20–21, 24, 28, 34, 39, 43, 47, 54, 56–61, 65, 67, 78, 83, 86, 90, 94, 96, 98, 103, 105, 107, 116, 121–2, 126–32, 136–7, 139–40, 143, 148, 152, 154, 162–76, 182, 185, 196, 200
'from' versus 'to' 126–7, 130–31

Locke, John 117

Madhyamaka School 3–4, 10, 12, 15, 17–18, 27, 40, 42, 47, 49, 52, 54, 62, 66, 69–70, 72, 74–5, 78–9, 81, 83, 88, 90, 92, 108, 111–12, 117, 134, 143, 155, 159, 175, 179, 190,
Marcaurelle, Roger 24, 48, 58–9, 97, 103–4, 182–5
māyā. *See* illusion
means of knowledge 41, 51–3, 57, 88, 101, 123–5, 134–5
means to liberation 20–21, 34, 61, 102, 106, 117, 124, 128
mental imprints. *See* tendencies, latent
merit 2, 34, 65, 76, 111–13, 115, 118, 130–31, 136, 139–40, 160, 163–4, 171–2, 175–6, 181, 191
  transference of 147, 152–3, 172
Metzinger, Thomas 3–7, 12, 15, 78, 92
Mill, John Stuart 30, 37–9, 67, 171, 174, 180–81
mind-only 10, 36, 50–51, 74, 81–5, 89, 116
mokṣa. *See* liberation
momentariness 10, 14–15, 50, 52, 84–5, 150, 154, 189
Mrozik, Susanne 34, 68, 72, 118, 161, 187–96
mukti. *See* liberation

Nāgārjuna 3, 5, 18, 49, 53, 62, 72–3, 84, 91–2, 108, 128, 131–2, 155, 164, 191
  in Śāntideva 128
Nietzsche, Friedrich 1–2, 41
nihilism 2, 4, 10, 27, 50, 154, 157–8
nirvāṇa 27, 32, 36–7, 128, 131, 134, 144–6, 152, 155, 157, 164, 173, 199
  brahma- 37, 163
  non-abiding 27, 152
  with and without remainder 56
Noble Truths 117, 131, 144–5, 151, 155
non-action 96, 106–7
non-difference 11, 13, 20, 52, 55, 57, 60–61, 122, 168
non-dualism 1, 9, 15–16, 22, 26, 35–6, 39, 47, 49–50, 52, 56–8, 61, 63–4, 94–5, 100–101, 121–2, 160, 164, 170, 183, 186
non-harming. *See ahiṃsā*
non-individuation 3, 16, 40, 96, 199
non-realism 54, 82
non-self 4, 9–10, 15, 17, 39, 44, 67, 77–8, 85, 90–92, 94, 111, 127, 135–6, 141–3, 146–50, 156, 160–62, 167, 189, 196, 201

old stage-structures 15, 20, 24, 162
Other, the 5–6, 11–12, 15, 25, 29, 31–2, 38, 40, 44, 61, 76–7, 86, 91–3, 117–18, 128, 135, 137, 142–63, 166, 172–9, 182–3
other-regarding ethics 1, 3, 5, 7, 9, 13, 15, 25, 31–2, 35, 37–40, 42, 44, 48, 71, 76, 93, 107–8, 113–14, 116, 127, 130–31, 135–6, 139–40, 146–57, 161, 164, 170–74, 182, 196, 201
  versus other-constructing ethics 142–3, 160, 199
Otto, Rudolf 1, 8, 39, 48–9, 63, 128, 171

pain. *See duḥkha / dukkha*
Parfit, Derek 3–4, 6–7, 10, 12, 15
personhood 3–16, 25–6, 40, 43–4, 66, 85, 92–6, 101, 111–12, 142, 149–51, 154–60, 201
prajñā, See wisdom
Prajñāpāramitā 4, 157, 160
pramāṇa. *See* means of knowledge
Prāsaṅgika 5, 42, 69, 134
provisional reality 3, 5, 13, 15, 24–26, 44, 47, 51, 54, 66, 87–9, 94, 96, 100–102, 112, 124, 129, 139, 160, 166–7, 172, 183, 186, 196–7
  and karma 112, 139, 142
prudence 5, 150–51, 156

Rāmānuja 34, 63, 100, 105
Ram-Prasad, Chakravarthi 4, 7–12, 31, 41, 51–4, 57, 65, 77, 79, 82, 86–7, 90, 92, 102–3, 122, 125, 128–30, 185
realization. *See* knowledge
reasoning
  as limited 19–20, 22, 94–5, 121–6, 131, 133–4, 137, 200

as necessary 62, 125, 133–4, 167
rebirth 8–9, 12–15, 65–6, 93–4, 111, 124, 129–32, 139–40, 144, 150–51, 164, 168, 176, 187, 189, 191
re-evaluation of 9, 15, 131
and Parfit 6
reconstruction 5, 40, 77, 92–3, 107–8, 157, 161, 199
Reductionism 4–6, 11, 15, 154, 157–8
relative truth. *See* conventional truth
renunciation 39, 56, 59–60, 68, 73, 95–97, 102–4, 108, 113–19, 126, 128–9, 133, 137, 147–9, 153, 160, 165, 169, 175, 184, 187, 190, 196–7, 200
'from' versus 'to' 103
'inner' versus 'outer' 59, 99–100, 103–5, 108, 116, 167
Kṛṣṇa's redefinition of 97–8, 105
'ultimate' versus 'secondary' 99–100, 103–5
revisionary metaphysics 3–4, 16, 41–3, 47, 53, 95–6, 139, 141

saṃsāra 1, 15, 27, 37, 65–6, 76, 89, 94, 99, 104, 112, 124, 128, 130–32, 135–7, 146, 164–5, 174, 179, 196
saṃskāras. *See* tendencies, latent
Śaṅkara
as an *avatāra* 69
as an exegete 48
as founder of Advaita 49
and God 1–3, 7–8, 19–20, 57, 60–61, 64–6, 100–101, 140, 163–4
Śāntideva
and buddha-nature 68
as a gradualist 70, 110–14
as a Mādhyamika 2, 12, 15, 18, 70, 72, 76, 159, 178, 190–92
as a Prāsaṅgika 5, 69
and tantra 67–8
satya-dvaya. *See* Two Truths
scepticism 1–4, 41, 53–4, 74–5, 82, 154, 166, 176, 190–93
self
individuated 2–4, 7–10, 13–14, 19, 25, 38, 41, 43–4, 47, 60–64, 76–8, 81, 90–96, 100, 105, 124, 128–9, 135–7, 142, 157–8, 167, 172, 201
as *paramātman* 94, 100, 168
as Self. *See tat tvam asi*
sense of 12, 77, 90, 92, 95, 117, 146, 149, 165
in Western context 3–12, 15, 25, 29, 35, 38–9, 90, 95, 142–3
selfless 4–5, 7, 9, 13–16, 25–6, 29, 37–44, 75, 77, 90, 93, 96, 98–101, 106–7, 117, 128, 135–6, 139–42, 146–9, 152–6, 160, 170–71, 177–8, 196, 199, 201
three meanings of 13–14, 42
self-love 5, 144–8, 150, 156, 177
self-luminosity 84, 88–9
self-sacrifice 37–8, 113, 143
Siderits, Mark 4–6, 9–10, 13, 15, 32, 108–9, 136, 156–8
Śikṣa Samuccaya. *See Compendium*
six perfections 20, 67, 70–71, 135–6, 159–60
skilful means 31, 60, 70–71, 96, 108, 110, 113–14, 132, 143, 157, 161
snake & rope, analogy of 64, 85–7
Śrāvaka 21, 71, 108, 117, 131–3, 143, 152–3, 155, 164
Śūdras 183–6
and non-duality 186
suffering. *See duḥkha/dukkha*
śūnyatā. *See* emptiness
Suthren Hirst, Jacqueline 1, 41, 48, 53, 63, 104, 165, 184
svabhāva. *See* inherent existence

tat tvam asi 61–2, 164–5
teacher, the need for 124, 164–5, 168–9
tendencies, latent 6, 9, 22–4, 57, 96, 124, 129, 184
tension 26–30, 44, 53–5, 60, 66–7, 76–7, 98, 111, 156, 161, 199
versus risk 29
tenth boy, the 127
testimony 47, 51–2, 57, 124, 132
transcendency thesis 32, 111–12
transcendental argument 52–4, 190
transmigratory existence. *See saṃsāra*
Triple Canon of Vedānta 48
two moons, analogy of 23
Two Truths 5–6, 14, 18–19, 26–30, 36, 44–5, 47, 49, 51, 53–4, 61–2, 76,

92, 94, 135, 141, 147, 150, 156, 159, 177–9, 183, 185–6, 189–90, 193, 197, 201
versus Two Realities 19, 24, 44–5, 167, 172

ultimate truth 6, 14, 19, 47, 199
universal consciousness 2, 9, 11, 14
Upadeśa Sāhasrī
as authentic non-commentarial work 48
Upaniṣads 6, 39, 47–8, 55–6, 58–62, 90, 96, 101, 104, 106, 122–6, 140–41, 163, 172, 175
as source of authority 36, 47–8, 50, 61, 124–6, 141, 185
Upāyakauśalya Sūtra 70–71, 108
Utilitarian 30–39, 143

varṇa. *See* caste
Vasubandhu 82–5
Vedānta 8–9, 17, 34, 36, 48–50, 56, 59–60, 73, 97, 122, 125
Neo- 104
Vedas, The 13, 47–54, 84, 102, 122–6, 130, 137, 141, 166–70, 183–4, 188
as authorless 49
as conventional truth 57, 141
vidyā. *See* knowledge
Vijñānavāda. *See* Yogācāra
Vimalakīrti-Nirdeśa Sūtra 108–9
Vinaya 71–2, 111, 114–15, 153
Bodhisattva- 71
not to be disregarded 72, 115
Śrāvaka- 71
Virtue Ethics 30–40, 109, 111, 114, 117
Viśiṣṭādvaita 49, 100, 105
Viveka Cūḍāmaṇi
as not by Śaṅkara 2
voluntary delusion 15, 23, 43–4, 68, 76, 112–13, 129, 135, 156–7, 162, 172, 191

wavering 21, 28, 100, 136, 161, 196
as opposed to flickering 28
Williams, Bernard 29, 162
Williams, Paul 5, 28, 67, 69, 71–2, 75–6, 84, 108, 115, 129, 142–3, 151–9, 162, 178, 195
wisdom 2, 14, 19–22, 36–7, 65–7, 70–71, 103, 107–8, 113, 131–6, 145, 148, 152, 155–7, 160, 181, 188, 196
women
as *brahman*-knowers 175
and emptiness 95, 111, 189–96
excluded for renunciation 184, 186
as foul 189–93, 195, 200
included in the *Saṅgha* 188
and non-duality 23–4, 55, 95, 186, 197
and past tendencies 23–4

Yājñavalkya 58
Yogācāra 10, 18–19, 21, 45, 49–50, 53–4, 64, 69, 74, 81–9, 112, 116, 133, 195

Zen (Ch'an) 52, 195